D0722435

# Greening the Media

# Greening the Media

Richard Maxwell

Toby Miller

OXFORD
UNIVERSITY PRESS

# OXFORD
UNIVERSITY PRESS

Oxford University Press, Inc., publishes works that further
Oxford University's objective of excellence
in research, scholarship, and education.

Oxford    New York
Auckland    Cape Town    Dar es Salaam    Hong Kong    Karachi
Kuala Lumpur    Madrid    Melbourne    Mexico City    Nairobi
New Delhi    Shanghai    Taipei    Toronto

With offices in
Argentina    Austria    Brazil    Chile    Czech Republic    France    Greece
Guatemala    Hungary    Italy    Japan    Poland    Portugal    Singapore
South Korea    Switzerland    Thailand    Turkey    Ukraine    Vietnam

Copyright © 2012 by Oxford University Press, Inc.

Published by Oxford University Press, Inc.
198 Madison Avenue, New York, New York 10016
www.oup.com

Oxford is a registered trademark of Oxford University Press

All rights reserved. No part of this publication may be reproduced,
stored in a retrieval system, or transmitted, in any form or by any means,
electronic, mechanical, photocopying, recording, or otherwise,
without the prior permission of Oxford University Press.

Library of Congress Cataloging-in-Publication Data

Maxwell, Richard, 1957-
Greening the media / Richard Maxwell, Toby Miller.
p. cm.
Includes bibliographical references.
ISBN 978-0-19-991467-8 (cloth :alk. paper) — ISBN 978-0-19-532520-1 (pbk. : alk. paper)
1. Mass media—Social aspects.    2. Mass media—Political aspects.    I. Miller, Toby.    II. Title.
HM1206.M3759 2012
302.23—dc23
2011035713

For Luke and Caitlin and their friends

# CONTENTS

# ACKNOWLEDGMENTS

We'd like to thank everyone who encouraged us to write this book and provided opportunities for us to publish some of our earlier research or share our ideas in public venues: Jane Arthurs, Jody Berland, Tammy Boyce, Pat Brereton, Mari Castañeda, Jorge Castillo, Alex Champlain, Drew Davidson, Matt Davies, Robert De Chaine, Nick Couldry, Michael X. Delli Carpini, Michael Curtin, Anamaria Tamayo Duque, Kelly Gates, David Theo Goldberg, Miriam Greenberg, Larry Gross, James Hay, Mette Hjort, Peter Labella, Scott Lash, Justin Lewis, Tania Lewis, Bob McChesney, Shannon McLachlan, Robin Mansell, Guillermo Mastrini, Vicki Mayer, Katherine Miller-Rowan, John Philips, Emily Potter, Marc Raboy, Chad Raphael, José Carlos Lozano Rendón, Luis Reygadas, Andrew Ross, Ned Rossiter, Anita Schiller, Mila Sterling, Luis Alberto Urrea, Frank Webster, and Yuezhi Zhao. Richard Maxwell's students in Political Economy of Media and Media and the Environment courses helped to shape many ideas for this book. Jamal Bilal, Jennifer Chang, Krystal Gomola, Bree Kessler, and Christina Vlahos provided valuable research assistance to Richard Maxwell, as did a small grant from the Professional Staff Congress/CUNY Research Award Program. Karen Mandoukos, Bridget Holdbrook, and Shireen Ali helped Richard Maxwell find time to write, while Tamara Evans, as Dean of Arts and Humanities at Queens College, offered needed moral and research support. Finally, we'd like to thank Brendan O'Brien, Samara Stob, Molly Morrison, and their teams at Oxford University Press for guiding the book through the final stages of production.

# INTRODUCTION

In the eager search for the benefits of modern science and technology we have become enticed into a nearly fatal illusion: that through our machines we have at last escaped from dependence on the natural environment.

—Barry Commoner, 1971, 12

The increasingly faster and more versatile computers, appealing mobile phones, high-definition TVs, Internet, tiny music players, ingenious photo cameras, entertaining games consoles and even electronic pets give us the idea of a developed, pioneering and modern world. It is indeed a new era for many; but the dark side of this prosperous world reveals a very different reality, that far from taking us to the future, takes us back to a darker past.

—Centre for Reflection and Action on Labour Issues, 2006, 4

We Have Met The Enemy and He Is Us.

—Pogo, *Earth Day*, 1970

*Greening the Media* focuses on the environmental impact of the media—the myriad ways that media technology consumes, despoils, and wastes natural resources. It introduces ideas, stories, and facts that have been marginal or absent from popular, academic, and professional histories of media technology.

Readers may not be surprised to discover that media technologies contain toxic substances, or that the workers who assemble their cell phones and computers do so under hazardous conditions. But if you are like us, you will be startled by the scale and pervasiveness of these environmental risks. They are present in and around every site where electronic and electric devices are manufactured, used, and thrown away, poisoning humans, animals, vegetation, soil, air, and water.

What follows is a list of the problems we examine in this book. They represent just a few of the ways that media technology has contributed to climate change, pollution growth, biodiversity decline, and habitat decimation—the constituents of our global ecological crisis.

In 2004, the Political Economy Research Institute shamed media owners by placing them at Numbers 1, 3, 16, 22, and 39 in its report *Misfortune 100: Top Corporate Air Polluters in the United States*. By 2007, a combination of information and communications technologies (ICT), consumer electronics (CE),[1] and media production accounted for between 2.5 and 3 percent of greenhouse gases emitted around the world. At that time, the Environmental Protection Agency (EPA) of the United States, a statutory authority, estimated that US residents owned approximately three billion electronic devices. The country's Consumer Electronics Association (CEA), which represents the industry's corporations, says $145 billion was spent on its sector in 2006 in the United States alone, up 13 percent from the previous year. Since then, there has been an annual turnover of 400 million units, with well over half such purchases made by women.[2] The CEA refers joyously to a "consumer love affair with technology continuing at a healthy clip." In the midst of a recession, 2009 saw $165 billion in sales, and households owned between fifteen and twenty-four gadgets on average. By 2010, the country was spending $233 billion on electronic products. Three quarters of the population owned a computer, nearly half of all US adults had a Moving Picture Experts Group Audio Level 3 (MP3) player, and 85 percent used a cell phone. Overall CE ownership varied with age—adults under forty-five typically boasted four gadgets; those over sixty-five made do with one.[3]

By all measures, the amount of ICT/CE on the planet is staggering. The investigative science journalist Elizabeth Grossman summarizes the situation this way: "No industry pushes products into the global market on the scale that high-tech electronics does. And no other industry employs a comparably complex global supply chain, both for manufacturing and for end-of-life materials recovery."[4]

Rapid but planned cycles of innovation and obsolescence accelerate the production of electronic hardware and the accumulation of obsolete media, which are transformed overnight into junk. Today's digital devices are made to break or become uncool in cycles of twelve months and counting down (check your warranty). This may appear to be a welcome sign of abundance, a support for the idea that technological turnover is necessary and efficient—a good thing. But such growth comes at a cost. While it has helped enlarge the world economy by five times since the mid-twentieth century, the corresponding degradation of the globe's ecosystems has been 60 percent. If that rate is maintained, the economy will be eighty times its current size by 2100; and the Earth's ecosystems?[5] Even the Organisation for Economic Co-Operation and Development (OECD), perhaps the world's leading proponent of growth, acknowledges that prevailing "patterns of growth will compromise and irreversibly damage the natural environment."[6]

A sizeable amount of this invidious growth is linked to ICT/CE. By 2007, between twenty and fifty million tons of electronic and electric waste (e-waste) were being generated annually, much of it via discarded cell phones, televisions, and computers. E-waste has mostly been produced in the Global North (Australasia, Western Europe, Japan, and the United States) and dumped in the Global South (Latin America, Africa, Eastern Europe, Southern and Southeast Asia, and China) in the form of a thousand different, often lethal materials for each electrical and electronic gadget, though this situation is changing as India and China generate their own deadly media detritus.[7]

The extent of e-waste is truly astonishing. Twenty million computers fell obsolete across the United States in 1998; the rate was 130,000 a day by 2005. It has been estimated that the five hundred million personal computers discarded in the United States between 1997 and 2007 contained 6.32 billion pounds of plastics, 1.58 billion pounds of lead, three million pounds of cadmium, 1.9 million pounds of chromium, and 632,000 pounds of mercury. The EU is expected to generate upward of twelve million tons of e-waste annually by 2020.[8] In 2007, the EPA reported that "of the 2.25 million tons of TVs, cell phones and computer products ready for end-of-life management, 18 percent (414,000 tons) was collected for recycling and 82 percent (1.84 million tons) was disposed of, primarily in landfill." Although refrigerators and refrigerants account for the bulk of e-waste from the EU, about 44 percent of its most dangerous e-waste measured in 2005 came from medium to small ICT/CE: computer monitors, TVs, printers, ink cartridges, telecommunications equipment, toys, tools, and anything with a circuit board.[9]

Enclosed hard drives, backlit screens, cathode ray tubes, wiring, capacitors, and heavy metals pose few risks while these materials remain encased. But once discarded and dismantled, ICT/CE have the potential to expose workers and ecosystems to a morass of toxic components. Theoretically, "outmoded" parts could be reused or swapped for newer parts to refurbish devices. But items that are defined as waste undergo further destruction in order to collect remaining parts and valuable metals, such as gold, silver, copper, and rare-earth elements. This process causes serious health risks to bones, brains, stomachs, lungs, and other vital organs, in addition to birth defects and disrupted biological development in children. Medical catastrophes can result from lead, cadmium, mercury, other heavy metals, poisonous fumes emitted in search of precious metals, and such carcinogenic compounds as polychlorinated biphenyls (PCBs), dioxin, polyvinyl chloride (PVC), and flame retardants.[10]

One might think that understanding the enormity of the environmental problems caused by making, using, and disposing of media technologies would arrest our enthusiasm for them. But many intellectual correctives to our "love affair" with technology—our technophilia—have come and gone without establishing much of a foothold against the breathtaking flood of gadgets and associated propaganda promoting their awe-inspiring capabilities.[11]

It is difficult to comprehend the scale of environmental destruction when technology is depicted in popular and professional quarters as a vital source of plenitude and pleasure, the very negation of scarcity and dross. In economies in which the watchword is growth, consumerism has become virtually uncontestable as the cultural norm. A high-tech version of this consumerism assumes people to be calculating machines designed for shopping and pleasure seeking.[12] Perhaps the obsession with immediacy and interactivity via networks induces an ignorance of the intergenerational effects of consumption, inhibiting our awareness of the long-term harm to workers and the environment. Could constant connectedness be actively diminishing our ethical ability to dwell on interconnections between the present and future, between media and the Earth?

The enchantment with media technology certainly clouds much of the received history on the subject, making it hard to perceive its material connection to ecological decline. Social scientists have argued that widespread resistance to a critical, secular view of technology can be attributed to the *technological sublime,* a totemic, quasi-sacred power that industrial societies have ascribed to modern machinery and engineering. The emergence of the technological sublime has been connected to the Western triumphs of the post–Second World War period, when technological power supposedly supplanted the power of nature to inspire fear and astonishment.[13]

Media history is replete with similarly mad visions of technology's potent blend of magic and science. In the nineteenth century, people were supposedly governed by electrical impulses. Telegraphy was conceived of as a physical manifestation of human intellect that matched the essence of humanity with the performance of labor. In the early twentieth century, radio waves were said to move across "the ether," a mystical substance that could contact the dead and cure cancer. During the interwar period, it was claimed that the human "sensorium" had been subjected to "training" by technology. By the 1950s and '60s, machines were thought to embody and even control consciousness.[14] In our own time, this strange enchantment has attached itself to wireless communication, touch-screen phones and tablets, flat-screen high-definition televisions, 3-D IMAX cinema, mobile computing, and so on.

Three qualities endow the media with unique symbolic potency—volume, verisimilitude, and velocity. The media proliferate everywhere and all the time; they are good at producing the truth; and they are increasingly quick at doing so. In addition, the technological sublime that governs their reception and use is reinforced by what media scholars Tammy Boyce and Justin Lewis call the "virtual nature" of media content, which diverts attention from the industry's "responsibility for a vast proliferation of hardware, all with high levels of built-in obsolescence and decreasing levels of efficiency."[15] This is a longstanding tendency. According to Grossman, built-in or planned obsolescence entered the lexicon as a new "ethics" for electrical engineering in the 1920s and '30s, when marketers, eager to "habituate people to buying new products," called for designs to become quickly obsolete "in efficiency, economy, style, or taste."[16] Fast fashion and short life span certainly characterize ICT/CE products, with cell phones and computers leading the charge. And as planned obsolescence, fast fashion, and short life span reach "dizzying new heights," there is an overstated sense of preeminence and newness attached to whatever the latest media gadget happens to be. Sociologists have identified a "cult of the present," comprised mainly of cyberenthusiasts, who fetishize novelty as if each new version magically reboots their hipster identity into a perpetual now-ness.[17]

References to the symbolic power of media technology are so ubiquitous that they incite minimal if any scrutiny. The hymnal can be found across the internet, the press, children's textbooks, and academia. Although the litany is banal, its repetition is somehow exciting: technologies change us; the media will solve social problems or create new ones; monopoly ownership no longer matters; the internet killed journalism; social networking enables social revolution; the planet must be comprehensively wired; every child must have a laptop; cell phones must proliferate; the media deliver a cleaner, postindustrial capitalism; and we must all become cultural producers.[18]

Here is one commonly heard assessment of media technology from the twilight zone of the technological sublime:

> A major feature of the knowledge-based economy is the impact that ICTs have had on industrial structure, with a rapid growth of services and a relative decline of manufacturing. Services are typically less energy intensive and less polluting, so among those countries with a high and increasing share of services, we often see a declining energy intensity of production... with the emergence of the Knowledge Economy ending the old linear relationship between output and energy use (i.e. partially de-coupling growth and energy use).[19] (Houghton, 1)

Such statements are filled with technologists' jargon. They mix half-truths and utter nonsense. In reality, old-time, toxic manufacturing has moved to the Global South, where it is ascendant; pollution levels are rising worldwide; and energy consumption is accelerating in residential and institutional sectors, due almost entirely to ICT/CE usage, despite advances in energy conservation technology. As we will show, these are all outcomes of growth in ICT/CE, the foundation of the so-called knowledge-based economy. ICT/CE are misleadingly presented as having little or no material ecological impact.

## GREENING THE MEDIA

We have written this book knowing that a study of the media's effect on the environment must work especially hard to break the enchantment that inflames the popular and elite passion for media technologies. We understand that the mere mention of the political-economic arrangements that make shiny gadgets possible, or the environmental consequences of their appearance and disappearance, is bad medicine. It's an unwelcome buzz kill—not a cool way to converse about cool stuff. And it won't win us many allies among high-tech enthusiasts and ICT/CE industry leaders.

We do not dispute the importance of information and communication media in our lives and modern social systems. We are media people by profession and personal choice, and deeply immersed in the study and use of emerging media technologies. But we think it's time for a balanced assessment with less hype and more practical understanding of the relation of media technologies to the biosphere they inhabit.

This book is our attempt to present the issues in a critical manner with an eye to how media consumers, activists, researchers, and policy makers can move ICT/CE production and consumption toward ecologically sound practices. In the course of this project, we have found in casual conversation, lecture halls, classroom discussions, and correspondence consistent and increasing concern with the environmental impact of media technology, especially the deleterious effects of e-waste toxins on workers, air, water, and soil. We have learned that the grip of the technological sublime is not ironclad. Its instability provides a point of departure for our investigation and critique of the relationship between the media and the environment. As we will show, there is no place for the technological sublime, technophilia, or technological fads in projects to green the media.[20]

Chapter 1 addresses media consumers in order to clarify the material and ethical issues attendant to the rapidly growing rates of ICT/CE production and consumption. Our prognosis for individuals and institutions encourages a more-considered judgment of the relation between the environment and technology. The way technology is experienced in daily life is far removed from the physical work and material resources that go into it. In this sense, consumers experience the technological sublime in a manner reminiscent of what Karl Marx called "the Fetishism which attaches itself to the products of labour" once they are in the hands of a consumer, who lusts after them as if they were "independent beings."[21] There is a direct but unseen relationship between technology's symbolic power and the scale of its environmental impact, which the economist Juliet Schor refers to as a "materiality paradox"—the greater the frenzy to buy goods for their transcendent or nonmaterial cultural meaning, the greater the use of material resources.[22] We think that ecologically sound uses of media are possible without the overblown emphasis on technology's wonders, but reenchantment with both low-wattage culture and nonhuman nature are prerequisites. To that end, we introduce three forms of ecological ethics for assessing attitudes and actions that affect the environment—one that is human centered, another that is Earth centered, and another somewhere in between. With an eco-ethical turn away from the technological sublime, and technophilia more generally, we pose some key questions for readers to consider as they work through the book. The first and most important question to ask is how much media technology is socially necessary, not only on an individual or household basis but also on institutional and social scales. In addressing this question, our focus moves from the limitations of green consumption onto key case studies of the media's environmental and labor problems, concluding with possibilities for green governance, green citizenship, and green media design.

In chapters 2 and 3, we assess the material environmental impact of media technologies—from paper to tablet computers—by investigating the ecological context of "words" and "screens" respectively. We have built brief historical accounts of media technology from an ecological perspective into chapters 2 and 3. When we began our research, there was no tradition of ecological media history to draw on. But although this story has yet to be comprehensively documented, we discovered evidence of a fascinating, infuriating, complex, and contradictory historical relationship between media, environment, and society. In parallel to a succession of key moments in capitalist development, environmental effects of media technology began to emerge in small, incremental stages in the fifteenth century. The volume of toxic drips and harmful puffs increased over four centuries, spreading across the Earth in a pattern of uneven development established by merchants, mercenaries, and missionaries. The Industrial

Revolution brought crucial transformations in the scale and scope of media technology, as the convergence of chemical, mechanical, and electrical processes accelerated the accumulation of toxins in the environment. In the twentieth century, these innovations launched the era of electronic media and US hegemony while increasing the burden borne by the Earth's ecosystems.[23]

In chapter 4, we examine the relationship between the environment and labor in the global assembly lines and salvage/recycling yards where media technologies are built and dismantled. We draw on supply chain research to comprehend the global scale and intersectoral linkages that characterize ICT/CE "labor convergence."[24] We find that the greening of ICT/CE labor will require a broad international effort to bring about structural changes in the production, distribution, and disposal of media technologies. This necessitates greater transparency in working conditions throughout the ICT/CE supply chain, a goal that can unite workers, activists, researchers, policy makers, and unionists.

In chapter 5, we evaluate the environmental effects of bureaucratic thinking in the design, deployment, and regulation of ICT/CE. We focus on the gains and obstacles to green global governance enacted by decision-making bureaucrats, who play an important gatekeeping role in determining the ICT/CE we get and how their production, consumption, and disposal is regulated. We offer a brief historical account of bureaucratic thinking about technology and an assessment of the eco-ethics upon which such thinking is predicated. We use two case studies to illustrate current business strategies for large-scale green projects, and in a final section we review global policies that reflect bureaucratic approaches to green governance. We find some promising changes in state and corporate governance, but the bulk of bureaucratic thinking remains anchored to the belief that unfettered economic growth is necessary and good, with the eco-ethical limitations that this implies.

We sharpen this critique in chapter 6 by turning to green citizenship and governance. Here, we had to modify fundamental notions of citizenship, which are rooted in ideas of national rights and responsibilities, to account for the transterritorial nature of ecosystems and the global division of labor around ICT/CE. We offer examples of three emerging forms of green citizenship identified by the eco-political economist John Barry: he suggests that *environmental citizenship* is practiced part-time within such institutional settings as schools, offices, and other workplaces; *sustainability citizenship* strives for broad systemic change, with examples found in a mix of the research- and policy-oriented work of critical advocacy groups, scholars, unionists, and activists; and *resistance citizenship* involves direct action designed to pressure corporate and government bureaucrats to revolutionize their behavior, policies, and practices, and is enacted by groups like Greenpeace.[25] This chapter concludes with the fictional odyssey of a green citizen on a quest to uncover the environmental and labor conditions within the global supply chain of ICT/CE This scenario is also something of a synthesis of the book's analysis. It helps us imagine not only the obstacles faced by a dedicated green citizen but also many of the conditions needed to green the media.

We hope to make a convincing case that the media are, and have been for a long time, intimate *environmental participants*. In researching this book, we have learned that technology is yesterday's, today's, and tomorrow's news, but rarely in the way that it should be. The prevailing myth is that the printing press, telegraph, phonograph, photograph, cinema, telephone, wireless radio, television, and internet changed the world *without* changing the Earth. In reality, each technology has emerged by despoiling ecosystems and exposing workers to harmful environments, a truth obscured by both symbolic power and the power of moguls to set the terms by which such technologies are designed and deployed. Those who benefit from ideas of growth, progress, and convergence, who profit from high-tech innovation, monopoly, and state collusion—the military–industrial–entertainment–academic complex and the multinational commanders of labor—have for too long ripped off the Earth and workers. The implications are stark. They inform what is to come in this volume.[26]

·  ·  ·

As teachers and researchers, we are concerned with how media studies and the related fields of communication, film, literary, and cultural studies have addressed the environmental impact of media technology. You may choose to follow us into this review of media studies. If you're more interested in the book's ecological analysis of media technology, do turn to the next chapter!

Although these disciplines have distinct traits and traditions, they have all largely ignored the physical environmental effects of media (spoiler alert) because of their overriding interest in consciousness. They focus on how books, newspapers, magazines, advertisements, films, programs, games, conversations, and sites reflect, refract, or create states of mind in audiences. This is so whether the topic is media effects, psychoanalysis, ownership, control, imperialism, play, interpretation, or textuality. The field has largely neglected the physical environment. Can it be nudged toward a materialist ecology?

## MEDIA STUDIES

The central event of the 20th century is the overthrow of matter. In technology, economics, and the politics of nations, wealth—in the form of physical resources—has been losing value and significance. The powers of mind are everywhere ascendant over the brute force of things. (Esther Dyson, et al., 1994, 1.)

Most media experts would find little to criticize in this quotation from the modestly entitled *Magna Carta for the Knowledge Age*. For them, the principal role of the media is to inform, entertain, and involve the public, providing a grand conduit of knowledge and hence consciousness, a universal, devolved system of making meaning that transcends the centralized model of the mass media, transforming each consumer into a producer in the process. Information has been supplemented, and in some ways supplanted, by participation, with an emerging cacophony of democratic urges. The power of the mind is supposedly ascendant, thanks to the liberating role of ICT/CE.

Due largely to a surge of interest in the internet, books on technology make up over a fifth of media studies titles available in the United States.[27] Underlying this tendency is a tacit understanding that the materiality of technology—and its magical qualities—come prior to accompanying topics: Before there can be a story to analyze, a message to decode, or a pattern to identify in collective or individual media use, there has to be a physical medium, a technical means of communication. Books, magazines, money, and other printed media rely on a chain of production that begins with papermaking and printing. Similarly, radios, televisions, computers, cell phones, and music players arrive in our homes and offices with assembled and packaged parts derived from materials that have been excavated and manufactured, and delivering them relies on an array of electrical and electronic technologies. Cable and airborne networks are comprised of technologies that make the media possible. In short, apart from the immediate surroundings of offices, factories, forests, homes, vehicles, underpasses, jungles, stadia, prisons, mountains, parliaments, deserts, oceans, skies, hospitals, cemeteries, cinemas, and campuses where people engage the media, the physical foundation of media studies is machinery that is created and operated through human work, drawing on resources supplied by the Earth.

Despite this fact, media students and professors generally arrive at, inhabit, and depart universities with a focus on textuality, technology, and/or reception; they rarely address where texts and technologies physically come from or end up. Media critics for newspapers, podcasts, magazines, blogs, television, or radio may be more attuned to this political economy, at least in terms of how corporations promote their wares, but they rarely share such knowledge with their audiences.

Media studies abstains from deep analysis of technology's materiality in part because the field remains in thrall to two largely distinct but eerily compatible discourses: First, a cult of humanism adores the cultural devolution afforded by consumer technologies that generate millions of texts and address viewers and users as empowered. Second, a cult of scientism adores the mathematicization of daily life afforded by the digital and its associated research surveillance of everyday life.[28]

The humanistic side treats media technology as an enabler of human understanding, a tool for extending our capacities for expression and exchange. The mechanistic side draws on the scientific impulse to break down components of machines and study the entirety of communication. The former looks at relationships, relying on metaphors and pictorial codes; the latter looks at audiences, relying on linguistic codes and algorithms. The humanistic thinker emphasizes that technology is "a central character and actor in our social drama";[29] the mechanistic one emphasizes its linear progression from the Stone Age to computing.

Humanistic forms of inquiry have focused on themes raised in the content of texts and genres in the context of authors and societies, with a basis in rhetorical and novelistic writings from the principal Romance languages. Literary studies has provided a template through its claim to produce citizens imbued with national values. The history of printing has been peripheral to the mission of the study of English; thus, technological history has been a recent innovation across the humanities, largely being introduced in media studies. But a deeper ecological materiality has eluded the humanistic knowledge of media technology.

The humanistic bias that nature "is there for people to exploit" feeds into a binarism between nature and culture. It forgets the oneness of matter that René Descartes recognized, and the truly radical dimension of Darwinian evolutionary theory—not that we have ascended from others, but that we are inextricably related to them, logocentrically interdependent with forms of life that were previously deemed inferior.

What would happen to the humanistic approach if an ecological context were highlighted? Its focus on the symbolic environment would be enhanced by articulating links between the environmental impact of media technology and, say, media representations of the environment, from Romantic ideas of machines in the pastoral idyll to depictions of technological remedies for natural disasters in popular film, fiction, and TV. Such a transformation could link the humanities to the synthetic chemical ecology that people have introduced to the Earth as they have developed the media.[30]

What would become of the mechanistic tradition, which has been a core element of the social sciences' claim to generate useable knowledge that can improve life, if an ecological context were focused on? This approach has paralleled and sometimes mimicked the rational-scientific methods of media engineers and designers. It drew early inspiration from telecommunications systems to envisage a network of compartments that would connect senders, channels, and receivers. Interest in the first two aspects faded quickly, and communication research began a decade-long concentration on reception. This served two powerful constituencies. In the 1920s and '30s, research on radio and film responded to anxieties about unruly domestic and insurgent international populations. Media technologies were perceived as persuasive machines that could influence people's worldviews to shape political and commercial outcomes. Much US social science research on the media, for example, developed as an extension of foreign policy (propaganda studies) and as academic support for the capitalist media (market research and audience studies).[31] Methods were shared across commercial, academic, and governmental enterprises, creating a range of quantitative tools for observing large-scale social phenomena. This tradition envisioned technologies in narrower and more fragmented ways than humanistic media studies. Quantification of a medium's use, type, spatial distribution, component composition, and other related data was scarred by highly partial but pseudo-objective analytical contexts. The weakness of such knowledge is exposed when it is applied without a humanistic compass for direction—and via simplistic experiments whose results an eight-year-old could foretell.[32]

One of the most influential ideas guiding both wings of media studies is that new technologies redefine the social and cultural relationships that earlier media helped shape. As the economic historian Harold Innis put it in the middle of the twentieth century, "The demands of the new media" are "imposed on the older media."[33] Old media cannot carry certain new content, such as streamed words and images in print. They are displaced by new media delivering higher-potency versions of old content through new channels (words and data are transmitted via telegraph and telephone; words, data, and music via radio; words, data, music, and images via TV and the internet; and so on). Some theorists regard these new media as additive rather than subtractive, cross-referencing one another and serving different as well as overlapping people and interests in "peaceful coexistence." For others, the arrival of the internet changes the story. They proclaim, for example, "la fin de la télévision" [the end of television] or even that "la televisión ha muerto" [television is dead].[34] It is true that most forms of new media have supplanted or supplemented earlier ones as central organs of authority and pleasure: newspapers versus speeches, films versus plays, and records versus performances. TV blended what came before it and became a warehouse of contemporary culture. Today, the model of incorporation continues, but without necessarily terminating earlier forms. Television models the internet and vice versa, while print and telephony expand due to their convenience and durability.[35] And established cultural producers dominate across these media. Cybertarian true believers commonly refer to other forms of knowledge as "legacy media" and celebrate the idea of audiences transformed into producers. But many people visit websites that are really rather distant from these dreams, such as the BBC for news, which employs a lot of professionally trained journalists; YouTube for drama, which features material from TV; and Wikipedia for background, which follows the eighteenth-century format of an encyclopedia.[36]

Sometimes these changes and predictions are celebrated; sometimes they are denounced. On the one hand, media studies buys into the individualist fantasy of reader/audience/consumer/player autonomy—the libertarian intellectual's wet dream of music, movies, television, and everything else converging under the sign of empowered fans. On the other, it buys into the corporate fantasy of control—the political economist's arid nightmare of music, movies, television, and everything else converging under the sign of empowered firms. Those antinomies shadow the fetish of innovation that informs much discussion of media technology, while ignoring the environmental destruction and centralized power that underpin it.

Media studies *does* provide a political-economic framework for understanding media technology, but the tendency is marginal, especially in the United States.[37] A few scholars have addressed the nexus of management, empire, labor, and the media from an ecological point of view.[38] But such a focus remains largely neglected next to the fulsome joy with which the "new" is made welcome. Consider the "new Right" of media studies, which invests in Schumpeterian entrepreneurs, evolutionary economics, and "creative industries" with unparalleled zest. It never saw an app it didn't like, or a socialist idea it did.[39] Innovation animates economic growth as new products and services destroy existing ones, with anyone left standing the beneficiary. For example, Manuel Castells's discussion of environmental movements fails to identify information technology's polluting side, even as he details the movement's reliance on such technology.[40] The irony of exemplary ironies.

The philosopher John Dewey may have been the first to suggest that communications exerted an environmental influence upon the organization of society[41]; the literary critic Marshall McLuhan went on to speak of the environment as a central concern of "media study." For McLuhan, a

"TV is environmental and imperceptible, like all environments." This was the medium's famous message, the expert analysis of which McLuhan hoped would elevate media studies as a discipline (helping the fish become conscious of the water, as it were).[42] Although the fortunes of McLuhanism waned academically, in the United States at least, by the 1970s, the idea had taken hold that media analysis was "resolved with a metaphor" of environments.[43] This substitution by the metaphorical still obscures the ecological context of media technology (search any database for media and environment, environmental impact of media, media and ecology, or related phrases, and you will see what we mean). And McLuhan's belief that "as software information becomes the prime factor in politics and indus-try... suddenly *small is beautiful*"[44] continues to hold sway over the demate-rializing fantasies of cybertarians.

Orthodox histories of media technology provide non-ecological, tele-ological narratives of heroic business innovators and plucky independent inventors dialing up freedom and fun for consumers, ringing in new forms of public knowledge to satisfy an innate desire for progress and artistic realism. Film critic André Bazin, for instance, tells us that film emerged as "an idealistic phenomenon," with economic and social relations following the lead of desire—the desire for realism in cinema.[45] This mimetic fallacy assumes that the power of artists' and audiences' desires drives technologi-cal innovation in the media.[46]

In accordance with these foundation myths, conventional accounts chart successive new media technologies appearing along relatively autonomous and benign paths that are as additive as they are competitive, as syntagmatic as they are paradigmatic. This history is rife with narcissistic accounts from the media themselves, which often tell us that digitization derived from the laid-back musings of California dreamers (what we sometimes refer to as "fun stuff") rather than the military–industrial–entertainment–academic complex. Digitization supposedly fused the media in the 1980s to create today's *Aufklärung*, delivering text, voice, data, video, and music to consum-ers and enabling them, *Gestalt*-like, to become producers.[47] "Prosumers" allegedly emerged from the dream to take over the means of production, streaming onto computers of every size and resolution—from tiny cell phones through middling laptops to large flat-screen TVs.[48] The cultural historian Andrew Ross describes prosumption as referring to "consumers who do more and more of the work that producers used to pay employ-ees for."[49] The prosumer is subject to the simultaneous triumph and emp-tiness of commodity aesthetics, in which signs substitute as sources and measures of value. The symbolic power of media technology is enhanced by the idea of a liberated consumer, which, like the commodity sign, provides no residual correspondence to a reality other than its own.[50] In embracing

MAXWELL, RICHARD, 1957-

GREENING THE MEDIA.

Cloth    246 P.
NEW YORK: OXFORD UNIVERSITY PRESS, 2012

AUTH: QUEENS COLLEGE, CUNY. EXAMINES VARIOUS WAYS
MEDIA TECHNOLOGY NEGATIVELY IMPACTS ENVIRONMENT.
LCCN 2011-35713
  **ISBN** 0199914672      **Library PO#** AP-SLIPS

|  |  | **List** | 99.00 | USD |
|---|---|---|---|---|
| 9395 NATIONAL UNIVERSITY LIBRAR | | **Disc** | 14.0% | |
| **App. Date**  3/20/13  SOC-SCI  8214-09 | | **Net** | 85.14 | USD |

SUBJ: 1. MASS MEDIA--SOC. ASPECTS. 2. MASS MEDIA--
POL. ASPECTS.
AWD/REV: 2012 COYB
CLASS HM1206        DEWEY# 302.23        LEVEL ADV-AC

---

**YBP Library Services**

MAXWELL, RICHARD, 1957-

GREENING THE MEDIA.

Cloth    246 P.
NEW YORK: OXFORD UNIVERSITY PRESS, 2012

AUTH: QUEENS COLLEGE, CUNY. EXAMINES VARIOUS WAYS
MEDIA TECHNOLOGY NEGATIVELY IMPACTS ENVIRONMENT.
  LCCN 2011-35713
  **ISBN** 0199914672      **Library PO#** AP-SLIPS

|  |  | **List** | 99.00 | USD |
|---|---|---|---|---|
| 9395 NATIONAL UNIVERSITY LIBRAR | | **Disc** | 14.0% | |
| **App. Date**  3/20/13  SOC-SCI  8214-09 | | **Net** | 85.14 | USD |

SUBJ: 1. MASS MEDIA--SOC. ASPECTS. 2. MASS MEDIA--
POL. ASPECTS.
AWD/REV: 2012 COYB
CLASS HM1206        DEWEY# 302.23        LEVEL ADV-AC

simulation, "human needs, relationships and fears, the deepest recesses of the human psyche, become mere means for the expansion of the commodity universe."[51] Sociologist Jean Baudrillard laments a "submission to technology and to the crushing virtual reality of the networks and programs." He argues that this dependence "is irreversible as it is the result of the fulfillment of our desires."[52] Likewise, for the philosopher Max Horkheimer, the supposedly resistant consumer is susceptible to a new mastery, and a new servitude, to those who labor to serve and shape that consumer—who, in another role, might be a different kind of person.[53] Meanwhile, marketers delight in selling this historical achievement as, for example, a "new TV ecosystem."[54]

Such odes to keyboard dexterity are hardly novel. Seventy years ago, Walter Benjamin wrote of photography that "a touch of the finger now sufficed to fix an event for an unlimited period of time." Since the 1970s, "knowledge workers" have gained in status among economists thanks to information-based industries that promise endless gains in productivity and the purest of competitive markets. They form what geographer Joel Kotkin calls a putative "aristocracy of talent" elevated by the meritocratic discourse of progress, informatization, and the "creative industries," luxuriating in ever-changing techniques, technologies, and networks. According to sociologist Armand Mattelart, because their work is abstracted from physical, dirty labor, knowledge workers thrive in the twilight zone of the technological sublime. Literary critic Michael Hardt and philosopher-politician Antonio Negri graphically, romantically, and inaccurately refer to the exchange of information, knowledge, and emotion that happens on computers as "immaterial labor."[55] Business people love this form of talk, even dreaming up the term "virtual workers."[56] Right-wing futurist Alvin Toffler invented the related concept of "the cognitariat," which has since been taken up and redisposed by progressives. Negri uses the term to describe people mired in contingent media work who have heady educational qualifications and a grand facility with cultural technologies and genres.[57]

This Pollyannaish decoupling perhaps reaches its acme in telecommuters, who not only have paper-free offices, but office-free work. Like the defense attorney Mickey Haller in Michael Connelly's hardboiled Los Angeles novels, who works in a Lincoln Town Car driven by an ex-client, they operate from wires rather than buildings. But, according to the Institution of Engineering and Technology, the net amount of energy saved from telecommuting in the United States is, at best, 0.4 percent, because while people no longer drive to work, they end up living in suburbia and hence travel sizeable distances to experience actual life, in addition to increasing their domestic power use monumentally.[58]

The cognitariat plays key roles in the production and circulation of goods and services by creating and coordinating media technologies and texts. It is defined by a narrow focus on consciousness:

- artists, comprising musicians, directors, writers, and journalists
- artisans, including sound engineers, editors, graphic designers, and cinematographers
- impresarios, connecting proprietors and executives to artists
- proprietors and executives, controlling employment and investment, negotiating with states
- audiences and consumers, paying for content, interpreting it in order to give media meaning, and eliding real barriers of entry to media production through their dubious anointment as producer-consumers (prosumers)

These groups operate within institutional contexts:

- private bureaucracies, controlling investment, production, and distribution across the media
- public bureaucracies, offering what capitalism cannot, while comporting themselves in an ever-more commercial manner
- small businesses, run by charismatic individuals
- networks, fluid associations formed to undertake specific projects

Most writings in media studies constrict the ambit of media labor such that the industry mavens and spectators listed above define production. This mirrors the growth ideology and apolitical enchantment with media technologies found in most trade publications, entertainment news outlets, and fan culture.

In contrast, a growing body of critical scholarship into media labor is generating information from below the line of elite industry research, drawing on more diverse and independent sources, including labor unions and policy analysis, to consider the physical nature of work and what it does to people and the environment. Examples include Luis Reygadas's account of how television sets are made in Mexico, Jefferson Cowie's study of RCA's "seventy year quest for cheap labor," Pun Ngai's time spent on the electronics production line in China, and Vicki Mayer's investigation of similar workers in Brazil.[59]

And the novelist Ralph Ellison tells a tale that doesn't suit the triumphalism of the new that impels conventional media history:

> Like so many kids of the Twenties, I played around with radio—building crystal sets and circuits consisting of a few tubes, which I found published in radio magazines.

At the time we were living in a white middle-class neighborhood, where my mother was a custodian for some apartments, and it was while searching the trash for cylindrical ice-cream cartons which were used by amateurs for winding tuning coils that I met a white boy who was looking for the same thing. I gave him some of those I'd found and we became friends.... I moved back into the Negro community and ... was never to see him again. (quoted in Smith, 2003, 93)[60]

Ellison's story about scavenging for parts to build crystal sets reminds us that the history of media technology is rarely written as a sequence of happy or harmful accidents, or the outcome of searing racism. In this case, chance brought two young radio enthusiasts together, then discrimination kept them apart. Such an anecdote requires that we rethink standard explanations. The mimetic fallacy, a sweet story of art, markets, realism, or innovation that purportedly shapes technological change in the media, does not explain, for example, why film stock once privileged white skin tones over black. This occurred because the development of dye couplers to highlight darker-toned skin was not a priority for the movie industry. Whiteness came cheaply and early, at the nexus of aesthetics, chemistry, commerce, and race—a nexus that should disturb causation myths of immanent realism, pure supply and demand, or apolitical technological progress.[61]

Those of us who study, write, and teach about the media have an historic responsibility. Media studies must erase "the tenacious division that for so long separated sciences of description and sciences of interpretation, morphological studies and hermeneutical analysis," recognizing with the cultural historian Roger Chartier that the "world of text ... [is] a world of objects and performances." The media must be traced through "their different and successive materialities," accounting for both their open, malleable, polyphonic qualities and their closed, fixed, monaural ones.[62] Media texts and technologies accrete and attenuate meanings on their travels as they rub up against, trope, and are troped by other fictional and factual texts, social relations, and material objects and as they are interpreted by readers—all those moments that allow a book, for example, to become a "literary thing."[63]

Understanding the media requires studying them up, down, and sideways, as found in notable anthropological approaches such as Laura Nader's ethnography of the powerful, George Marcus's multisited analysis, and Néstor García Canclini's insistence that "macrosociological approaches, which seek to understand the integration of radio, television, music, news, books, and the internet in the fusion of multimedia and business, also need an anthropological gaze, a more qualitative perspective, to comprehend how modes of access, cultural goods, and forms of communication are being reorganized."[64] This means knowing which companies make media technologies and texts; the physical processes of production, distribution, and consumption; the systems of cross subsidy and monopoly profit making; the complicity of media coverage, regulation, and ratings with multinational corporations' business plans in the circulation of texts; and press coverage of stars and awards, inter alia.

These approaches fruitfully connect media analysis to what literary critic Ian Hunter calls an "occasion...the practical circumstances governing the composition and reception of a piece," or as in the communicologists Alec McHoul and Tom O'Regan's description of a "discursive analysis of particular actor networks, technologies of textual exchange, circuits of communicational and textual effectivity, traditions of exegesis, [and] commentary and critical practice," with links to models of sender–message–receiver and encoding and decoding information.[65] These authors attempt to deliver us from the clutches of "immanence, from the imprisonment in corpuses considered as unique dispensers of meaning," as do the ethnographer Bruno Latour and his followers with their actor network analysis of contemporary life as the sum of equal and overlapping influence among natural phenomena, social forces, and cultural production.[66] Latour notes: "Every type of politics has been defined by its relation to nature, whose every feature, property, and function depends on the polemical will to limit, reform, establish, short-circuit, or enlighten public life."[67] The linguist Stephen Muecke puts it another way: "We have only ever managed to philosophise with the help of things: the turning stars, apples which fall, turtles and hares, rivers and gods" and, for media studies, "cameras and computers."[68] Just as objects of scientific knowledge come to us in hybrid forms that are coevally affected by society and culture, so the latter two domains are themselves affected by the natural world.[69]

Media technologies are creatures, then, of ideology, symbolic power, "corporations, advertising, government, subsidies, corruption, financial speculation, and oligopoly."[70] Yet they are not mere epiphenomena arising from this nexus of political and economic forces; nor are they simply channels of meaning and pleasure or dumb industrial objects. Rather, they are all these things. They are hybrid monsters, subject to rhetoric, status, and technology—to value, power, and science—all at once but in contingent ways.[71] Thus, engagements with media technologies and texts must account for the conditions under which they are made, circulated, received, interpreted, criticized, and disposed of, considering all the shifts and shocks that characterize their existence as commodities—their ongoing renewal and disposal as the temporary "property" of varied, productive workers and publics. As a medium passes across space and time, it is remade again and again by institutions, discourses, and practices of distribution, reception, and disposal. That takes us beyond the rather musty corridors of academic labor and media critique; it hauls us into the polluted corridors of material production and death that derive from a risk society.

Early modernity was about producing and distributing goods in a struggle for the most effective and efficient industrialization, with a devil-take-the-hindmost mentality and little consideration of the environment. We can see instances of this in capitalism's imposition of time discipline over working-class life. The risks posed by the unruliness of both capitalism's basic nature and the proletariat had to be managed to serve growth and progress. The result improved the productivity of industrial labor but introduced potential and actual harms to workers' minds, bodies, and communities. The increasing velocity of production and an unprecedented variety and volume of commodities fostered a fetishism that was detached from the natural environment.

Today, risk society is about enumerating and managing those threats via probability, by imagining possible outcomes. Rather than being an occasional factor, risk is now part of what it means to be modern. This aspect of modernity is characterized by having ever-more sophistication in measuring risks, even as their range and impact grow less controllable, because the technologies and markets that "improve" life also add unforeseen dangers. Risk societies admit and even promote the irrationality of the economy as a means, paradoxically, of governing populations. They naturalize despoliation, global labor competition, cyclical recession, declining life-long employment, massive international migration, overreaching technologies, and diminished welfare-state protections.[72]

Ironically, the future orientation of risk society lacks the revolutionary sensibility of forward-thinking politics. Denizens of risk societies factor costs and benefits into everyday life as never before, while their sense of being able to determine the future through choice is diminished. The obsession with risk as inevitable weakens ideological commitments to Marxism, feminism, and anti-imperialism, for unlike the notions of a broad Left that once infused the struggles involved in these movements, political and social issues are delinked from a central organizing critique. A position adopted on, for instance, ecologically sound consumption says nothing about a position on popular democracy. The calculation of chance worsens the odds for radical change.[73]

We think media studies can counter such approaches by relinking probability to politics. But, to do so, it must rethink the displacement of *meta-récits* such as Marxism, since that preference ironically mirrors capitalism's focus on microeconomic theory, privileging the firm and the consumer as units of analysis over attempts to understand cui bono.[74]

Rather than the sender–message–receiver models of US communication studies, the circuit-of-culture methods of British cultural studies, or

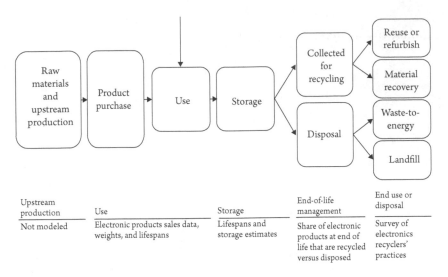

| Upstream production | Use | Storage | End-of-life management | End use or disposal |
|---|---|---|---|---|
| Not modeled | Electronic products sales data, weights, and lifespans | Lifespans and storage estimates | Share of electronic products at end of life that are recycled versus disposed | Survey of electronics recyclers' practices |

**Figure I.1:** The Life of Electronic Objects

the active-audience pleasures of feminist media studies, we need to look at what happens to objects as much as at brains (see Figure I.1).

This means following some surprising tacks, such as the critical path outlined in the US federal government's 2011 report on e-waste.[75] And the implications of doing such work are uncomfortable—as ironic as the massive proliferation of "green" branding skewered by *The Onion*'s "Obligatory Green Issue," an "all-paper salute to the environment," and as paradoxical as the fact that environmental scientists use energy to undertake and disseminate research that shows we must use less energy. After all, many of us grew up driven—or orchestrated—by the tenet that when we "add writing" to evolution, "history proper begins."[76]

Can a single critic or academic do such work? Collaborative scholarship is mostly frowned upon—or at least not understood—beyond the sciences. A commitment to the single-authored monograph's aesthetic-monastic model of knowledge entrenches such backwardness. We must get beyond that to create teams of scholars and activists from right across the human and other sciences, especially given the paucity of cradle-to-grave media work, using Chartier's fascination with archives and libraries and Latour's focus on factories and laboratories.[77] Core research subjects for this type of analysis include:

- policy documents from public bureaucracies (international, national, regional, state, and municipal governments) and private bureaucracies (corporations, lobby groups, research firms, nongovernment organizations, religions, and unions) on media subvention, awards, raw materials, and recycling

- debates (congressional/parliamentary, press, lobby-group, activist, and academic) pertaining to cultural and environmental policy
- budgets (for paper makers, printers, and publishers, for example)
- laws (relevant legislation and case law about labor, copyright, environmental impact, importation, and censorship)
- histories (acknowledging what came before and what is new)
- places (analysts in the Global North and South contextualizing their findings as partial, not universal, by examining other examples)
- people (who is included and who is excluded, who is highlighted and who is hidden, when technologies and texts are made)
- pollution (the environmental costs of textuality)
- science (independent, not just corporate, research)

Moving agilely between systems of subsidy, forms of policing, plans for commodification, methods of governmentality, and practices of waste disposal will help media studies intervene in the environmental relation between technologies and texts. As the current celebration of media technology inevitably winds down, perhaps it will become easier to comprehend that digital wonders come at the expense of employees and ecosystems. This would return us to Max Weber's insistence that we understand technology as a "mode of processing material goods." Conversation analyst Harvey Sacks explains that "the failures of technocratic dreams that if only we introduced some fantastic new communication machine the world will be transformed" derived from the very banality of such introductions—that every time they take place, one more "technical apparatus" is simply "being made at home with the rest of our world."[78] Media studies can join in this banality or withdraw the welcome mat for media technologies that despoil the Earth and wreck lives of those who make them. It is time to green the media by greening media studies.

# CHAPTER 1

✧

# Consumers

If you…want the latest and greatest…you have to buy a new iPod at least once a year…Apple has a really strong environmental policy.
— Steve Jobs, quoted in Slade, 2007, 76[1]

Only recently have we started to understand the negative impacts of digital electronic equipment worldwide. Most of us, overwhelmed by the technological wonders that these devices are capable of, forget to ask ourselves, "How have they been made?" "By whom?" "Where?" "Under what conditions?"
— Centre for Reflection and Action on Labour Issues, 1996, 4

S hop 'til you drop![2] For anyone growing up in a culture oriented toward consumption, these are the marching orders that explain why we work and define who we are. They exemplify the all-encompassing idea of consumerism: to get inside us; to determine many if not most of our personal aspirations; and to reflect our sense of belonging in a capitalist society, in which virtually every public official, business leader, teacher, family member, work mate, and lover agrees that a high-consumption lifestyle is the norm. Even the word "consumer" is now regularly "used interchangeably with person in the 10 most commonly used languages, and most likely in many more."[3]

It's easy to forget what Marx, our greatest ethnographer of shopping, noted: that commodities originate "outside us," where they begin their life as an amalgamation of natural resources, energy inputs, labor, production processes, and political and economic arrangements.[4] Accounts of the work, raw materials, and exploitation that go into media technologies are generally displaced by representations of the leisure, style, and equality that supposedly come out of them. Apple thus refers to the iMac as a "modern art installation" and advertises "Do-It-Yourself Parts for iBook," even though the company is notorious for sealing its products from inspection and customization.[5] The Hong Kong–based advocacy group Students & Scholars Against Corporate Misbehaviour (SACOM) explains that "We are consuming the blood and tears of workers, a fact hidden from us by fancy advertisements."[6]

Adorned with human characteristics of beauty, taste, serenity, and the like, media technologies compensate for the absence of these qualities in everyday capitalism via a "permanent opium war" of symbolic intoxication.[7] They woo us with an attractive appearance in ways that borrow from romantic love, but reverse that relationship, teaching people about romance from commodities, which become part of them through the double-sided nature of advertising and "the good life" of high-tech luxury. Cultural critics capture this paradox with terms like "commodity aesthetics" and notions of "the *promesse du bonheur* that advanced capitalism always holds before…[people/consumers], but never quite delivers."[8] The intense come-hither stare of media technologies endows them with totemic power—they appear in the sublime form of fetishes that we should pursue with frenzied ambition.

This is not to propose that consumption is eradicable, pointless, or unpleasant. Fifty years ago, the renowned Jamaican cultural theorist Stuart Hall wrote about the spread of consumer electronics among the poor as part of "a legitimate materialism, born out of centuries of physical deprivation and want."[9] The point is to find ways to transcend the shallow roles assigned to us as consumers by marketers, microeconomists, and other boosters of unbridled consumption. To them, we are "desiccated calculators…rational-choice rodents moved exclusively by the short range and the quantifiable." Our liberty is thereby reduced to the "freedom to choose" after "major political, economic, and social decisions have already been made." Even the "time society has gained through technology is organized in advance for the [consumer]."[10]

These negative, system-serving ideas of consumption are ironically underpinned by a libertarian idea that says deregulated, individuated media making turns consumers into producers and subcultural rebels. Examples include blogging or posting videos online to riff on commercial culture or right-wing demagoguery, clicking on a link to endorse antiwar or environmental activism, mocking bourgeois manners, goading the law in the safety of cyberspace, or simply celebrating alternative lifestyles. These "prosumers" are supposedly freed from social confinement to experiment with new subjectivities as they are rewarded for their intellect and competitiveness by the capacity to network with people across cultures in a postpolitical cornucopia.[11] The idea of a proactive consumer is quite capacious, though its claims don't stand up once we understand the limits imposed by technology and the political economy the consumer inhabits. For example, the possibilities for green prosumption can be seen in the growing number of media users concerned about the material effects of commodities on the planet. A 2002 study reveals that half the US population engaged in consumer boycotts and their opposite, buycotts. These actions were frequently inspired by environmental concerns. But the next stage is for merchandisers to find ways to benefit from the boom of shoppers willing to pay more for goods labeled "green." New markets equal new markups, so they have joined the green-is-good chorus.[12]

These market-oriented notions of green prosumption hardly aim to advance the goals of environmentalism; they are branding opportunities for retailers and other advertisers. A more significant movement toward green consumption is growing out of a widespread political aspiration to form a greener society. This is reflected in the global doubling of membership in environmental groups between 1980 and 2000. At the beginning of the new century, such participation rivaled "that of political parties" and exceeded "membership levels of other important civil society sectors." These numbers and events do not indicate an absolute swing away from the cultural paradigm of consumerism; but they do reflect people's readiness to know what goes on "outside" the commodity and, by extension, what relationships might flourish beyond the network of things that circumscribe our immediate surroundings.[13]

More important, consumer curiosity about the material provenance of commodities has begun to pose new ethical challenges to corporate defenders of the consumer society. For instance, there is evidence that green customer demand can push media businesses toward ecologically sound practices.[14] This is part of a new understanding of accountability—called corporate social responsibility (CSR) by public relations managers. Such accountability, once applied to political organs and their responsiveness to their constituencies, has expanded in the early twenty-first century to encompass the relationship of corporations to their customers and the wider world.[15] Among numerous examples of this trend is the Hearst Corporation's consumer magazine, *TheDailyGreen.com*—"dedicated to green living"—which stands in for the hundreds of firms waiting to do the bidding of the conscious consumer. There are also consultants who stand ready to aid corporations involved with ICT/CE that seek consumer approval for their green credentials and are looking for subtle ways of asking for it. International Shareholder Services (ISS), a proxy advisor for many large institutional investors such as mutual and pension funds, astonished outsiders in 2002 by recommending that ExxonMobil stockholders vote in favor of renewable fuel research and anti–sexual discrimination policies and against child labor in Marriott hotels. Previously a right-wing stalwart, ISS had determined that "being perceived as a good corporate citizen might affect shareholder value" by appealing to socially concerned investors. Put another way, for the first time, ISS judged that being on the same side as environmentalists and unions made sense and cents, in keeping with studies that correlate stock valuations of companies with environmentalism. Whereas growth in professionally managed assets in the United States was about 15 percent annually before the global financial crisis, the figure was 40 percent for assets with mandates for "social responsibility." Indeed, over 90 percent of *Fortune* 500 companies appear in "socially responsible" investing portfolios, which use the Dow Jones Industrial Average.[16]

Signs of a burgeoning institutional embrace of environmental ethics should not relieve us of our critical sensibilities. For starters, there are many obvious shortcomings to greening business-as-usual: It is contradictory, valorizing "a green commodity discourse" that promotes the magical fusion of environmentalism with growth, profits, and pleasure; it is transient, narrowly focused on what is right for investors and short-term gains, and therefore untrustworthy as an environmental partner; and it is superficial, guarding carefully against the acknowledgement of what is already known—that accelerating innovation, rising energy consumption, and government and business policies promoting a growth ideology are responsible for scarcity and climate change. In short, it is an inadequate response to consumers' environmental worries, a shallow ethics that is inherently flawed by its faith in a doctrine of unending economic expansion and plutocratic form of participation, where money does not so much buy votes as qualify voters.[17]

The only upside, for the foreseeable future, is that persistent consumer demand for corporations and governments to take greater responsibility for environmental harm has forced self-described green businesses to generate a steady stream of documentation on supply chains and other physical processes in which commodities are produced. In combination with the increased publicity of science journalism that is focused on ecological problems, the sharing of publicly available information on the material reality of the life cycle of ICT/CE has begun to dampen popular enchantment with media technology.[18] Despite some one-dimensional ethical displays on the part of green media businesses, consumers can now get a wider range of probing answers to the environmental questions set forth in the second epigraph above: How have media technologies been made? By whom? Where? And under what conditions?

The answers to these questions necessitate both desire and method if we are to understand the intimate relationship between media technologies and ecosystems. For a green consumer, this means learning some basics of environmental science and becoming comfortable with a relatively small but new vocabulary of consumption, which we draw on in this and forthcoming chapters. Green consumers will need to be familiar with processes that take place behind their screens yet at some distance from their media use, such as the environmental impact of prior inputs to media technologies from the Earth, extracted via mining, logging, and drilling; and subsequent outputs from technology into the Earth from emissions into air, land, and water whenever a media device is made.

Input effects involve the Earth's ability to provide resources whose quantities are either renewable or not (soils, forests, water, minerals, and so on). Ecologists call this the *source function* of the environment. Output effects involve the ability of the Earth's ecosystems to absorb and recycle wastes from media technology's electrical and chemical products and processes. Ecologists call this the *sink function* of the environment.[19] As we show throughout this book, the effects of such inputs and outputs outlive the technology's existence, in some cases for generations, through deforestation; water pollution; carbon dioxide $(CO_2)$ emissions; PCBs; dioxin; and other destructive processes, substances, and byproducts.

Perhaps the most important idea for green media consumption is environmental *sustainability*, which can be defined as the "nonnegotiable planetary preconditions" that set limits on how much the Earth can give to and absorb from economic, social, and cultural activities.[20] In its most radical interpretation, the idea of sustainability thoroughly discredits the growth model that subtends capitalism itself, though soft versions of sustainable development seek an accommodation with growth (we address these in chapter 5).[21] For now, consider the tougher stance expressed by many environmental economists: there can be no compromise in the fusion of growth and sustainability. The idea of sustainable growth is "a bad oxymoron—self contradictory as prose and unevocative as poetry." The economy is an "open" subsystem of the Earth's ecosystems, which are "materially closed."[22]

Human transgression of the limits of sustainability has led to the contemporary ecological crisis, which consists of four interrelated environmental problems:

- climate change (global warming), caused by historical overproduction of greenhouse-gas emissions (carbon dioxide, methane, and nitrous oxide);

- pollution in the overdeveloped world, including the effects of industrial dumping from the Global North to the Global South; with the rising levels of poisons disrupting biological development and immuno-logical, endocrinal, neurological, and hormonal systems of "virtually all organisms";
- reduced biodiversity—the Earth's "sixth great extinction," unique for being caused by one species; and
- disappearing habitat—50 percent of the Earth's forests and 25 percent of sea habitats gone.[23]

Throughout this book, we review the ways that media technologies have contributed to and deepened the eco-crisis. In this chapter, electricity usage by media technologies provides the first illustration of the scale of the problem facing green consumers. We follow that with a discussion of how consumers can connect to and think about the relationship between the environment and media technologies through an ecological-ethical ori-entation. We end with a brief case study of the cell phone, which brings several threads of the consumption problem together. Mobile telephony consumes us and the environment: it mixes sublime qualities into social conditions that make it indispensible; it is an exemplar of planned obsoles-cence; and it is an energy guzzler that brings hundreds of toxic compounds into the environment.

## POWERING MEDIA IS A DIRTY BUSINESS

Integrated circuits will lead to such wonders as home computers—or at least terminals connected to a central computer—automatic controls for automobiles, and personal portable communications equipment. (Gordon E. Moore, 1965, 114)

In a famous article from the 1960s, the Fairchild Camera and Instrument Corporation chemist and future Intel founder Gordon E. Moore framed what has come to be known as "Moore's Law." It states that the number of transistors arrayed on an integrated circuit chip will double every two years for the foreseeable future, at minimal additional cost. His predic-tion was based on a semilog graph that extrapolated from developments between the invention of the integrated circuit in 1958 and 1965. Moore's estimates have largely been exceeded. His work is cited approvingly every day, even as Intel is criticized for abusive, avaricious business practices that have led to massive antitrust cases, resulting in a billion euro fine levied by the European Commission.[24]

A small section nestled in Moore's article has not been mentioned as enthusiastically or often as his saccharine promise. It addresses the consequences of a "heat problem" that could occur if computers became so small that they essentially had the same mass as their components. Moore suggested that this might make them "glow brightly with present power dissipation." He ultimately decided that the subsequent cost (always Moore's principal concern) would be manageable, thanks to the space available for cooling. But by 2011, the energy demands of the latest chip generations were reaching the limits of the electrical power supply, while the only way to avoid destructive heat levels was to create a kind of chip, known as dark silicon, on which some transistors were left unpowered while others were running.[25]

The environmental impact of the media's energy consumption has a long history, beginning with the invention and deployment of telecommunication. We examine this history in more detail in the next chapter. Here, we focus on contemporary environmental concerns with electricity consumption.

The spread of a national electric grid across the United States entailed the inclusion of large transformers to regulate electricity flow and large capacitors for energy storage (microversions of capacitors are in all electronic devices; they make the current generation of touch screens work). Between 1930 and 1980, these devices used PCBs to cool and insulate— until they were banned. But the US Toxic Substance Control Act of 1976 (section 761.2) allowed these flame retardants to be used until 2025 in "nonleaking" transformers, capacitors, cables, and other enclosed equipment, as well as in "non–totally enclosed" older equipment still in use and in need of refits. PCBs are carcinogenic. Like dioxin, they are known as persistent organic pollutants because they do not degrade easily, travel great distances in waterways, and are absorbed into food chains through bioaccumulation.[26]

The electrical industry has been one of the biggest emitters of PCBs into the environment—General Electric (GE) holds the record for PCBs dumped in US waterways.[27] Until 2011, GE was also one of the largest media companies in the country via its ownership of the massive TV network NBC and associated properties. Acting as clinically as one can imagine, GE announced a twenty-first century policy of "eco-imagination," a word that emerged from $90 million of product development along with advertisements of trees growing from smokestacks and a computer-generated elephant dancing around a rain forest and a "clean" factory. The intention was to show that the company was "addressing the problems of tomorrow, today"—in reality, a response to regulations imposed in Europe (see chapter 5).[28]

As we noted in the introduction, between 2.5 and 3 percent of the world's greenhouse-gas emissions in 2007 resulted from electricity consumed by media technologies, including personal computers, data monitors, printers, fixed and mobile telecommunications, televisions, local-area networks, and server warehouses. At that time, this level of emissions was virtually the same as aviation, if the energy required for ICT manufacture is included.[29]

Electricity consumption at server warehouses worldwide doubled between 2000 and 2005. By 2006, they accounted for 1.5 percent of the use of the US electrical supply, which is about $4.5 billion worth. In 2010, US server warehouses consumed between 1.7 and 2.2 percent of the total supply. In 2006, Google's server warehouse in Oregon was using the same amount of power as a city of 200,000 people, even though Google is considered more efficient than the bulk of the data center industry. By 2008, Microsoft was adding 20,000 servers a month. Google had perhaps half a million servers, while eBay and Amazon maintained such facilities by the thousands. The number of federal government data centers increased from 432 in 1998 to over a thousand in 2009, with a projected consumption of twelve billion kilowatt hours in 2011. The energy required to run them keeps going up. British data disclose that in the 1980s, 400–800 watts per square meter was typical; during the heyday of the dot coms, it was 750–1000 watts per square meter; and 1000–1200 watts per square meter between 2004 and 2006. A few years later, 1500–2000 watts per square meter became the norm. It is not surprising that the number of power stations being built around the world also began increasing—by 150 percent a year.[30]

Although server warehouse power consumption grew at slower rates with the contemporary economic crisis, the industry continued to expand its overall energy demands. Assuming that server warehouses return to pre-crisis trends, their electricity consumption in the United States and the European Union could double every five years. Yet their existence and impact are largely immaterial to consumers. For example, cloud computing might as well result from invisible magic for all that we can see of it. Conversely, customers were able to visit or at least visualize telegraph and telephone exchanges, post offices, and so on, the buildings of which were as readily identifiable as was the labor to construct, maintain, and use them.[31]

According to the International Energy Agency (IEA), residential electricity consumption for powering ICT/CE is also growing at unprecedented rates, accounting for about 15 percent of global residential electricity consumption by 2009. By 2011, upwards of ten billion devices needed external power supplies, including two billion TV sets, a billion personal computers, and cell phones, which reached five billion subscriptions in 2010, including 85 percent of the US public.[32] In 2011, nearly three-quarters of the world's population owned one, and three-quarters of these accounts were held in the Global South. By 2009, about 40 percent of US homes had video-gaming consoles, which collectively consumed electricity at the same annual rate as San Diego, the ninth-largest city in the country. If media usage continues to grow at this rate, the IEA estimates that electricity consumption by electronic equipment will rise to 30 percent of global demand by 2022, and 45 percent by 2030.[33]

## WHAT CAN CONSUMERS DO ABOUT IT?

The amount of electricity needed to power media technologies seems to dwarf individual attempts to make media consumption environmentally sustainable.[34] Efforts to unplug this or that device appear insignificant in comparison to institutional consumption of electricity by business and government. Moreover, the environmental legacy of past electricity consumption presents consumers with a poisonous inheritance via PCBs, inter alia, that only large-scale cleanups could mitigate. The cost of repairing long-term damage to the environment adds weight to the argument that change must come from the top down—from laws, international accords, institutions, and technological fixes. It is particularly difficult for green consumers to formulate a point of intervention when gadgets are built with components that have seemingly disconnected production histories, such that they are manufactured all over the planet. Unlike boycotts and other consumer action against such merchandise as sporting apparel, one would be hard pressed to pinpoint individual action against many of the firms that operate in the globally dispersed electronics manufacturing sector. Consider Greenpeace's methods, chronicled in *Ethical Consumer* magazine as an "economic vote" via "shareholder activism," whereby social movements purchase a financial stake in polluting companies in the hope of changing corporate conduct.[35] It is clear that humiliating giant multinationals in a very public way induces apoplexy in fossil-fuel capitalists and their political and intellectual allies. But we should note the premise of Greenpeace's strategy: it assumes the futility of consumer decision making as a basis for massive change.[36]

These conditions militate against a focus on individual consumption as the key area for people to enact their environmentalism.[37] For this reason, it is important to elaborate a political vision that cultivates connectedness among consumers via green citizenship—a shared commitment to confront the eco-crisis and press for greener governance through media policy. This book proceeds towards that end.

Nevertheless, we wish to preserve a role for individuals and households as part of a larger movement to reorient society away from growth and toward sustainability. Small changes from the ground up can draw from existing cultures of sustainability in which routines, rituals, norms and taboos incarnate ecologically sound quotidian practices.[38] At the heart of these practices is a deepening ethical regard for the intimate bond of human and nonhuman nature. This ecological ethics can be combined with political-economic critiques of a growth-based, consumerist system to develop ethico-political tools and commitments and move us from green consumption to green citizenship.[39]

## ECOLOGICAL ETHICS AND MEDIA TECHNOLOGY

> After seeing electricity, I lost interest in nature. Not up to date enough.
> (Vladimir Mayakovsky, quoted in Macauley, 1996, 114[40])

The discourse of consumer ethics can be a poorly disguised effort to slough off responsibility for saving the environment onto individual consumers who, as we have argued, are in no position to effect change on their own at the scale that is needed. Moreover, business strategies have adopted "ethical" environmental rhetoric to placate regulators, stave off further regulation, or argue that self-regulation makes government regulation irrelevant.

It is important to reiterate that the cultivation of an eco-ethics within media consumption can fire up challenges from below by providing evaluative standards against which to judge manufacturers, policy makers, bureaucrats, and activists who play a role in greening media technologies. By ecological ethics, we mean the subset of ethics concerned with "how human beings ought to behave in relation to non-human nature."[41]

Three ethical orientations define the way we might collectively evaluate a particular ecological dilemma posed by the production, consumption, and disposal of media technologies. At two extremes are anthropocentric ethics and eco-centric ethics, with an intermediate ethics combining elements of the others. The lines separating these categories are often blurred in practice; like all ethics, there are no ironclad rules of operation. But each in its own way has virtues and limitations that inform how we can evaluate the relationship of the environment and media technologies. The three schools can be distinguished by their answers to questions across three themes: (a) value: what is valued, which entities qualify for moral consideration, and what matters most?; (b) rights: what are the duties and rules that protect valued individual and collective entities?; and

(c) consequences: what are the utilitarian considerations of actions and motives that affect the well-being or happiness of those valued?[42]

For anthropocentric eco-ethics, nonhuman nature has no value and hence no rights, except in relation to how humans are affected by changes to it. Although anthropocentric eco-ethicists see humans as ruling the Earth by virtue of their intrinsic value, they need not rule out an ecological ethics that helps humans flourish by finding instrumental value in nature as a means to happiness. For example, green consumers might prefer to purchase paper products composed mostly of recycled materials, because they understand that deforestation negatively affects their well-being. Anthropocentrism has provided the most politically expedient form of ethical discourse shaping environmental policy, at least in capitalist societies—namely, self-interest. But even this is a complex matter, for the narrow confines of self-interest can allow for a virtuous ethics oriented toward protecting nonhuman nature. Many consumers inferentially endorse virtuous ethics when favoring an ecologically sound life. Green consumption is perceived as a way to accumulate ethical substance in one's character.

In contrast to this human-centered ethics, eco-centric ethics holds that nature is the "ultimate source" of all value and should guide judgment of right/wrong and good/bad human action in relation to the environment. Eco-centrists are convinced that "some or all natural beings, in the broadest sense, have independent moral status."[43] They believe that human domination of nature is fundamentally wrong/bad and that there is a right/good way to live an ecologically healthy life by putting the Earth's well-being first. For some eco-centrists, putting the Earth first is a matter of having an ethical regard for the integrity and ineffability of nature—for example, the ecologist Aldo Leopold's "land ethical" wonder at the sleepy skunk stirring during a midwinter thaw, or political theorist William Connolly's polytheistic "affinity of affect" for an unruly Australian cockroach.[44] In Gaia theory, eco-centric ethics reside in the notion of the Earth as one-big-organism. Eco-centric ethics also informs critiques of class, race, and gender oppression. Left biocentrists and ecofeminists argue that there is an inextricable link between the capitalist/masculinist subjugation of nature and doctrines of growth.[45]

An intermediate form of ecological ethics accords some intrinsic value to nonhuman nature, but not so completely as ecocentrism. Nor is this "midgreen" ethics fully anthropocentric, though it rests on the principle that humans' "moral considerability" can be extended to other (sentient) beings, primarily nonhuman animals. Proponents of such an intermediate eco-ethics can be found among philosophical and ecological advocates of animal liberation (Peter Singer) and animal rights (Tom Regan) as well as biocentrism or life-centered ethics (Paul Taylor). However, when there is a conflict between humans and other life forms, the intermediate position tends to privilege the former.[46]

Anthropocentric eco-ethics includes many conflicting interpretations of how humans should value nonhuman nature. Some philosophers see human beings in absolute instrumentalist terms. For Horkheimer, we are a "rapacious race, more brutal than any previous beasts of prey," preserving ourselves "at the expense of the rest of nature, since [we are] so poorly outfitted by nature in many respects" and must survive through violence. Thomas Hobbes holds that as part of "the war of all against all," it is right for people to domesticate or destroy nature.[47] Georg Wilhelm Friedrich Hegel argues that a person can put his or her "will into everything." An object or place thereby "becomes *mine*" since humanity "has the right of absolute proprietorship." In his philosophy, people are unique in their desire and capacity to conserve objects and represent them, and a strange dialectical process affords them a special right to destroy as well. Willpower is independent of simple survival, which sets humanity apart from other living things. Humans' semiotic power confers the right to destructive power, so "sacred respect for...unused land cannot be guaranteed." The capacity to restrain oneself and master one's "spontaneity and natural constitution" distinguishes people from animals. The necessary relationship between humans and nature asserts itself at the core of consciousness as a site of struggle for people to achieve freedom from risk and want. Nature's "tedious chronicle," where "nothing [is] new under the sun," is rightly disrespected and disobeyed by the progress that comes with human dominion over it.[48]

And there are endless examples of captains of industry and techno-science enacting this harsh moral code: Henry Ford argues that "unused forces of nature" must be "put into action...to make them mankind's slaves," and Vannevar Bush, US Director of the Office of Scientific Research and Development during World War II, speaks proudly of the drive to release humanity "from the bondage of bare existence."[49]

Writing against the dominant view of technology as "a means and a human activity," Martin Heidegger argues that technology stages a more powerful social struggle. It makes "the unreasonable demand" that nature "supply energy which can be extracted and stored" in a way that challenges seasonal rhythms, bending them to the demands of work, growth, and competition. In this regard, Heidegger shares the Hegelian view of nonhuman nature as an instrument of humans. However, Heidegger's discomfort opens up the possibility of a midgreen ethical consideration of non–human nature and a critique of instrumentalism. Similarly, David Hume maintains that animals, like people, "learn many things from experience," developing "knowledge of the nature of fire, water, earth, stones, heights, depths, etc." in addition to receiving instruction as part of domestication.

Rather than being merely sensate, advanced animals apply reason through inference. Jeremy Bentham did not go so far, but appositely asked of our duty of care to animals: "The question is not, Can they *reason*? nor, Can they *talk*? but, Can they *suffer*?" Here again, the impact of technology is not merely a human problem; it is a problem for other inhabitants of the Earth as well. There is a duty of care to the weak on the part of the strong to preserve their lives as denizens of shared space.[50]

As we'll see in later chapters, most environmental activism and policy directed at media technologies employ the least harsh of anthropocentric sensibilities, for example, by focusing on the cost of environmental degradation to collective human life. This characterizes the consequentialist assumptions of research on e-waste, global warming, alternative energy, air and water pollution, greening of industry, and so on, in which humanity is seen as the ultimate loser of bad ecological behavior.[51] In this eco-ethics, media technologies carry both promise and peril for the environment. Media technologies are worthwhile because they enhance people's ability to act and communicate as green consumers and concerned eco-citizens. But they work against our well-being when they pose hazards and deposit toxins into the environment or diminish our enjoyment of nature (for example by using ugly towers or cables) or otherwise foul the lives of creatures who share the Earth with us. Likewise, intermediate eco-ethics has implicitly guided judgments of media technology's environmental threat to animals, such as in regard to birds killed by communication towers, habitats disrupted by chemical effluents and electromagnetic fields, declining biodiversity resulting from pollution, and climate change caused by ICT/ CE production and use. Such midgreen eco-ethics is limited by the presumption of moral extensionism, in which rights are extended to individual species perceived to be more like humans and denied to those perceived as alien. Dogmatic animal-rights activists displace a human chauvinism with animal chauvinism.[52]

By far the most disruptive ethical orientation for consumers of media technology is eco-centric ethics, which calls for a paradigm shift toward sustainability that is far more radical than either anthropocentric or intermediate eco-ethics. This position rejects technologies that can only flourish on the planet by damaging it. That's a real deal breaker for most users of media technology, because they would have to undergo a fundamental conversion to give the Earth's well-being preeminence over their beloved gadgets. For the eco-centrist, our environmental crisis necessitates the rejection of moral self-righteousness about the value or revolutionary potential of media technology. More generally, it means defending the rights of the Earth against the claims of human-centered progress via new technologies and growth-based expansion. Although eco-centric

ethics must work alongside light- and mid-green eco-ethics, the principles it embodies can inspire fresh approaches to green consumption
of media technologies and problematize unthinking technophilia.[53]
And its disenchantment with media technology necessitates a welcome
re-enchantment with nonhuman nature, forming the basis for an expansive eco-ethical critique of business-as-usual as per Herbert Marcuse's
signal recognition that:

> the demands of ever more intense exploitation come into conflict with nature itself, since
> nature is the source and locus of the life-instincts which struggle against the instincts
> of aggression and destruction. And the demands of exploitation progressively reduce
> and exhaust resources: the more capitalist productivity increases, the more destructive
> it becomes. This is one sign of the internal contradictions of capitalism.... [Nature] is
> a dimension *beyond* labor, a symbol of beauty, of tranquility, of a nonrepressive order.
> Thanks to these values, nature was the very negation of the market society.
>
> (1972, 11; also see McLaughlin, 1993)

We understand why Marcuse posits a "nonrepressive order" of nature,
but we would modify his perspective with something beyond human consciousness, calling for eco-centric precaution even in the face of nature's
beauty. An eco-ethical orientation toward nonhuman nature must advocate
for more than humanistic categories of value. Beauty in a pristine landscape
might appear to be a semiotic negation of market society, but it may also
misrepresent the invisible chemical burden of a crystal flowing waterway or
lush green mountainside created by human aggression against nonhuman
nature.

Even among reactionary voices, an appreciation of nature and a mistrust
of people and technology can lead to careful thinking. Plato admires the
capacity of natural disasters to destroy social and technological advances,
especially "crafty devices that city-dwellers use in the rat-race to do each
other down." Once such "tools were destroyed," new inventions and a
pacific society could emerge in the absence of mass violence, permitting
the redevelopment of a legal system based on restraint. Similarly, Edmund
Burke's cautionary words against the popular will and democracy's present-
ism endorse a rule of law that acknowledges each generation as "temporary
possessors and life-renters" of the natural and social world. Society must
maintain a sense of "chain and continuity" rather than act ephemerally like
"the flies of a summer." There must be "a partnership not only between those
who are living, but between those who are living, those who are dead, and
those who are to be born" to sustain "the great primeval contract of eternal
society." This notion of intergenerational responsibility remains a hallmark
of sustainability.[54]

The lesson of eco-ethical green consumption is that without a moral obligation to the environment (and, as we show in later chapters, to labor) we become "devices of our devices." Commodity signs and preconfigured opinions urge us to "settle mindlessly into the convenience that devices may offer us."[55] There is no better example of this devotion in the present than the cell phone.

## THE WONDROUS CELL PHONE

"I want you to come and see me."

Vashti watched his face in the blue plate.

"But I can see you!" she exclaimed. "What more do you want?"

"I want to see you not through the Machine," said Kuno. "I want to speak to you not through the wearisome Machine."

"Oh, hush!" said his mother, vaguely shocked. "You mustn't say anything against the Machine."

"Why not?"

"One mustn't."

"You talk as if a god had made the Machine," cried the other. "I believe that you pray to it when you are unhappy. Men made it, do not forget that. Great men, but men. The Machine is much, but it is not everything. I see something like you in this plate, but I do not see you. I hear something like you through this telephone, but I do not hear you. That is why I want you to come. Pay me a visit, so that we can meet face to face, and talk about the hopes that are in my mind."

She replied that she could scarcely spare the time for a visit.

(E. M. Forster, 1997, 88)

Cell phones have been praised for broadening channels of communication, securing personal safety, integrating family life, developing peer groups, speeding up rendezvous, making users feel important, and confirming what Castells calls the "timeless time" and "space of flows" that characterize people's experience of communication in a network society.[56] There are additional benefits that are claimed about the features of cell phones: They allow users to produce content, create their own languages, and draw personal meaning from design characteristics. On the other hand, cell phones cause a new form of inequality, because without one you lack access to the new sociality. In addition, they are biased toward young eyes and dexterous fingers, can spread rumors quickly, are vulnerable to viruses, distract drivers and pedestrians, can cause interpersonal conflicts between callers, and so on.[57]

Cell phones are promoted as being crucial to democracy, economic efficiency, and green jobs. A dual discourse of virtue holds that cell phones and other ICT/CE will save the two "ecos"—the economy and ecology—along the lines of Barack Obama's largely forgotten "Green New Deal."[58] Mainstream economists claim that cell phones have streamlined markets in the Global South, thereby enriching people's lives in zones where banking and economic information are scarce, thanks to the provision of market data. Exaggerated claims include "the complete elimination of waste" and massive reductions of poverty and corruption through the empowerment of individuals. Industry magazines such as *Advertising Age* positively salivate over the prediction that by 2013, there will be 4.5 billion users, well over half the world's population, as the absence of conventional telecommunications and financial infrastructure is overcome thanks to digital wallets and micro-payment systems.[59] This happy state of affairs finds the world's leading media ratings company, Nielsen, publishing an unimaginably crass account that begins "Africa is in the midst of a technological revolution, and nothing illustrates that fact [more] than the proliferation of mobile phones" then notes casually that "more Africans have access to mobile phones than to clean drinking water."[60]

Media historian Dan Schiller offers a contrasting view of mobile telephony. He challenges cell phone enthusiasts to query the way social stresses fuel new consumer needs, as people rush to buy inferior services at a high cost. This is particularly the case in the United States, where a decline in government oversight of media industries since World War II has resulted in increased privatization and diminished quality guarantees, standards, and regulation of competition. Schiller argues that poor-quality cell phone service in the United States is a function of telecommunication companies' abilities to exploit a need for connectedness in times of social fragmentation.[61]

Schiller draws on Raymond Williams's cultural analysis of television in the 1970s to describe the experience of displacement and deracination in modern life, a mode of sociality in which individuation (separateness and privacy) combined with mobility (transport and access). Williams suggests the term "mobile privatization" to capture the paradoxical feelings of being distinct from others yet capable of continuous connection with them.[62] Whereas broadcast technology, in Williams's view, is a social product of this industrial form, much like the suggestion of Castells and his acolytes that mobile technology is the network society's structure of feeling, Schiller argues that political-economic arrangements allow mobile telephony to emerge in a form befitting divided societies. Perhaps this is what the musician Billy Bragg is referring to in "Levi Stubbs' Tears" when he sings, "She bought herself a mobile home/So at least she could get some enjoyment/Out of being alone" and the sentiment underpinning the band Straight Outta Junior High's arch song "Cell Phones Suck." Or maybe it echoes Benjamin's Proustian lament for the loss of art's aura because of photographic technologies that look back at us and carry our images and statements into a reciprocal loop. It certainly captures the ironic advent of the telephone as a commercial apparatus in 1870s Paris, in which it supposedly exemplified and countered the depersonalization of modern life by simultaneously helping to make the public private and the private public.[63] And it informs Weber's understanding, from almost a century ago, of the role of the phone in fictive capital:

> The "arbitrager" seeks a profit in that he simultaneously sells a good at a place where it is, at that moment, able to be sold at a higher price, while he buys it at a place where it is to be had more cheaply. His business is therefore a pure example of calculating the numbers. He sits at a telephone . . . and, as soon as he notices the possibility of, for example, making a profit from buying Russian notes or notes of exchange drawn on Russia available in London and then selling them in Paris, he places his orders. (2000, 344)

None of the research outlined above, worthy though it may be, engages the technology's environmental relationships. For example, scientific studies have linked long-term exposure to cell-phone radiation to two types of brain cancer—glioma and acoustic neuroma—salivary gland tumors, migraines, vertigo, and behavioral problems in children. Various European health agencies have issued warnings about cell-phone radiation exposure (see chapter 5). As we will see in subsequent chapters, there are abundant toxic by-products and workplace hazards throughout the supply chain from cell phones and other ICT/CE, in addition to their life-cycle energy requirements (the "no-load" burden of plugged but empty chargers) and postconsumer existence (spent batteries, disposal, and recycling). The source materials used in cell phones vary among manufacturers. They all: contain lead or tin solder and plastic (circuit boards and casings); involve chemical processing, including the use of detergents and etchants in chip production; and use tantalum, the mining of which has caused social and environmental harm in Africa. Most include mercury, though this is changing, and many require flame retardants made of polybrominated diphenyl ethers, which are bioaccumulative synthetic chemical compounds that cause neurological problems, though they are not well-understood. These phones also need batteries, the contents of which are toxic, including nickel cadmium, lead acid, nickel metal hydride, lithium ion, and lithium polymer components. Like generators, batteries are not primary energy sources but require raw materials and energy inputs prior to production and distribution.

Their environmental costs must be measured against their energy provision during their lifecycle.[64]

Finally, cell phones carry dread post-consumption risks. As the environmental health scientist Oladele A. Ogunseitan warns: "In a phone that you hold in the palm of your hand, you now have more than 200 chemical compounds. To try to separate them out and study what health effects may be associated with burning or sinking it in water—that's a lifetime of work for a toxicologist." More than a hundred and thirty million of these devices are trashed annually in the United States alone, where people purchase replacements once a year, on average—a direct outcome of the business strategy of planned obsolescence.[65]

We conclude here by wondering what the green consumer might say about the eco-ethical challenges posed by the cell phone.

Eco-centrism would remind us that the eco-crisis demands the immediate termination of all unsound ecological practices associated with the cell phone, letting the Earth's well-being take precedence over human interests. Intermediate eco-ethics would include in this argument calls for action to stem the bodily and environmental burden of cell-phone manufacturing, use, and disposal. Studies of the persistent organic pollutants in land, air, and water would accompany epidemiological research to help guide solutions. Manufacturers might help reduce environmental burdens by looking for nontoxic source materials, and together with distributors create buy-back or recycling programs to keep spent phones and batteries out of landfills, as per 2006 legislation in California—not merely consumer/user repurposing outlined in the Castells study cited above. Along this mid-green line of thought, some life-cycle analysis (LCA)[66] concludes that the greenest phones would share the following design principles: the end of miniaturization, which leads to thoughtless disposal, as smaller gadgets falsely connote harmlessness; the use of standardized components to reduce the number of devices needed, which would discourage disposal and encourage reuse via replaceable modular parts and upgrades; the discontinuance of disposable phones; the substitution of green chemicals; and the expansion of and incentives for take-back programs. Of course, such LCA findings contradict business-as-usual in the ICT/CE industry. Progress in regulating the industry has been slow, hampered by such bureaucratic rigmarole as cost-benefit analysis (CBA) and risk management (see chapter 5).[67]

Finally, anthropocentric eco-ethics might offer a range of responses, including application of the precautionary principle, a "better safe than sorry" guideline that requires withholding potentially toxic devices from entering the environment until there is scientific consensus about the consequences; or some form of CBA that settles for compromises and slow reforms to ensure greater technological efficiency in the manufacture and disposal of the cell phones without disrupting profit and growth, with risks distributed along existing lines of socioeconomic stratification.

In the end, these eco-ethical options are not merely about the kind of phone a green consumer might wish were available; they are also starting points for a discussion about the kind of society we want to live in. The cell phone is a very odd thing when seen in this light—built upon the stressful fragmentation of social life, toxic high-tech industrialism, the searing divisions between rich and poor, and the false promises of consumerism.

## CONCLUSION

The woman came back carrying a small cardboard box. She went directly to Bosch and handed it to him, then bowed as she backed away. Harry opened it and found the remains of a melted and burnt cell phone.

While the woman gave Sun an explanation, Bosch pulled his own cell phone and compared it to the burned phone. Despite the damage, it was clear the phone the woman retrieved from her ash can was a match.

"She said Peng was burning that," Sun said. "It made a very foul smell that would be displeasing to the ghosts so she removed it." (Michael Connelly, 2009b, 243)

This chapter has focused on both individual and institutional modes of technological consumption, examining how media technology and the environment are intimately related through electricity production and use, whose legacy and rising levels contribute massively to the ecological crisis the world faces in the twenty-first century. The collective problems were presented in the aggregate levels of consumption that have grown without interruption over decades. The problems for green consumption incurred by the individual consumer pale in comparison to those brought about by institutional consumers, although both individuals and institutions are slowly incorporating a green moral code into their respective worlds of media use. By far the biggest change has been in consumer awareness of the environmental impact of the products they buy, including ICT/CE. And although such green consumption has not been lost on marketers and manufacturers, who are finding ways to profit from it, the consumer demand for greater corporate and government accountability in addressing environmental harms is having real effects on business-as-usual. We identified a conflict that will persist for the foreseeable future between large institutional consumers, which promote an unstable and contradictory idea of sustainable growth, and eco-ethical orientations based on sustainability and rejection of the growth doctrine. The stakes appear extremely high for anyone who understands the extent of the ecological crisis.

We will continue this argument in our chapter on citizens, in which we seek to subsume notions of consumer engagement into more effective political forms of environmental citizenship. In doing so, we challenge the conventional terms of national citizenship that think of the citizen and the consumer as alter egos of each other—the *national* subject versus the *rational* subject. In the late twentieth century, proponents of neoliberalism (or market liberalism) sought to redefine the current understanding of citizen engagement in politics as an artificial and meaningless endeavor, while framing consumption and individual acquisitiveness as a natural, god-given freedom.[68] The idea of "voting with your pocketbook" became a way for neoliberal citizenship to be expressed through consumption. But by adopting the tenets of the consumer, this citizen is reduced to a bundle of material desires. Though seemingly self-actualizing, they conform to general patterns of controlled market behaviors. If green citizenship were limited to this neoliberal idea, the green citizen would be nothing more than a self-limiting, self-controlling subject who conforms to a lifetime of purchasing behavior—shop 'til you drop. In this chapter, we have presented a number of arguments against this view of media consumption, which is not only demeaning but presumes that the consumer is completely vulnerable to the ideological effects of media technologies and the mystical powers of the technological sublime. As Immanuel Kant said, "I need not think, so long as I can pay."[69] If we stop thinking about the eco-crisis, we'll pay dearly.

# CHAPTER 2

✧

# Words

When I was a boy—I'm that old—I used to read printed books. You'd hardly think it. Likely you've seen none—they rot and dust so—and the Sanitary Company burns them to make ashlarite. But they were convenient in their dirty way. One learnt a lot. These new-fangled Babble Machines— they don't seem new-fangled to you, eh?—they're easy to hear, easy to forget.
—H. G. Wells, 2003, 104

Written literature has, historically speaking, played a dominant role for only a few centuries. Even today, the predominance of the book has an episodic air. An incomparably longer time preceded it in which literature was oral. Now it is being succeeded by the age of the electronic media, which tend once more to make people speak. At its period of fullest development, the book to some extent usurped the place of the more primitive but generally more accessible methods of production of the past; on the other hand, it was a stand-in for future methods which make it possible for everyone to become a producer.
—Hans Magnus Enzensberger, 2003, 272.

For a long time, the publishing industry considered itself to be relatively innocuous environmentally. The "lightening rod" mining, energy and food sectors kept the eyes of the public diverted.
—Christy Collins, 2010[1]

When you think of words and the environment, your mind may turn to how written texts have depicted nature and pollution, as discussed by numerous distinguished eco-critics.[2] Rather than excavate literature that *represents* the environment, this chapter argues that we need to be aware of how the printed word *changes* that environment.

Media mythmakers and those who do not observe history ecologically tend to depict the early printing workshop as an odorless and tidy place, a golden-hued diorama in which a heritage was born. Today, we have a similar, though somewhat more prosaic, still life of garage geeks fueled on caffeine and instant noodles, soldering circuit boards and microchips to launch the *computing moment that changed the world*. These dreamy accounts are inadequate for understanding the ecological context of media technologies. The Print Revolution inaugurated new occupational hazards in workshops that were redolent with chemically altered natural elements and process residues of fumes, dust, and heavy metals, while later deforestation for industrial wood pulp production imposed grave risks to animal and plant diversity and habitats. Then came the turn of the telegraph operator, who risked exposure to acids used in batteries, among other dangers, while tapping commands and communiqués into singing wires from trading floors, army outposts, and newspaper offices. Each new medium has layered new environmental problems upon the old, with little regard for ecosystems or labor.

This chapter examines the intersecting histories of chemical, mechanical, and electrical processes in order to understand the ecological context of the printed word and the environmental problems that have been bequeathed to present and future generations. The first section discusses the current orthodoxy of "reading" books or other print media, which rests on enchantment with the printed word and the technologies that have revolutionized its dissemination. The next three sections offer short histories of the environmental impact of these technologies, from the industrialization of print to the advent of the electronic book (e-book)—paper/presses, telegraphy, telephony, long-distance cable, and plastic. The final section touches on the changes taking place in publishing as it moves toward "paperless" operations. Even if paper eventually declines as the primary delivery system for the printed word, the ecological context of its successor will share most of the characteristics that defined print's relation to the environment. We conclude with a brief look at e-books, before moving on in the next chapter to examine the provenance of this medium's screen-based technology in more depth.

## THE POWER OF WORDS

Throughout *Greening the Media*, we examine the different ways that the tendency to regard each emergent medium as awe inspiring and world changing relies on recurring myths of technological power in the absence of acknowledging environmental and labor realities. We can see this tendency in Socrates's dialogue with Phaedrus, as recorded by Plato. Socrates referred to this double-ness as the "propriety and impropriety of writing." He related the story of an Egyptian king complaining to the god who had invented the new art of writing, suggesting that it "will create forgetfulness in the learners' souls, because they will not use their memories; they will trust to the external written characters and not remember of themselves." Today, of course, literacy and knowledge are inexorably intertwined, and a prior reliance on oral and visual representations has been incorporated into Socrates's "writing."[3]

The spoken word, painted image, and written text were coeval sources of intellectual authority until the eighteenth century, although numerous French and Spanish artisans had relied solely on printed material to codify technical information two hundred years earlier. Some visionaries of that time saw that the life of the mind was changing irrevocably.[4] Francis Bacon's *Novum Organum* of 1620 declared that printing, alongside gunpowder and the compass, had "changed the whole face and state of things throughout the world" and Descartes made a defiant apologia in 1637 for choosing to write in the vernacular in search of new audiences rather than "those who only trust old books."[5] Faith in new media was solidified by Johann Creiling's lecture at Tübingen, Germany, in 1702, which alleged that teaching would be transformed by the magic lantern.[6] And it is certainly true that the acquisition of practical and conceptual knowledge came to be dominated by linguistic representations. From the nineteenth century, it was commonplace to hear that books contained the entirety of human knowledge, which was therefore available to all those who could read. Reading has long been valorized as an aide to contemplation, seriousness, profundity, and a higher joy; today's *Prospect* magazine hails books as "immutable, individual, lendable, cut off from the world."[7]

This utopia is matched, of course, by dystopic corollaries, largely concerned with the democratization of culture via literacy. In the late eighteenth century, Johann Georg Heinzmann wondered, "Why [should] things always be written and published for the ruined species of man who wants to be ever entertained, ever flattered, ever deceived?" In *The Art of Reading Books*, his contemporary Johann Adam Bergk makes a similar protest: "The results of such tasteless and thoughtless reading are ... senseless waste, unconquerable reluctance to exert oneself, limitless itch for luxuries, suppression of the voice of conscience, boredom with life, and an early death."[8] And only sixty years ago, critics railed at the way that individuated reading led to a production "emphasis on speed and action," an economy that militated against poetry and performance.[9] We can read similar infatuation and distaste transposed with regard to the internet.

Proponents of emergent media, both past and present, return obsessively to print in order to show its difference from what came before. They just can't help themselves. Semiotician Umberto Eco reminds us that "in Hugo's *Hunchback of Notre Dame,* Frollo, comparing a book with his old cathedral, says: 'Ceci tuera cela' [the book will kill the cathedral, the alphabet will kill images]." The notion that successive technologies destroy their predecessors remains strong, though writing's resilience engages as material and symbolic material. But how many pundits have seen the book as a destructive technology? One wonders what they would make of the humble pencil—approximately twenty billion are made a year in a vibrant and growing industry that has existed since the early 1600s and shows signs only of expansion.[10]

Of course, to the extent that the printed word's properties can be separated from a mode of production, they are not the problem. In the words of Hewlett Packard (HP) researchers, print and paper form "an exquisite technology" because they are stable, unerring, pleasurable, and have minimal environmental impact during their use. But the way that capitalism governs the book business poses grave ecological dangers. For example, 40 percent, or 1.5 billion, of the books on display in US stores are returned to publishers each year for recycling or destruction, due to the old nostrum that readers buy books when they are stocked in a large pile because this indicates their significance and popularity. Half of all book sales in the United States take place in the big-box retailers Target and Walmart.[11] Books, newspapers, and magazines are characterized by massive overproduction, occasioned by web promotion, offset lithography, and gravure printing and cavalier use of natural resources. US book publishers use just 5 percent recycled material in production, even though studies suggest more than three-quarters of US readers would happily pay more for books on recycled paper. If that overproduction were cut in recognition of the reality that most books are now purchased and read online, 60,000 acres of trees would be saved and carbon output diminished to the equivalent of two million medium-sized automobiles.[12]

Such stories and images inspire a counter-narrative to the prevailing myths of the printed word. This alternative history focuses on the environmental plunder and noxious sweatshops that have made old and new media possible, rather than celebrations or warnings of artistic expression or manipulated minds. Ecological issues must inform those of us who love print and enjoy reading, so that we learn to read beyond the text—not so much "against the grain" as with an appreciation of how the grain came to be there and what it has meant for the Earth.[13] Consider Heidegger's famous paradox of the forester, a man who participates in the destruction of the very environment that gives meaning to his life in order to supply a key resource to the bourgeois press, which in turn uses it to shape his opinions:

> The forester who measures the felled timber in the woods and who to all appearances walks the forest path in the same way his grandfather did is today ordered by the industry that produces commercial woods, whether he knows it or not. He is made subordinate to the orderability of cellulose, which for its part is challenged forth by the need for paper, which is then delivered to newspapers and illustrated magazines. The latter, in their turn, set public opinion to swallowing what is printed, so that a set configuration of opinion becomes available on demand. (Heidegger, 1977, 299)

As the forester's work is subsumed into modern pulp and paper production, labor and the environment are further disarticulated from one another. Paper mills and printing presses are hailed as revolutionary. Newspapers, magazines, books, and fine paper become signs of progress and intellectual life. They bear no relation to the role of the forester or their own environmental aftershocks. The underlying convergence of labor, environment, and media disappears from view.

This need not be the whole story. An ecological history that emphasizes managerial power and labor exploitation can restore the forester's severed connections and enlighten our understanding of the media, so that we come to see them as destructive as well as productive forces.

## THE ECOLOGICAL CONTEXT OF WORDS

Our account begins at a conventional point of departure in media history: the advent of the printing press, site of the technological "revolution" of moveable type that supposedly helped establish and enlarge Europe's global dominance between the fifteenth and eighteenth centuries. When introduced to China under the Qing Dynasty, it exemplified the imperial turn as an index of military power and missionary zeal.[14] Its antecedent was papermaking, a technology that traveled from China to the West via Islamic territories over the course of a thousand years. Paper mills operated in *al-Andalus* (the Iberian Peninsula) by the twelfth century and a papermaking industry emerged across Europe, from "the lawyers capital" Bologna in 1293, Basel in 1424, and Cracow in 1491.[15]

Two important properties of paper-mill technology deepened the printed word's relationship to the Earth's ecosystems, causing effects that are familiar to modern readers: water pollution and deforestation. Since at least the fourteenth century, papermaking has involved the location and provision of vast amounts of clean water as both a power source and ingredient.

The effluents that flowed into waterways increased in toxicity with each innovation in chemical processing of fiber. In the last quarter of the nineteenth century, new methods made it feasible to use wood fiber for industrial papermaking, initiating deforestation in the service of print technology. Prior to that time, the rag trade provided a primary source of raw material for making paper from recycled wool, linen cloth, old rope, and other materials. Cotton and linen were the preferred ingredients. Vellum and parchment (sheep or goatskin) were also used to make high-quality surfaces for writing and printing but at a cost too dear to support profitable printing businesses. Socially marginal workers, itinerant "rag-and-bone men," drew rags from the rubbish they collected on the streets of preindustrial European towns for use by publishers. In typically blunt yet metaphoric prose, Marx described them as an "undefined, dissolute, kicked-about mass."[16]

Movable type in various forms was used in China, Japan, Central Asia, and Europe before Johannes Gensfleisch zur Laden zum Gutenberg invented his eponymous method of printing in the mid-fifteenth century. That famous technique—which combined chemistry, mechanics, and metallurgy—was directly linked to the work that goldsmiths like Gutenberg undertook for wealthy bishoprics in Mainz and Strasbourg. Biblical printing consequently expanded the use of copper, lead, antimony, and tin. The typographer Beatrice Warde refers to the period between Gutenberg's invention and the late nineteenth century as "the five hundred years of the Printer," when "there was his way, but no other way, of broadcasting identical messages to a thousand or more people, a thousand or more miles apart." She suggests that that capacity created "the epoch that we have been calling 'modern times' by opening up a 'deep cleft-in-history' that made a time without print unimaginable." Warde attributes the spread of literacy and hence the universal franchise to further technological developments in making paper and printing on it.[17] This "age of the printer" exposed the latter to large amounts of poisons, such as lead, now considered one of the most lethal elements, though this would not have been widely discussed during Gutenberg's time or most of the subsequent five hundred years.

Demand for rapid and accurate reproduction of printed media grew as the number of readers began to outpace the supply of handmade documents produced by scribes, presaging the demise of manual lettering. A veritable "cluster of innovations" emerged: movable metal type, oil-based ink, and wooden hand presses.[18] The ink was composed of lampblack, turpentine, and boiled linseed oil—the first was harmful to the lungs and mucous membranes; the second to the nervous system, liver, and kidneys; and the third irritated the skin. For most of the nineteenth century, turpentine extraction and distillation in the southern United States depended on slave labor; after the Civil War, forced labor became the norm. Turpentine was extracted from living pine trees (as were other resinous substances referred to as naval stores) and became increasingly labor and forest intensive with industrialization.[19]

From the early 1800s, coal-burning, steam-powered presses not only multiplied the potential volume of printed pages by three to four times, they also added new synthetic elements to the environment. These new mechanical systems were soon accompanied by the chemical innovation of chlorine compounds, derived from the process for manufacturing sodium carbonate and caustic soda (lye), used in textile, glass, and soap production; on its own, soda production emitted toxic byproducts and generated carbon dioxide. The chlorine allowed the patterned and colored rags to be bleached prior to rag processing and pulping. In the United States, women workers did most of the rag preparation—the removal of buttons and the cutting and ripping of seams—"converting the tatters almost into lint," as Herman Melville wrote in "The Paradise of Bachelors and the Tartarus of Maids." In the rag room, the "air swam with the fine, poisonous particles, which from all sides darted, subtly, as motes in sunbeams, into the lungs."[20]

Cloth for papermaking was perennially in short supply in the late 1800s. New sources of fiber were drastically needed, especially after 1850 when paper demand exploded with the introduction of the rotary press, which made it possible to print millions of copies in a single day. Rag imports grew steadily, especially in the United States, until 1884, when imports thought to carry disease were embargoed.[21] The introduction of Linotype in 1886 cut the cost of composition in half. Meanwhile, the US state intervened to encourage massive piracy of British books under copyright legislation until 1891, a further stimulus, and mandated low postage rates for print regardless of distance from 1874 (for newspapers) and 1885 (for books). The International Paper Company, a monopoly formed in 1898 by nineteen former US competitors, brought additional pressure on the US government to eliminate tariffs on imported Canadian lumber, pushing Theodore Roosevelt to promote the company's campaign on conservation grounds, crying, "We are out of pulpwood."[22] These market stimulants caused substantial environmental trouble.

During this period two interrelated environmental issues emerged: wood pulp surpassed rags as the main source of fiber, and waste paper became a disposal problem for households and industry, escalating quickly with the surge of demand for the commercial print media and the advertising industry's requirement of "substantial amounts of paper for labels and cardboard" for packaging.[23] Wood was, and remains, a poor source of fiber compared to cloth and natural sources like hemp, but hemp could not be bleached white and cost more than rags at the time. The process of wood pulping was perfected in Germany, and US papermakers imported the machinery and

know-how that would make trees the primary material for modern industrial printing. Abundant forests offered a seemingly endless supply of cheap
raw materials to commercial papermakers; this natural resource contributed enormously to the reduction of newsprint's price from a little over 8.5
cents a pound in 1875 to 1.5 cents a pound in 1897.[24]

Between 1899 and 1919, as these and other innovations—such as illus-
trations and telegraph networks—were standardized, tonnage consumption of processed wood pulp expanded by 1,175 percent in the United
States alone. Advertising expenditures in print grew 742 percent in the
same period, fueling a "startling increase" in newspaper, book, and paper-
board consumption: from 25 pounds per capita in 1909 to 59 pounds in
1930. In 1925, a New York newspaper accounted for 2,000 acres of forest.[25]
By 1930, papermaking had become "one of the principal industries polluting water." Meanwhile, the ecological interdependence of North American
paper manufacturing deepened with the opening of the US market to the
Canadian pulp and paper industry, a bilateral trade arrangement brokered
as part of an antitrust investigation of the International Paper Company.
With this new political-economic reality in place, the "fever to publish and
advertise now infected Canadian waters."[26]

The United States and Canada remain the world's largest producers of
paper, due to their large reserves of softwood. By the end of the last century,
the southern states of the United States already comprised the world's biggest paper-producing region. Mexico, by contrast, is a net importer of paper
and so has been much more innovative in recycling newsprint, for example.
Canadian attempts to shift to wheat-straw pulp have been frustrated by the
fact that excess wheat isn't pulped there, so it imports pulped wheat and rice
from China to make paper, adding massively to carbon use through transportation. Countries whose forests are endangered by the paper industry
include Indonesia, Chile, Russia, and Brazil, though mining, agriculture,
and settlement also contribute to the devastation. The International Tropical Timber Organization is the principal governing body for the paper sector, allocating voting power to members based on their global share of the
timber trade, ensuring domination by the wealthy over actual custodians.[27]

Throughout the twentieth century, rising energy demands in the printing
industry increased the use of coal, and new chemical processes introduced
large quantities of sulfite salts, sulfur dioxide, caustic soda, sodium sulfate
(the malodorous kraft process), and bleaching chemicals into the environment. Innovations in chemical bleaching of pulp produced a number of
new synthetic byproducts, including dioxin—discovered eventually to be
a carcinogen that settles without decaying in the ground, waterways, and
the human food supply (making it a bio-accumulative toxin). Successive
refinements in the chemical pulping process deepened the environmental

impact of paper, amplifying the materials that could be cut down for paper-making and multiplying the chemicals contained in the "waste liquor" emitted into waterways.

In addition, over the course of the twentieth century, environmental hazards for print workers remained serious despite the introduction of new production techniques, such as "hot metal" typesetter technology (1886), analog photo typesetting (1949), digital photo typesetting (1965), and laser-image setting (1976). Early twenty-first century pressrooms contin-ued to expose workers to airborne and liquid toxins, including solvents, developing solutions, and inks, at the same time as they emitted lower atmosphere ozone (smog), heavy metals in ink, solvents, silver (film devel-opment), film and paper scraps, and wastewater into the environment. Chemicals released into the environment mainly come from solvents con-taining toluene, methyl ethyl ketone, xylene, and trichloroethane, exposure to which can disrupt the normal functioning of internal organs and nervous systems in humans and animals.[28]

By the end of the twentieth century, the pulp and paper industry was the "second largest consumer of energy" within the world's largest consumer of energy, the United States; the principal industrial consumer of water; and third largest greenhouse gas emitter across the wealthy democracies of the OECD. In 2006, US papermaking used seventy-five billion kilowatt hours of energy, lagging behind just one industry: petroleum. Greenhouse gases emitted from paper and pulp makers include carbon monoxide, nitrogen dioxide, particulate matter, sulfur dioxide, and volatile organic compounds. In some cases, these substances are released at significantly higher levels than from electronics and computer manufacturing, and in certain catego-ries, beyond even mining and petroleum. By 2011, the United States pro-duced nearly 100 million tons of paper annually, or about 663 pounds per person, of which approximately 90 percent was not recycled after use. This is a vastly greater amount of paper per capita than anywhere else—in 1994, a fifth of all paper made in the world was thrown out in the United States, where books and newspapers were responsible for felling 125 million trees in 2008, quite apart from carbon impact and water use.[29]

The US book industry estimates the annual carbon impact of books at between 11.3 and 12.4 million tons, equivalent to the total emissions from between two and seven million cars, depending on which account you trust. The figure is 1.8 million tons for Britain. Per-capita carbon emis-sions from books are 20.4 tons in the United States, 20 tons in Canada, 3.84 tons in China, 1.2 tons in India, 1.8 tons in Brazil, and 3.7 tons in Argen-tina. The Japanese book industry is notably less wasteful than that of the United States, in keeping with its economy's commitment to green supply chains.[30] Twenty percent of newspapers are recycled or end their time in landfills without even having been read, while each book produced in the

United States averages four kilograms of carbon dioxide emissions—eight times its average weight. Distributing and retailing account for five hundred grams of carbon dioxide emissions. Scholarly journals are responsible for twelve million tons a year worldwide.[31] The US Book Industry Environmental Council (BIEC) was formed in 2008 with the aim of reducing greenhouse gas emissions produced by the publishing industry by 80 percent over four decades.[32] London's newspapers and books make up 13 percent of the city's consumer carbon footprint compared to 10 percent for consumer electronics; the energy used to produce printed newspapers is greater than watching the news on television.[33]

Since 2000, high-end magazine publishing has eaten up forests at a higher rate than any other print medium. The glossier the magazine, the more new or virgin wood is needed. In 2001, the 18,000 US magazine titles comprised an estimated annual print run of twelve billion copies, of which just 20 percent was recycled. To publish that amount of magazines necessitates cutting down thirty-five million trees and emitting vast amounts of waste and greenhouse gas. Two-thirds of all magazines are not purchased, leaving 90 percent to be trashed within a year of publication, creating an abundance of waste—only 19 percent of which is recycled. The rest of the magazines (about two million tons) end up in landfills or are incinerated. In the United Kingdom, the Periodical Publishers Association (PPA) calculates that in 2008 the carbon footprint of 70–80 percent of British magazines came from paper supply, 13–25 percent from printing, and 6–8 percent from transportation.[34]

Table 2.1 illustrates some of the environmental burden that magazine publishing placed on the Earth's ecosystems in 2000.

*Table 2.1.* ANNUAL ENVIRONMENTAL IMPACT OF PRODUCING TWELVE BILLION MAGAZINES[35]

| Environmental Impact | Annual Amount | Annual Equivalent |
|---|---|---|
| Wood Use | 5,110,398 tons | Amount of copy paper used by 109 million people (39 percent of US population) |
| Energy Use | 72,220,086 million British Thermal Units | Enough to power 694,000 households |
| Greenhouse Gases ($CO_2$ Equivalents) | 13,408,395,941 pounds | As much as the emissions produced by 1.2 million cars |
| Solid Waste | 4,917,979,277 pounds | As much as the garbage produced by 1.2 million households |
| Wastewater | 34,241,543,545 gallons | As much as the sewage produced by 352,000 households |
| Particulate Emissions | 23,572,856 pounds | N/A |

Each ton of *Time* magazines emits 0.32 tons of carbon dioxide, mostly from pulp and paper mills. *National Geographic* generates 0.82 kg of carbon dioxide equivalents through the life cycle of each issue, and its greenhouse gas emissions are akin to those that come from driving three kilometers. (It is a somewhat unusual magazine, in that readers archive perhaps 60 percent of issues, with the remainder ending up in municipal solid waste.) *Discover* magazine accounts for the release of 2.1 pounds of carbon dioxide per issue, equivalent to the emission from twelve 100-watt light bulbs left on for an hour. The company arrives at this estimate based on the cumulative emissions that come from thirty-five employees traveling to its offices each day, in addition to other transportation costs, office energy use, paper production, inking, and printing (348,000 pounds of paper are used each month for the 1,000,000 copies printed) and distribution.[36]

## WIRED WORDS

Telegraphy involved the first major commercial application of electricity. It provided much of the financial and technical impetus to solve practical problems of large-scale electrification and set standards. Telegraphy's system of wires and devices allowed a person to turn electromagnetic impulses into code, which could be sent from one end of a wire to an endpoint, singly or via a web of interconnected endpoints, where it was decoded into words from dots and dashes that were either printed or rendered audible by a "sounder." The telephone enhanced this capacity by extending the power of the telegraph's sound-making device to send speech down the wire. Telegraph and telephone systems at first relied on local battery power, but by 1900 larger storage batteries, or "common batteries," were used to power telegraph offices and the central exchanges of the newer urban phone networks. Telecommunications still use industrial storage batteries charged from the electric grid, providing robust backup during power outages.[37]

The battery has martial origins. Benjamin Franklin coined the term after wiring together a number of Leyden jars (glass cells that store static electricity) to shoot jolts of electricity just as a "battery of cannons" fires its charges. Thirty years later, Alessandro Volta suggested that a charge from a Leyden jar could be used to fire a pistol from a long distance and went on to invent the chemical basis for the electrical storage battery. Batteries provided most electrical power prior to the commercialization of incandescent lighting systems in the 1880s, when primary currents began to be supplied by a generator (the dynamo). Chemical energy storage was considered cutting-edge technology, and many inventors thought of batteries as central components of urban electrification, with large telegraphic zinc mercury acid batteries for a time being considered a likely primary energy source. Before large-scale electrification in the United States, there were experiments with "battery in the cellar" home distribution systems, but size, cost, and emissions from sulfuric acid made them untenable.[38]

Sulfuric and nitric acid were used in each revision of battery technology in the nineteenth century and remained a problem for telegraph workers handling them. Liquid battery acid helped produce the chemical reaction that generated the electricity, and as the components (zinc, copper, and other materials, including mercury) dissolved, toxic gases (nitric oxide in the case of the early Grove cell used in US telegraphy) were produced. In addition to inhaling the fumes, which could damage lung and mucous membranes, contact with the battery acids harmed the skin and caused deep lining of hands (palmar fissures) into which other workplace filth became lodged. According to Gilbert Forbes, writing in a mid-twentieth century issue of the *Journal of Criminal Law and Criminology*, "Anyone working in sulphuric acid has his hands affected in this way."[39] Dry-cell batteries would reduce the problem of sloshing liquid acid, though the noxious components were still present in the form of a paste. As the zinc core of these early batteries burned away, which happened quickly, the batteries lost their charge. With the exception of valuable copper pieces, the spent components were discarded.[40] It was estimated that long-distance telegraphy (800-mile circuits) required fifty cells, whereas shorter closed-circuit systems used two or three. So-called gravity cells eventually replaced the Grove acid batteries after the 1860s. They continued to use zinc and copper metals, but replaced sulfuric acid with a layering of zinc sulfate and copper sulfate solutions of varying densities. Maintaining gravity cells remained difficult despite several designs to facilitate replacement of the spent parts and solutions, and they were useless for mobile telegraphy because the gravity action of the solutions required that they be completely still. But by 1886, Western Union used 12,500 gravity cells in its New York offices, consuming thirty-five thousand pounds of copper sulfate, nine thousand pounds of zinc, three thousand pounds of copper (most of which could be recovered) and eight barrels of battery oil each year.[41]

Rechargeable, or secondary, storage batteries were available by 1870, a time when steam-powered generators were also coming into use, but only large telegraph plants used these batteries. Larger storage batteries were based on a lead acid chemical reaction that allowed the action of the battery to be reversed for storing electricity drawn from a primary generator (like a car battery). The electrolyte solution was made of sulfuric acid, which was topped off with mineral oil to lessen evaporation and absorption of airborne elements that might interact with the electrolytes. Storage batteries were widely used in Britain and Germany as indispensible parts of central station electrical generation. The United States lagged behind, in part because of Thomas Edison's opposition—he once called rechargeable batteries "a catch penny, a sensation, a mechanism for swindling the public by stock companies."[42] Edison's stance held sway even though it was motivated by the rivalry between his incandescent lighting business and an arc lighting competitor who had invested in the manufacture of storage batteries (Edison later successfully marketed his own storage battery). Servicing these batteries involved either replacing worn lead plates and posts and cracked jars or removing any remaining oil or spent battery acid solution, which would have been dumped into a containment sump or directly into the ground. Workers were exposed to acids, acid vapor, and lead, and overflows from the sump entered the sewage system and waterways or soaked into the land under the buildings.[43]

By 1900, storage batteries used to back up central power were dominant even among Edison's companies as a result of a patent-sharing cartel of US, British, German, and French firms.[44] The cartel ensured transfers of technology and know-how to US battery factories but failed to transfer European standards that reduced workers' exposure to hazardous lead dust, fumes, molten lead, and lead oxide paste. In 1914, it was estimated that "18 percent of American battery workers had lead poisoning. This compared with a rate of three percent in the British battery industry and one percent in Germany's largest battery plant."[45] Research in the United States funded by battery factory owners consistently understated adverse health effects right up to the 1960s. Poisoning rates rose everywhere with the expansion of battery production: In France, 32 percent of battery workers were afflicted in 1924, up from 12.5 percent in 1921; battery manufacturing became the most dangerous lead industry in Britain, where 23 percent of battery workers were poisoned in 1925; and similar increases were recorded for Australia, India, and the United States. By the 1990s, US battery workers were still the group most at risk for occupational lead poisoning. Cases of lead poisoning spread worldwide with the expansion of battery salvage and recycling, affecting workers and their families in China, Colombia, the Dominican Republic, Germany, India, Iraq, Israel, Jamaica, Nicaragua, Russia, Taiwan, the United States, and Spain.[46]

The electrical generator, in contrast to the chemically based battery, uses electromagnetism to convert mechanical energy into electrical current. In its simplest form, a coil of copper wires turns around a magnetic core to create the current. This is not the origin of the energy—the rotational motion of the electrical generator requires its own source of mechanical power, which has historically been drawn from streamside waterwheels, hydroelectric turbines, and steam turbines powered by fossil fuels (coal, oil, and gas) and nuclear fission. The environmental impact of burning fossil fuels for electrical generation needs little comment here, other than to note that the historical growth and planetary spread of pollution from electrical consumption tracks the industrialization of capitalism across the Earth—from nineteenth-century Britain, to the United States after 1920, and on to China by the end of the twentieth century. Large-scale electrification transformed the ecological context of all media when commercialized electrification of industrial manufacturing took off after World War I.[47]

The wires inside the cables and generators used in telegraphy and telephony were primarily made of copper by 1900. The purity of the copper had been linked to conductivity around 1850, after which British telegraph companies pressured copper smelters to improve production techniques. In the United States, galvanized iron wire was the main cable used in telecommunication, even after high-quality copper became available. The eventual rise in copper use in the United States paralleled that of the country's emergence at the end of the nineteenth century as the "world's leading producer and consumer of copper" (displacing Chile) a status it maintained into the 1970s. The New York–Chicago telephone line consumed 870,000 pounds of copper.[48]

Copper demand, the growth of the copper industry, and environmental despoliation are intimately linked. Early mine deposits were relatively shallow veins of high-grade ore, and they were quickly exhausted by the early 1900s. To meet demand, the industry dug deeper into the Earth and extracted lower-grade ore in increasingly large volumes. In this business, "the tonnage of ore increases geometrically as grade decreases arithmetically," causing a number of organizational and technological changes that affect the environment. New technologies were instituted to improve drilling and milling to access deeper deposits and larger volumes of ore. At the same time, the mining industry expanded internationally, drawing in more territories and widening organizational problems of transport and communication. Rising capital costs accelerated large-scale commercial growth, the integration of smelting capacity to reduce transportation costs, and greater waste in mining techniques—the so-called unselective methods using large earth-moving trucks that indiscriminately shovel tons of material into the mills, saving money at the expense of the environment and its inhabitants. All this impelled "large mining and smelting companies to become even larger ... to finance, in a stable planning environment, the scale of operations necessary to sustain the growth in the world's demand for this raw material."[49] Central to this "stable planning environment" was the formation of cartels—a cooperation agreement among the largest firms to control market prices. In the United States, two cartels were organized under the Webb-Pomerene Act (in 1918 and 1926). A third, The International Copper Cartel, was formed in 1935 (ending in 1941) with mines in Latin America (US–controlled), the African copper belt (British- and Belgian-controlled), Spain (British-owned; a nonvoting cartel member), and Yugoslavia (French, nonvoting). Canadian copper owners were considered "friendly outsiders."[50] The size and power of the firms ensured that they held sway over an ecologically unsound political-economic arrangement. Their names should be remembered in media history: Kennecott, Anaconda, Rhokana, Mufulira, Katanga, and Rio Tinto. Their power is neatly indexed in the classic film noir *Gilda*,[51] in which Ballin Mundson (George Macready) runs a casino in Buenos Aires that provides money-laundering services for a global tungsten cartel run by German Nazis, which he in turn wants to take over. The casino and the cartel represent a return to international domination. In Mundson's words, "A man who controls a strategic material can control the world," which is "made up of stupid little people."

By the middle of the nineteenth century, copper smelters—and all metal smelting—were known to be major contributors of industrial pollution. The pollution could be seen in the vast quantities of copper smoke that hurt people's eyes and lungs. Toxicologists spoke of "metal fume fever" among the major occupational hazards of the time, the acids that formed in the moist air destroyed surrounding habitats and affected agriculture, and particulates of copper, sulfur, arsenic, lead, antimony, silver, and other byproducts dusted the nearby countryside. Estimates of the emission of deadly heavy metals in the 1860s in the Swansea region of Wales (nicknamed "Copperopolis") put levels at ten times those now considered safe by the European Union. This environmental problem was known in the United States, Spain, Germany, and Britain. In Britain, the problem was not eliminated by legislation or altered manufacturing techniques; rather, ore deposits had dwindled to nothing by the end of the nineteenth century, exporting the copper smoke problem, and by 1920 copper smelting was replaced by other metallurgical industries as a primary scourge.[52] In the United States, regulation of copper industry pollution began to reduce greenhouse emissions only in the 1980s, with deadlines set by the Clean Air Act.

Another historic advance of wired words with enormous contemporary implications came from undersea cable, which has been crucial to telegraphy, telephony, and the internet. The gun maker Samuel Colt developed one of the earliest applications of underwater cable for detonating bombs at a distance. Samuel Morse befriended Colt and used this underwater technology for his telegraph network, while lobbying the US government to lay transatlantic cable.[53] But the discovery of gutta-percha was "the greatest single factor making possible submarine telegraphy."[54] Gutta-percha, a form of latex drawn from the sap of the slow-growing *sapotaceae* tree family, is indigenous to the Rhio Archipelago, which crosses parts of the

Malay Peninsula, the Philippines, and Indonesia. Gutta-percha is relatively easy to refine and shape when heated, holds an electrical field without conducting electricity, does not degrade metal wire (unlike some rubbers) and becomes virtually indestructible when submerged in the cold, high-pressure seabed.[55]

Despite the fact that Dutch colonies produced the bulk of the raw material used to make gutta-percha, the United Kingdom obtained commercial control over latex because it ran Singapore, the international hub for the trade of the material, and cultivated close ties with Chinese merchants, who depended on British credit. The gutta arrived in Singapore via Chinese traders, who bartered with indigenous laborers for the raw material and coordinated fleets of junks to collect it across the region. The Malays worked outward from their villages into the jungle forests to gather gutta, using a technique that was wasteful but effective: they cut the trees down to milk the sap. The harvest could take the workers up to six months from the time they left their villages, because a fifteen- to twenty-year-old tree yielded less than a pound of gutta.[56]

By 1924, 237,000 miles of undersea cable had been laid, at the cost of some twenty-seven million trees—it took about sixty-nine pounds of gutta-percha to insulate one mile of cable. An estimated 675,000 trees were needed annually after 1924 to meet demand for new undersea cable, which had to be replaced every forty years. Most gutta flowed into Britain, which used more than half of all the production; France used less than a quarter; an eighth went to Germany; three percent went to the United States; and the rest to Asia, Italy, and Holland. Many forests of gutta had disappeared and new supplies were difficult to access, which gave rise to fake or low-grade gutta. By midcentury, when the first undersea telephone cable was laid, PVC had replaced gutta as cable insulation.[57]

Believed to be a benign use of the seabed, the laying of undersea cable has not attracted significant environmental regulation other than when a new rollout affects existing operations, shipping, marine life or fishing.[58] But undersea communication creates ancillary environmental problems due to copper mining and smelting and plastic production and disposal. The act of laying deep-sea cable also alters habitat and species colonization of coral, anemones, and certain fishes, and generates near-shore abrasion and snagging hazards for trawlers. Cable decommissioning and removal cause further seabed erosion through abrasion and the disruption or death of hundreds of thousands of organisms that have taken up residence on or around exposed cable. Geological events such as the 2006 earthquake near Taiwan, which severely disrupted internet communications between East Asia, China, and the United States, are reminders of the precariousness of this strategic medium.[59]

Both copper and undersea cable communication have been and will remain for the foreseeable future strategic assets in the global political economy. Copper has been essential in military weaponry and Communications, Command, and Control technology; in electrical and telecommunication networks; in electronics; and in construction (the primary user). Its importance dramatically outstrips its availability on the Earth, and as a scarce resource with high strategic value, dominion over copper deposits is key to geopolitical power in the twenty-first century. Likewise, undersea cable continues to be of crucial importance. It is not surprising that approval for landing undersea cable on US shores has historically been the responsibility of the Department of Defense.[60]

The wiring of words quickly enabled a massive acceleration and increase of information after the cables were deployed. Instantaneity substituted for deliberation, and serious public affairs became matters of private minutiae. As telecommunication became associated with new modes of sociability and exclusion, its connection to market sensitivities was blamed for everything from shocks in the prices of stock market shares to managerial neuroses, even as it was admired for transforming business efficiency. Such anxieties continue to haunt globally networked financial markets, which facilitate instantaneous trade continuously across the globe.[61] The technological impact on the environment has been left aside from such concerns.

## PLASTIC WORDS

The magnetic tape that was developed for the telegraphone, an 1898 invention that recorded speech, captured sound through microphones used in telephones. The basis of magnetic surface recording has varied little from the first telegraphone to computer tape drives, floppy disks, and hard drives. The recording surface of the early devices consisted of a magnetized steel wire or strip, which recorded fluctuations in electrical current from the microphone. The technology advanced somewhat in the United States and Britain, but an innovation in German recording technology in the 1930s led to the first use of magnetic oxide on coated plastic tape. The magnetophone was developed by Allgemeine Elektricitäts Gesellschaft for the German radio industry. At the end of World War II, the occupying US government seized technology, patents, models, and prototypes from Germany then made them available to US manufacturers through the Department of Commerce. Without concern for patent infringement, major US companies like 3M and Ampex were able to use these technical designs and reverse engineering to reproduce machines and magnetic tape—3M altered machinery it had already employed to make adhesive tape. Other entrepreneurs, some of whom worked for the occupying government in Germany, returned to the United States with leftover German supplies and set up smaller companies, as was the case of Oraddio. 3M packaged tape with its Scotch brand, while Orradio called theirs Irish Tape, burying any memory of its German origins.[62]

The ecological context of magnetic tape overlapped with raw film and pulp and paper manufacturing at the point when oxide emulsion was initially applied to strips of kraft paper. Cellulose acetate provided the film base (we shall see more on this in the next chapter). Demand for plastic magnetic tape grew during the 1950s in the radio industry; the military, oil, and mining sectors (for data collection and storage); and among consumers who could afford the novelty to record special sounds of domestic life, but the tape was hard to come by until it was mass-marketed in the 1960s. Early tape-making machines looked like large pasta makers. They mixed solvents, plastics paste, and iron oxide to produce strips of acetate tape. The technology for the magnetic tape passed through several phases—the base changed over time from cellulose acetate, to PVC, to polyester (the most stable); the magnetic film coating from iron oxide, to chromium dioxide, to a variety of different alloys found in compact and computer disks (which have a nonmagnetic base of aluminum or glass on which the emulsion is applied). Phonograph recording began by using fragile media like wax and shellac, but by the late 1940s recordings were pressed into PVC.

PVC was first manufactured commercially in the 1930s. Then as now, it was the most environmentally pernicious plastic in use, though knowledge of its toxicity was suppressed until the last quarter of the twentieth century. In the 1960s, the building block of PVC, vinyl chloride monomer (VCM), was found to cause cancer among workers in vinyl factories, but vinyl producers hid such information from the public and policy makers. VCM is an unstable, combustible compound that can cause brain, liver, and stomach cancers. The environmental risks of transportation for processing it into PVC were also well known by the 1980s after at least seventeen people reported accidents in the United States and Europe, causing increased regulation in its handling and transport. In addition to VCM, the manufacture of PVC uses ethylene dichloride, which is also a highly flammable pathogen that damages the liver, kidneys, and other organs. Because of its high chlorine content, PVC production and disposal release carcinogenic dioxin and hydrochloric acid into the environment, and some of the additives used in making various vinyl products produce further occupational and environmental hazards. PVC that is used to sheath and insulate electric and electronic wiring contains toxic phthalate-based plasticizers.[63]

## CHANGING BUSINESS, PERSISTENT ENVIRONMENTAL ISSUES

"450,000 Unsold Earth Day Issues of *Time* Trucked to Landfill"
  (Headline in *The Onion*'s "Obligatory Green Issue," an "all-paper salute to the environment")

Newspapers—the worst print offenders in carbon terms—are in crisis in some parts of the world. Yet in Japan and Brazil they continue to thrive and India's increasing literacy rate has stimulated new news outlets. Meanwhile, the German publishing company Springer boasted a 27 percent profit margin in 2010. But in much of the Global North, the story is very different. Per-capita paper consumption has declined, especially in the EU, though some British data is conflictual. From 2009 to 2010, dozens of US newspapers confronted bankruptcy, closed, moved exclusively online, or curtailed home delivery. Newsrooms shed a quarter of their staff between 2000 and 2010. In addition, readers are aging—many are retirees—and new readers are not coming forward. Sometimes, sizeable advertisers put pressure on newspapers to provide an audit of their carbon impact, as has happened to News Corporation with such retailers as Tesco and Walmart.[64]

There are numerous reasons for this decline. Thoughtless corporate owners such as venture capitalists, uninterested in public service, leverage newspapers against other debts; classified and other small-scale advertising revenues have fallen due to internet competition (a drop of 35 percent from 2008 to 2010); subscriptions drop as news coverage becomes poorer because fewer journalists are employed; and readers consume newspapers virtually rather than materially, leaving the newspapers without a proven means of charging them (other than in the case of the ur-ruling class, which is prepared to pay a premium for the *Financial Times* and even the third-rate *Wall Street Journal*). Also, several places in the Global South are seeing extreme weather that may correlate with climate change, which influences their capacity to produce and distribute newspapers. The *Fiji Times*, for instance, experienced severe disruptions from unprecedented cyclones in 2009 and 2010.[65] Its parent company News Corporation—elsewhere a stoic denier of climate change via Fox News Channel—cites this disruption as evidence of the need to deal with climate change. The aforementioned *Wall Street Journal*, which often espouses that the environmental concern is hype and denies climate change,[66] is part of the Dow Jones section of News Corp., which is powered through a solar photovoltaic facility.

Other companies work artfully to acknowledge their role in the emergent carbon disaster. The Hearst Corporation's guide *Being Green*, which we have already mentioned, announced that 75 percent of its magazines would be made from certified fiber by 2010 and 15 percent of its paper use came from recycling, though it should be noted that there is a debate about the ecological benefit of such practices.[67] The epigraph from *The Onion* quoted at the beginning of this section is apposite. *Vanity Fair*, the up-market lounge-lizard/coffee-table/hairdressing-salon magazine offered particularly notorious "green issues" from 2006 to 2008—until interest from advertisers declined. Whereas the decision to scrap the series was met with protest from those who favored its public-relations value for environmentalism, others pointed out that the special issues had necessitated flying Annie Leibovitz to Germany to photograph a polar bear, emitting 51 tons of carbon for a picture that was later digitally remastered, while the two planes that flew her, Leonardo DiCaprio, and their associates to Iceland accounted for 89 tons. The first two issues of *Vanity Fair* focusing on green topics were printed on virgin paper, requiring 2,350 tons of pulp and emitting 2,300 tons of carbon dioxide. The magazine industry now runs a "please recycle this magazine" campaign aimed at readers. The PPA estimates that the average recycling rate of British magazines is 70 percent.[68]

In the personal-computer era, of course, the paper-free office was supposed to prevail—we were told that by the 1980s, printed media and paper would be extinct. Instead, printing has become an everyday part of household and office work: World manufacture of paper for such purposes increased 44 percent from 1990 to 2008. US workers print over 60 kilos of paper per year, and Europeans average thirty pages per day.[69] Printers come to us as material objects, with complex histories to their steel, plastics, cardboard, cartridges, copper, aluminum, and wiring. The implications for pollution through plastics, ink mist, household ozone clouds, and flame retardants are serious: each year, 575 million printer cartridges are thrown away in North America alone. Modern chemical processes involved in printing have produced new synthetic byproducts, including dioxin. High-end office printing still proliferates in wealthy countries as people produce color and high-resolution prints. London's Sustainable Development Commission estimates that about 5 percent of carbon emissions in the city result from office paper. Consider academia. Most researchers seek out portable document formats of the papers they download. It seems likely that researchers now print more articles than they once read as hard copies in libraries (which were also shared with countless others). As they do so, they are also incurring something of an opportunity cost: HP Inkjet ink is seven times as expensive as a 1985 bottle of Dom Pérignon (a fabulously Bondian calculation).[70] Is it any wonder that the Electronics TakeBack Coalition rated HP a C– and Canon, Epson, and Brother an F in its 2010 "Report Card"?[71]

## CONCLUSION

The cosmic ambivalence and interdependency between older and newer media was cleverly expressed in the New York tabloid *Newsday*'s 2010 commercial for its new iPad application. The advertisement begins serenely enough: a white heterosexual family is enjoying breakfast. Its patriarch reads the paper on his iPad and an offscreen narrator extols the virtue of this new means of subscription by contrast with the old. Then a fly starts buzzing around the table. The father does with the new device what he would do with his old newspaper—he tries to squash the fly. The tablet shatters—and the fly keeps buzzing. While the advertisement's humor was meant to convey *Newsday*'s popular appeal, Apple reacted with a threat to withdraw the relevant application and make the newspaper unreadable on iPads in the form advertised if the commercial wasn't withdrawn. *Newsday* complied.[72]

Similar if less dramatic struggles emerged with the advent of e-books, which came on the market late in 2006 with the Sony PRS-500. Much is made of the fact that December 25, 2009, was the first day Amazon dispatched more books to its Kindle e-readers than to mailboxes. Revenue from downloaded books in the United States rose 150 percent that year, three million e-book readers were sold, and e-books accounted for perhaps 3 percent of the market. It was estimated that four million Kindles were sold in the first three years after their launch in November 2007. For the first time, over a billion dollars was spent in the United States on e-book readers in 2009, when more than two million e-books were sold. About 8.25 million iPads were sold in the nine months after Apple introduced them. And the northern summer of 2010 saw Amazon sell 143 digital books for every hundred print copies in the United States. But the e-book segment of the overall market remained around 6 percent, whereas book sales were up 22 percent. Simon & Schuster predicts the proportion of e-books to print books will be a quarter by 2015. Amazon is now the world's biggest bookseller, with 2009 sales of $24.5 billion and overall growth of 28 percent that year, aided by a stock of two million titles and a policy of 50 percent discounts on best sellers. There are now more iPhone applications for books than for games, the previous market leader, and HarperCollins sells hundreds of thousands of cartridges of books that can be read on Nintendo consoles.[73]

Common sense suggests that electronic books will diminish the carbon footprint of the industry: 80 percent of British book buyers believe electronic communications are less environmentally destructive than paper ones. Early comparisons between the environmental impact of printed newspapers and electronic consumption support this view. Sixty-five percent of publishing's carbon footprint comes from paper, and e-book readers require one-off transportation (obtaining the devices) and no pulping, bleaching, or printing. The Kindle is supposed to offset the carbon footprint of its production within a year and over a lifetime purportedly saves the carbon needed to make twenty books, and solar-charged devices were expected by 2012. However, when side-by-side comparisons are made, the environmental costs of production for one e-reader (including raw materials, transport, energy, and disposal) far outweigh those of one book printed on recycled paper: the e-reader uses 33 pounds of minerals, including tantalum, versus a paper book, which uses two-thirds of a pound; 79 gallons of water versus 2 gallons; 100 kilowatt hours of fossil fuels versus 2 hours, with proportional emissions of carbon dioxide; and the health effects of exposure to internal toxins is estimated to be seventy times greater for the e-reader. Of course, these are rough, short-sighted estimates that do not account for the environmental impact of recycled paper manufacture or the environmental benefits of reducing book production as more volumes are published directly on e-readers, which we are told begin to pay back their environmental costs somewhere around a hundred book downloads.[74]

But there is no accepted measurement system for readers, publishers, scholars, policy makers, librarians, and salespeople to calculate the renewable virtues of paper versus the electrical vices of electronics, while there are dozens of competing environmental-certification systems.[75] Because young trees are the most efficient at absorbing carbon emissions, regularly replenishing them rather than relying on elderly branches and roots may be effective. And we know that the use of digital devices in the United States generally relies on coal-powered electricity at some point in the supply chain (much of it responsible for removing the Appalachian mountaintops). Ordering books online involves individual packaging and delivery, and numerous midpoints of distribution, by contrast with bookstore purchases; plus while US consumers are rare in wealthy nations because they use cars to shop for books, when they do so, they generally purchase several at a time, by contrast with online delivery patterns. Although web publishing does not encourage planting of trees, it does nothing to remove carbon from the atmosphere, unlike printing. And when comparisons are made, the amount of time per day that electricity is used for reading, especially via the power grid, must be factored into determining environmental impacts. Current research indicates that reading online for half an hour equates to ninety minutes of watching television or the printing of a newspaper. Perhaps public libraries can mitigate some of these environmental costs, by socializing access to e-books, centralizing distribution, and providing community-centered forms of sociality—in the aggregate they may be a better target for research and development in new forms of greening the printed word, quite apart from their capacity to reach those excluded from needy, nerdy private consumption.[76]

This chapter has examined the ecological context of the printed word and the mechanical-chemical processes that characterize its relation to the environment. By thinking of the interconnections of the Earth's ecosystems and the political economy of print media, we have again posed the question of sustainability—in this case, how much can the Earth provide to create print media and how much can it absorb from its production, distribution, and waste. It is clear that there is an urgent need for renewable sources of fiber, the reduction and elimination of toxins and waste in production and consumption, reinvestment in national public libraries, and more rational organization of the publishing industry, which is a thoroughly wasteful business perpetuated by wholesale distributors, market-research firms, and retail sellers who appear uninterested in sustainable publishing.[77] Our next task is to examine how screen technologies have extended these problems through film and the electronic media.

# CHAPTER 3

✧

# Screens

George Clooney

On the ground: George favors a Tango, an electric car that gets a whopping 135 miles to the charge.

In the air: Los Angeles/Tokyo, 5500 miles in a private jet.

Gas guzzled: 7,000 gallons of jet fuel.

Electric shocker: Even with his super-saver Tango, he'll have to drive over 57 oceans—Pacific Ocean[—]to break even.

So George says: Clooney's rep, publicist Stan Rosenfield, tells TMZ, "You clearly have no understanding of certain people's need for private transport," and points out that Clooney often has "no control" over his travel schedule.

—TMZ Staff, 2006, "*George Clooney*" section

In 1968, I came to California and didn't know why my eyes were constantly filling with tears. I quickly learned about smog and bad-air days. These days, the air is much cleaner thanks to the Clean Air Act and technologies that resulted from it, such as catalytic converters on cars and particle traps on diesel exhaust. Those toxic smog days motivated everyone to act.

Today, I have tears in my eyes again but for a very different reason. Some in Washington are threatening to pull the plug on this success. Since January, there have been more than a dozen proposals in Congress to limit enforcement of our clean-air rules, create special-interest loopholes, and attempt to reverse scientific findings. These attacks go by different names and target different aspects of the law, but they all amount to the same thing: dirtier air.

—Arnold Schwarzenegger, 2011

Media screens come in all shapes and sizes. They may feature touchable or untouchable features and take the form of phones, tablets, flat- or fat-screen TVs, standard analog and high-definition digital screens,

3-D images on flat or spherical surfaces, computers, camera viewfinders, and so on. Depending on their configuration, when they are turned on or off, they typically display references to the brands that sell them and/or the distributors that fill them with content.

Instead of these corporate images standing in for the provenance of each screen or its contents, imagine a green banner framing a tightly edited, sixty-second video showing the working conditions, environmental inputs, and toxic waste that occur throughout each particular screen's life cycle. The video would end with the line "Demand Greener Media" before beginning "regular programming." In this chapter, we show why this green public service video would be a better index of the origins of screen technology than corporate logos, those familiar enticements from the fantasy world of the technological sublime that are out of place in an ecologically sound media system. After a preliminary discussion of the more prevalent sorts of green on the screen, we delve into the history and status of the ecological context of Hollywood's silver screen and other electronic screens that dominate media consumption.

Ecological issues and environmental realities do, of course, appear on screens in popular and journalistic depictions of nonhuman nature, environmental catastrophes, tourist idylls, and the like. But because these subjects rarely act as calls to arms against the eco-crisis, it's easy to criticize them as mere spectacles of "objectifying recreation," akin to a video loop of an undersea world designed to prettify the dreary domestic life of the urban dweller.[1] There's an ugly version of this in the landscape encountered by Tom Hanks's character in the film *Cast Away*,[2] a Robinson Crusoe throwback set on a desert island. His only companions are the detritus of global capitalism, exemplified in their pointlessness by unplayable videotapes. We also have global disaster films like *The Day After Tomorrow*,[3] *An Inconvenient Truth*,[4] and *2012*,[5] which have either misled or informed the public about climate change, depending on the environmental scientist, zoologist, ornithologist, geographer, or pundit one endorses.[6]

Robert Redford, actor, director, producer, founder of the Sundance independent film market, and doyen of environmental stardom, was inspired toward environmentalism as a teenager working at the Standard Oil refinery in El Segundo, California, where he "saw the oil seeping into the sand dunes. Now all that [oil] sits underneath the big buildings they've built there."[7] As our epigraphs suggest, by far the biggest onscreen boosters of environmental content are celebrities like Redford who endeavor to win public acclaim for environmental causes. Hollywood stars love to add awareness of their shrinking carbon footprints to their enviable personal traits, even as they jet around the world. Frugal is finally fabulous, and the ecorazzi—paparazzi on the eco-celebrity beat—oblige audiences with nonstop, if sometimes rather arch, coverage. Meanwhile, talent agencies allocate executives to identify suitable causes for celebrities to endorse, based on visibility, publicity, subjectivity, interest, availability, and other pragmatic factors. By 2005, celebrity endorsements were said to amount to over a billion dollars in expenditure. They were based on the assumption that audiences infer qualities from stars that can be transferred onto themselves. Marketing mavens call this "associative learning," whereby the "matchup" between commodities and stars habituates consumers to thinking that the celebrity lifestyle can be purchased along with an endorsed product. It is not clear if this works for environmental advocacy, but celebrities certainly attract public attention to environmental issues.[8]

Consider Pierce Brosnan. On his website, piercebrosnan.com, causes, corporations, and characters are fused to promote a green lifestyle, illustrating a seamless link between the actor's multiple incarnations as a star brand and his public-service endeavors. His celebration of Earth Day allows visitors to click on a link to petition the California government to prevent offshore gas production near his luxurious gated community in Malibu. His tips on purchasing products reinforce the consumerist message in a way that furthers his family's "quest to be environmentally conscience [sic]." He favors an "eco-friendly gardening or car service" and proudly notes that the Brosnan Trust has donated over $1 million to schools, activists, charities, and third-sector environmental bodies. This has become a key part of his public image. The Sustainable Style Foundation named him, along with fashion model Angela Lindvall, the "most stylish environmentalists on the planet," and he's a member of the "celebrity cabinet" of the American Red Cross.[9] Brosnan appeared in the documentary *Whaledreamers*,[10] and lobbied Congress and the administration on behalf of the International Fund for Animal Welfare.[11] He and his wife Keely also blogged about the film *The Cove*[12] to great effect. Their post on the TakePart website bears quoting at length:

There is a cove in Taiji, Japan that is completely off limits to the public. Activists have long suspected that dolphins and porpoises were entering the cove and not coming out, but there was little evidence of what took place in those closely guarded waters. Film director Louie Psihoyos and prominent dolphin advocate Ric O'Barry assembled a team of activists, divers and special effects experts to embark a on [sic] covert mission to infiltrate the cove in the dead of night. It sounds like the plot of a Hollywood spy thriller; but in this film the danger is real.... We have long been passionate about marine mammal protection. After watching *The Cove*, we were astonished to discover that more than 20,000 dolphins and porpoises are slaughtered in Japan each year, and that their meat—which contains toxic levels of mercury—is sold to consumers and in grocery stores across Japan. Without this kind of investigative journalism, the plight of dolphins and the safety of some of Japan's seafood may not have been adequately reported. This powerful and moving film is an urgent cry for help—and now that the public finally knows the truth, we *must demand change.*

That roster of eco-ethical commitments fits Brosnan's fourfold "definition of citizenship": "get informed…take a stand…get involved…give your support"[13]—inspired, one hopes, by James Brown's song "Get Up, Get Into It, Get Involved."

The "blogroll of eco-celebs" at ecorazzi.com lists many Hollywood stars, events, and resources and also features these examples: twenty-five celebrities arriving at the 2006 Academy Awards in Toyota Priuses; the 2007 Emmy Awards show's red carpet being made from 95,000 recycled soda bottles; a "Hollywood Goes Green" summit meeting being held the same year; *Hollywood Today* praising actors who give green gifts of "vintage-inspired" camisoles and recycled jewels; the 2008 Academy Awards ceremony being designed to cut 630 tons of carbon emissions from similar affairs; a relatively new Environmental Media Association honoring green celebrities with a Green Seal (this is Hollywood, so the awards are self-nominating); the producers of *Evan Almighty*[14] boasting about it being "the first big movie comedy to zero out its impact on the environment," because of a prop ark made from recycled wood, a bicycle riding crew, and tree planting to offset carbon emissions; and *The Day After Tomorrow* receiving CarbonNeutral status, a global proprietary offsets seal, because director Emmerich paid perhaps $200,000 to plant trees to mitigate the projected 10,000 tons of carbon dioxide emitted by the production.[15]

Not everyone working the eco-beat is impressed by this activity. For example, msnbc.com admonished the superficiality of green celebrity, for which "the Prius reigns supreme as the current status symbol," suggesting that air pollution would be a more apt symbol of Hollywood life, as "trucks that carry equipment from studios to locations and back continue to emit exhaust from diesel engines," as do generators on set.[16] MSNBC was not expressing misdirected jealousy or sour grapes at the eco-elite. The environmental burden of screen production is very real.

The first major scholarly study on this topic, conducted on behalf of the Integrated Waste Management Board from 2003 to 2005, concluded that the motion-picture industry is the biggest producer of conventional pollutants of all industries located in the Los Angeles area, thanks to its massive use of electricity and petroleum and release of hundreds of thousands of tons of deadly emissions each year. In California as a whole, film- and television-related energy consumption and greenhouse-gas emissions (carbon dioxide, methane, and nitrous oxide) are about the same as those produced by the aerospace and semiconductor industries.[17] Spectators are also major producers of pollutants, from auto emissions, including chemical runoff from parked cars, and the energy required to run home-entertainment devices.[18] There is a structural homology between this disposable attitude to film production and forms of consumption oriented to fast fashion, fun, and a throwaway culture: "Every movie, every broadcast program, or issue of a newspaper or magazine must be quickly forgotten, rendered obsolete." This will "clear the way" for the next models, "each of which is unique, unprecedented, unparalleled, extraordinary, exceptional—even though indistinguishable—from what has gone before."[19] As we argued in the introduction, this cult of the present fosters a perception that the environment and media technology are disconnected. To counter this idea and reconnect screen and Earth, consider the following examples.

Millions of cartridges of Atari's failed electronic-game adaptation of *E.T.: The Extra-Terrestrial*[20] were buried in a New Mexico landfill, broken up by a heavy roller, and covered in concrete to consign them to history. Microsoft and Nintendo have appalling game-console environmental records. They have sold seven generations of frequently non-interoperable home consoles with poisonous flame retardants, plastics, chemicals, and heavy metals as components. This built-in obsolescence is justified via a "utopian mythology of upgrades."[21]

Much of Fox Studios' film *Titanic*[22] was shot in a Mexican water tank in the village of Popotla in Baja California. During the making of the picture, the national film studio Estudios Churubusco was renovated and a national film commission established with satellites across Mexico, providing *gabacho* moguls trips in governors' helicopters, among other services. Restoring Mexico to the Hollywood map gained the director, James Cameron, the Order of the Aztec Eagle from a grateful government. *Titanic* was, in this context, a screen testimony to the 1994 North American Free Trade Agreement [Tratado de Libre Comercio] (NAFTA [TLC]), which has seen offshore film and television production in Mexico increase thanks to easy shipment of film stock and special-effects equipment, especially for low-budget shoots. Studio owner Rupert Murdoch approvingly cited the number of workers invisibly employed in making the film: "This cross-border cultural co-operation is not the result of regulation, but market forces. It's the freedom to move capital, technology and talent around the world that adds value, invigorates ailing markets, creates new ones." Meanwhile, local Mexican film production spiraled downward, from 747 titles in the decade prior to the Agreement to 212 in the decade after.[23]

There is a cruel irony to this globalization of cultural labor: People submerged in the credits to *Titanic* (or not listed at all) supposedly benefited from the story of a boat that had been sunk by invisible ice and business bombast eighty years earlier. During filming, Popotla was cut off from the sea and local fisheries by a six-foot-high and five-hundred-foot long movie wall, built to keep citizens away. Fox's chlorination of surrounding seawater decimated sea urchins, which locals had long harvested, and reduced overall fish levels by a third. The cost of the film could have provided safe drinking water to 600,000 people for a year.[24]

In collaboration with artists like Jim Bliesner, the Popotlanos decorated the wall with rubbish to ridicule the filmmakers and adopted the rallying cry "Mariscos libre" [freedom for shellfish].[25] This nifty environmental critique, and fish ethic, largely eluded journalistic and scholarly analysis, though Ars Electronica awarded the Popotlanos a prize for "symbolic low-tech resistance to real high-tech destruction" that was in keeping with the movie's textual—if not industrial—class politics. The award was itself a fraction of the money Ars Electronica gave the film's producers for their innovative special effects! The Popotlanos' view of Cameron's putatively green, proindigenous, anti-imperialist film *Avatar*[26] is not yet on record, but their town is currently vilified by the likes of *The Washington Times* as a site for "illegals" seeking to enter the United States.[27] Cameron acknowledges the need to change his own filmmaking in light of the ecological crisis and is quick to point out that "*Avatar* was an enormous battle film that took place in a rainforest but it was 100% C[omputer]G[enerated by] a few people working on a performance capture stage, so the footprint compared to the visual impact of the movie was really tiny."[28] When he lectured in the Pacific Northwest about oil from tar sands, the *Edmonton Sun* editorialized in its best un-Canadian fashion that "James Cameron is a hypocrite" for working in California, where energy comes from power companies that use coal from elsewhere.[29]

Three years after *Titanic*, Fox Studios made *The Beach*,[30] in which a modern-day Asian Eden suddenly turns nasty for jaded tourists. The film was shot in Maya Beach, part of Phi Phi Islands National Park in Thailand. Natural scenery was bulldozed because it did not fit the studio's fantasy of a tropical idyll: sand dunes were relocated, flora rearranged, and a new strip of coconut palms planted. The producers paid off the government with a donation to the Royal Forestry Department and campaigned with the Tourism Authority to promote the picture and the country together. The damaged sand dunes of the region collapsed in the next monsoon, their natural defenses against erosion destroyed by Hollywood bulldozers. Thai environmental and prodemocracy activists publicized this arrogant despoliation. The director, Danny Boyle, claimed that the film was "raising environmental consciousness" among a local population whose appreciation of these things lagged "behind" US "awareness."[31] Director Boyle heroically announced his intention to "give something back to Thailand" by hiring Thai apprentices but then complained that "we were hauling 300 fucking people around wherever we went. And you know how hard it is to learn Thai names. Every lunchtime was like a prime minister's reception."[32]

Before the film was released—but no doubt after having had their consciousness raised courtesy of Fox and Boyle's actions—the Ao Nang Tambon Administration Organisation, the Krabi Provincial Administration Organization, and various environmental groups filed suit against Fox and local officialdom for contravening the National Parks Act and the Environmental Protection Act. It took seven years, but the Thai Supreme Court ruled in their favor in 2006.[33] The reaction of the "300 fucking people" who were being "hauled around" during production is not on record.

The political-economic background to such ecologically destructive filmmaking has been shaped in part by economic-structural adjustment peddled by neoliberal high priests at the World Bank, the International Monetary Fund, the World Trade Organization, and the sovereign states that dominate them. They have encouraged the Global South to turn away from subsistence agriculture and towards tradable goods—beyond their manufacturing capacity, in the direction of service exchange. In much of Southeast Asia, for example, structural adjustment pushed people into littoral regions in search of work. Fish-farming corporations created a new aquaculture, displacing the natural environment of mangroves and coral reefs that protect people and land. The requirement to constitute themselves as entertaining heritage sites and decadent tourist playgrounds induced Thailand, Indonesia, and Malaysia to undertake massive construction projects of resorts located at the points where high tides lap, attracting more and more workers and decimating more and more natural protection. Areas that had not been directed to remove natural barriers suffered dramatically fewer casualties in the 2004 tsunami.[34]

The screen business has played its part in the global spread of this dirty neoliberal work. But its egregious impact on the environment predates the 1970s and '80s, when neoliberal economic doctrines became mainstream. For decades, Hollywood and the electronics sector followed a grotesque economic model that ravaged the environment in the name of entertainment, enlightenment, growth, and progress.

## THE SILVER SCREEN

The US film industry's ecological context was established in the late nineteenth century, a few decades before the merger of warring movie moguls, who had been allied with either technology or content. Today, Hollywood's private bureaucracy boasts that the earliest studio owners were ragpickers and junk dealers in New York, but this mythology hides the reality of a rapidly managerializing, professionalizing class in the 1920s and '30s. Much of Hollywood was run not out of the remnants of the Lower East Side of Manhattan, but alumni associations of the Ivy Leagues engaged in intra-class conflict over the primacy of mercantile versus manufacturing capital. Those ties to secondary industry are crucial to understanding the environmental impact of Hollywood's silver screen, its mass-production techniques, its financial interests in techno-scientific research, and its standards for the development of plastics and other harmful products.[35]

The type and volume of chemical waste emitted into the air and waterways by large-scale film production is traceable to the chemical process for extracting cellulose from cotton and wood pulp, which was invented in the 1800s for papermaking. Guncotton, or cellulose nitrate, was the first synthetic commercial plastic and the first celluloid base, upon which an emulsion of light-sensitive silver crystals was applied to make film for photography and motion pictures. The chemical-mechanical process for manufacturing cellulose nitrate film required large volumes of clean water and a variety of chemicals, including alcohol, sodium hydroxide, camphor, and nitric and sulfuric acids. Cellulose nitrate was originally marketed as imitation ivory for making billiard balls, combs, and sundry personal items, but film stock became its defining application.[36]

Cellulose nitrate was closely linked to explosives through nitrogen-based chemistry; film stock was famously combustible. Many precautions were put in place from the earliest days of its production, transportation, and film exhibition, including fireproof enclosure of projection rooms and training projectionists in handling the flammable material. A substitute of cellulose acetate, a less flammable product known as safety film, was available in the 1920s and prescribed for lightweight 16 mm filmmaking and screenings in "homes, schools, churches, factories, lecture and assembly halls."[37] Both materials were replaced in mid-century by triacetate and polyester.

The main ingredients of cellulose nitrate film manufactured after 1890 were cotton and silver. Cotton supplies were abundant in the United States, rising very rapidly in the early decades of the twentieth century. Eastman Kodak consumed five million pounds of cotton annually in 1926 and almost twice that amount ten years later. While most commercial manufacturers of cellulose nitrate used cotton-mill waste, it is not clear whether Eastman Kodak favored mill waste or a mix of available supplies. To remove impurities, the cotton was bleached with sodium hydroxide (lye or caustic soda). Used also in wood-pulp bleaching, this chemical base is harmful to skin and eyes. The treated cotton was then immersed in nitric and sulfuric acids as it rotated in large perforated vats that allowed the acids to be drawn off. After this acid wash, the nitrated cotton was put into large centrifugal washers that rinsed the remaining acids with large quantities of water, a process repeated over weeks. Once the water was spun off, the cotton was fed into mixers that added a solvent of camphor and alcohol to produce a paste with the viscosity of honey. The camphor was used as a softener or plasticizer that kept the film from becoming brittle. Cellulose acetate film was made in a similar way, using acetic acid and other chemicals.[38]

The silver arrived at Eastman Kodak's Kodak Park Plant in Rochester, New York, in forty-two–pound bars of bullion. By 1926, Eastman Kodak was the second-largest consumer of pure silver bullion after the US Mint. The plant was processing five tons of silver in 1936 and remained one of the metal's largest purchasers in the world even after 2000, when it began to focus on digital photography. The silver bars were dissolved in nitric acid to obtain pure crystals of silver nitrate, which were mixed into an emulsion with potassium iodide, potassium bromide, and gelatin (the latter made from cattle bones and hides). The emulsion was then applied to the film base.[39]

From the mid-1920s, the Kodak Park Plant was churning out 200,000 miles of film stock annually, sucking more than twelve million gallons of water daily from Lake Ontario and spewing the used water, along with chemical effluents, into the Genesee River. At the end of the century, when it supplied 80 percent of the world's film stock, Kodak Park was using thirty-five to fifty-three million gallons of fresh water a day. By then, the company was the primary source of pathogens (mainly carcinogenic dioxin) released into New York State's environment. Rochester was "ranked number one in the U.S. for overall releases of carcinogenic chemicals" from 1987 to 2000, despite the fact that since the 1970s, most of the wastewater had been collected in a treatment plant in order to comply with the Clean Water Act.[40]

By this time, Kodak was dumping "methylene chloride concentration as high as 3,600,000 parts per billion" into New York groundwater. That was 720,000 times the permissible levels of this pulmonary and skin irritant that humans metabolize into carbon monoxide. The company halved this amount by 2003 as a result of pressure from regulators and its own reduction of celluloid-film production and expansion of its digital-media business. Three years later, the ties of film to paper came full circle when Kodak announced a process for high-speed digital printing that could be customized by publishers. This new process included one of the first commercial applications of nanotechnology in the media sector. *Business Week* called it "as important an evolution in printmaking as movable type." It is unclear how this innovation addressed the scant scientific literature on the health risks of nanotechnology; the precautionary principle was clearly not applied.[41]

Kodak Park exposed its workers to acids and acid vapors as well as other irritants. The waste from this process also sent bleaches, traces of silver, and acids into the Genesee. Silver is not considered dangerous to humans, although high levels of it are toxic to fish and other aquatic life, but employees at Eastman Kodak were exposed to abnormal levels of silver dust or fumes, which can irritate the upper respiratory tract and eyes. The cotton dust also affected workers' respiratory systems, and if exposed constantly to high levels, they might contract byssinosis, or "brown lung," which reduces lung capacity. Byssinosis was recognized as an occupational hazard in Britain by the 1940s but not in the United States until the 1970s, largely because cotton-mill owners had moved operations to non-unionized southern states, where worker protections were weak. Workplace hazards and noxious by-product waste were common at Kodak's chemical plant in Tennessee, set up after World War I to produce solvents, cellulose acetate, and plastics.[42]

The competition effect of capitalism—its paradoxical tendency toward monopolization—propelled environmental exploitation and despoliation in the raw-film business as much if not more than the rising commercial demand for film stock. For example, George Eastman was very keen to maintain his monopoly in raw-film supply. He worried that German and French competitors might capture part of the market with improved product, specifically nonflammable cellulose acetate film, which the French film equipment and production company Pathé and the German firms AGFA, Bayer, and BASF were developing between 1904 and 1909. So Eastman infringed the patent rights to acetate film held by his European rivals. Rather than settle for a cartel arrangement offered by the German companies, he leveraged contracts and credit deals with European customers to obstruct sales of German film stock, especially by AGFA, which he saw as his main competitor. AFGA expanded during World War I, and survived to reestablish its business with European customers.[43]

Eastman experienced less competition for his control over the supply of silver, which was solidly in the hands of US and British interests. In the interwar years, Mexico, the United States, Canada, and Peru were the largest producers of silver ore, and the United States controlled 73 percent of refinery production, including the Guggenheim Exploration Company's ownership of Mexican refineries.[44] China and India were large consumers. China was on the silver standard, which made it vulnerable to US silver interests. The latter sought and won a favorable purchasing and subsidy agreement from the Federal government in 1933, forcing China into a political crisis.[45]

Camphor was another story. By 1932, 80 percent of the world's supplies went into film and celluloid products. At that time, virtually all camphor came from Taiwan, then known as Formosa, which Japan colonized between 1895 and 1945. Japan set up a government monopoly on the compound, fixing prices to maintain its dominance of the market against growing competition from synthetic camphor producers. Natural camphor would eventually be replaced by synthetic camphor, derived from turpentine in a process developed in Germany. By the end of the twentieth century, Taiwan had become home to Formosa Plastics, the world's largest producer of PVC.[46]

Today's silver-halide film stock is under threat by the imminent move to digital printing/filmmaking. Film will be around as long as millionaire aesthetes and movie moguls insist on its superiority, but digital production is fast becoming the new standard. The question is whether the digital transition will make motion pictures less ecologically destructive, a subject addressed in the next section.[47]

## ELECTRONIC SCREENS

The ecological context of electronic screens was established with practical applications of wireless communication that built upon experiments to describe, detect, and measure electromagnetic waves. While electromagnetic fields (EMFs) exist in nature and had already been exploited for the mechanical generation of electricity, wireless communication was the first large-scale attempt to generate EMFs. Early wireless signaling used spark-gap transmitters or continuous current generators to send messages from antenna to antenna to convert radiation into an intelligible code. Newfangled gizmos like the coherer (made of metal shavings in a glass tube) would react visibly to the signal and enhance its conductivity; in contrast, the crystal detector used a piece of crystal to steady the oscillating frequency and make it audible, a process known as rectification (crystal would later be understood to have semiconducting properties).

By the 1920s, electro-mechanical means of generating radio frequencies (a large generator, or alternator) were replaced by a novel electronic device: a vacuum tube wherein electricity heated a filament (a cathode) to produce a cloud of negatively charged electrons that flowed to a positively charged plate (an anode) via a grid that dictated the flow according to the voltage applied to it. Known as a triode vacuum tube (or valve in the United Kingdom) this device made it possible to amplify the signal, switch signals off and on, improve signal detection, and control frequency generation. Both long-distance cable and wireless telecommunication were improved by this breakthrough, and a greater portion of the spectrum of electromagnetic waves could be used for the emerging system of radio broadcasting and multidirectional wireless radio communication—both of which profited from the increased wartime demand for tube production and trained radio operators.[48]

By 1929, radio set manufacturers had learned to exploit acquisitive individualism as consumers upgraded their radio sets as often as twice a year in order to boast about having the model with the most tubes; this coincided with the moment that engineers working for such commercial firms as GE embraced the idea of planned obsolescence.[49]

The electromagnetic spectrum is comprised of ionizing radiation (ultraviolet rays, X-rays, gamma rays) and nonionizing radiation (extra-low and very low frequencies; electrical power lines, radio waves, microwaves). Prior to World War II, radio broadcasts, telecommunications, and medical uses of low-level radiation (radio-diathermy) were practically the only human-made sources of nonionizing electromagnetic radiation (electrical power lines became additional sources of radiation soon after the introduction of the triode vacuum tube). Nonionizing radiation occurs at the atomic level when sufficient energy excites electrons and molecules, such as the electron clouds that light an incandescent bulb, without knocking the electrons out of orbit, as ionizing radiation does. The earliest attempts to understand the biological effects of EMFs occurred in the first decades of the twentieth century, when the heating properties of radio waves were studied for radio-diathermy applications, but this work was soon overshadowed by concerns about the adverse effects of X-rays and other sources of ionizing radiation, including fallout from atomic bombs.[50]

During and after World War II, the rapid development and deployment of radar systems using high-power electronic tubes paved the way for the utilization of the EMF microwave range for wireless communication in both civilian and military spheres. Radio and microwave frequencies are used in all the communications media that we are familiar with today—from garage-door openers and remote controls to cell phones and satellite systems. The ecological context of wireless media includes the same material basis as wired communication (batteries, electricity, copper, etc.) but the electronic contrivance added a new element to the ecological history of media technology. The artificially created EMFs introduced by electronics into the Earth's natural EMFs created radiation exposure with "no counterpart in man's evolutionary background."[51]

The proliferation of electronics in the post–World War II period prompted the US Department of Defense (DoD) to fund research into the dangers of EMFs, especially radar and other microwave communications technologies. The DoD's Tri-Service Research Program, which lasted from 1957 to 1961, set safety standards for occupational exposure to nonionizing radiation, at the points when the heating of soft tissue causes localized burning, heat stress, skin irritation, and the internal disruption of normal functioning of organs and the hormonal, neurological, and endocrinal systems.[52] Because the DoD program focused only on the thermal effects of

EMFs, it created the perception among US radiation experts that non-thermal hazards from low-level EMFs were nonexistent. This research diverged radically from that being conducted at the same time in the Soviet Union, which placed harmful exposure levels a thousand times lower than the US standard. In the late 1970s, research agreements between US and Soviet scientists corroborated the effects of low-level, non-thermal EMFs, including their disruption of biological development (learning ability and immunological systems) eye and brain deterioration, and possible genetic and birth defects.[53] Research in the USSR found microwave workers to be suffering from "chronic exposure syndrome," which consisted of

> headache, eyestrain and tearing, fatigue and weakness, vertigo, sleeplessness at night and drowsiness during the day, moodiness, irritability, hypochondria, paranoia, either nervous tension or mental depression and memory impairment... sluggishness, inability to make decisions, loss of hair, pain in muscles and in the heart region, breathlessness, sexual problems... trembling eyelids, fingers and tongue, increased perspiration of the extremities, rash, and, at exposures in the 1 to 10 mW/cm² range, changes in electro-cephalogram (EEG) patterns. (Massey, 1979, 120)

Additional research has shown that the important parameters of exposure to EMFs are the energy level of signal generation, proximity to the signal source, radio-wave frequency resonance with affected bodies (EMF absorption rates vary among species and body sizes) pulsed versus continuous wave forms, and duration of exposure.[54] By 1980, there was consensus about a number of adverse effects associated with EMF radiation; namely, bio-thermal damage to organisms located in close proximity to transmission towers and signal generators—this includes not only media workers continuously exposed to radio, TV, and telecommunication equipment but also office workers on top floors of buildings within range of high-power transmission antennae (determining the size of the danger zone depended on whether one used the Soviet or US minimum standard). In addition, by then, it was known that interference with other sensitive electronic equipment created health and safety hazards, and there was evidence suggesting that TVs and radios also introduced nonionizing radiation into the environment.[55]

With the advent of electronic television in the 1930s, ionizing radiation (X-rays) entered into the ecological context of screen technologies. The television camera tube was developed to serve as an electronic means to record and display images. These tubes, like all cathode-ray tubes (CRTs) were built to take advantage of the properties of ionizing radiation to focus and manipulate a beam of electrons within a glass enclosure. The electron beams inside television sets generate EMFs in the X-ray portion of the spectrum, using high energy to excite cesium to create the electron cloud. The glass tubes containing the electron beams were designed to inhibit the escape of X-rays; creating these protective shields involved adding large quantities of lead to the glass (between four and eight pounds per monitor). Monochrome TV sets were tested in the 1950s and 1960s for X-ray emission and found to be relatively safe. In contrast, the first generation of color-television receivers leaked so much X-radiation that GE recalled 90,000 sets in 1967. GE and other manufacturers expressed surprise in finding this "defect" in their TV design, even though researchers had established the existence of X-radiation leakage from color sets years earlier.[56] The publicity about X-ray leakage from TV receivers helped consumer advocates convince the US government to pass the Radiation Control for Health and Safety Act of 1968. Television camera technology would eventually switch from using CRTs to using semiconductors by the 1990s, but household CRT-receiving sets and computer monitors remain in use.

War research propelled further advances in electronics: the standardization and mass production of tubes and development of silicon as a semiconductor material. The post-WWII period saw the escalation of Federal funding for Cold War technology, prompting the build up of a military-industrial-academic nexus of engineers, designers, and high-tech manufacturing in and around Stanford University in Santa Clara County, California.[57] Efforts to miniaturize the triode, using solid-state electronics rather than vacuum-tube electron clouds, revived older crystal-set technology and led to the discovery of the transistor effect. Transistor arrays on printed circuit boards produced further miniaturization in the form of microelectronics. The integrated circuit fused all electronic components (active transistors and passive elements like resisters and capacitors) into a single wafer of crystal. Integrated circuits avoided the drawbacks of vacuum tubes, including leaks, heat, burnout, high electricity consumption, and the space needed to employ large numbers of tubes: in 1946, the first big digital computer used 18,000. Tubes were still prevalent well into the 1960s, though by 1965 the new integrated circuitry of microelectronics had compressed fifty transistors into one small circuit, a number that would reach 500 million on a single chip forty years later.[58] Miniaturization continues to be a key goal of military-funded electronics for use in ever smaller, ever lighter munitions.

At the heart of microelectronics was high-grade silicon crystal, which was produced in semiconductor factories in the United States, Britain, Japan, and Germany by the end of the 1950s. General Electric made silicon material from a mix of purified silicon powder and chemical impurities essential for creating the transistor effect—this would later be called doping. By 1957, Texas Instruments had developed a process for making electronic-grade silicon, dominating the largely military market for semiconductors to become one the top three silicon makers in the United States by the mid-1960s.[59] This was the period when construction of semiconductor factories "radiated outward" from Stanford University to transform the surrounding regional economy, soon to be rechristened "Silicon Valley."[60]

With the refinement of electronic-grade silicon production in 1962, the ecological context of media technologies changed once again. Toxic by-products began to flow into the environment, from mining and chemical processing, and high-grade silicon wafer production required 160 times more energy per kilogram than regular industrial-grade silicon. Mining raw silica, silicon, and ferrosilicon damages and pollutes the land, though it is believed to cause less harm to the environment than copper and gold mining because it doesn't employ chemical acids. Nevertheless, silicon dust is a pathogen that can scar miners' lungs, inhibit breathing, lead to incurable lung disease (silicosis) and increase susceptibility to diseases like tuberculosis and emphysema.[61] Processing mined silica begins by grounding it into a powder, purifying the powder in a chlorine solution then heating it to remove the chlorine. Because the crystal material "is the device," the next stage determines the exact characteristics of crystal composition.[62] The crystal is "grown" from a molten solution containing different chemical impurities that set conductivity levels of electrons (doping); the common dopants are antimony, arsenic, boron, and phosphor. Military specifications for microchips not only required that such toxins be built into the chips but also that other known biotoxins and pollutants be employed in manufacturing.[63] The crystal rods are then polished into cylinders from which microthin wafers are sliced, cleaned, and polished with acids and caustics. Throughout the doping and polishing stages, vast amounts of poisonous by-products are emitted into water and air. It wasn't until the 1980s that the extent of pollution from US silicon manufacturers was disclosed—and this only after hundreds of workers in Silicon Valley and people living close to semiconductor factories had developed cancer, reproductive disorders, and other illnesses.[64]

Transmission and reception towers also posed new environmental problems that persist into the present. These relate to some of the hazards already mentioned in regard to EMFs; additionally, the configuration of the towers, guy wires, and transmission cables brought about changes to land use, obstruction of the flight path of migratory birds, and aesthetic issues with the alteration of the landscape. Communications towers and wires kill tens of millions of birds (over two hundred species) in North America every year and an estimated 174 million annually across Europe and the United States.[65] This problem worsens with the proliferation of ever-taller towers. The US Telecommunications Act of 1996 mandated the acceleration of tower construction as part of its communication infrastructure expansion. By 1999, there were more than 40,000 towers in the United States over two hundred feet tall. Between 1990 and 2000, the number of cell towers and antennae in the United States grew to 130,000; and since 2000, with the transition to digital television, there is a growing number of broadcast towers a thousand feet in height.[66]

Higher even than these towers, satellite dishes share the chemical and electrical characteristics of all electronics and microelectronics, including nonionizing EMF radiation from high-power ground stations. Satellite dishes add at least two toxic aspects to the ecological context of screen technology: internal nuclear power sources and fuels, along with batteries, fuel cells, and solar panels; and basic rocketry, which emit messy discharges and scrap to the electronic waste stream. A lot of "space junk" has accumulated since the launch of the first satellite in 1957. Most of it emerged in the 1980s, when the satellite industry was deregulated, commercial satellite companies proliferated, and direct-satellite broadcasting began to win customers away from cable services. A "debris belt," predicted in the 1970s, now encircles the planet.[67] By 2007, there were over 330 million pieces of debris orbiting the Earth at speeds that erode satellite surfaces and optics and, if large enough, could puncture the skin of an operational satellite. A speck of a paint chip four-hundredths of one millimeter could damage a space-shuttle window; a dot of debris one tenth of one millimeter could puncture an astronaut's protective suit. By 2007, there were between 140 and 150 million fragments whizzing around in low-earth orbit with diameters of a millimeter or more; only ten thousand pieces of this measuring one centimeter or more had been catalogued. In 2009, Iridium 33 crashed into Cosmos 2251. The result was hundreds of ten centimeter pieces of shrapnel, flying every which way at eight kilometers a second.[68]

## THE SCREEN'S FUTURE

> When I grew up in LA, there were all these days you weren't allowed to go outside during recess; you had to stay inside, or red flags. Or you would wake up and your chest would hurt. It's so much dramatically better now than it was 25 years ago.
>
> ( Josh Mark, Fox Broadcasting Company[69])

Very basic technical problems associated with screen production, distribution, and storage created these environmental risks. To make matters worse, the rapid pace of innovation has persistently outrun efforts to track all the risks that accompany new models of screen technology. This problem is exacerbated by the computer-electronics industry's strategy of planned obsolescence, which designs a short life span into drives, interfaces, operating systems, and other ICT/CE of questionable physical integrity. This has fostered high levels of electronic garbage and energy use, with related waste, pollution, and dangerous working conditions.[70]

The television set is emblematic of this problem. TVs are relentlessly marketed as perpetual novelties, which are simultaneously part of the established daily routine and upgraded (i.e., increased) consumption. In 2007, 207.5 million television sets were sold around the globe; 56 percent were old-style, fat-screen analog TVs with CRTs. The estimated number for 2011 was 245.5 million, with just a third being analog fat screens, and the remainder flat-screen, digital TVs. Flat-screen consumption has been a problem of the Global North until recently: the Asia-Pacific region continued to buy old-style sets in much greater numbers than consumers elsewhere until 2009–10, when sales of CRTs plummeted and liquid crystal displays (LCDs) and plasma screens proliferated. Marketing for flat-screen TVs stresses the pleasures of higher resolution and a slimmer profile—which derive from their intense energy use. And as the cost of the sets drops, their uptake increases, with little regard for electricity consumption or the chemical dangers of discarded sets. Depending on the screen size, flat-screen TVs can use more than three times the electricity required for older CRT sets. In Britain, it was estimated that flat-screen TVs would add 700,000 tons of carbon emissions a year by 2010, an increase of 70 percent on 2006 levels.[71] As noted in chapter 1, the increasing time people around the world spend staring at screens is feeding an unsustainable rise in global demand for residential electricity. In terms of overall environmental impact, "The CRT screen is almost always one order of magnitude higher than that of a LC display (renewable resources, energy use, solid waste, hazardous waste, radioactive waste). Only in the cases of aquatic and terrestrial eco-toxicity is the impact score of the LC display larger" because of mercury content. This appears to be declining with the advent of light-emitting diode (LED) screens, though these have not been as extensively tested as CRT and LCD screens.[72] CRTs contain zinc, copper, cesium, cadmium, silver, and lead. Major environmental problems occur when CRTs are created and thrown away because their components seep into groundwater at both stages, leaving a base history of heavy metals and lethal chemicals. This worsened with 2009's transition to digital broadcasting in the United States, when many analog sets, perhaps the hardest of all devices to recycle, were discarded.[73] Plastics and wires were burnt, monitors smashed and dismantled, and circuit boards grilled or leached with acid; the toxic chemicals and heavy metals that flow from such practices have perilous implications for local and downstream residents, soil, air, and water. No matter how you look at this, TVs do dreadful harm to the environment.

There are signs of hope from the screen industries, though they offer scant reasons to celebrate, just yet. Many firms are clearly feeling the pressure of public disdain and internal dissent and are joining countless others in search of "green IT." Nearly every major film company has a program of corporate responsibility aimed at saving money and the planet simultaneously (we cover this in the next chapter). The Motion Picture Association of America has a Solid Waste Task Force. The Association claims that the Task Force collectively diverts tens of thousands of tons of waste from landfills to recycling and reuse, thereby preventing the emission of even-more greenhouse gases. It encourages carpooling, water-based versus volatile-compound paints, reusable sets, green construction, cyan optical soundtracks, and so on, via the *Best Practices Guide for Green Production* in film and TV.[74]

News Corporation is vigorously re-examining its disastrous environmental record, thanks to an unlikely source—Rupert Murdoch, he who funded *Titanic* and *The Beach*. In 2007, Murdoch convened a meeting of employees across the world. The sole agenda item was his goal of making the company carbon neutral by the end of 2010 via a Global Energy Initiative (GEI) that would counter its annual carbon footprint of almost 650,000 tons. Murdoch told his employees that "if we are to connect with our audiences on this issue, we must first get our own house in order," and "climate change poses clear, catastrophic threats." The GEI has a tripartite strategy to reduce energy use, employ renewable power when "economically feasible," and buy carbon offsets when necessary.[75]

Every unit of News Corporation has been given an "energy team leader." The company has "multiple full-time dedicated managers," and there is regular intervention from on high. The dedicated managers are paid for this work. Other participants receive nonmonetary recognition. The impacts have been real. The *Futurama* TV series was released on carbon-neutral DVDs, and Fox's far-right vigilante TV show *24* became the first carbon-neutral US TV drama in 2009, with offsets calculated against the impact of car chases, air travel, and coal-generated electricity, and wind and solar power from LA and the Pacific Northwest used where feasible. The Fox lot in Hollywood buys renewable energy certificates from facilities across the country to offset its carbon footprint, and broadcast studios in Turkey use natural cooling and heating.[76]

The entire project is formally couched in terms of risk—risk of regulation, risk of financial peril, risk of reputation, "lost viewership/readership," and "lost revenues from business partners and advertisers for companies that that [sic] have a poor reputation on environmental issues."[77] In effect, science and democracy are sources of risk, not truth and justice. Words like "aggressive" denote value, whereas "risk" has a more negative connotation.

A social and environmental duty to care for other living creatures is absent from the rhetoric. One of Murdoch's several beneficiaries of filial piety, über-nepotist James Murdoch, published the embarrassingly titled op-ed "Clean Energy Conservatives Can Embrace" in the *Washington Post*, boasting that: "At News Corporation, we have saved millions by becoming more energy-efficient.... This has yielded savings that help us invest more in talent and has inspired us to look for further opportunities to improve."[78]

Rupert Murdoch's "journalists" at Fox News Channel barely covered his policy speech or the GEI. The Initiative applied to them in terms of industrial production, but it did not suit their audience targeting, which focused, inter alia, on climate-change deniers. Who knows what they made of the company's Green It, Mean It campaign and whether they avail themselves of the $2.75 paid to employees who ride buses or $4000 for purchasing a Prius?[79] After selecting Murdoch as the corporate executive most responsible in 2010 for blocking efforts to stop global warming, *Rolling Stone* succinctly summarized News Corps' contradictory efforts: "Murdoch may be striving to go green in his office buildings, but on the air, the only thing he's recycling are the lies of Big Coal and Big Oil."[80]

For its part, Time Warner's 2008 Corporate Social Responsibility Report proclaims "Energy efficiency at the studio lot since 2002," announcing that it had saved "over 8 million kilowatt-hours of energy and approximately $1 million annually" via efficient lighting, heating, and air-conditioning, occupancy sensors and timers, and so on. The corporation even undertook a carbon-footprint analysis in 2007 to determine the greenhouse-gas impacts of its DVD manufacture and distribution. Warner Bros. studios installed Hollywood's first photovoltaic energy system and the first soundstage in the world to be gold certified by the US Green Building Council for Leadership in Energy and Environmental Design (LEED). The company's HBO headquarters received an Energy Star Award from the federal government, and its CNN studios have reduced energy use by a quarter since the early 1990s and carbon emissions by three and a half million tons.[81]

There is a long history of attempts by Disney to greenwash its activities. *White Wilderness*[82] created the mythology that lemmings commit mass suicide as part of its "documentary" stature.[83] In 1990, the corporation trademarked the term "environmentality" as part of this "commitment." But it does have a corporate greenhouse-gases emissions inventory, the Set Reuse Program at ABC Television, and recycled packaging of some DVDs. Disney says that it "makes concerted efforts to embed environmental stewardship into the decisions and actions of our employees." But let's be honest: the offensive, patronizing tone adopted toward workers, as if they were animals or children in need of tending and direction (entirely other to what would be done by a benevolent and mature firm) is breathtaking.[84]

These and other studios have initiated environmental programs, including accounting for a film's overall pollution; installing low-energy LEDs to illuminate buildings and outdoor signage; reducing paper utilization; composting organic waste; retrofitting buildings with computer-controlled air and heating systems and environmentally friendly materials; paying for reforestation from production budgets; teleconferencing; reducing or eliminating hazardous materials, eliminating and recycling wastewater; introducing solar and other renewable energy sources; networking with green suppliers and organizations like the Greencode Project (funded by the National Film Board of Canada); managing chemical use and disposal; and recycling wood, paper, recording media, metals, film stock, electronics, and printer and toner cartridges.[85] Many corporations have joined founders Google and Intel in the Climate Savers Computing website.

Various governmental and professional trade initiatives have supported such private-sector activities. For instance, the defunct UK Film Council's environmental strategy helped "trade bodies and individual companies" reduce the environmental impact of the British film industry, where so many nominally Hollywood products are made. Similar film-commission initiatives exist in Canada, New Zealand/Aotearoa, and the United States.[86]

The Producers Guild of America Green began the PGA Green website in 2010, offering advice on cruelty-free mascara and recycled sets and a carbon-footprint calculator, available at greenproductionguide.com. The Science and Technology Council of the US Academy of Motion Picture Arts and Sciences presses for industry-wide models to deal with aspects of the digital transition that could alter Hollywood's relation to the environment in positive ways. Though its recommendations do not explicitly mention the environment, they are indirectly linked to environmental risks posed by the industry. The Council rejects the current "store and ignore" and "save everything" attitudes of producers and studio managers and recommends reducing wasteful practices through better-organized responses to technical obsolescence—for instance, standardization and nonproprietary technical collaborations and using open-source systems to extend the utility of digital platforms.[87]

Meanwhile, major CE brands like Sony are routinely touting new flat-screen TV sets that would require much less power than others, in part by going to sleep when they were not being watched thanks to motion-sensor surveillance of viewers. Such plans obviously play environmental politics against economies of scale—to charge green consumers a premium and hence counter the tendency for high-definition TV prices to fall. This is all at once a business plan, an element of the company's environmental policy that markets its corporate responsibility, and an attempt to elude democratic regulation.[88]

## CONCLUSION

Sebeck was surprised at how warm and stuffy the room had become. The AC hadn't
been off that long. He glanced around at the dozens of rack-mounted computers
clicking away. That was a lot of BTUs [British Thermal Units]. That's probably why
they had an entry vestibule—to keep the cold air in. He turned to the engineer.
"What are these machines for, anyway?"

"People playing games with each other over the Internet. My grandson plays." Sebeck
had heard of this sort of thing. He had no idea it involved so much hardware.

(Daniel Suarez, 2009, 18)

Suarez's novel *Daemon* illustrates that the sheer materiality of the internet
can stymie and astonish a neophyte who assumes that electronic games
are simply the product of a few wires and pieces of plastic. Picking up on
that character's astonishment, we have recast screen technology in light
of its ecological context by rewiring the historiography of innovations
to indicate how they have deepened the media's environmental burden.
Screen technologies come from the Earth, generate waste in the environment, exploit work deployed to harness mechanical-chemical and electronic technologies and processes, and leave a legacy of ecological harm
in their wake. Other novels show a similar appreciation. Jesse Detwiler,
Don DeLillo's UCLA professor and "waste hustler" in *Underworld* who
scams for film properties, tells his students that garbage was an incentive
for civilization, its progenitor, rather than a distasteful byproduct.[89] And
the grizzled detective Martin Beck remarks in the social-realist classic
*Roseanna* that "Americans were wasteful with film. Weren't they known
for that?"[90] Even James Bond has e-waste villains.[91] Yet it has taken a
century for the screen industry's peak organization, the Motion Picture
Association of America, to take seriously the "trash production of the
film industry."[92] Hollywood now knows that mise-en-scène has a carbon
footprint.

As we have seen, there is some good news at the frontier of both movi-
emaking and digital television. Risks to the environment are being factored
into spreadsheets, location shoots, Styrofoam cups, and headlines. We still
need more research and press coverage to widen the debate.[93] We dig more
deeply into these matters in the remainder of this book, considering how
manufacturers, regulators, unionists, environmentalists, and scholars might
establish a broader dialogue about the relation of media technology to the
eco-crisis. In the next chapter, we examine the frontline of labor involved in
the global production of ICT/CE.

# CHAPTER 4

✧

# Workers

In the factory, I assemble five computer cards per minute. More than 3,000 cards in my 11-hour daily shift. But I have never used a computer myself, I don't know how to; what's more, I don't even know what the computers I make look like when finished.

—unnamed Mexican worker[1]

I work like a machine and my brain is rusted.

—19-year old female worker from Guangxi at the Compeq printed circuit board factory in Huizhou City, China[2]

The San Remo of my childhood springs to mind, and I see the dustbin man with his sack on his back walking up the hairpins of the drive as far as the villa to collect the rubbish from the zinc bin: our genteel lifestyle seemed guaranteed for all eternity by the availability of cheap labor.

—Italo Calvino, 1994, 99

We began the last chapter looking at how celebrities, with help from the ecorazzi, represent environmental concerns via screen technology. Such top-billed actors are part of a creative workforce whose careers in Hollywood reside "above the line," a term in accounting hierarchies that demarcates writers, producers, executives, directors, and actors, among others, from those who work "below the line," where a sizeable group tend to the mostly unglamorous side of media making—middle management, assistants, set dressing and design, electrical and physical plant workers, machine operators, hair and make-up, costumers, and so on. This chapter looks beyond the small set of above-the-line creative personnel—who are already well studied by media scholars and journalists and hyper-familiar to people around the globe—in order to understand the contemporary reality of "labor convergence" that has accompanied the global spread and technical convergence of ICT/CE manufacturing.[3]

Our approach to understanding the relation of the environment to working conditions compresses lessons from first-, second-, and third-wave environmental movements, which initiated action-oriented research, respectively, on the ways industrial capitalism despoils the Earth, endangers people's health, and distributes such hazards to the least advantaged populations.[4] We examine workers affected by source materials, chemicals, and compounds in ICT/CE supply chains, drawing attention to global instances of environmental racism and other injustices where the poorest populations and regions involved in media production suffer a disproportionate share of environmental harm. Unfortunately, the present situation in media production mirrors the findings of epidemiological studies, which mostly correlate income inequality with poor health and unhealthy working conditions.[5]

As we have seen, since the "age of the printer," media technologies have needed and emitted environmentally critical substances, creating modern risks to ecosystems and workers. Print workers, past and present, must contend with poisons from solvents, inks, fumes, dust, and tainted wastewaters. Similar conditions affected workers in film-stock manufacture, where cotton dust has added the additional risk of "brown lung." Occupations involving batteries have historically been some of the most dangerous, with exposure to lead and other pathogens causing fatal injury to the lungs, skin, and nervous system. These illnesses not only make battery workers in the United States the top risk group for lead poisoning, but the expansion of production, salvage, and recycling has extended the problems around the world. Plastics have caused increasingly greater damage, with brain, liver, kidney, and stomach cancer all associated with manufacturing, and disposal of plastics with high chlorine content releases carcinogenic dioxin and hydrochloric acid into the environment. Plastic flotsam accumulating in the open waters of the North Pacific (nicknamed the great Pacific garbage patch), North Atlantic, and Indian Ocean have threatened habitats and drawn attention to the unthinking habits of consumers addicted to plastic, which is recyclable but not biodegradable—it breaks down into ever smaller fragments but isn't absorbed into the Earth's sink and can last for thousands of years. We've seen how microwave workers can suffer from "chronic exposure syndrome," and there is growing concern with lower-level radiation emitted from televisions, computers, electronic games, computer monitors, cell phones, laptops, networks of telecommunication and electrical towers, and power lines. Bio-thermal risks exist for workers continuously exposed to radio, TV, and telecommunication equipment, as well as high-rise office workers near high-power transmission antennae.

Workers bearing the burden of environmental harms in high-technology systems may be barely visible in double-entry bookkeeping, but they are not always inconspicuous. The Luddites, for example, were a social movement of British textile laborers in the early nineteenth century that fought against the machinery and social relations of the Industrial Revolution. They recognized that capitalists who did not do productive work controlled machinery, which controlled the lives of those who *did* work. Their name is used today to disparage workers suspicious of technology's capacity to induce job losses, deskilling, and health risks. Such workers realize that at any moment technology may control their labor, spy on them, or shift their jobs.[6]

Of course, the conditions of industrial labor have long formed a focus for critical minds, famously for Marx and Frederick Engels in *The Communist Manifesto* and their contemporary Abraham Lincoln, who said in his first annual message to the Congress in 1861: "Capital is only the fruit of labor, and could never have existed if labor had not first existed. Labor is the superior of capital and deserves much the higher consideration."[7] Marx also perceived links between environment and labor when he wrote that industrial progress was "progress in the art, not only of robbing the labourer, but of robbing the soil ... ruining the lasting sources of that fertility." Capitalist technology and associated social relations sapped "the original sources of all wealth—the soil and the labourer."[8] Engels was one of the first to document in vivid detail the environmental ugliness of industrialism, albeit in anthropocentric terms, as a shameful blight on English workers' lives.[9]

Since the nineteenth century, capitalism has largely treated labor and the environment as things to be controlled long distance, connected to transnational textual and military domination but also set against themselves via an ever-grander division of labor and a growing perception that human and nonhuman nature were disconnected. The imperial division of labor kept costs down through the formal and informal slavery of colonialism (the trade in people and indentureship) and cheap expropriation of raw materials. Value was added in the form of finished goods manufactured in the metropolitan countries. Successful action by the industrial working class in the twentieth century eventually redistributed wealth downward in the richer industrialized regions. The response from capital was to create multinational corporations and export production, focusing increasingly on exploiting the labor of young women workers. Folker Fröbel and his collaborators christened this trend the "new international division of labor" (NIDL), dating it from the post–Second World War era.[10] The NIDL model suggests that in a major industrial economy, goods are initially made and consumed in the center, then exported to the periphery, and finally produced and consumed "out there" once technology is standardized and savings can be made on the labor front.

As capitalist expansion drove the uneven geographical enlargement of this division of labor, it simultaneously altered people's relation to the global environment, as resources supplying industry were increasingly drawn from outside local ecosystems. As a result, local populations could not readily experience the growing environmental burden of capitalist production occurring in far-flung places. This caused both the transformation of "ecosystem people" into "biosphere people" and a parallel disenchantment with the intrinsic value of both labor and nonhuman nature.[11] As we have seen, the modern wonders of rail, electricity, telegraph, and telephone stepped into the breach with great ideological effect to elevate the status of technology while further diminishing the importance of human labor, nonhuman nature, and pre-modern ways of seeing nature. Throughout the twentieth century, popular and official accounts depicted labor and the environment, along with indigenous cultures, as either noble national spectacles or objects of scorn, suitable for domination and exploitation.[12] The deployment of modern communication technologies thus played a paradoxical historical role by at once enabling long-distance human interaction, facilitating command and control over the division of human labor, and obscuring the intimate relationship between human and nonhuman nature. Both forms of nature were reduced to resources for industrial production.

The workers who actually make media technologies are rarely discussed in academic, business, or journalistic accounts of high-tech's provenance—the technologies all seem to come from the geniuses at Apple, Sony, Google, and their ilk, who form an aristocracy of creative talent. The disappearance of labor is a classic illusionist effect of the fetish that Marx described over a century ago[13]: the dirty work is concealed within the toys and machines that others use to relax as they fuss over "the tidy finished exterior of this equipment," its power, and its speed.[14] To disrupt that technological sublime, we examine media technology's life cycle from production to disposal, with an approach predicated on a deep regard for workers and the Earth and an equally profound disregard for technological hype. We begin by identifying the ecological contexts of ICT/CE production, drawing from supply-chain research to comprehend the global scale and the intersectoral linkages of work in these industries. We offer a brief case study of Mexican maquiladoras, exemplary sites of dirty international ICT/CE work. Our final section focuses on salvage workers and recyclers, who dismantle the toxic technological dross flowing massively from rich to poor regions of the world—what the Basel Action Network (BAN) describes as "effluent for the affluent."[15] The figure of the ragpicker provides us with a critical perspective on the distance that consumers, activists, and policy makers must travel intellectually, morally, and geographically in order to green the media.

## MEDIA ON THE GLOBAL ASSEMBLY LINE

At the start of the twenty-first century, there were approximately 61,000 multinational corporations worldwide, with links to 900,000 other firms. By definition, multinationals search the world for competitive advantage in state incentives, weak labor organization and protection, minimal environmental regulation, favorable exchange rates, low wages, and sparse human-rights enforcement. By the mid-1980s, the value of offshore production by multinationals had begun to exceed trade between states.[16] Most economists love this allocation of resources, loathe opposition to it, and tacitly endorse the racism, sexism, and other injustices implicit in its model of growth and progress. Among the thousands of examples of their hubris, here are two that speak to their vision of the value of workers around the world:

> What do I say to the young woman on the steps at Georgetown University who was so concerned about the evils of the race to the bottom, so concerned about where and how her T-shirt was produced? I would tell her to appreciate what markets and trade have accomplished for all of her sisters in time who have been liberated by life in a sweatshop. (Rivoli, 2008, 215)[17]
>
> I think the economic logic behind dumping a load of toxic waste in the lowest wage country is impeccable and we should face up to that. (Lawrence Summers, internal memo, World Bank, December 12, 1991, quoted in "Let Them Eat Pollution," 1992)[18]

In the late 1970s, big ICT/CE firms set about departing first-world factories for the sweatshops of developing countries, in accordance with the NIDL; by the 1990s, the electronic waste from their overhyped, badly engineered products began to stream into salvage yards that formed a newly created final stop in the life cycle of high-tech wonders. Core players in the NIDL include such major ICT/CE brands as Apple, Dell, HP, IBM, Kodak, and Sony. They are known as original equipment manufacturers (OEMs).[19] Before media technologies appear under OEM's name brands, they travel along a supply chain. Mines supply metals to foundries and factories, which make parts for assembly, packaging, and so on.

Figure 4.1 is a modification of an academic paean to the iPod that referred to the MP3 as the latest triumph of Apple's "thriving ecosystem."[20] In some ways, Apple's metaphorical "ecosystem" duly describes its relation to the environment: by 2007, it was an $8 billion corporation with half its liquid assets held by overseas subsidiaries from Ireland to Singapore. It took advantage of the NIDL to assemble i-gadgets across Korea, Japan, Germany, China, Singapore, Taiwan, and the United States. The tin solder in its circuit boards allows armed groups in Congo to earn over $90 million annually, while its wee phone also relies on Chinese tungsten mining, Bolivian salt-flats excavation, and monumental exploitation of assembly workers.[21]

OEMs like Apple are lords of the electronics supply chain, controlling intellectual property and technological research, design, and marketing. Below them lie extractive industries, small-scale cottage assemblers, and contract manufacturers. The latter have grown massively since the 1990s, with about 75 percent of global electronics manufacturing and 60 percent of cell phone production subcontracted to them by OEMs.[22] In 2011, the following five major contractors controlled this section of the chain:

- Foxconn Technology (a subsidiary of Hon Hai Precision Industries) of Taiwan (Apple, Dell, HP, Nintendo, Nokia, Sony Ericsson, and Amazon)
- Flextronics of Singapore (Cisco, Kodak, Sony Ericsson, HP, Microsoft, and Motorola)
- Jabil of the United States (Cisco, Philips, and HP)
- Celestica of Canada (Motorola, Palm, Research in Motion, Sun Micro-systems, and HP)
- Sanmina-SCI of the United States (Cisco)

These multinational ICT corporations operate factories in scores of countries, employing tens of millions of workers.[23] Throughout the supply chain, both the environment and workers are vulnerable. For example, the semi-conductor, the heart of all electronic equipment, is produced by hundreds of companies around the world for a market dominated by such OEMs as IBM, Intel, Samsung Electronics, Toshiba Electronics, Texas Instruments, Qualcomm, and ADM. Microchip production requires millions of kilowatt hours of electrical power, half a trillion gallons of deionized water, hundreds of millions of cubic feet of bulk gases (much of it poisonous), and millions of pounds of acids and solvents, which expose workers to skin irritants and dangerous toxins and carcinogenic chemicals that can injure mucous and pulmonary tissue and the reproductive system.[24] Data from the Norwegian silicon-carbide industry's smelters indicate elevated risks of stomach and lung cancer for workers by contrast with the wider population, as a consequence of exposure to crystalline silica, dust fibers, and silicon-carbide particles.[25]

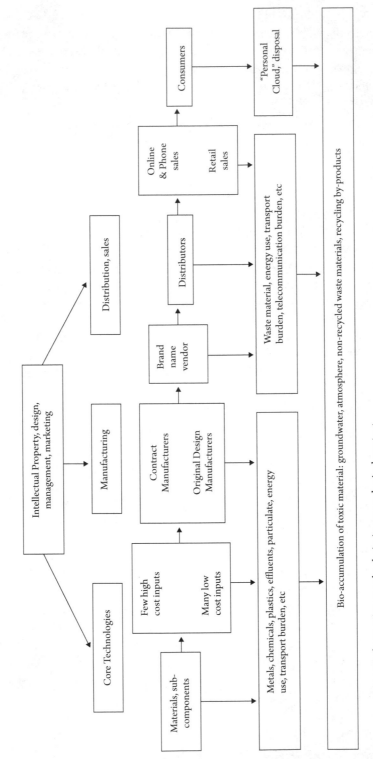

**Figure 4.1:** Generic electronics supply chain in an ecological context

Most OEMs are forced to confront environmental problems in production and devise internal codes of conduct to meet guidelines on worker safety established by the International Labor Organization (ILO). With the exception of Sony, which commenced environmental audits in 1994, the major companies only began to consider the ecological impact of their production process this century. To minimize state regulation and gain green public credibility in their home countries, OEMs adopted a strain of public relations pioneered in the 1990s by textile and footwear industries to address workplace hazards, human rights, and environmental damage. CSR became their watchword as the companies audited working conditions across global supply chains, disclosing their findings and efforts at remediation. In 2004, Dell, HP, IBM, and the contract manufacturers Flextronics, Solectron (bought by Flextronics in 2007), Sanmina-SCI, Celestica, and Jabil developed an "electronic industry code of conduct," which set benchmarks that gave watchdog groups like SACOM tough standards with which to judge OEMs like HP (which earned high marks) and Apple (which earned low marks).[26]

Two of the main trade groups representing OEMs are the Electronic Industry Citizenship Coalition (EICC) and the Global e-Sustainability Initiative (GeSI). These groups conduct supply-chain audits of labor and environmental conditions in the mining industries that extract and process the metals used in electronics (tin, cobalt, palladium, gold, copper, silver, and aluminum). These metals travel the supply chain via buyers, brokers, and refiners. In 2008, the proportion of the world's metals going into media technologies was 36 percent of all tin, 25 percent of cobalt, 15 percent of palladium, 15 percent silver, 9 percent of gold, 2 percent of copper, and 1 percent of aluminum.[27]

There are about 4,100 major mining companies, though the top hundred and fifty control 80 percent of global output. Tracking workers in the metals supply chain is complicated by a globally diffuse informal sector—which consists of artisanal and small-scale mining (ASM), a notoriously harsh, low-tech, poverty-driven sector. The ILO estimates that while there are upwards of thirteen million workers in ASM worldwide, the total number is closer to two hundred million if we include populations whose jobs depend on it (porters, buyers, transporters, smugglers, exporters, and so on).[28]

ASM is concentrated in Africa, Asia, and Latin America, where about a million children labor in mines. In the Democratic Republic of Congo, which has a third of the world's columbite tantalite (coltan), over 90 percent of eastern mines are controlled by mercenaries, many of whom are also members of the Congolese Army. These soldiers have used threats, intimidation, murder, rape, and mutilation to enslave women and children for

work in the mines, extracting profits to buy more weapons. Over five million people have perished in the country's civil war over the past decade.
Congolese "conflict" metals and minerals, such as coltan, are processed in
Chinese-owned plants in the Congo or exported for smelting in China.
The processed ore is then mixed with the overall global supply and sold on
the international commodities market as tantalum, a core component in
capacitors that end up in phones, computers, games, and media-production
equipment. The United Nations Security Council set up a panel of experts
on the topic, and the US Senate took up the issue in 2009 with its biparti-
san S.891, the Congo Conflict Minerals Act. The Dodd-Frank Act of 2010
mandated increased oversight of ICT/CE producers to ensure that they do
not purchase conflict minerals. In response to the Dodd-Frank Act, image-
conscious OEMs, fearful of being associated with African warlords, reacted
with a de facto embargo on Congolese minerals, a catastrophe for those
mining communities not under militia control.[29]

Inconsistencies in OEM audits are coupled with a lack of sociological
and historical understanding of the changes that have accompanied the
rapid growth of contract manufacturing in Asia and elsewhere. The internal
audits give us Dell and HP's suppliers' names, for example, but don't tell us
that Apple petitioned the Federal Communications Commission (FCC)
to hide the government's review of the iPad, which would have disclosed to
the public the way that it exploits multinational labor. Only after continual
pressure from Greenpeace and other nongovernmental watchdog groups
did Apple begin to green its business model. Until 2009, the company had
no plans to protect iPod production workers (who work in at least four different countries) from mercury, lead, solvents, and flame retardants. It produces annual *Supplier Responsibility* reports, but unlike the best examples of
such investigations, refuses to name all subcontractors that break the law or
ignore Apple's guidelines.[30]

Investigations into its Chinese suppliers have shown that Apple was
aware of its subcontractors' unsafe and illegal operations. Examples include
chemical (n-hexane) poisonings of 137 workers at the factories of Lian
Jian Technology Group in the eastern city of Suzhou (owned by Taiwan-
based Wintek, Lian Jian is an iPhone touch-screen supplier). N-hexane
poisoning causes damage to the peripheral nervous system, which is not
only extremely painful but leads to numbness in the limbs, chronic weakness, fatigue, and hypersensitivity to heat and cold. In 2010, workers were
poisoned while degreasing the Apple logo with n-hexane at the Yuhan Lab
Technology Company and the Yun Heng Hardware & Electrical factory.
Both subcontractors were among dozens of "suspected Apple suppliers"
poisoning workers and surrounding communities in China, according to
the Beijing-based Institute of Public and Environmental Affairs.[31] Apple

also acted indifferently to the searing conditions behind twelve reported suicides that took place in 2010–11 at the Chinese Foxconn factory making iPhones and the first iPads.[32] *Bloomberg Businessweek* called Foxconn "a postmodern industrial empire." That year, Foxconn boasted close to a million employees across China and was responsible for almost half the world's electronics manufacturing, using military-style discipline characterized by verbal and physical abuse (many line supervisors are ex-army officers from Taiwan). When the iPad was launched outside the United States in 2010, protestors in Hong Kong responded to the suicides with ritual burning of iPhone photos.[33]

Apple finally responded in its 2011 annual supply chain audit by welcoming improved wages, safety measures, and counseling services at Foxconn and admitting to the poisonings at the Lian Jian factory and other violations of codes of conduct, including the employment of underage girls by some of its Chinese subcontractors. However, while Apple ordered subcontractors to halt these unsafe and illegal practices, the company representatives never met with affected workers or committed any support, financial or otherwise, to help rehabilitate them or compensate them for their physical and emotional losses.[34]

The suicides are also evidence of a malicious ethico-political orientation that infects management in the global supply chain of ICT/CE manufacture. They point specifically to the brutality of combining twenty-first century means of producing media technology with the mass mobilization of rural Chinese youth to work in these factories—the largest migration in history, by some measures. In the words of the manager of a Chinese electronics factory, "There are … plenty of girls with good eyes and strong hands. If we run out of people, we just go deeper into China."[35] These types of stresses are symptomatic of contemporary industrial organization; post-Fordist factory systems are geared to meet OEMs' demand for rapid innovation through just-in-time production. But there is also an inhuman dimension to the way Chinese contract manufacturers implement this system: these young people are removed from family, friendship, freedom of association (they are prohibited from talking to one another on the assembly line) and forms of cultural enjoyment and release, which might help them adjust to sequestration in high-tech, high-speed, high-security compounds. The suicides supposedly followed a pattern of suicide clusters discernible at moments of industrial takeoff, which was first noted two hundred years ago in Europe.[36]

From a US business perspective, "Foxconn's suicides are a reminder of the human cost that can come with the low-cost manufacturing US tech companies demand." For "image-conscious companies with which Foxconn does business … the suicides were a public-relations nightmare and a challenge to offshoring strategies essential to their bottom lines." Indeed, Foxconn responded to the suicides with a new business plan that included outsourcing management of its factories' living quarters, relocating more of its manufacturing to inland China and Vietnam, and automating assembly lines with a million robots. The first action reduced the company's responsibility for worker satisfaction, the second action allowed it to return to lower-wage regions where workers could remain close to families, and the third action reduced employment in a labor market where wages have been steadily rising. This is the suppressed dark side of the neoliberal push of ICT/CE production in China, which has contributed 15 percent annually to the country's gross domestic product. Concepts such as those of knowledge worker, immaterial labor, creative industries, and cognitariat are of little use to explain the situation in Foxconn's Shenzhen factory, where wages were at the minimum allowable by law before the suicides, overtime exceeds legal limits and is often not paid, a totalitarian polity and company controls everyday life, and the first iPads were made under such pressure that shifts were twelve hours a day/seven days a week for six months with a rest day every thirteen days and no weekend overtime premium.[37]

Meanwhile, Foxconn's Indian facility in Chennai, which was making phones for Nokia, worked with the state of Tamil Nadu to imprison trade-union leaders following a major demonstration in which over a thousand workers sought the right to negotiate with management through a union, a situation complicated by a demarcation dispute. A few weeks earlier, the Indian government had suspended operations at the plant after workers were overcome by nausea and giddiness.[38]

With labor so geographically dispersed via international subcontracting, union density in the ICT/CE industries is "startlingly low around the world." Although this does not prevent spontaneous forms of labor solidarity and agitation—such as Foxconn employees in Guadalajara supporting their counterparts in China—low levels of unionization in the global supply chain of media technology severely hamper research that could empower labor organizers, environmental activists, and industry audits aiming to oversee and improve working conditions and eliminate environmental hazards. Without widespread union representation and improved associational rights, production workers lack independent institutional sources of information, "casting doubts on the prospects of raising labor standards through codes of conduct alone."[39] This is certainly one reason why existing ICT/ CE audits have been unsuccessful in reaching the part of the supply chain where thousands of labor-intensive component makers provide contractors with resisters, capacitors, cables, switches, microchips, unfinished circuit boards, wires, connectors, power supplies, clips, screws, and so on. Part of this activity is internalized within large factories, where it can potentially be monitored, but a significant amount takes place in people's homes. As long as political-economic arrangements militate against unionization, it will be difficult to find reliable and representative statistical and qualitative analyses of workers' exposure to toxic materials and other workplace hazards.[40]

It should also be noted that settled patterns in the international division of labor are changing with new formations in the structure of the global work-force. The late–twentieth-century system assigned poor regions to make the "low-value" constellation of pieces and parts of a device, whereas richer regions were given "high-value" research, development, and marketing. That imbalance remains largely intact, but the rapid pace and expansion of sub-contracting is making stark distinctions of this kind increasingly unreliable as guides for present-day research and analysis. By 2004, for instance, 35 per-cent of ICT/CE manufacturing jobs were in China, as compared to 7 percent in the United States, 9 percent in Japan, and 10 percent in Western Europe. By 2011, Foxconn had already begun to increase investment in its research and development and retail operations. As our example of the maquiladoras will show, this trend suggests further concentration of manufacturing jobs in Asia at the expense of jobs in competing countries like Mexico, once a pre-ferred labor market for outsourcing low-wage ICT/CE manufacturing.[41]

## LAS MAQUILADORAS: "HEADSTONES FOR THE GRAVEYARD OF AMERICAN UNION LABOR"

The National Coalition of Electronic Industry Workers, declares that five years after the publication of the Electronic Industry Code of Conduct: the same companies that signed the Code are the ones violating the human labor rights. The Code states ... that the signing companies should respect the workers' freedom of association. This right, in our Federal Labor Law, is constantly violated. We recall two recent cases. The first one: the dismissal of more than 10 workers of Flextronics, only because they demanded transparency on the issue of profit shares.

The second case was the dismissal of Aureliano Rosas Suárez, Omar Manuel Montes Estrada and Vicente de Jesús Rodríguez Roa, sacked because they demanded their right to have their wages leveled. They also worked for the company Flextronics.

We inform the International Electronic Industry that the members of the National Coalition of Electronic Industry Workers will continue to use this mask as a symbol of our repression. But the coalition will continue demanding and defending our human labor rights. (National Coalition of Electronic Industry Workers, quoted in CEREAL, 2009, 28)

This statement comes from a group of Mexican electronics workers who stage protests in white masks around the employment agencies that govern casualized labor in assembly plants. The coalition is the solitary civil-society voice that is connected personally to workers on the line and those who have been dismissed. The official trade unions that address working conditions in Mexican ICT/CE plants are neither representative of workers nor interested in their grievances. Instead, they help manufacturers bypass laws covering contract negotiations and prevent labor from forming independent unions. As CEREAL (Centre for Reflection and Action on Labour Issues) puts it: "90 percent of workers belong to a trade union; but 90 percent of those do not know it."[42]

In his surfing mystery novel, *Tijuana Straits*, Kem Nunn depicts the world of violence, misunderstanding, indifference, sacrifice, and redemption represented by maquiladoras and their deadly, unforgiving impact on occupational and residential health and safety:

> The community in question occupied a tract of land at the foot of the mesa. Above it hunkered the remains of *Reciclaje Integral*, a deserted smelting and battery recycling plant. For years the residents of Vista Nueva had reported skin ulcers, respiratory ailments, birth defects. A number of children had died. ... When it became apparent that charges would be brought against him in a Mexican court, however, the owner, an American, simply filed for bankruptcy in Mexico, left the factory as it stood, and withdrew across the border, where he continued to prosper ... He lived in a million-dollar house somewhere in San Diego County while his deserted plant continued to poison the residents of Vista Nueva. (2005, 25)

Like Nunn, Luis Alberto Urrea blends sociological observation, *roman à clef*, and ethnography in his blistering account of cultural difference and destruction:

> *Maquis*, of course, are binational or multinational factories. They sit on their bulldozed hills like raw-concrete forts, and the huts of the peasants ring their walls. Some of them have Japanese names on them, some of them have American names. All along Tijuana's new high-tech highway, *el Periférico*, you can see them up there, receding into the hazy distance. Headstones for the graveyard of American union labor. (1996, 5, 25)

Urrea wryly notes that Mexican progressives have dubbed the Mexico–US western border region "Palestijuas" (in other words, Palestine-Tijuana).

The maquiladoras exemplify Fröbel et al.'s theorization of the NIDL. When a *bracero* (guest-worker) program between Mexico and the United States was terminated in the 1960s, the Mexican State introduced import-tax exemptions to stimulate in-bond input assembly, and Washington, DC permitted duty-free return of assembled components that had originated north of the border. What began as a temporary initiative became of massive economic significance during the 1980s and '90s, with ICT/CE at its heart. In 1993, maquiladora exports amounted to $21.9 billion; in 2000, the figure was $79.5 billion. The maquiladoras' proportion of Mexico's overall exports grew from 37.8 percent in 1995 to 47.1 percent in 2006, when the country employed upward of 1.2 million people, a labor force generated through the migration of poor rural people to the North. There was no equivalent growth in social services, education, public health, housing, or water in that period.[43]

The key policy instrument of this exploitation has been NAFTA/TLC, discussed briefly in the previous chapter. Since the treaty's adoption, trade between the United States and Mexico has grown, without an equitable distribution of wealth or economic development. The junction of the two countries sees "greater income disparity ... than at any other major commercial border in the world." Electronic industry warehouses, managers, and researchers are generally based in San Diego. Complex components are exported from there or Germany, Korea, Japan, Taiwan, Malaysia, and Thailand for basic assembly in Mexico. So, "high value" is created in the United States and elsewhere, while dangerous, dull, and poorly remunerated work is done across the border. The 1983 La Paz Agreement between Mexico and the United States mandates that maquiladora waste be returned to its country of origin, but enforcement has been lax, and statistics about the flow of contaminated goods and the environmental side effects of production have been spotty. Since NAFTA/TLC, the failings of these environmental and labor protections have been compounded by both increased output and the rising number of workers exposed to unhealthy chemicals and gases, low wages, and labor-law violations—a toxic life in every sense.[44]

Tijuana has been dubbed "TV capital of the world" because so many TV sets are assembled there. In 2002, Mexico accounted for 30.42 percent of TV and video-equipment exports to the United States and China 18.5 percent. But competition increased due to tax incentives and lower wage and energy costs in China, Thailand, Malaysia, and Vietnam. By 2006, the proportions of TVs made in Mexico and China were virtually equal (35.07 percent compared to 34.76 percent). Maquiladora employment fell each year from 2000 to 2003. The global recession, evident by 2008, slashed employment and investment. The nearly two hundred companies that assembled ICT/CE in Mexico decreased production by almost 40 percent from the middle of that year. Sony announced the closure of a TV plant in Mexico in 2009, with the loss of six hundred positions. The maquiladora slide slowed later that year as firms looked to cut the time wasted exporting parts and importing sets across the Pacific. Production was boosted and job growth accompanied it, but not at pre-recession levels. In all, 144 plants closed in the twelve months prior to October 2009 and 122 new ones opened. This was in keeping with the NIDL moving toward a more regional pattern of outsourcing in response to capacity shortages in shipping and gridlock in hub ports.[45]

It's not as though labor costs were high in the maquiladoras: Wages consistently declined as productivity increased from 1993 to 2006. Two full-time workers in a Mexican plant received just two-thirds of the wages needed to support a family of four prior to medical and educational expenses. Not surprisingly, the workers who make gadgets can't afford to purchase them. Because a flat-screen TV sold in San Diego is exempt from customs duty, it costs less there than where it was made, across the border in Tijuana.[46]

Of course, manufacturing television sets is just one part of Mexico's electronics production. HP, Hitachi, IBM, Nokia, Siemens, Phillips, and Motorola all have businesses there, not to mention such subcontractors as Foxconn, Solectron, Flextronics, and Jabil Circuits. Mexico is also Latin America's second-biggest consumer of electronics, accumulating between 100,000 and 180,000 tons of electronic waste each year.[47]

Women have long been at the forefront of the electronics labor processes in maquiladoras. For instance, when RCA moved its radio and TV plants from New Jersey, to Indiana, to Ciudad Juárez in search of ever-lower wages, company elders sought a workforce of young, mostly unmarried women. This strategy had little to do with biological kinesiology, as caricatured by the docile, nimble-fingered girls found in managerial playbooks. It was about gender and power.[48] Revelations of workplace hazards in these plants provide heartbreaking evidence of the contract manufacturers' indifference to women's exploitation:

> I was three months pregnant. I told them when I was one month pregnant; I asked my facilitator to move me, but she said no, not until they have found someone else. I worked from 3:30 to 12 p.m. On November 17, 2005, when I arrived at work, I started to feel unwell. I went to the lavatory and noticed I was bleeding. I went straight to the infirmary and the doctor told me it was nothing, that it was normal. I went back to the production line and told my supervisor I was feeling quite sick, and asked him for permission to leave. He talked with the doctor over the phone and then told me "I'm not letting you out, don't be a wimp." ... The baby wasn't growing properly. [The doctors] told me it was because of the lead, and I believe that; that's why I wanted to be moved when I found out I was pregnant, but I wasn't allowed. ... I lost my baby. ... I got very depressed and spent all those days crying. I was only given two days sick leave. (Rosa, twenty-one years old, ICT production worker for contract manufacturer Jabil in Chihuahua, Mexico, quoted in *CEREAL*, 2006, 23)

CEREAL interviewed thousands of workers across the Mexican electronics sector in 2008 and 2009, disclosing systematic sexual harassment and other forms of discrimination. Employees were often subjected to invasive interviews, body searches, and pregnancy tests; illegally excessive working time was common and uncompensated; contracts were nonexistent or highly precarious, temporary agreements; some managers were using psychological violence; workers were exposed to hazardous chemicals and fumes, with little or no training about these hazards or proper protection from them; and there was no freedom to form independent unions or other organizations. Despite each woman preparing over a hundred central-processing units an hour in factories, the women were categorized as "temporary" employees, enabling employers to elude regulations and contracts that govern full-time workers.[49] Civil-society groups on both sides of the border remind authorities of their responsibilities and encourage citizen activism, notably Voces de la Maquila, Colectivo Chilpancingo Pro Justicia Ambiental, Greenpeace, Women in Informal Employment: Globalizing and Organizing, Self Employed Women's Association, and the Environmental Health Coalition; and the Maquila Solidarity Network has close ties to SACOM to monitor similarities between exploitation in China and Mexico.[50]

Consumers reliant on business journalism for their news of the world are dutifully informed that maquiladoras are positive features of foreign direct investment, local employment, and technology transfer, rather than sources of pollution, exploitation, and stratified gender relations. The *New York Times*, for example, has headlined TV-set manufacture as "A Boom Along the Border." Such accounts presumably regard "*maquiladora* diseases ... that bloom in wombs and spinal columns" as acceptable costs outweighed by benefits.[51] Lacking a media watchdog on the ICT/CE beat, US consumers can turn to records of class-action lawsuits to track the occupational health-and-safety impact of these processes. If they do so, they will discover that the relevant authorities have neglected to acknowledge the dangers of chemical compounds or prohibit their use.[52]

## RAGPICKERS AND ELECTRONIC WASTE

Foul and adventures-seeking dregs of the bourgeoisie, there were vagabonds, dismissed soldiers, discharged convicts, runaway galley slaves, sharpers, jugglers, lazzaroni, pickpockets, sleight-of-hand performers, gamblers, procurers, keepers of disorderly houses, porters, literati, organ grinders, rag pickers, scissors grinders, tinkers, beggars. (Marx, 2003, 63)[53]

Before the Spanish invasion, Mexico had many *pepenadores*—people who managed waste.[54] Their policies and practices were disrupted by the conquest, which saw more and more urban dross accumulate over three centuries as commodification took hold and put an end to rural recycling norms.[55] In Europe, according to the historian Alain Corbin, ragpickers were among the ranks of urban untouchables: "sewermen, gut dressers, knackers, drain cleaners, workers in refuse dumps, and dredging gangs." Such ragpickers and junk dealers had been assigned "to sort and order domestic rubbish from houses; to collect organic remains, the bones and corpses of small animals, and so complete the work of cesspool clearers." By the mid–nineteenth century, the volume of waste removal from city centers to city peripheries had grown because the urban rich condemned the "odor of crowded bodies" and the "rising tide of excrement and rubbish." Removal meant the displacement of waste but not its elimination: as a living, malodorous reminder of urban filth, the lowly ragpicker foiled bourgeois fantasies of cleanliness.[56]

Literary reactions to the Euro-ragpicker can be found in the work of Charles Dickens, E. T. A. Hoffmann, and Émile Zola. Vincent van Gogh called The Hague's city dump "a paradise for the artist," while Manet's *Ragpicker* trudged disconsolately toward refuse he could not resist. Ragpickers continue to fascinate writers of fiction from China (Ah Cheng), Italy (Italo Calvino and Paolo Teobaldi), Austria (Christoph Ransmayr), the United States (Nunn, Paul Auster, and Donald Barthelme), Canada (Daniel Brodeur and Margaret Atwood), France (Michel Tournier), the Czech Republic (Bohumil Hrabal and Ivan Klíma), and Costa Rica (Fernando Contrera Castro), among others.[57]

Calvino's elaborate *aperçus* about his life include a lengthy meditation on "taking out the rubbish," which stands alone among "housework" as a task that he undertook with both "competence and satisfaction." At the same time, the *poubelle agréée*, the model Parisian rubbish bin, "proclaims the role that the public sphere, civic duty and the constitution of the polis play in all our lives." Without that object, and the institutions and work associated with it, Calvino "would die buried under my own rubbish in the snail shell of my individual existence." The daily task of sloughing off the abject permitted the middle class to "begin the new day without having to touch what the evening before we cast off from ourselves forever," consigned to an alien status that was clearly apart from the authentic self. For Klíma, the street is an alternative to the state. Unable to write due to governmental cultural policies that silenced him, he literally takes to the streets; not in formal protest, but to work as a street sweeper for all the world like the far-humbler subject of Jimmy Buffett's "It's My Job," which features a man proud to be cleaning up mess and hence "better than the rest." His example makes the protagonist ponder his banker uncle, who is unable to take pleasure in anything.[58]

We are often told that the ultimate figure of Euro-modernity was the *flâneur*, whose roving gentlemanly eye viewed the city with a mixture of distraction and immersion—in contemporary terms, a true cognitarian working above the line. But another person, also to be found on that street, could ill afford such gazes and glances: This was an intensely practical *bricoleur*, for whom recycling was a way of life. In his poem "Le vin des chiffonniers" [the ragpicker's wine], Baudelaire famously portrayed the ragpicker "drunk with the splendor of his own virtues ... bent double by the junk he carries/ The jumbled vomit of enormous Paris" as he champions the poor in the face of an uncaring bourgeoisie.[59] This evocative vocalization and mimesis has drawn commentary from fans and idolators ever since: Gustave Flaubert, Marcel Proust, T. S. Eliot, Walter Benjamin, Jean-Paul Sartre, and Georges Bataille were all taken with Baudelaire's poetry at the limit. For Benjamin, the ragpicker became a motif for philosophical and historical method in times of chaotic change that could not be captured adequately by social-scientific controls. One might say the same of Humphrey Jennings's project of explaining industrialization in cultural fragments lost and found at the coalface.[60]

"Le vin des chiffonniers" was translated on the World Bank's PovertyNet website, because it is said to "develop a greater sensitivity to the tragedy, the challenges, and the urgency of poverty." This is surely a sign that ragpickers remain embarrassing embodiments of postindustrial "progress." Not surprisingly, the World Bank and its kind show no interest in actually engaging ragpickers, whom they want to transform from a distance. Ragpickers themselves seek a dignified recognition of their contribution plus material improvements to their lives, as Fernando Solanas's 2005 documentary *La dignidad de los nadies* [dignity of the nobodies] tellingly shows.[61]

The ragpicker also erupts in popular culture. He was a figure of pathos in the British situation comedy of the 1960s, *Steptoe and Son*. In the show, the Steptoes and their horse and cart looked for gems among the discards of "swinging London," throwbacks to a time that had not really passed for working people. Steptoe Jr. spent his evenings dreaming of transcending their life together, as he devoured the works of Marx and George Bernard Shaw. But he could never leave his sub-proletarian status behind. The Labour government of the day even invoked the Steptoes to show that it blended old-style workerism with creative innovation—but the world it depicted lay some distance from Pete Townsend's Union Jack coat and John Lennon's glasses. The series resonated internationally: It was remade as the 1970s US sitcom *Sanford and Son* and influenced the Nigerian *Basi and Company* (1985–'90), which subsidized the literary career of Nigerian environmental activist Ken Saro-Wiwa. Mos Def and Jack Black play similar characters in *Be Kind Rewind*[62] and Mark Knopfler released a 2002 album named "The Ragpicker's Dream" that celebrates indigent people making do. The song "Why Aye Man" hails "nomad tribes, traveling boys" who are found in the "dust and dirt and the racket and noise." The film *Waste Land*[63] chronicles the artist Vik Muniz's "Pictures of Garbage Series," which reimagines the lives, labors, and dreams of the *catadores*, pickers working in the world's largest garbage dump on the outskirts of Rio de Janeiro.

Ragpickers derived further visibility when they were defined as statistical problems in need of resolution. They became a living index of chaotic urban growth, as illustrated by Delhi's or Mexico City's sprawling deterioration and regeneration—even though research indicates they produce the least waste of all urban groups. Perhaps one percent of people in the Global South now live as ragpickers—approximately fifteen million people worldwide. By the end of the twentieth century, a growing portion of ragpickers everywhere were mopping up the deadly detritus of the information society as the electronic salvage business expanded globally, poisoning land, air, water, and bodies in its wake.[64]

The location of most digital-age landfills follows a pattern set in the nineteenth century, when the urban rich could barely tolerate the everyday sight and smell of their own waste. The "deodorization of public space" remains highly stratified in the twenty-first century, as the richest regions of the world use those of the poorest as dumping grounds for noxious electronic junk—by 2007, over 80 percent of e-waste was exported to Asian, African, and Latin American sites.[65] Most salvage and recycling has been carried out by preteen girls working with discarded ICT/CE to find precious metals and then dump the remainder in landfills. Exportation of these hazardous materials from the Global North is driven by the characteristic business logic of the NIDL: avoid the higher costs and regulatory oversight of recycling in wealthy countries and (selectively) punish destruction to the environment and workers. And businesses with corporate policies that forbid dumping in local landfills are all too happy to send it elsewhere.[66]

California alone shipped about twenty million pounds of e-waste in 2006 to various nations, including Mexico, Malaysia, Brazil, South Korea, China, Vietnam, and India, even as an internal audit disclosed that state workers and agencies had no idea what they were doing. By 2007, over one-hundred-thousand personal computers were being dumped monthly in Lagos, Nigeria, a country where "around half a million second-hand computers are dumped ... every month," three-quarters of which are unusable and end up in toxic-waste dumps, and the continent lacks safe waste-management systems. Ghana reported similar numbers and proportions.[67]

E-waste generates serious health and safety risks for salvage workers: brain damage; headaches; vertigo; nausea; birth defects; diseases of the bones, stomach, lungs, and other vital organs; and disrupted biological development in children. These conditions result from exposure to heavy metals (lead, cadmium, and mercury, among others); dioxin emitted by burning wires insulated with polyvinyl chloride; flame retardants in circuit boards and plastic casings containing polychlorinated biphenyls or newer brominated compounds; and poisonous fumes emitted while melting electronic parts for precious metals such as copper and gold.[68]

Yet there are many willing recipients of e-waste, because along with these hazards, it also generates new streams of capital that overwhelm and surpass traditional livelihoods. Thousands of small firms clustered along the Chinese coast specialize in this illegal trade, notably in the deltas of the Pearl and Yangtze Rivers. The latter was importing upward of 700,000 tons of e-waste by 2001, hidden as scrap metal and similar items. The number of people involved in e-waste recycling has been hard to pin down. There may be over 700,000 workers collecting and disassembling e-waste in China, with an estimated 98 percent in the informal sector. The nation's two major recycling centers in 2007 were Luqiao in Zhejiang Province and Guiyu in Guangdong Province. Guiyu was once a farming town. That changed in the 1990s with the arrival of e-waste from the "creative industries" of the West. E-waste has transformed Guiyu in three ways: 80 percent of local families have left farming for recycling; soil and water contaminants from recycling saturate the human food chain; and the saturation of land and water with persistent organic pollutants has prohibited the safe return of affected agricultural lands to future generations.[69]

Dioxin at these Chinese sites has been found at levels fifty-six times higher than World Health Organization standards. In 2008, perhaps 20 percent of salvage workers lacked basic protection against toxic metals, with lead exposure at fifty times the "safe" levels. People living in proximity to the sites were carrying lethal dust residue on their clothing and into their homes. Contaminants from incineration and landfill of residual waste had saturated local dust, soil, river sediment, surface and groundwater, and air. Of Guiyu's more than five thousand ragpickers, many were preteen girls, picking away at dangerous materials with little or no protection. Eighty-two percent of the city's children under aged six suffered lead poisoning.[70]

Epidemiological studies of Indian ragpickers and junk collectors, or *kabaadiwala*,[71] who number in the hundreds of thousands, disclose an unprecedented prevalence of low hemoglobin levels, high monocyte and eosinophil counts, gum disease, diarrhea, and dermatitis. In Brazil, where it's estimated that there are half-a-million e-waste workers, extraordinary levels of physiological disorders and psychological distress have been reported. Ragpickers in Medellín, Colombia, work well over eight hours a day for less than $11 and with minimal capacity to move on from their parents' livelihoods into healthier and more remunerative occupations.[72]

By 2010, many former employees or family members of maquiladora workers had become e-waste pickers, who collect, separate, catalogue, and sell materials from spurned consumer and business products that have made their way to rubbish dumps and low-income areas. They operate beyond taxation, labor laws, and police; do not earn wages from employers; and are not in registered cooperatives or small businesses. This informality mirrors the conditions we have described in the maquiladoras, which use temporary-employment agencies to hire workers who are never deemed full-time and hence lack contractual protections and rights.[73]

## CONCLUSION

Having perishable things (consumer goods) sprout again remains a privilege of the god Capital who turns the soul of those things to money and in the most favourable of circumstances leaves us their mortal remains for our use and consumption. (Calvino, 1994, 112–13)

This chapter has shown that before directors call "action," or editors mix sound and image, a thousand assembly lines from all over the world have streamed into media production. By some estimates, there are nearly two hundred million ICT/CE workers, a number that doubles if we add mining and related labor-intensive work. This chapter has only glimpsed the organizational relationships, geographical bonds, and interlocking occupations in supply chains that currently link computer scientists, engineers, designers, marketing researchers, miners, mineral brokers, refiners, chemists, factory laborers, server-warehouse employees, telecommunications workers, truck drivers, logistics workers, salespeople, office clerks, and anyone else whose job has been "informationalized" with ICT tools or who has contributed innovation, time, blood, sweat, or death to making, distributing, receiving, or rejecting media devices or texts. Blood and sweat are not just metaphors; real bodies are at work, and in profoundly unequal ways.[74]

Because the "informal working class" of e-waste labor lacks monetary and social influence, it has not received the same attention in media-production research and policy circles as even conventional below-the-line workers have. This leaves a growing number of ICT/CE salvage workers off the agendas of policy makers, unions, and many nongovernmental organizations. This informality does not mean they are entirely disconnected from the macro-economy, as they suffer massively during recessions when the price of scrap diminishes.[75] The story is not dissimilar for the lowest-wage assemblers that piece together the miscellany of widgets that hold high-tech gadgetry together and only slightly better for workers in the extractive industries that feed minerals into the supply chain. There must be more attention, research, and respect for work on the margins of media-technology production so we can all move toward a greener media system.

By contrast, there is increasing activity in the upper reaches of the supply chain. At companies such as Australia's Global Renewables, which is typical of an affluent nation's recycling operations, the facilities include optical scanners, wind sifters, electrical-eddy currents, robotic arms, vacuums, air jets, computer-controlled cameras, percolator tanks, digesters, and electromagnets, thereby diminishing the need for individual judgments by workers and ensuring a safer environment for the people it employs. Thus, some facilities in the Global North recycle safely, but they are expensive. This is not to imply that first-world lands and waterways are no longer filled with the detritus of rich city centers—millions of tons of e-waste are thrown into US landfills each year, and British landfills host 1.5-million new personal computers a year. And in addition to sending the problem overseas, the United States uses cheap, indentured labor in unsafe conditions in Federal prisons. Prison laborers, paid between 23¢ and $1.15 an hour, hide recycling of hazardous materials from public view on behalf of UNICOR, a corporation of the Federal government that "employs" seventeen thousand inmates. E-waste has been a staple since 1997 and its unsafe methods and corrupt ways have led to so many complaints that the Department of Justice mounted a massive evaluation that uncovered extraordinary malfeasance, not least misleading prisoners about the risks they were facing.[76]

The number of firms addressing the problems of reusing and recycling old or discarded electronics is growing, while bodies such as the ILO and the International Organization for Standardization (ISO) seek greater transparency and uniformity in the way ICT/CE corporations do business, as do international legal agreements to reduce the toxic content of electric and electronic goods, such as the EU's Waste Electrical and Electronic Equipment (WEEE) Directive and the Directive on the Restriction on the Use of Certain Hazardous Substances in Electrical and Electronic Equipment (RoHS)—policies that aim to recover 75 to 80 percent of e-waste and recycle 50 to 75 percent of it. Yet without such regulatory force reaching the lowest rungs of work throughout the supply chain of media technologies, global working conditions in the informal salvage and recycling sector will remain marginal to such audits.[77]

Revisiting the NIDL thesis a decade later, its authors added the following wishes: "to rectify the disastrous levels of air and water pollution, chemical depredation of the soil, toxic devastation of forests, and associated morbidity and mortality; and to increase the autonomy of national economic choices, by lessening vulnerability to integrated world production structures."[78] The greening of ICT/CE labor depends in part on such essential structural changes. But a deeper transformation will be contingent on the success of activists, researchers, policy makers, and unionists seeking greater transparency in working conditions throughout the ICT/ CE supply chain. For consumers, this transparency can fuel their understanding of electronics workers' experiences in China, India, Mexico, and elsewhere—knowledge necessary for cultivating empathy with workers who disappear in the twilight zone of the technological sublime. It is telling and moving that a body such as the Chintan Environmental Research and Action Group in New Delhi collaborates with ragpickers to undertake research. The results are copyrighted, with a marvelous proviso: "Feel free to use this information to promote the decent and secure livelihoods of the urban poor everywhere." That speaks to a globalization that is very different from the one that has created and sustained the NIDL.[79]

We built this chapter upon an expanded meaning of "below-the-line" workers that includes occupations throughout ICT/CE supply chains worldwide. This approach is unorthodox to the extent that we have examined working conditions that industry and academic experts have largely ignored or undertheorized in studies of media production, from those involved in mining metals and assembling low-value parts to the salvage and disposal of e-waste.[80] Further research is obviously needed to comprehend both labor and technological convergence from an ecological perspective. This will require greater attention to occupational hazards across the vast interconnecting nexus of work, environment, and production practices that define the life cycles of media technologies. For now, this and the preceding three chapters have provided a point of departure for consumers, activists, union organizers, policy makers, and managers seeking to green the media. Our next chapter turns to those whose decisions play key gatekeeping roles in achieving that goal.

# CHAPTER 5

✧

# Bureaucrats

The revolution in information technology and the internationalization of production processes have helped to bring about an extraordinary convergence of methods and perceptions among business communities everywhere. Despite the continued relevance of national and regional characteristics, business circles today are definitely sharing a common code of procedures and concepts, much to the benefit of general levels of productivity.

—former Brazilian President, Fernando Henrique Cardoso, 2005, 8

Remaining non-union is essential for survival for most of our companies. If we had the work rules that unionized companies have, we'd all go out of business.

—Robert Noyce, cofounder of Intel

The following current and/or anticipated regulatory risks are relevant to News Corporation and its operations: carbon taxes; cap and trade schemes; emissions reporting obligations; fuel/energy taxes and regulations; product labeling regulations and standards.

—News Corporation

P revious chapters have shown that ecologically sound practices are needed at institutional levels of producing and consuming media technologies, at the personal level of consumption, and across the international division of labor that feeds a toxic supply chain with workers who make, distribute, and take care of the gadgets' destruction. In this chapter and the next, we argue that a new kind of global governance is needed to establish and foster these green practices. Here, we focus on the bureaucrats who make crucial decisions in these areas.

We define the bureaucrat in simple terms to mean a decision maker who works from a desk or an office to set, influence, or enforce policies at the state and interstate level, whether inside the state apparatus or within corporations and their trade organizations, with the capacity to link large bureaucracies whose actions delimit what kinds of ICT/CE are produced. In some cases, bureaucrats are undemocratic (or at least unelected) elites, others are part of the military-industrial-academic complex, and others have corporations stand in as their fictitious representatives; in all, they have played and will continue to play an important gatekeeping role in defining not only the design and deployment of media technologies but also the limits and possibilities for those seeking to create a system that supports sustainable ICT/CE without compromise with the idea of growth.

The first section of the chapter is a brief history of bureaucratic thought on ICT/CE and the ideological effects of media technology that have influenced elite decision makers. This is followed by an examination of the eco-ethical orientation in bureaucratic thinking about the environment. The third and fourth sections provide case studies of green corporate strategies directed at new electricity distribution known as smart-grid technology and at large-scale greening of retail distribution at Walmart,[1] a point-of-purchase destination for consumers of ICT/CE and a potentially influential rule maker in ICT/CE supply-chain operations. Both business strategies are designed to implement ecologically sound practices without making fundamental changes to business-as-usual—a contradictory effort, as we shall see. The final section examines global-media policy and governance as a prelude to the next chapter on green citizenship.

## A BRIEF HISTORY OF BUREAUCRATIC THINKING ABOUT MEDIA TECHNOLOGY

Media technologies have generated terrific popular excitement since the eighteenth century, as far-flung communities were connected via road, wire, and eventually wireless systems of communication. By the early twentieth century, dread and wonder at social and technological transformations inspired many emergent European artists, who imagined homologies and analogies between their creations and the revolutionary urban environment of people and things. We can see modernity's love of mastery and perfection, the application of reason to better the world, in Surrealism, Dadaism, Futurism, and projects such as Le Corbusier's.[2] Newly urbanized dwellers met dislocated social relations with technologies that supplanted old ways with a technological wonderland that Weber imaginatively refers to as follows:

> The modern metropolis, with its railways, subways, electric and other lights, shop windows, concert and catering halls, cafes, smokestacks, and piles of stone, the whole wild dance of sound and colour impressions that affect sexual fantasy, and the experiences of variations in the soul's constitution that lead to a hungry brooding over all kinds of seemingly inexhaustible possibilities for the conduct of life and happiness. (2005, 29)

Proud human achievement made it easy to forget the natural habitats that were destroyed in the name of progress and growth. This hubris brought the transcontinental railroad, the knife that cut the US bison herd in half and facilitated Native American genocide. Forgetting about the environment enabled media technology to converge—with hardly a voice of opposition—around chemico-mechanical processes; water and steam power; deforestation; mining; smelting; and toxic emissions into air, soil, and water, a pattern established by print and paper industries in nineteenth-century North America and Europe. In the electric age, chemical batteries powered telegraphy and telephony, and fossil-fueled national grids made radio, television, and telematic networks buzz with information and pleasure.[3] For the bureaucratic mind, a mechanistic one, these changes can be readily packaged into stages of economic progress in which technologies of dirt/culture evolve into technologies of knowledge/culture, passing through the necessary evil of industrialism's smokestack.

In this scenario, we arrive inevitably at the knowledge worker and the creative economy. These are terms loaded with ideological effects, the main one being to obfuscate the reality of environmental and working conditions in the haze of the technological sublime. Here is an exemplary snippet of this bureaucratic *idée fixe*:

> In a First Wave economy, land and farm labor are the main "factors of production." In a Second Wave economy, the land remains valuable while the "labor" becomes massified around machines and larger industries. In a Third Wave economy, the central resource—a single word broadly encompassing data, information, images, symbols, culture, ideology, and values—is actionable knowledge. (Dyson et al., 1994, 1)

Adherence to this glossy view of technological developments dooms the bureaucrat to "think inside the box" of very established practices, where worker and environment are reduced to exploitable resources, if they are acknowledged at all. In his seminal study of modern bureaucracy from almost a century ago, Weber describes the bureaucratic mind as an "instrument of 'societalizing' relations of power ... an attitude-set of the official for pre-cise obedience ... in public as well as private organizations," adding that the advance of bureaucratic systems "rests on 'technical' superiority."[4] As the founding president of today's European Bank for Reconstruction and Development, Jacques Attali, approvingly puts it, systemic power accrues "wherever a creative class masters a key innovation from navigation to accounting or, in our own time, where services are most efficiently mass produced, thus generating enormous wealth."[5] When media technologies are added to the tool kit of bureaucratic techniques, they intensify and spread managerial coordination from above; hence the consulting firm of Henry Kissinger, master of the dark arts of US foreign policy, advising that the United States must "win the battle of the world's information flows, dominating the airwaves as Great Britain once ruled the seas."[6]

Herbert I. Schiller, an incomparable critic of the interlocking bureau-cracies that shaped the development and deployment of US imperial communications, argues that media technologies were vital to the "infra-structure of socialization" that synchronizes the interests of dominant strata in both core and periphery via common business cultures, institu-tional networks, organizational models, and modes of communication and cultural production.[7]

As we saw in the previous chapter, this command-control function of capitalist organization extends throughout the supply chain and into the waste stream, where salvage workers recycle and dispose of electronic garbage. Waste was essentially unknown in subsistence societies, but the nineteenth-century capitalist city put an end to automatic, unreflexive recycling, thanks to bourgeois manners, technological innovation, unequal living conditions, and the division of labor that swept the latter out of sight. One of the first bureaucratic responses to the ragpicker's world of waste and filth focused on European health reforms, which linked sanitation and disease from the 1840s, when urban environments became collective rather than individual responsibilities. Fifty years later, even the United States got the message that intense industrialization coupled waste to sick-ness.[8] The economic historian Karl Polanyi referred to this as "the discov-ery of society"—that moment in the nineteenth-century transformation of capitalism when Marx's "kicked-about mass" gained recognition as mem-bers of society, deserving of aid and inclusion and vulnerable to critique and exclusion.[9] Their well-being became a right, a problem, a statistic, and a law, juxtaposed to the self-governing worker or owner. When merged with class activism and philanthropic moralism, the positive side of this bureaucratic intervention was that it legitimized social-welfare principles and held society to be simultaneously within and beyond market precepts and controls.

By 1930, industrial waste was widely known to pose risks to workers and the waterways used by nearby populations, though local bureaucrats rarely enforced the relevant nuisance and riparian laws for fear of chasing away industries and jobs—a familiar refrain among growth ideologues to this day. Businesses became increasingly arrogant about dumping waste into rivers and sewage systems; landfills were not widely used until after 1945, though US municipalities had solid-waste disposal programs by the time of the Depression. As we have seen, manufacturers of media technology presumed that the reduction or elimination of waste would slow production and erode profits. To them, "managing" waste meant dumping it on-site or into waterways. The dilemma was not "how to dispose of process residue safely" but "how least to interfere with the manufacturing process."[10] The story continued in this vein over seven decades.

By the time we get to the 1970s and '80s, pundits, politicians, and academics in affluent nations were entranced by a new kind of chrome-plated electronic convergence. Built on microchips, digital gadgetry, and planetary networks, it would spark unending prosperity and growth throughout the market system. Such gilded bureaucratic thinking was a stark rebuke to the reality of industrial capitalism's unsustainable growth model, which the energy crisis and the oil-price shock had pressed into public awareness with great ferocity during this period. Instead, the crisis provided the impetus for capital to reverse the downward redistribution of wealth in the First World that had come about after 1945 through working-class organization and politics. Neoliberals took the reins of economic restructuring and crowned the "information economy" as a royal road to crisis management, paying no attention to the environment as they asserted control over the technical capacity and operating materials of ICT/CE and the NIDL.[11] Polluting industries seemingly no longer represented the dynamic core of industrial capitalism; instead, market dynamism radiated from a networked intellectual core of creative and informational activities. ICT/CE catalyzed the new information- and knowledge-based economies that would rescue First-World hegemony from an "insurgent world" that lurked within as well as beyond itself.[12] Business professors, coin-operated think tanks, and management gurus said it was feasible; the commercial business media concurred; and leaders of the advanced market economies bet their treasuries on it. The boosterism was shameless—the very idea of "high technology" was actually the invention of business journalism rather than science.[13]

This beguiling discourse had been incubated in the 1940s in one of the largest engineering projects ever to unite state, military, industrial, and academic bureaucrats. In testimony to the US Atomic Energy Commission, the noted physicist J. Robert Oppenheimer, who led the group that developed the atomic bomb, talked about the instrumental rationality that animated the people who created this terrifying technology. He suggested that once these scientists saw that it was feasible, the device's impact on the Earth and its inhabitants lost intellectual and emotional significance for them. They had been overtaken by what he called its "technically sweet" quality.[14]

The bureaucratic aspiration for building technically sweet machines locked out the social and environmental effects in order to animate innovation, adoption, and the mix of the sublime—the awesome, ineffable, godlike power over all—with the beautiful, made up of the approachable, the attractive, the pliant, the soothing. In philosophical aesthetics, the sublime and the beautiful are generally regarded as opposites. The unique quality of media technology has been to combine them at both industrial and popular experiential levels. For instance, many of the companies involved in the development of broadcast TV in the United States, such as Westinghouse, GE, and DuPont, also participated in the development of nuclear energy and weaponry—and advertised *on* television from the earliest days. The US Ad Council even sponsored coverage of the bomb tests in 1952, under the auspices of the Atomic Energy Commission.[15]

The go-go years of the information economy were in full swing when Ronald Reagan entered the White House in 1981. Reagan—who twenty years earlier told TV audiences to "live better electrically!" as GE's lead spokesperson—seemed a perfect technically sweet bureaucratic creation. And indeed, he was as destructive as they come. As president, he replaced welfare-oriented state control and risk management with a militant anti-government style of governance that hypocritically used state power to intervene in the name of the free-market economy.[16] Under his watch, the United States led the way in dismantling domestic and international regulation of the media and eviscerated public policies and programs that promoted alternative energy and protected the air, water, and soil. Intolerance of green policy was (and remains) a powerful rallying point for the political Right, as symbolized by Reagan, who claimed that trees caused pollution. His first act after being reelected in 1984 was to order the removal of solar panels from the White House, where his predecessor had installed them.[17] Fortunately, he could not undo legislation that limited dumping hazardous wastes, such as the 1976 Resource Conservation and Recovery Act and the 1980 Comprehensive Environmental Response Compensation and Liability Act.[18]

Reagan wasn't the first Hollywood creation to be drawn into the higher circles of "technological nationalism," or the last. One contemporary manifestation was a 1996 workshop for academia, Hollywood, and the Pentagon held by the National Academy of Sciences of the United States on the subject of electronic games. The next year, the National Research Council announced a collaborative research agenda on popular culture and military needs.[19] The DoD, by far the globe's leading polluter and killer, depends on electronics, information technologies, games, and special effects as much as it does on fossil fuels, destruction of terrain and infrastructure, radiation, conventional pollution, buried ordinance, defoliants, land use, antipersonnel mines, carcinogenic chemical deposits, and toxic effluents. Despite the Pentagon's latter-day claim that it is "going green," the DoD is the world's largest user of petroleum—a million gallons a day in both Iraq and Afghanistan in 2009, for instance, and a 2008 fuel bill of $20 billion—and each battalion produced a ton of waste a day.[20]

Bodies such as the University of Southern California's (USC) Institute for Creative Technologies merrily exploit this convergence of war, media, and environmental ruin in their search for the technical sweet spot. The Institute convenes scholars, film and television producers, game designers, and the military using Pentagon money, Hollywood connections, and faculty desire to test homicidal technologies in narrative scenarios, in a workspace lovingly laid out by the set designer for *Star Trek*. Formally opened by the Secretary of the Army and the head of the Motion Picture Association of America, the institute was started with $45 million of the military's budget in 1998, a figure that was doubled in its 2004 renewal. USC collaborates on major motion pictures, for instance *Spider-Man 2*,[21] and produces such Pentagon recruitment tools as the popular electronic game "Full Spectrum Warrior," which double as "training devices for military operations in urban terrain." The Pentagon even boasts that the game "captured Saddam" because the men who dug Hussein out had been trained by playing it.[22] To propagate admiration for the Institute's work, DoD's website, Armed with Science, offers downloadable podcasts called *Armed with Science: Research Applications for the Modern Military*. A typical podcast explains how the Pentagon and USC were developing the software-based simulation system UrbanSim to improve "the art of battle command" as part of the United States' imperial wars. They claim that this is only a small shift from commercial gaming: "Instead of having Godzilla and tornados attacking your city, the players are faced with things like uncooperative local officials and ethnic divisions in the communities, different tribal rivalries," to quote an Institute scholar in the podcast.[23]

We are writing in the midst of the greatest global economic crisis in seven decades, one that exceeds the 1970s version in its reach and impact, and accompanies an equally forbidding and more dramatically present ecological crisis. But powerful strains of bureaucratic thought continue to stress the virtual elements of ICT/CE in terms of "dematerialization," which purports to describe the purely positive economic impact of these technologies.[24] The promised "dematerialization of society" (we're still waiting) is based on the notion that electronic commerce, teleconferencing, telecommuting, and the virtual administration of health and taxes reduce the environmental burden of business-as-usual.[25] The trouble is that each time this dazzlingly dematerialized future seems to be upon us, it keeps inconveniently rematerializing and failing to spark renewed growth.[26]

Moreover, crestfallen boosters of dematerialization must contend with environmentalism's spreading influence in policy circles and the tension it places on bureaucrats trying to promote ICT/CE at the same time as acknowledging their environmental impact. For example, the International Telecommunication Union (ITU) has recognized that the proliferation of electronic gadgets for productivity and pleasure also has negative effects on ecosystems. Hamadoun Touré, Secretary General of the ITU, hails ICT/CE for their potential to connect six-and-a-half billion residents of the Earth by 2015, so that "everyone can access information, create information, use information and share information" and suggests that the "ICT sector will take the world out of financial crisis, because it's the only industry that's still growing," thanks to developing markets.[27] But Touré has also pressed for "climate neutrality" and greater efficiency in energy use, while venues such as the World Telecommunication Standardization Assembly 2008 in Johannesburg encouraged its members to reduce the carbon footprint of communications in accordance with the United Nations Framework Convention on Climate Change.[28]

In a similar vein, the OECD says ICT will play a pivotal role in developing service-based, low-polluting economies in the Global South, offering energy efficiency, adaptation to climate change, mitigation of diminished biodiversity, and decreased pollution. The organization is quick to caution that technological advances can produce negative outcomes, warning, for example, that remote sensing of marine fisheries enables unsustainable levels of fishing.[29] Likewise, satellites monitor environmental changes (deforestation, desertification, earthquakes, volcanoes, climate modeling, and so on) help fisheries and species-migration research, and inform marine ecosystem protections. But space junk is a growing problem, with over three hundred million pieces orbiting the Earth, discharging poisonous chemicals and compounds and nuclear waste, and threatening operational satellites, as we saw in chapter 3. Other media that balance the virtues and vices of ICT/CE include so-called smart technologies, which use radio controls and "internet protocols" to reduce consumption of natural resources and shrink greenhouse-gas emission and conventional pollutants. Some of these communication systems now operate irrigation systems and smart-electricity grids, a subject we'll discuss shortly.

## THE ECO-ETHICS OF BUREAUCRACY

The anthropocentric-ethical orientation dominates bureaucratic think-ing on the environment. In the United States, for example, environmental policy is based entirely on CBA, a risk-management technique that lies at one extreme of human-centered eco-ethics.[30] CBA is used to determine whether a particular regulation justifies its cost. This type of analysis can influence decisions about whether mandated recycling is an efficient use of resources or if stemming losses to a lagging economy outweighs the benefits of protecting endangered wildlife. CBA works by monetizing human and nonhuman life through various methods, such as "hedonic pricing," which would find the market value of a forest, for example, by correlating housing prices with proximity to undeveloped land. In this case, the benefit of not developing *all* of a forest would justify mandated conservation of *part* of it. Critiques of this approach include the arbi-trariness of assigning monetary value to human life and other nonmarket goods, the failure to account for intergenerational equity, and the eleva-tion of technocratic decision-making at the expense of public input and participation.[31]

CBA also practices a spatial politics that fails to address inter-territorial equity. Its eco-ethics presumes that the zones of the biosphere in which it is applied have merely relative connections to zones beyond the boundaries of its analysis. For example, CBA reinforces the logic that the processes of dumping waste in the Global South are efficient and effective for the North and South alike. This view allows for a number of other cultural assumptions about the relative value of human communities living across multiple lines of difference, territorial or otherwise.[32] As we saw in the previous chapter, there are grave consequences when such a shallow moral code guides the treatment of e-waste.

Underlying the tensions between "bean counters" and "tree huggers" is a techno-scientific ideology that determines how environmental risk is dis-tributed. The discourse of risk management masks the fact that decisions are actually made to define the number of habitats and creatures that will die or be sickened by environmental despoliation. Science (or more nar-rowly, techno-science) plays a role in this moral detachment by providing legitimacy via the measurement of "safe amounts" of exposure to toxins and pollutants.[33] The language of risk management puts ethical considerations in an apolitical frame of technocracy, as compared to language that denotes in more precise terms the ethico-politics of what institutions like the EPA do: determine how the impact of harm is allocated. This is why some have called managerialism one of the ecological "curses of our time"—for its "belief that human beings have not only the 'right' but the ability, even if only potentially, to successfully manage the world."[34]

Although anthropocentric eco-ethics implicitly underpin CBA and risk management, they also contain alternatives, including the precautionary principle, absolute prescriptions, sustainable development, and cost-benefit shortcuts.[35] The precautionary principle holds that "our knowledge of the effects of our actions is always exceeded by our ignorance." This standard lays the burden of proof of value and safety on those who would introduce potentially toxic substances or dangerous practices into the environment in circumstances where there is no scientific consensus about such actions' consequences.[36] This principle is very strong in international agreements and offers the most serious challenge to CBA bean counters. Absolute prescriptions are unconditional bans on known pollutants and toxins; this was the standard that informed much of 1970s environmental law. As discussed in chapter 1, sustainable development refers to efficient use and equitable distribution of natural resources for long-term, intergenerational socioeconomic development. CBA shortcuts include technological fixes that offer qualitative improvements without strict adherence to quantitative factors of regulation.[37]

Of all these alternatives, sustainable development has been the most controversial, due to its casual overuse by actors across the political spectrum, from free marketeers to eco-centrists on the Left. Ideally, the term denotes a standard that "rules out all practices except those that are indefinitely sustainable" by the Earth's ecosystems. Sustainability is more commonly deployed to signify a balance between economic development and environmental protection, though this tends to mean qualitative development rather than pure quantitative growth. The virtues of sustainable development are as follows: It accounts for intra- and intergenerational equity; it allows for open participation, if not by affected communities, then at least by their representatives; and it is recognized in international agreements to assure a certain inter-territorial equity, even when the parties disagree on its meaning. It thus offers a more equitable alternative to CBA's comprehension of the world.[38]

The disadvantages of sustainable development emerge at the point at which the question of quantitative economic development overtakes other concerns. In its weakest form, sustainable development becomes "little more than 'sustainable' capitalism."[39] Economic self-interest pushes eco-ethical self-interest into a little corner of sustainability. Herein lies a key vulnerability of anthropocentric eco-ethics. Self-interest that does not perceive the intimate relation between human and nonhuman beings will tilt the balance toward the satisfaction of human needs. The following case studies exemplify this problem.

## THE GRID: "WISER WIRES"?

At a 2009 meeting in India with government and business leaders, US Secretary of State Hillary Clinton outlined her country's plan to foment ecologically sound consumption on a global scale. Clinton spoke of "the challenge" for international environmental policy to recognize "the different needs and responsibilities of developed and developing countries alike." Sovereign states must not ignore the global ecological crisis: "The times we live in demand nothing less than a total commitment," she declared, adding that the "statistics are there for everyone to see." Clinton went on to identify an ethical dilemma at the base of US policy: On the one hand, the "United States and other countries that have been the biggest historic emitters of greenhouse gases should shoulder the biggest burden for cleaning up the environment and reducing our carbon footprint." On the other hand, developing countries should not give up their dreams of emulating US industrial production and consumption: "The United States does not and will not do anything that would limit India's economic progress" but will work collaboratively to "devise a plan that will dramatically change the way we produce, consume, and conserve energy" in order to "develop sustainably" and "eradicate poverty."[40]

Clinton gave her speech at India's ITC Green Centre, one of the largest buildings in the world to receive a top LEED rating. Built for the second-largest cigarette maker in India, the ITC Green Centre is known for its green construction—and corporate greenwashing.[41] With that backdrop, Clinton described the sustainable society the United States would like to see: one where "the private sector can play a role, along with government" in an "innovative and entrepreneurial spirit" to create "smart design," with green buildings modeling the "smart design of whole communities" to renovate entire nations. The message was clear: a smart-design economy would be warmly welcomed by US leadership, provided that its political-economic arrangements suited the US government and "private sector" and rejected China's example of locking out solar and wind technology from the Global North to favor national producers.[42]

We have seen how such high-flying rhetoric can reveal the power elite's political and economic aspirations. Grand bureaucratic pronouncements about the "selection, investment and development" of new technologies are linked to each generation's delimiting "social relations and cultural forms," as Williams puts it. In his time, radio exemplified how new ideas of scientific experimentation—Hertzian waves, the conduction of electricity—were pressed into existing social patterns encouraged by private enterprise and military (in telegraphy and telephony, and later wireless). In the 1920s, when it was clearly possible to transmit messages wirelessly over very great distances, northern warlords in China monopolized the radio spectrum for military purposes. In the United States, this privilege fell to the Navy, while newly established corporations sought to use radio for entertainment and marketing.[43] What transpired gives us some clues into the strategic designs that led to the earliest forms of technological convergence in media systems. By 1930, US telecommunications executives were planning to merge diverse technologies into single business operations. A bureaucratic rationale to increase profitability and reduce risk fostered a desire to fuse the media industries through the systematic accumulation of patents in electricity, chemistry, and telecommunications. Strategic convergence on the corporate drawing board found support among engineers, who had demonstrated that common physical properties allowed telegraphy, telephony, and wireless to use electrical energy for "intelligence transmission." These engineers had influential allies among business consumers: new telecommunication systems were "disproportionately used by large-scale enterprises oriented toward a truly national political economy: banks, commodity traders, news agencies, and railroads."[44]

We can see signs of the same power structure emerging today to define new "smart-grid" electricity distribution systems. Conventional power grids are centralized and use "dumb wires." When a major outage occurs, no one knows where or why it happened until it is reported and physically investigated. In addition, the existing grid is not designed to manage fluctuations in availability of power that come with geothermal, solar, and wind sources.[45] New technologies are creating a smart grid that meters, analyzes, regulates, and charges for electricity usage in homes and office buildings via internet protocols that can alert grid operators instantaneously to fluctuations in demand from networks and appliances. The *Economist* engagingly alliterates this as "wiser wires." It explains that there were sixty million smart meters operating worldwide in 2009, with plans announced for an additional eight hundred million in pilots across the OECD.[46] Google has marketed software for the computerized smart grid, while GE offers a metering system for it, along with hardware and services to create and run a green home.

Utility customers that use smart-grid metering to reduce consumption turn off air conditioning during peak times or power some appliances down while running others at lower rates, and their electronics are automatically plugged and unplugged from the grid as needed. This marginally reduces living standards, due to a greener relation to the environment, but does not involve radical changes in lifestyle by either companies or people. An effective smart grid promises to lower electricity usage and reduce emissions, but what awaits commercial-energy producers whose business will suffer from diminishing demand? And what if there is a "rebound effect," such that policies designed to reduce energy consumption, cut prices, and increase efficiency, have the opposite effect and encourage consumption to increase?[47] The answers offer further examples of what happens when private-sector bureaucrats dominate the smart-design economy.

Metering the grid between customers and central systems through internet protocols allows system managers to track fluctuations of supply and demand moment to moment. This is important for balancing the load and saving energy. But commercial energy producers in the United States see another value in this technology. They have proposed to use research data on fluctuations in consumption in pilot programs to convince regulators to approve real-time price fluctuations. Utility companies offer a bogus "green" rationale for fluctuating rates: that they encourage conservation and keep inessential energy use down during peak demand. They suggest that lower demand will mean lower rates, peak prices will follow peak usage, and overall consumption will decline. It looks as though energy producers are willing to accept the social gains of smart design only if they make money as a consequence.[48] US commercial utilities aren't alone in resisting change or seeking regulation to help them preserve profit growth in the smart-design economy. In France, the main energy producer (which is majority owned by the state) faced declining profits as a result of eco-ethical consumption combined with smart-grid metering. Regulators there have approved a system to compensate the utility for its losses by taxing smart-grid company revenues. Consumer advocates consider this to be an unjustified reward for energy producers that will ultimately be paid by consumers in higher rates for smart-metering services.[49]

So, smart-grid technology promises to reduce both cost and global warming. But consumers who might otherwise feel comfortable with smart design should be wary, not only about the dodgy pricing structure but also about the indirect ways that taxpayers are funding utilities through government programs designed to ensure that the largest private firms shore up their expertise and deepen their hold on emerging computerized energy-management systems. For despite their professed love of laissez-faire, profit-seeking utilities are not above receiving largesse from governments. For example, the US Department of Energy (DoE) has funded private utilities and other businesses like IBM, Cisco, and GE to implement and study pilot programs for smart-grid projects. IBM has positioned itself "as a strategic advisor to Washington's top policy makers and bureaucrats" based on the need for a national "smart infrastructure." GE and Google, among others, have lobbied Congress for investment in the smart grid. Cisco and IBM partnered for a smart-grid project in Amsterdam to reduce greenhouse gas emissions, while Cisco and GE planned to build smart grids in parts of Miami.[50]

GE's "eco-imagination" policy for the twenty-first century brought its supposedly "green" business into the race to acquire some of the $400 billion in "economic stimulus" allocated in 2009 for alternative-energy projects around the world, and hoped to grab subsidies for a new industrial battery factory in New York State. The backdrop, as we have seen, is that GE holds the record for PCBs dumped into US waterways. The "eco-imagination" brand earned $17 billion in 2008. Part of that revenue came from the hundreds of millions of dollars GE received from municipalities, the DoE, and the DoD to develop smart-grid systems. GE's CEO, Jeffrey Immelt, served on the President's Economic Recovery Advisory Board until 2011 when Obama appointed him chairman of his panel of economic advisors, which was renamed the President's Council on Jobs and Competitiveness upon Immelt's ascent.[51]

Such corporate welfare *should* force its beneficiaries to recognize their indebtedness to a mixed-economy model and the legitimacy of democratic control of their activities. Yet it would be foolish to expect corporate-welfare recipients to tolerate taxpayers' claiming the status of stakeholders in their businesses. To recognize taxpayers as investors would mean they were owed a return on investment. In the context of green ICT/CE, that would mean intergenerational equity, realistic environmental accounting, and public-sector involvement in setting standards for infrastructure design, access, and maintenance. The "private sector" pretends instead that it imagined, paid for, and created the technology, the application, and the market. In the foreseeable future, it appears that rewards for eco-ethical action through taxpayer investment and ecologically sound living will be externalized as the price of services charged by energy companies, with social gains, public investment, and internal cost savings welcomed by energy businesses. This will happen on the condition that profit continues to grow at rates enjoyed during the pre-green era.

We are routinely told that consumption will diminish as media usage moves to handheld devices that show first-run movies, headline sports, child care-center workers, and happy-family photo albums. The smart-design economy will bring about fewer switching centers, without the need for air conditioning and with low-power and sleep functions. The movement from desktop to laptop computers means 40 percent less electricity used per appliance, while the proliferation of multicore processors also reduces energy use. There are other power-saving applications, such as LED monitors, flash drives that replace hard disks, and so on. But they all bring with them a "rebound effect" of increased consumption of such capacious and efficient systems. We see this already with very high-speed digital subscriber lines and gigabit passive optical networks, which have massively expanded the capacity for transmission and power usage. So far, data centers are set to become even-bigger carbon emitters as corporations and governments move to the supposedly immaterial atmosphere of cloud computing.[52]

## WALMART

In the same week that Clinton visited India, Walmart announced a new environmental strategy. The largest retailer in the world, with almost eight-thousand stores, it tops the *Fortune* 500, had 2008 sales that were one-third of India's GDP, and boasted 2009 revenue of $401 billion, dwarfing the combined income of its three biggest competitors. Handling a million trans-actions every sixty minutes, Walmart's data needs are managed through sys-tems with a capacity of 2.5 peta-bytes (a peta-byte is a quadrillion bytes) and growing—that's equal to 167 times the content of the Library of Congress. The company has its own television network, which is broadcast over three thousand stores in the United States. One hundred and forty corporations advertise on its six channels, and the model is being emulated in China, Bra-zil, and Britain. As a commentator for Harvard Business Publishing notes, "Once Wal-Mart is involved, everything gets much, much larger."[53] That was certainly the view of demonstrators, who protested vigorously when the company gained entry to Indian markets and tried to enter Teotihuacán, Mexico. And it has led to productive debates about an exploitative employer that appeals to poor consumers worldwide because of its convenience and pricing. As an idea of both the immensity of Walmart and the dimension of popular opposition to it, the company proposed over 1,500 new US stores between 1998 and 2005; more than five hundred were massively opposed, and in two-thirds of those cases, the plans were abandoned.[54]

In 2007, Walmart announced that it intended to reduce its energy con-sumption by a third. This was part of a "going-green" policy, apparently in reaction to critical press coverage, exemplified in the excoriating documen-tary *Wal-Mart: The High Cost of Low Price*,[55] and rendered costly through a succession of lawsuits for violations of labor and antidiscrimination legisla-tion as well as social movements such as the United Food and Commercial Workers International Union, which runs a site exposing the workings of Walmart.[56]

Walmart's Sustainable Product Index proposed a three-stage plan to assess its suppliers' green characteristics, build a free and open database on the life cycle of materials used in the products it sells, and enable con-sumers to make choices based on the environmental impact of the prod-ucts they buy. The toxicity of components, workplace hazards, and other issues related to labor and environmental justice were absent from Walmart's assessment of sustainability, leaving its reputation for exploitation of human and other resources largely intact.[57] Nor does Walmart plan to set performance standards to pressure suppliers into making greener products—the existing plan does not rank companies or list champions chosen for their greenness. The Index will, however, generate information about suppliers and, eventually, about product content, so that green-conscious consumers can factor in the environmental footprint associated with making a purchase at Walmart, thinking about pollution at the same time as price, availability, and satisfaction. If consumers favor green products, the market will force suppliers to mend their dirty ways. The other major big-box retailers, such as Carrefour (France), Tesco (Britain), and Metro Group (Germany), are also pursuing environmental strategies as part of corporate responsibility.[58]

There are already numerous databases that provide LCAs[59] of products' chemical and other contents, as well as websites like GoodGuide that help consumers identify the green credentials of producers and products. But if Walmart's Index develops as its proponents have claimed, it could expand ethical consumption of media technologies in three ways: First, Walmart plans to build the database of the Index with the participation of nongovernmental organizations, university researchers, and government agencies, as well as its usual business partners. Second, unlike most LCA databases, which are often privately held by corporations and vended at vast cost, Walmart claims it will open its database to free public access. Finally, because of the firm's domination of the retail market, the Index could expose the internal operations and environmental impact of most consumer-goods manufacturers. And if it creates an alliance with other big-box retailers, as some reports claim, the Index could have wider application.[60]

That said, in trying to balance green supply and demand, Walmart's Index recapitulates the discredited idea that green consumption can coexist with market efficiency through the magical fusion of growth and sustainability. The Electronics TakeBack Coalition rated Walmart a C+ in its 2010 "Report Card," because the firm lacks a national recycling program for the ICT/CE it has sold to people, does not disclose information on the size of its existing schemes, fails to offer television trade-ins, keeps its recycling requirements of vendors secret, and does not support legislation to regulate the environmental impact of the media. In addition, of course, there are appalling reports of the way its subcontracted workers are treated in adjacent sectors. SACOM has revealed extraordinary infractions of national and international law in the manufacture of the toys Walmart sells, a critique we've seen applied to Disney despite its "environmentality." So, while Walmart's program includes laudable goals to reduce "white pollution" (through paper advertising and packaging) and emissions from operations and transport and to encourage consumption of lower-emission goods through labeling of "small-footprint" products, the corporation remains ethically challenged on too many levels to make it a trustworthy environmental partner.[61] Green consumers, activists, policy makers, and unionists will have to continue to pressure this monolith's bureaucrats if real transformation toward sustainability is to happen.

Consistent with Clinton's vision of the smart-design economy, Walmart represents a "private sector" that empowers consumers to make green choices, with economic growth oddly coupled with sustainability. Walmart depicts itself as a leader in green-business strategies, as if governmental policies weren't responsible for changing the rules by which such mega-retailers must operate. It's hard to find mention in Walmart's own documentation of the political process that shaped its makeover, though one can find explicit reference on its website to the EU's RoHS, adopted in 2003—three years before Walmart set out to green itself. So, once we get beyond the rhetoric of Walmart's Sustainable Product Index, the catalyst for change turns out to be political intervention and green governance in the world's biggest economy. The retailer's commitment to eco-ethical consumption indicates that Walmart may in fact be positioning itself as a leading "private-sector" agent, or agenda setter, in shaping regulations of its industry, much as IBM, Google, GE, Cisco, and other utility and ICT corporations have been doing in the smart-grid economy.

## POLICY MAKERS

This reinforces the need to address state policies as key places where corporate action is determined. Hundreds of accords aim to protect workers, waterways, plant and animal life, fisheries, archaeological and other cultural-environmental heritage, and atmospheric and ground air quality through the regulation of waste management, trans-border flows of heavy metals, airborne and waterborne pollutants, forests, nuclear energy, and exported hazardous waste. These local, regional, national, and global ecological policies have intersected with the media's impact on climate change, pollution, biodiversity, and habitat. For instance, in the case of storage batteries that power electronics of all shapes and sizes, hundreds of laws regulate their production, contents, disposal, and transportation, overlapping with court decisions and international agreements, notably the Stockholm Convention on Persistent Organic Pollutants, the Kyoto Protocol, and the United Nations Framework Convention on Climate Change.[62]

Multilateral environmental accords date from the 1920s. But prior to the first United Nations Conference on the Human Environment in Stockholm in 1972, only Britain, France, and Canada had cabinet-level environment ministries. The 1972 event marked the UN's attempt to create global governance of the environment, and the 114 countries that attended responded to the conference and other pressures in remarkable ways. By the second UN conference, United Nations Conference on Environment and Development, known as the Earth Summit, in 1992, there were over a hundred such bodies. Of the approximately hundred and fifty international ecological agreements, over half emerged in the years after the first Stockholm event. In 2009, there were almost five-hundred relevant multilateral accords involving at least 198 environmental ministries, agencies, or directorates, with participation by many intergovernmental organizations as well as international nongovernmental organizations like Greenpeace, BAN, and the Silicon Valley Toxics Coalition (SVTC).[63]

As we mentioned above, policies adopted in the 1970s stressed absolute prescriptions for conservation, water quality, and air-pollution controls. There has been a shift since that time toward precautionary principles and a less efficient and effective form of environmentalism via policies that emphasize CBA and risk-managerial governance, based on setting standards and evaluating performance through self-regulation. Just as the period since the 1992 Earth Summit has intensified the standing of nongovernmental organizations, it has also seen corporations claiming civil-society stature. They favor a deregulated, corporate-audited form of governance, in keeping both with the neoliberal triumphs of the era and the limited sovereignty of states over global problems. Big polluters dedicate massive resources to lobbying and, as in the examples of smart-grid and big-box retailing, jockey for advantage in markets regulated by a growing number of environmental laws, accords, and agreements.[64]

The remainder of this chapter focuses on specific policy problems, suggesting ways that ecologically oriented media policy might make print and ICT/CE production, consumption, and end-of-life management more sustainable.

## PAPER

The early ecological history of paper and pulp included a few voices of resistance calling for legislation to protect waterways and forests, but the pro-business lobby successfully limited debate. In 1920, Congressman Charles J. Thompson, an Ohio Republican, introduced legislation to tax advertisers 10 percent on column inches they purchased in periodicals "to teach advertisers to tell their stories in less space and thus conserve the use of paper and curtail enormous waste now quite evident and admitted."[65]

The legislation failed, and the threat of further conservationist challenges to advertising provoked the Association of National Advertisers to redouble its efforts via lobbying and public relations to stave off future attempts to tax its members' use of the media.

For most of the twentieth century, conservationists were told that it was antibusiness to claim that the pulp-and-paper industry should bear full responsibility for their pollution. Meeker proposals tried to nudge pulp and paper makers to look for profit in waste management; even the most noxious pulping processes must be able to monetize some toxic by-product, so the argument went. Such milquetoast politics set a pattern of accommodation with the industry that persists in much contemporary environmental policy. In the United States, court action has brought little more than a cynical response from the pulp and paper manufacturers, who plead that they would be happy to act if someone would step forward to show them how to dispose of waste without polluting. By the 1970s, this situation resulted in some "cooperative action between state authorities and pulp and paper manufacturers" to develop techniques to recycle by-products from waste, but nothing came of this effort at the time. The EPA formed a "pulp and paper cluster group" in the 1980s, and enforced Clean Water Act and Clean Air Act updates since the 1990s to regulate deadly media effluents. In the early 2000s, the California Department of Education was required by Assembly Bill 2532 of 2002 to set maximum limits on the weight of textbooks pupils could be expected to lug around. And the British government pressed newspapers and newsprint producers to set a target of using 60 percent wastepaper by the end of 2001 and 65 percent two years after that; targets that were surpassed a year early.[66] A handful of trade organizations have also been involved in efforts to rethink print's relation to the environment.[67]

The patchwork of certification programs claiming to ensure responsible paper use that can sustain forests is extremely confusing—there are about fifty such systems in play, with a handful routinely used in the United States, for example. In the midst of the global recession that began in late 2007, one might have anticipated an uptick in recycling, as frugality's virtues rivaled consumption's pleasures, but prices for virgin paper and plastics dropped along with fuel costs, ironically imperiling the financial footing of many recycling companies. The impact of future carbon taxes, new technologies, and deforestation may diminish the printing industry's size; alternatively, massive developments in nanotechnology (a neat paradox) could dematerialize paper manufacture. Along with new water-management techniques, and subtractive rather than additive electronic methods, such innovations might make printing sustainable.[68]

## SALVAGE AND WASTE

As we saw in the preceding chapter, corporations and governments in the Global North dispatch e-waste hazards to other countries, deliberately globalizing a problem that is always already trans-territorial, because its impact on air, water, and land transcends its origins. Greenpeace estimates that 75 percent of e-waste is "disappeared" via inadequate or illegal salvage. The 1992 Basel Convention on the Control of Transboundary Movements of Hazardous Wastes and Their Disposal prohibits international transportation of hazardous material, even between non-signatories of the accord (such as the United States) and signatories (such as Mexico). But powerful polluters like Japan, Canada, and the United States engage in "venue shopping," seeking out dumping grounds wherever feasible (in 2010, it cost approximately $5000 to ship a forty-foot container of e-waste from the United States to Africa). They justify such actions on a neoliberal basis, invoking doctrines of comparative advantage and the notion that every nation has a certain amount of e-waste it can bear.[69]

In 2008, the US Government Accountability Office (GAO) reported that the United States had done virtually nothing to impede illegal and harmful exports apart from laxly enforcing bans on exporting CRTs. GAO operatives "posed as foreign buyers" in search of the tubes. Forty-three US corporations offered to sell them, and just one bothered to submit the forms required of such recyclers. The office monitored two e-commerce trading sites for three months and found 1.3 million CRTs exchanged between the United States and the rest of the world. Experts say that a vastly bigger trade is enacted in secret. In 2010, the British government announced charges flowing from its biggest-ever investigation into illegal e-waste exports to West Africa by companies and individuals. Criminal Intelligence Service Canada is seeking to control a thriving illegal trade disposing of electronic waste alongside the country's other global organized crime. And the EU's European Waste Shipment Regulation licenses e-waste exporters, traders, dealers, and brokers. Everything sold abroad must be certified as functioning.[70]

While workplace and environmental hazards abound in media production, the need for global media policy based on principles of environmental justice is most evident in e-waste. The experience of China, a major player in the entire life cycle of electronic technologies, is illustrative. A typical trajectory is for computers made there to be sold, used, and discarded in Australia; disassembled in the Philippines; sent back to China for partial reassembly; then returned to Australia for the extraction of valuable metals. Because imports of e-waste have been illegal in China since 1996, there are no official figures on the amount being smuggled into the country's informal e-waste recycling economy, but estimates range from one to fifteen million tons annually. Enforcement and data are similarly inexact in the case of India. Banning the illegal e-waste salvage business will require multilateral policy and enforcement, with the costs of administration, enforcement, health care, and other forms of remediation paid by the corporations responsible. No single nation can ensure effective ripostes to this trade in disease. China introduced new regulations in 2011 that may make a difference, in concert with those listed above.[71]

In addition to the Basel Convention, RoHS and WEEE are significant protocols that restrict corporate "freedoms." RoHS limits the use of carcinogenic metals and compounds (lead, mercury, cadmium, and hexavalent chromium) and fire retardants that endanger humans and wildlife (polybrominated biphenyls and polybrominated diphenyl ethers). The WEEE accord, introduced in 2002 and due for full implementation in 2011 after several postponements, involves national and local authorities, producers, distributors, consumers, treatment operators, recyclers, collectors, transport, and "producer responsibility organizations" that police corporations. It is meant to eliminate e-waste, or at least ensure that whatever cannot be eliminated is recycled in an ecologically sound manner. In allocating responsibility to producers, WEEE follows a regulated-market logic, in that an incentive is created for manufacturers to design and make ICT/CE with an eye to downstream residues.[72]

Although some costs of e-waste collection are to be paid by municipalities, WEEE is largely financed by electric- and electronic-equipment producers, including EU-based manufacturers and resellers of imported and own-brand equipment. This doctrine of "extended producer responsibility" (EPR) requires producers to take responsibility for end-of-life management of their products, thus internalizing the environmental costs of inefficient and wasteful design that were once treated as "negative externalities" in the electronics sector. Although costs paid by producers are initially transferred to consumers in the price of electronic equipment, EPR encourages new designs that cost less to collect, treat, and recycle. Similar schemes have been mandated across other parts of Europe, such as in Switzerland, Norway, and the Baltic States, as well as South Korea, Taiwan, and Japan. It perhaps goes without saying that the United States has no national legislation of this kind. Fortunately, the EU is big and wealthy, so its confident movement into regulating hazardous goods and services should punch big holes in an already-tattered neoliberal doctrine.[73]

The WEEE and RoHS directives promise to reshape e-waste management within the EU and in countries where manufacturers produce electronic equipment for the European market. They envisage implementation benefiting the EU as well as non–European residents affected by e-waste flowing illegally from the region. However, a number of practical problems emerged during the initial years of the WEEE Directive. One difficulty has been how to measure waste that disappeared because it was either tossed into bins as garbage or resold illegally in the global e-waste salvage market. Raising consumer awareness might improve e-waste recycling at home. But to confront increased pollution caused by the global e-waste business, major changes in the political-economic system would be needed to make illegal trade also unprofitable, starting in the biggest source of revenue, the United States.

Other problems have occurred as unanticipated side effects of RoHS. RoHS bars the use of cadmium in battery production and prohibits the transport of cadmium outside the EU. These policies caused a rise in production of other battery types, provoking a shift of most nickel-cadmium battery production to China. In Jiangsu Province in 2007, twenty battery workers were diagnosed with cadmium poisoning in a factory contracted by a US company to make nickel-cadmium batteries for the Japanese multinational Panasonic. The manufacturer had used the NIDL because "no one in the United States wanted to deal with the waste from cadmium," which Japan also prohibits.[74] As this example demonstrates, important advances in environmental protection can be hindered by failures to address inequities in the NIDL. In such cases, policies must embrace principles of environmental justice and human rights on a global scale in order to transform the structural conditions of ICT/CE production, consumption, and the end of life-cycle operations. An ecologically sound policy would ensure that OEMs create "*closed-loop* supply chains," such that the original supply chain maximizes reutilization of materials via refurbishment, cannibalization of spare parts, and remanufacturing.[75]

## ICT/CE AND NETWORKS

By 2009, radiation from ICT/CE had become the focus of increasing concern; in particular EMFs emitted by cell phones and other wireless electronic equipment. As we pointed out in chapter 1, scientific studies have linked long-term exposure to cell-phone radiation to two types of brain cancer (glioma and acoustic neuroma), salivary-gland tumors, migraines, vertigo, and behavioral problems in children. This research led health agencies throughout Europe to issue warnings about cell-phone radiation exposure and prompted EU lawmakers to discuss new legislation that would require lower radiation for cell phones. Regulators in a number of European countries have recommended caution to adult users and in most cases extreme caution for children, pending ongoing research. Taking this precautionary principle further, the French Senate proposed legislation to ban cell phone use by children under six as well as related advertising directed to children under the age of twelve.[76] The European Parliament's resolution on "health concerns associated with electromagnetic fields" (INI/2008/2211) affirmed the potential risks of EMFs from a range of wireless electronic devices, including Wi-Fi/WiMAX, Bluetooth, and cordless landline phones. This resolution also called for governmental oversight of scientific research and campaigns to educate citizens on precautions, including safe techniques for using electronics and how to avoid exposure to EMFs, for example, by using maps to avoid transmission towers and high-voltage power lines.

At the intergovernmental level, the International Commission on Non-Ionizing Radiation Protection has appealed for public policy to set limits on "simultaneous exposure" to multiple EMF-emitting devices. The European Environment Agency followed up a major scientific review by the Bioinitiative Working Group of radiation from Wi-Fi, cell phones, and masts by announcing in 2007 that immediate action was needed lest the latest fad end up as damned for its health impact as lead and tobacco were in the previous century. Even the OECD promoted EPR and acknowledged the risk of electing to "target a single point in the chain" and put eco-ethical responsibility on consumers alone. Meanwhile, the FCC had "all but ignored evidence that long term cell phone use may be risky."[77]

Humans are not the only creatures imperiled by this technology. As we have noted, wildlife is poisoned by toxic emissions, and communication towers and wires kill birds, affecting over two hundred species.[78] The United States has guidelines regulating placement and size of communication structures, many of which overlap with zoning rules that prohibit communication towers from being built in protected habitats, wildlife refuges, historic or heritage locations, or near places where children play or attend school. Such ecologically sound policies rarely arise from a green consensus in which bureaucrats willingly embrace the principle of a bird's right to exist, which is guaranteed by a number of international agreements that protect migratory birds and endangered species.

There is evidence that global accords are poor safeguards given the impact of EMFs on wildlife and lax human enforcement of protections of other species. For example, when experienced media companies seek to erect communication towers with stabilizing guy wires and aerial power and communication lines, they experience little friction from regulatory agencies because of their skill in minimally meeting criteria set out in national environmental policies. An added problem for the birds is that regulators may not be on their side. As we have seen, the Telecommunications Act of 1996 mandated the acceleration of tower construction. Its neoliberal framework barred "states and local governments, explicitly or effectively, from imposing unreasonable" regulation on the growth of cellular and other mobile services.[79] When the American Bird Conservancy and the Forest Conservation Council took the FCC to court over the way it authorized these communication towers, the DC Court of Appeals found that the Commission had failed to abide by key environmental laws. The decision enhanced the capacity to challenge the FCC on the basis of environmental law and procedure, but it took dedicated citizen action to make these bureaucrats do their job.[80] Of course, this is far more significant than a domestic US matter because birds are the most experienced and determined of globalizers, with boundaries set by geography rather than sovereignty.

## CONCLUSION

> We have no idea, now, of who or what the inhabitants of our future might be. In that sense, we have no future. Not in the sense that our grandparents had a future, or thought they did. Fully imagined cultural futures were the luxury of another day, one in which "now" was of some greater duration. For us, of course, things can change so abruptly, so violently, so profoundly, that futures like our grandparents' have insufficient "now" to stand on. We have no future because our present is so volatile. ... We have only risk management. The spinning of the given moment's scenarios. (Hubertus Bigend, founder of the Blue Ant advertising agency [(another brilliant fiction concocted by William Gibson, 2003, 57])

Civil society adopts and adapts policies issued by bureaucrats working in large governmental and corporate organizations. So it is vital that bureaucrats comprehend the global scale of environmental decline and hazards caused by human ambition to create ever-expanding systems of ICT/CE, no matter how awe inspiring. It is a positive sign that parts of the business sector have pursued strategies and design innovations in response to the crisis we have outlined, rather than denying its existence. The smart-design economy appears to promote ethical electronic consumption, greening inputs and production processes, and disposing of electronic gadgets responsibly. And there is clearly a link between attempts to counter the economic crisis and the struggle against global warming through publicly funded programs that shift investment to renewable sources of energy generation such as solar, wind, and biomass and reduce energy consumption by retrofitting buildings.[81] But, thus far, the largest-scale activity has been in reducing the electricity consumption that powers ICT/CE, though in this case innovations might be losing ground to the rebound effect in which energy savings are either negative or lower than expected. Meanwhile, major energy and media-technology firms are positioning themselves with state aid to dominate the global smart-design economy, offering services that claim to green energy consumption while protecting profit growth and shoring up barriers of entry to competitors in alternative-energy generation.

And as we have seen, greenwashing "astroturf" shenanigans abound, making much ICT/CE self-regulation a dubious affair. The GeSI Supply Chain Working Group and the Electronic Industry Code of Conduct, for example, seek to ward off international legislation and enforcement by proclaiming the industry's capacity to regulate itself through the "good governance" mantra, which proved so successful as business rhetoric until the recent financial crisis. Likewise, the *Smart2020 Report* was produced by a front organization for Deutsche Telekom, Cisco, T-Mobile, Intel, Vodafone, and other firms keen to influence and create international policy. Seemingly ubiquitous, it has been endorsed by Infosys, the California EPA, the UN Environment Programme, the China Development Research Foundation, and the China Mobile Communications Corporation. The report tells us that travel, work, and electricity will all diminish their carbon impact, thanks to the benign businesses that paid for and backed up the report.[82] The limiting factor to these business strategies is their proponents' profit motive and desire to avoid the democratic controls of public policy and regulation, plus the fact that national legislation is difficult to coordinate across jurisdictions.

From the Left, the Institute for Sustainable Development outlines strategies for using ICT to create sustainable development and ameliorate poverty levels in South Africa, Kenya, Costa Rica, Brazil, and Egypt. Since 1994, the ITU has also called for an "increasing role" for ICT in monitoring climate change and natural disasters, communicating information to those affected via collaboration with the World Meteorological Organization's World Weather Watch, and reducing business travel through teleconferencing. As of now, however, the policy calculus for dealing with e-waste takes as a *sine qua non* that there are "three dimensions of sustainability: people, planet, and profit."[83]

If we are to press an ethico-political orientation into policy discussions on the environmental impact of ICT/CE, it must be without the pretensions of risk managerialism and CBA. The next chapter begins this effort with an examination of alternative, citizen-based notions of green governance.

# CHAPTER 6

✺

# Citizens

The ecological crisis reveals the urgent moral need for a new solidarity, especially in relations between the developing nations and those that are highly industrialized.
—Pope John Paul II, 1989

We envision a toxic-free future, where each new generation of technical improvements in electronics products includes parallel and proportional advances in social and environmental justice. Our goal is environmental sustainability and clean production, improved health, and democratic decision making for communities and workers most affected by the high-tech revolution.
—Silicon Valley Toxics Coalition, 111[1]

As I've said many times, the future is already here—it's just not very evenly distributed.
—William Gibson, 1999

In the beginning of this book, we examined the challenges of green-media consumption at individual and institutional levels. While preserving an important role for green consumers imbued with eco-ethical defenses against technophilia, we have shown in subsequent chapters that the project of greening the media must be scaled to match the level of ICT/CE responsibility for the eco-crisis. From a political-economic perspective, the biggest problems of eco-ethical consumption do not begin at home, and hence cannot be addressed conclusively at that level. Absent an ongoing fabric of democratic control, consumer activism will always be an irritant rather than a counter to corporate destructiveness. For one thing, "consumer democracy" gives the wealthy more votes than the poor. Most First World activists are affluent and highly educated, so the practice ironically mirrors the unrepresentative plutocracies of the International Monetary Fund and the World Bank. The impact on, and inclusion of, working people in such actions is frequently problematic. Boycotts and buycotts require high levels of organization and sustained commitment, and they often end with apparent success, only for corporations to resume polluting activities in a quietly efficient manner.[2]

The eco-crisis clearly necessitates an international political undertaking that is aimed not just at rethinking media consumption but also at pushing media production toward the ecologically sound deployment of resources and labor. To that end, we propose a new understanding of green citizenship, defined as a shared commitment to confront the eco-crisis and press for greener governance through media policy. As we will see, this commitment can inform local duties within a green-ruled workplace as well as global obligations to counter systemic environmental harms through radical critique, organization, and resistance. Each form of citizenship can effect policy changes at varying scales of need—from enabling domestic and local initiatives of recycling and green infrastructure, to research and advocacy for environmental justice and the protection of biophysical rights of all inhabitants. And, where necessary, forms of direct action can be deployed to confront powerful forces intolerant of scientific and popular demands for new political and economic conditions that serve the Earth. In one way or another, all forms of green citizenship outlined here work against the unsustainable pursuit of growth in ICT/CE businesses.

Preceding chapters have examined the material properties of media technologies in order to draw attention to the environmental impact of their production, consumption, and disposal. We have shown how the global reach of ICT/CE systemically links bureaucrats, miners, electrical engineers, maquiladora workers, e-waste handlers, technophiles, and green-conscious consumers, among others.

This chapter explores the political commitments of environmental citizenship along this international division of labor, from local forms of citizenship to those that transcend national borders, seeking to enact or influence global green governance. In the first section, we examine some underlying contradictions of environmental citizenship, which are linked primarily to the porous foundation of the national, or territorial, citizen. The next section proposes what a universal notion of environmental citizenship might look like and describes key characteristics of three forms of green citizenship that are emergent today: *environmental citizenship*, which is tied to institutional behaviors in green-ruled organizations (schools, workplaces, and movie studios, for example); *sustainability citizenship*, which promotes advocacy and research predicated on the interconnectedness of people, eco-systems, and generations; and *resistance citizenship*, which takes the forms of protest and direct action aimed at greening institutional practices and state policies.[3] Then we revisit our chapter on bureaucrats with a summary of existing and potential forms of green governance to regulate ICT/CE production, consumption, and disposal. The chapter will show that while green citizenship and green governance are ascendant, they still have some distance to travel before they can move polities and the ICT/CE processes they govern into a greener world.

We end with a speculative account of what could happen if the ideal green citizen emerged in the near future to take on business-as-usual. We have selected the unlikely figure of the accountant—a bureaucrat—to provide the basic DNA for this green citizen, because in existing media organizations, bookkeepers are privy to the environmental costs of media production. For this accountant of the future, we have created an approxi-mate world synthesized from the analysis and arguments presented in this book. In our scenario, accountants of the future draw on environmental and union activism, scholarship, and public policy to free themselves from the bonds of business-as-usual in movie studios or site-specific shoots. The new accountants' odyssey leads to illuminating and frustrat-ing encounters with the international political economy, which transform their perception of green media and how to measure it. As these future accountants are challenged by ecological questions that cannot neces-sarily be answered by measurement alone, greener media are envisioned. The chapter ends there, and we take up the threads in the general conclu-sion that follows.

## CONTRADICTIONS OF GREEN CITIZENSHIP

Across the nineteenth century and most of the twentieth, businesses and governments shared an instrumental, acquisitive, "productive" orientation toward the environment, leaving virtually no room for the concerns, the-ories, and experiences of conservationists, native populations, or slaves. Nonhuman nature was deemed to obstruct nation building and profit mak-ing. Like labor, it was to be overcome, controlled, fetishized, and exploited: the drive and skill to generate new commodities were matched only by the passion and capacity to raze anything in their way.[4] Managerial efficiency depended on the domination of labor and nature and gained legitimacy from a largely unchallenged growth narrative that said all new and good things must be built by pillaging the old: "free" resources of land, forests, air, and water.

A rare counter-discourse of the nineteenth century was "settler environmentalism," a variant of conservationism that idealized colonial Edens. In the twentieth century, we find examples of environmental-activist groups led by women, such as the US Progressive-Era reformers and conservationists, who promoted "municipal housekeeping" of clean air, soil, and water, alongside the struggles of such workers as the US "Radium Girls" of 1927. The Radium Girls died from cancer within a few years of filing suit against their employers, but their example taught the public to beware the atom and distrust radiation (in this case, the use of radium for faddish glow-in-the-dark watch dials, though it was also widely promoted in cosmetics). The idea of saving the national patrimony gained influence in the same period. People considered questions of environmental heritage and legacy—thinking backward and forward rather than just contemporaneously. When tied to chauvinistic campaigns of "blood and soil," however, this nascent environmental citizenship was easily co-opted by nationalist movements steeped in racism and xenophobia. Extreme examples of the "greening of hate" include Nazi Germany's pairing of a pure nonhuman natural world with the genocidal program of ethnic cleansing.[5] We can find similar attempts in the twenty-first century to mobilize environmental citizenship in the name of racial purity: Consider such anti-Mexican groups as Californians for Population Stabilization and the Federation for American Immigration Reform, with its loathsome *Environmentalist's Guide to a Sensible Immigration Policy*.[6] In Britain and France, environmental arguments have also been appropriated by the Right, as the British National Party and the Groupement de Recherche et d'Études pour la Civilisation Européene [research and study group on European civilization] argue against development and on behalf of wildlife and national tradition as a means of humanizing themselves to voters. Migrationwatch UK also opposes immigration on environmental grounds.[7]

Internationalist versions of environmental citizenship were similarly fraught. Basic notions of citizenship were often seen as cultural forms of imperialism, when Washington began exporting citizenship to the rest of the world in the 1940s and '50s. The idea was to build strong national political and legal institutions and robust civil societies in Western Europe and ensure that the decolonizing world did not embrace Maoism or Marxism-Leninism. These ideological exports were compromised by critiques in the 1960s and '70s that charged the United States with being narcissistic, militaristic, and blind to the history of governmental and commercial powers annexing states and their labor forces—not to mention its Pollyannaish misrecognition of civil society in its own racially divided, patriarchal home. The idea of citizenship was unpopular with the international Left, other than in the terms sought by movements of anti-colonialist liberation.

By the end of the twentieth century, traditional political allegiances of once-formidable opposition forces to US models were splintering. The international Left was questioned for seeing class position as the principal axis of social suffering and historical transformation. Marxists were criticized by feminists and Third Worldists. The collapse of dictatorship in Latin America and state socialism in Europe, and the emergence of capitalism in China, challenged actually existing fascism and leftism and explanations of them. And feminists who posited a uniform female experience confronted critiques from women of color, lesbians, the Global South, and the working class, who pointed to differentiated gender relations, strategic alliances with subjugated men, and multi-perspectival notions of oppression. Newly established constituencies and emerging identities seeking representation and political franchise found citizenship's focus on the "common good" to be a safe haven, especially in forms that enabled social justice. Environmental justice and sustainability crossed lines of class, race, gender, interregional, and intergenerational difference.[8]

Unsurprisingly, right-wing ideologues and neoliberal policy makers attacked the notion of citizenship predicated on the common good. They denied the existence of a common good and posited in its place a world of deserving haves and slothful have-nots in which aggregate wealth accumulation benefited the general public. The erroneous reasoning and political opportunism behind this position have been well documented: there is no magical market mechanism that ensures the trickle down of wealth from the haves to the have-nots; the claim that publicly funded welfare programs inhibit "opportunities" and "efficiencies" for wealth creation is false and masks the reality that the gap between rich and poor has grown, not lessened, as government programs aimed at improving general well-being, or the common good, have been slashed. The corollary claim that taxing capital and corporations is inefficient and debilitating in a capitalist society has proven to be a scam to shift the tax burden from the rich to the poor, while an enormous tax-avoidance industry, sometimes called "wealth management," creates massive inefficiency and further trickle-up outcomes.[9] In most versions of this worldview, correcting the social harm of market failure—exemplified in our study by what economists call "externalities" like toxic waste, pollution, and anthropogenic climate change—is not the responsibility of corporations, and only minimally of governments. These phenomena are regarded as unavoidable costs that attend to wealth creation. Again, the present is all that matters; future generations must fend for themselves.

Other political-economic shifts that have enhanced green citizenship's standing include the intensification of globalization, regional trading blocs, globally-oriented cities with supranational ambitions, international media markets, and conflicting religious relations. These developments have helped remove citizenship from the narrow confines of the sovereign state and link it to universal rights and responsibilities. In the context of environmental citizenship, these rights include clean air, water, and land and healthy biological processes, whereas green responsibilities focus on the care of ecosystems, inhabitants, and the Earth's wellbeing.[10] This changing political economy has been challenged by right-wing nationalists pressing for environmentally tinged protections that are racist and chauvinist, neoliberal economists arguing for the "logic" of dumping First-World waste into the poorest regions of the planet, and recalcitrant governments claiming sovereignty protections for their polluting industries. Some Third Worldists regard concerns about the environment as crypto-colonialist. From their point of view, anxiety about climate change is an alibi for shutting down development in the Global South. And the minuscule Far Left fears that eco-panic might be a last, desperate post–Cold War lunge for money by the remnants of "big science."

Despite these critics, green citizenship has continued its ascent, as noted in our chapter on consumers. Along with expanded environmental activism has come the growing influence of green citizenship and governance, expressed in claims for public rights to clean air, soil, and water that supersede the private needs of industry; responsibilities for the environment that transcend national boundaries and state interests; and the espousal of intergenerational caring rather than policies that discount the health and value of future generations.[11]

These are hopeful signs that the neoliberal era would end up being a brief, if traumatic and destructive, moment of mismanaging the Earth during a half century that otherwise saw an ever-stronger environmentalism. It was indeed a remarkable symbolic coincidence that 1989 saw the Berlin Wall demolished at the same time as the first major congresses on planetary ecological survival were being convened in France, Britain, and the Netherlands, and the slow-food movement was emerging in Italy: at the very moment of its victory, market liberalism's dominance was compromised. The environmental side-effects of unhindered, globalized growth were recognized as unsustainable aspects of progress.[12]

## FORMS OF GREEN CITIZENSHIP

Green citizenship introduces anthropocentric eco-ethical aspirations into the global public sphere to counter the environmental despoliation that threatens human life. Still, as the experience of mainstream environmentalism shows, a human-centered focus has the possibility of being tilted toward concerns with the risks to nonhuman nature posed by the mounting ecological crisis. This allows a number of influences to shape the environmental politics of green citizenship—Left eco-centrism and eco-feminism as well as technocratic, anthropocentric forms. The pluralization of environmental citizenship opens up possible points of alliance at which political commitments to greening the media might converge.[13]

We can map green citizenship over the three zones of citizen rights posited within the liberal-democratic tradition: *political citizenship*, which confers the right to reside and vote on territorial terms; *economic citizenship*, which allocates the right to work and prosper; and *cultural citizenship*, which grants the right to know and speak. These rights correspond to the French Revolutionary cry "Liberté, égalité, fraternité" [liberty, equality, solidarity] and the Argentine Left's contemporary version "Ser ciudadano, tener trabajo, y ser alfabetizado" [citizenship, employment, literacy]. Each form of citizenship has assumed the capacity to appeal to national jurisdictions, but as we have seen, national boundaries and interests are brought into question by the border-crossing reality of ecosystem welfare and the impact of environmental despoliation. More than an addition to the rights of territorially based citizenship, green citizenship is a critique of them, a corrective that looks to saving infrastructure, ecosystems, and heritage from capitalist growth—a stand taken as early as 1739 when Franklin argued that "public rights" over Philadelphia's air and water should supersede the private rights of industry. Greening these rights extends green governance to cover policy, work, and communication channels. Green citizenship also introduces the right to biophysical health—a right to a body free from dangerous biotoxins.[14]

Green citizenship has a different perspective on civil-republican notions of citizen duties too. Examples of such duties include collective support of ecologically sound regulations that protect the right of workers to enjoy safe working conditions or vote on environmental matters, as opposed to leaving it up to governments and corporate "experts" to decide. Green citizenship would suggest that if an individual were accorded the right to biophysical health, this would be matched by everyone else's green obligation not to poison ecosystems, food chains, and so on. Bypassing localism and contemporaneity to enter the sphere of universal and future obligations, the responsibilities claimed by green citizenship transcend conventional political economic space and time, extending beyond the here and now toward a globally sustainable ecology. Green citizenship looks generations ahead, refusing to discount the health and value of future ecosystems and opposing elemental risks created by capitalist growth in the present.[15]

The environmental rights and responsibilities sketched here emerge in workplace policies, industrial codes of conduct, and national, regional, and global regulations. All scattershot. As we saw in the previous chapter, CBA and other risk-management tools constrain the ability of bureaucracies to meet most challenges of the eco-crisis, in particular the interconnected and intergenerational scope of environmental problems facing the planet. Conventional economic models omit the environmental and human costs incurred by toxic chemicals, fossil-fuel energy consumption, plastics, and pollution across the supply chains and life cycles of media technologies. In this primitive state, green citizenship has been subordinated to economic citizenship, which places environmental welfare outside the economic system. Crucial externalities do not "count" when growth serves as virtually the sole index of human well-being.[16] Also unaccounted for is the social impact of the anxiety and frenzy that accompany acquisitive individualism. The dictum "more is better" recapitulates the growth logic within not only economic citizenship but its political and cultural variants as well: to advance democracy, media channels must proliferate; to prosper, ICT/CE must be ubiquitous; to enhance pleasure, media technology must spread far and wide; there must be more outlets, more proprietors, more publics, more social networking, more use, more discourse. Economic citizenship must be modified to provide a creative basis for green citizenship.

One way to start would be to add environmental assets and costs into welfare accounts of prosperity and plenitude. Such environmental bookkeeping could improve the prospects for economic citizenship to claim rights to biophysical health, safe working conditions, and the like, transforming it into greener forms.[17] There are already methods of environmental accountancy that push for more accurate measures of the value added to national economies from environmental source-and-sink functions.[18] But the prevailing norms leave environmental and human "expenses" off the books, with net revenues tallied up to measure growth in media and technology markets, adding to the illusion that these sectors are ecologically benign drivers of economic expansion. Were we to consider ecological and human liabilities as vital financial information, green accounting would reveal "fictitious incomes and real costs that haven't been reckoned with yet," demonstrating the need for sustainability and regulated limits to growth. Such write-downs to correct accounts for environmental liabilities could further discredit the growth ideology fueling business-as-usual in ICT/CE.[19]

Economic citizenship can be further greened through institutional forms of *environmental citizenship* that set out rules to engage people in green practices within schools, neighborhoods, housing, workplaces, offices, and other settings.[20] Examples include the thousand US communities with electronics-collection services, the six-hundred colleges across Canada and the United States involved in the Campus Climate Challenge to make their schools carbon neutral, and the companies looking to send workable second-hand computers to Africa for re-use rather than recycling, via such agents as Computers for Schools Kenya and Digital Links International. We can also count industrial-workplace changes that force employees to alter their routines: Britain's BT has diminished carbon emissions by 58 percent in the decade since it began measuring such things. Telefónica, the dominant telecommunications force across much of Latin America, Africa, and Europe, has a climate-change office charged with reducing workplace electricity use by 10 percent and network use by 30 percent by 2015. NTT Communications in Japan and Britain's Vodafone Group Plc have similar goals.[21]

Environmental citizenship is emerging in serious ways across the US, Japanese, and European culture industries. Workers are being urged to follow environmentally sound practices on the job and in their non-work time as well. As we saw in chapter 3, major movie studios have programs that reduce paper use, lighting, communication, and heating costs and wasteful construction and disposal practices, including managing chemicals and hazardous materials; and their bookkeeping rules raise employee awareness of individual environmental impacts. These developments encourage environmental citizenship, even though the cultural industries came late to the realization that a slash-and-burn attitude to the environment was unsustainable.

Although these forms of environmental citizenship are important for shaping eco-ethical attitudes and routines among media workers, bureaucrats, and consumers, they are part-time commitments that do not cultivate a holistic understanding of the global scale of the eco-crisis and media and ICT/CE's role in it. An emergent form of green citizenship presses beyond these institutional limits: *sustainability citizenship*, which Barry describes as a critique of the "underlying structural causes of environmental degradation and other infringements of sustainable development such as human rights or social justice."[22]

We have already provided examples of groups whose actions represent sustainability citizenship: The students and professors at SACOM exposed corporate malfeasance when they went undercover to document life at Foxconn.[23] Activists in Latin America successfully mobilized on behalf of ragpickers' citizenship rights. In 2009, Colombia's constitutional court ruled that cooperatives of ragpickers were legal businesses, thus permitting them to bid for waste-management concessions from local government. That decision initially elevated the status of *recicladores*, decriminalized their actions, and protected their livelihood. Colombian activists have had to fight a subsequent reversal in state policy that marginalized the cooperatives by various means including criminalizing the opening of trash bags, a common method of sorting available to those without the capital to operate collection trucks. Sustainability citizenship in this context champions the poorest of the *reciladores* who seek means to participate competitively in Colombia's $2.5 billion waste market, which is dominated by five large private corporations, one of which is owned by the president's sons.[24] California-based ragpickers were pioneers in establishing cooperatives and held the world's first global conference of their fellow workers in 2008, including Brazilian ragpickers, whose work is now recognized by the labor ministry.[25]

Another example of sustainability citizenship is SVTC's campaign against toxic electronics, begun in the 1980s, a signal moment in the struggle to challenge the ICT/CE "clean-industry myth." Activists, public-health advocates, workers, and policy makers exposed the environmental impact of the electronics, electrical, and energy industries in Silicon Valley and elsewhere.[26] A founding member of SVTC, Ted Smith, offers further instances of sustainability citizenship:

> Community and worker based movements began to emerge in other countries—PHASE II in Scotland, Asia Monitor Resource Centre in Hong Kong, TAVOI in Taiwan, CEREAL in Mexico, etc. as the grassroots efforts began to grow into a global movement. Many of these groups are now working together internationally through various networks to develop worker training on occupational health and safety, to clean up and prevent air and water pollution, to press the electronics industry to phase out use of the most toxic chemicals.[27]

Sustainability citizenship works around the globe to monitor, analyze, and publicize dangerous environmental practices, including poisonous waste and workplace hazards in ICT/CE production and disposal. Involvement cultivates a broader view of the interconnections between sectors, workers, institutions, and the bureaucrats who people them. This form of green citizenship is exemplified by SVTC, BAN, CEREAL, SACOM, and other organizations we have mentioned. Their work is all the more laudable for having faced sizeable political-economic obstacles in their fight to ensure that electronic technology is built on ecologically sound principles. Their struggle to clear the air of misinformation has weakened the ideological effect of media technologies, the clean-industry myth, and the symbolic power of ICT/CE that clouds understanding in a technological sublime.

Complementing sustainability citizenship, but going beyond it to use confrontational tactics to expose the environmental impact of media technologies, groups like Greenpeace have engendered a third form: green *resistance citizenship*.[28] There are many well-known examples of such direct action: Greenpeace mounted a major protest in 2009 against HP, a leading manufacturer of computer and printing technology, because the company had postponed from 2009 to 2011 its commitment to phase out brominated flame retardants and PVC plastics, which can release carcinogenic dioxin when burned. With safe children's paint, activists drew an 11,500-square-foot message on the rooftop of HP's headquarters in Palo Alto that read "Hazardous Products." In addition to the graffito, automated phone calls recorded by William Shatner to employees protested HP's failure to abide by its undertakings. His phone message spoke directly to workers from a consumer's perspective that was also an activist's one. He even perorated politely: "Wishing you an enjoyable day."[29]

Greenpeace's direct, spectacular action deployed the power of celebrity culture, with a *Star Trek* hero as its pitchman. In a highly ironized way, Shatner parodied his own *persona* as a lapsed Shakespearian, ageing idol, and ponderous spoken-word performer. At another level, the action borrowed from political spectacle by trespassing in order to deface the bland but seemingly secure property of a powerful corporation, demonstrating street-level (and higher!) activism. Finally, it utilized the discourse of consumerism to avow the right of users to materials that are safe for all.[30]

When Greenpeace bought a stand at the three-day Mac Expo in London in 2006, it was quickly censored—in fact shut down. But the environmental organization's "Green My Apple" campaign against Apple's appalling environmental record drew enough protestors that 2007 saw the corporation phase out many toxic substances faster than was hitherto the case and provide recycling (but only in the United States).[31] This happened right as Apple was trumpeting its new iPhone. That same year, the Chinese computer-manufacturer Lenovo, which had bought IBM's CE business two years earlier and had previously ranked poorly for its environmental practices, topped Greenpeace's table of electronic production and recycling because it offered a global buyback system for personal computers at the end of their lives.[32]

While all three forms of green citizenship tend to be overwhelmed by technocratic or corporate bureaucracies, they offer strategies for change that can be channeled to representative government. This has happened for both good and ill in environmental debates over everything from bald eagles to building codes, albeit rarely representing the interests of birds or the land.[33] Our next section examines the status and promise of green governance.

## GREEN GOVERNANCE

Because issues of green citizenship transcend both state boundaries and commercial rents, they must be managed by international organizations. This is neither new nor dissociated from national citizenship. Away from the utopic hopes of world government on a grand scale, international organizations have been working for a very long time, both quietly and noisily, to manage particular issues.[34] Their business is sometimes conducted at a national state level, sometimes through civil society, and sometimes through both. In almost every case, they encounter or create legal and political instruments that make them accountable to the popular will of sovereign states, at least in name. We saw instances of this in the previous chapter. At the same time, it is clear that national and international organizations and accords have not put a stop to environmental destructiveness.[35]

The clearest and least compromising instances of green governance seek to enhance an ethico-political commitment to the Earth and its inhabitants by making human rights subject to eco-centric values. An example can be found in articles 71–74 of the 2008 Ecuadorian Constitution, which guarantees the rights of nature, or "Pacha Mama," and the rights of citizens to demand that public authorities protect nature and sanction those who defy their constitutional obligation.[36] The Ecuadorian example is unique, in that most mainstream green governance is human centered, focused on saving lives, infrastructure, and heritage from environmental risks. This was the framework for sustainable development established by the 1987 World Commission on Environment and Development, which the 1992 Rio Declaration on Environment and Development enshrined as a human right "to a healthy and productive life." The declaration accords equivalent value to economic growth, social progress, ecological health, and, in more recent interpretations, cultural and informational sustainability.[37]

Anthropocentric governance necessitates a difficult balancing act. Despite scientific consensus that "warming of the climate system is unequivocal,"[38] the twenty leading economic powers treat climate change and other ecological hazards as one more variable of international relations, ignoring decades-old warnings about the fast-closing circle of remedies for environmental ills.[39] This is one of the most volatile contradictions of our time: whereas the interpretation of economic, social, and cultural needs is fraught with political conflict and requires negotiations at multiple scales of global governance, the "scientific prerequisites for ecological sustainability" are not a matter of political agreement or "individual values" because "nature does not conduct consensus talks."[40]

Green global governance must match the scale and variation of environmental problems caused by media technologies within and across ecosystems. This necessitates changes to the old tripartite model wherein peak councils of capital, labor, and government set policy. A green model must involve advocates for our fellow animals and other life-forms that have significance in people's lives, and make room for environmental scientists, leaders of disenfranchised minorities and indigenous communities fighting for environmental justice, and representatives of workers on worldwide assembly and recycling lines whose expertise resides outside the rule of law, an especially important condition given the low density of unionization in global factories. Without this trans-territorial concern for the biosphere and the participation of those conventionally excluded from media policy, we shall simply burn one more page in an unsustainable playbook. At this scale of governance, policies such as EPR become truly global, rather than being applied spottily within the Global North.[41]

To succeed, global efforts will depend on sovereign states adopting and administering omnibus and specialized laws that ban the harmful practices of ICT/CE sectors within national ecosystems. The interdependence of supra-state, interstate, and state governance over environmental matters can already be found in numerous policies, laws, and agreements; the EU example outlined in chapter 5 represents the most evolved instance in which states harmonize governance to meet trans-territorial aspirations. Several options can then be called upon to regulate multinational ICT/CE corporations and empower citizen action trans-territorially: "soft law [protocols of international organizations], hard law [nationally based legislation], codes of conduct [transnational norms], and voluntary self-regulation." However, as we have seen in preceding chapters, these strategies have not matched the transfer of technology with the transfer of practices for using it safely. Safe use would necessitate universal standards of health and safety across sites, from policy regimes in the Global North to those in the South, in addition to contractual deals between multinationals and their territorial hosts.[42]

The state has a further role to play: It must create conditions for green governance to be decentralized so that small-scale institutions can autonomously design and monitor sustainable practices, in particular where governmental oversight and management are neither feasible nor efficient. For example, a national government could lay out a legal framework that funds self-organized local recycling associations to monitor best practices and sanction violations by their members, which could result in greater compliance with national and international laws. Such self-organized enterprises could be developed across lower tiers of the supply chain, from mining and transport to low-value, high-volume component production. National regulation is difficult to implement in these areas, and green compliance audits by manufacturers like Apple, Dell, and HP have little influence. There would be benefits for government and ICT/CE businesses if they supported and financed enterprises at this scale of governance, at least in locales where such enterprises could flourish.[43]

As a complement to trans-territorial and state levels of green governance, this model of managing resources moves away from the monadic selfishness envisioned in such defining works as "The Tragedy of the Commons,"[44] because the evidence does not support corporate beneficence and consumer selflessness as solutions.[45] Well-organized local institutions have a higher rate of success in resource management if external laws provide for their autonomy and involve "users in their choice of regulations so that these are perceived to be legitimate" because such policies encourage organizational relationships between the enterprises and communities that share an eco-system. Relationships focused on ecologically sound resource management could be extended up and down a supply chain to involve resource users across many ecosystems to monitor what works and what fails, to eliminate harmful waste, to modify methods of resource acquisition, and to share information that increases benefits "derived from a sustainable use of local resources."[46] Research on "enclave deliberation among the disempowered" provides further evidence that decentralized, participatory governance can play a vital role in policy making, for example by generating wide agree-ment on key policy recommendations through a consensus-conference that involves community members, resource users, experts, and elites.[47] Such models transcend the now-discredited Anglo-Saxon neoliberal policy framework that has propagated the ideology of growth, favoring instead the recognition that rational outcomes may derive from a stakeholder approach to managing the commons.

## IMAGINING GREEN CITIZENSHIP FOR THE FUTURE

Thus far, we have sought to understand citizen and governance alternatives to consumer action, corporate responsibility, and government bureaucracy. We believe that green citizenship and green governance promise transfor-mative roles that can lead to a greener media that give precedence, or at least moral consideration, to the Earth and all its inhabitants. For that to happen, we need to depart from an anthropocentric eco-ethics, in both its technocratic forms and its more pragmatic and pluralistic ones, pressing the politics of green citizenship to think harder about media production, consumption, and disposal. What kinds of changes would overcome the human-centered pragmatist faced with the systemic problems of the eco-crisis we have outlined to this point? As promised, we imagine answers to this question by asking a key bureaucrat from the media industries, a fic-tional accountant, to take on the responsibility of personifying this green citizen of the future.

Why did we pick on the accountant for this experiment? In most large organizations, the accounting office operates as an informational nodal point between management and labor, particularly where the audit of material expenditures details inputs of capital and energy into production.[48] It is thus a matter of expediency to make accountants working in media firms responsible for tracking carbon emissions and other costly by-products via purchases entered into debit columns on spreadsheets. A particular set of transactions denotes carbon emitted from filmmaking and TV production—gallons of fuel, nights at hotels, feet of lumber, air miles traveled, kilowatt hours burned, and so forth. Hence, the accountant, even one with no inherent yearning to be green, has taken on a vast and growing responsibility for measuring and reporting the media's impact on the environment, thereby leading the effort to habituate employees in their roles as part-time environmental citizens. But while such green accountancy marks a salutary turn to environmentally friendly practices in the culture industries, its confinement to the site-specific budgets of individual films or studio operations diminishes its ability to assess the external environmental costs of ICT/CE and media usage.

By the early twenty-first century, studio accountants could tell you how much carbon movies typically emit: short films were said to generate 145 tons; middling shoots, 970 tons; fast and furious ones, 4,000 tons; and so on.[49] This knowledge is not used to downsize filmmaking, however, because the institutional codes of business-as-usual push such information into the service of profit, which means that if dirty air can be quantified, it will be monetized. Ethics are just another word for nothing left to regulate. Enter the market for carbon offsets (indexed to a firm's reduction of carbon dioxide and other greenhouse gas emissions) in which organizations seek investment for green innovation or buy credits to plant trees or fund someone else's green company. Carbon offsets serve as the primary currency paid by or to a media firm to cover environmental behavior.

This bureaucratic arrangement limits the scope of environmentally sound production practices in the culture industries, because whatever can't be counted also can't be included in the accountant's impact assessment; for example, material or labor costs outside the production sites overseen by accounting or supply chains that are upstream or downstream of creative productions. Accountants know the price of electricity and phone calls but cannot include an audit of carbon emissions generated by their suppliers in the energy and telecommunications sectors. They know how much hazardous waste a film or TV shoot produces but have no way to tally and monetize off-site environmental emissions from recycling, incineration, long-haul transport, or the costs associated with dumping dangerous waste into landfills. Working conditions, resource materials, and other inputs beyond local production are not among the green accountant's line items. It doesn't help matters that existing environmental accountancy focuses entirely on natural resources as an asset in general economic-welfare accounts.[50] One study from 2010 said that even "*estimating* waste flows is not an easy task ... [and] has to be determined on the basis of often scarce information."[51] Another investigation from the same period worried that existing "accountancy rules, purchasing policies and reporting standards do not consistently require attention to environmental externalities—including social costs due to impacts on ecosystems and biodiversity."[52]

In order to implement an accounting system that is adequate to the global scale of an ideal green-media accountancy, a new kind of accountant is needed to take the virtue of accountancy's *modus operandi*—count everything!—and dedicate it to finding out how cultural labor and the environment connect beyond the gates of the studio. In our fictional account, a different sort of accountancy will materialize. This is that story, told before it happens.[53]

· · ·

Accountants of the future will begin by identifying international flows of toxic materials, inter-sectorial and trans-border carbon emissions, and other environmental harms that accompany ICT/CE production and labor worldwide. Their first shock will be the scale of the problem they face. There appear initially to be tens of millions of workers in the world's ICT sector alone, with the numbers growing in accordance with the NIDL.[54] As they search for information on these workers, the accountants of the future will run up against obstacles erected by Right-wing nationalist polities and global business lobbies who work to obscure workplace and environmental data. Media owners will justify their stance with a mixture of legal arguments about proprietary information, business freedom, and respect for national sovereignty (the Chinese owners being most adamant, deploying sovereignty arguments to protect illegal e-waste businesses in the ecological dead zones of the Pearl and Yangtze river deltas). Faced with such powerful resistance, the accountants will be tempted to abandon their project, at which point, they will make a radical—for them—decision to turn away from traditional sources in order to form an alliance with labor unions, environmental activists, and researchers already engaged in the battle to gather accurate statistics on workers and working conditions in the global media and ICT/CE sectors. This will mark the beginning of a long revolution for the new accountancy, leading eventually to the transformation of the existing system of bookkeeping. Their goal will be to reach numerical transparency, not for the bosses but to reestablish the ties of workers (if only statistically at first) up and down the interlocking supply chains of media and ICT/CE production.[55]

Their first success will come with a systematic correction of spreadsheets in the global human-resources system, which had hitherto depicted occupational extremes between a total system of surveillance of workers and those "disappeared" from the rosters. For the first time, the new accountancy will include data on the number of people extracting the metals that go into electronic media devices. The new data will include biographies of a growing portion of the thirteen million people said to work in the informal mining sector in Asia, Latin America, and Africa. With the help of labor unions, nongovernmental organizations, local activists, policy-oriented journalists, and even some CSR audits and social-networking sites, the new accountancy will revise the count of ICT and media workers to find over two hundred million worldwide—a far cry from earlier estimates of seventy million.[56]

Despite constant interference and threats from corporate lawyers, the American Civil Liberties Union, company security agents, and non-independent (company) trade unions, a statistical picture will emerge that reveals organizational relationships, inter-sectorial linkages, and regional points of alliance unacknowledged by the old accountancy. Eventually, the new accountants will identify assemblages of interconnected labor in global media production and measure the impact of the chemico-mechanical processes attendant to each line of work; including, among other careers, computer scientists, engineers, designers, market researchers, miners, mineral brokers, refiners, chemists, factory laborers, server-warehouse employees, telecommunications workers, truck drivers, salespeople, office clerks, and above- and below-the-line media-production workers. Not only will the new accountants identify and count vast numbers of workers throughout the supply chain; their technique will also track emerging constituencies of workers, from elemental stages of mineral extraction to home assembly.[57]

The data will eventually disclose collective and individual stories that show the faces and struggles of real people working in the global assembly lines. The accountants of the future will try to imagine unorthodox ways to combine ecological perspectives with these biographies to find the right algorithm for measuring the environmental cost of geographical co-presence in the global assembly line. They will have no trouble budgeting for the gaffer in Hollywood eating sandwiches on biodegradable bamboo plates while on breaks from handling cables, monitors, and advanced electronics. And they will easily perceive how that gaffer relates to the teenage girl in Mexico who assembled those technologies for companies that denied her lunchtime luxuries and exposed her to toxic materials. But they will fail to find a way to enter these relationships into their calculus.

Such challenges will not stop the new accountancy from developing new methods of calculation, unknown to old green audits. To the accountant of the future, these earlier procedures appear ludicrously narcissistic, because they focused on media producers' own growth-based criteria for evaluating the economic performance of the "creative industries" (a term from the early twenty-first century that summed up the narrowness of this worldview). The old-school criteria had valued such environmentally harmful economic activities as building new electricity-guzzling server warehouses in preference to green innovations.

Scientific knowledge will pose a second major challenge to the new accountancy. The accountants of the future will have to learn about bio-thermal risks to workers and consumers exposed to human-made EMFs and scientific parameters for human tolerance to these forces. They will have to understand the basic toxicological properties of carcinogenic and noxious gases, metals, and chemicals used in ICT/CE manufacturing, unpacking a daunting array of chemical elements, synthetic compounds, and their effects on human health. These chemicals include aluminum, antimony, barium, beryllium, cesium, chromium, cobalt, copper, lead, mercury, molybdenum, nickel, platinum, silver, tin, titanium, tungsten, zinc, acidic cupric chloride, alkaline ammonia, sulfuric peroxide, argon, arsine, silane, phosphine, arsenic, selenium, polychlorinated biphenyls, trichloroethylene, ammonia, methanol, glycol ethers, methylene chloride, nonylphenols, and more.[58] For all along the international division of cultural labor, workers will have been exposed to these materials, with serious consequences for their health.

The accountants will learn that some chemicals have short-term effects, such as skin and eye irritation, headaches, vertigo, and nausea. Others are absorbed into the bloodstream over longer periods, before life-threatening disorders can be diagnosed. And there are bio-accumulative toxins that collect in workers' and consumers' fatty tissue; these flow up the food chain through land and waterways before being consumed by humans and taking up residence in their bodies. They will learn about another class of toxins called endocrine disruptors, found in many plastics, which upset normal functioning of the endocrine system by acting as if they were human hormones, leading to cancers and other problems with reproductive systems, thyroids, and metabolic rates. One of the most dramatic ways the new accountancy will find to illustrate the longevity of these pathogens in the environment will come from research on e-waste, which provides a testing ground for the effects of open exposure to the chemical and heavy-metal content in ICT/CE.[59]

The accountants of the future will determine various ways to calculate the environmental cost of toxins that outlasted the devices containing them. They will not only track the sources, volume, and destination of discarded media technologies—the e-waste of dead or obsolete computers, printers, peripherals, music players, cell phones, ink cartridges, and other tools of contemporary media production. They will learn how to quantify the environmental liabilities of e-waste's chemical legacy. This will be an important achievement, given that past methods for determining the environmental cost of toxic e-waste consisted primarily of data from sales and incomplete records of units registered for disposal.[60] The accountants will also learn how the longevity of pathogens can be quantified and entered into ledgers along with other risks associated with damages to ecosystems. The valuation will be carried out using a model that assesses ecosystem services and biophysical benefits as economic inputs. For example, they will show how multiple relevant ecosystems add value to media and ICT/CE production, from the marine and desert biomes that endow the Southern Californian climate to the ecosystems providing food, water, and housing to cultural workers worldwide. This new bookkeeping will track costs incurred when waste, poisonous by-products, or other neglectful practices devalue ecosystem services.

The new accountants will successfully use this method for short-range projections of environmental costs, but will discover that it is useless for the long-range calculations. They will realize this when they have to deal with the problem of setting a discount rate that compares the present and future costs of environmental damage. Faced with the dilemma of determining the value of ecosystem services for future generations, the new accountants will be forced to accept the impracticality of long-term projections based on conventional economic models, which assume future technological fixes reduce the cost of ecosystem repair—for example, yet-to-be discovered nano- or bio-technology that consumes plastic or neutralizes toxins. They will not like it, but they will have to give up older cost-benefit methods in order to calculate future outcomes. Unlike climate scientists, who look to the geological past to help predict changing atmospheric conditions, the accountants of the future can only offer probabilities based on political trends and business-as-usual, which produce a list of general changes in the relationships of the environment to media and ICT/CE production. And the new accountancy will not be happy with such generalities. Even if such projections alert policy makers to the importance of energy-efficient production plants, smart grid/residential metering, and abundant low-wattage entertainments, there will always be unpredictable outcomes, from scientific discoveries to catastrophic events.

The new accountancy's faith in old economic models will eventually erode as they accept that long-term cost assessment is not quantifiable. They will learn that this shortcoming results from the physical difficulty of establishing and measuring the risks faced by all planetary inhabitants.[61] This will be difficult for them, and they will attempt to fuse old quantitative and new qualitative methods through "sensitivity analysis of cost-benefit-ratios using a range of different discount rates ... to highlight different ethical perspectives and their implications for future generations."[62] Eventually, a novel kind of bookkeeping will emerge from this compromise. It will take the new accountancy into the unfamiliar realm of ecological ethics.

The eco-ethical turn will improve their ability to evaluate the interconnectedness of labor over longer periods and wider geographical distances. They will continue to count the numbers of workers everywhere, from US federal prisoners to preteen Chinese, Nigerian, and Indian girls picking apart electronics for precious metals or reusable parts.[63] But they will rely more upon qualitative thinking to pinpoint the human and environmental costs of such dangers as dust laden with toxic heavy metals from circuit boards and other components inhaled or blown afield from recycling sites or those associated with exposure to multiple sources of electromagnetic radiation. They will no longer trust in the discourse of risk management, which can only tell them how particular pathogens are allocated across populations. Their embrace of eco-ethical principles will teach them to value human and nonhuman nature alike, making it hard for them to carry on with business-as-usual. The new accountants will come to see ideas like "safe amounts" of toxins and pollution as part of a dirty ideological game, a remnant of washed-out "modernity," wherein everyday life can only progress under persistent threats to well-being. They will reevaluate the idea of "risk society," which naturalizes environmental threats using future-oriented scenarios based on a cocktail of fragile numbers and faith-based predictions. They know too well how such calculations of chance can freeze critical thinking and rouse thoughtless decisions that sustain dangerous conditions.

Ecological ethics will offer them a considerate and sensible alternative: assuming that humans are ignorant of the future effects of present-day action, they will adopt a deep regard for the natural world and act with caution rather than hubris when working on projects that place a human presence within it. The new accountancy will generate guidelines with an extremely rigorous burden of proof on media and ICT/CE producers who claim that their business strategies do not introduce dangerous substances or practices into the environment. In some cases, where there is scientific consensus about chemical-mechanical processes used in the supply chain, the approval process will be streamlined. Many progressive producers will come to embrace the "better-safe-than-sorry" environmental principle introduced by their green "bean counters." Others will resist; among them a very vocal, obstinate group of climate-change denying media owners whose self-interest is legitimized by business-school accounting methods of the 1970s. This group will be squeezed by an unlikely coalition of twenty-something and eighty-something media makers who will join in the green transformation of the global cultural industries.

This division between eco-ethical producers and business-as-usual will manifest itself in an ideological battle. The former group will promote sustainable media making. The latter will promise abundant electronic pleasures of sublime design. The business-as-usual types will have the upper hand in this war for hearts and minds and enjoy some success in fighting the spread of the new accountancy through union-busting and monopoly practices that will lock out green competition. But the sustainability coalition will grow exponentially as green alliances form across the political spectrum. Increasing numbers of media owners and policy makers will come to understand that the information, entertainment, and educational aspects of the media can still prosper within a modest revenue model based on environmental accounting and sustainable practices. The business-as-usual faction will continue to reap huge profits from selling ever-more ingenious gadgets built by suppliers in regions unregulated by green guidelines and sold in markets where environmental regulation is seen a threat to freedom, choice, and identity.

Once the new accountancy crosses the threshold toward legitimacy on a multinational scale, there will be a dramatic and immediate effect on the outlook of global business. The transformation of the bottom line by environmental accounting will create an epidemic of "write downs," which will cause green firms to operate in the red for over a decade. At first, this will boost the business-as-usual faction, which will enjoy a rush of investment from financial markets that are historically intolerant of environmentalism. This will appear to weaken the green faction, which will further suffer as business-as-usual briefly defeats it on political and economic fronts. Eventually, however, three major institutional changes will propel green practices into the forefront of a new, vibrant media economy: First, policy makers in key regions—China, India, the EU, Brazil, Canada, and Japan—will establish social funds from which green-media organizations can draw in order to invest in long-term, sustainable practices. This will counter other market pressures that favor business-as-usual. The second change will involve large conglomerates closing their worst-polluting properties or investing in resource replacement, turning formerly wasteful, toxic practices into efficient, clean operations. The debt incurred by firms will be high at first, but lower environmental costs would follow. Simple changes in chemistry and fiber resourcing, for example, will make paper production viable again. Small- to medium-sized media and ICT/CE producers will begin to buy polluting properties and transform them through available technologies funded by environmentally oriented venture capitalists. The thinking here will be that the green accountancy was right (on the money) for medium- to long-term revenue generation and that only a fool would believe that ignoring environmental costs in bookkeeping can provide lasting advantages in the marketplace.

The final change will involve the asymmetrical take-up of green products in the largest consumer markets—the EU, the United States, India, China, and Brazil—as marketers realize that the European practice of consumer education in green product quality does not diminish sales. US regulations will, of course, remain unchanged for decades, allowing a continuous flow of poisonous products to be sold there. In the EU, however, regulators will have ensured that media products and consumption are indexed to ecological enhancements, which improve the quality and lifetime of technological goods, reducing the consuming frenzy for ephemeral fashion/style in consumer goods, and underwriting EPR for electronic and electric devices. Consumers will love the result: they will have high-quality media technology built on green-service principles; brand owners will upgrade or replace devices at prices tied to changes in new components or that were paid upfront in the original purchase (most top brands in Europe would have eliminated virtually all waste and discovered designs that allowed for routine reuse of components). It will take some time for production practices throughout the supply chain to reach ecologically sustainable benchmarks, but eventually even the brands designed as well as made in China and India, both egregious polluters but early innovators in state-based green-technology, will surpass the United States in green-media production. This will happen even as the Republican and Democratic Parties cling to massive corporate agricultural subsidies, unearthly underwriting of manufacturing via their war budgets, and oxymoronic opposition to state intervention in a green economy.

Green accountancy will establish a new paradigm for ICT/CE and media economies. Institutional changes will generate a steady stream of information about successful green cultural labor and technologies, with fact-filled reports shared widely in business and government circles. But this hegemony will remain vulnerable to challenges from business-as-usual, which will persist in its ambition to end the "reign of tree huggers." This highly capitalized faction of media owners will not yield to the growing consensus on sustainability lest it ruin their empires.

As in the past, business-as-usual will rely on parallel lines of attack—mass persuasion and control over political processes—focused primarily in the United States, where it will be easiest to control political discourse and where domination of a huge consumer market will fund political ambitions. Through media and communication channels, business-as-usual propaganda will seek to convince consumers that green media-technology is a scam. Its media will depict suffering and hard-working consumers locked out of the good life by expensive green technologies, while portraying its own proponents as providing affordable electronic and electric pleasure to the downtrodden. "The green companies must think you are chumps," will be one typical retort from a business-as-usual–sponsored commentator. That rhetoric of economic self-interest will be a powerful distraction from the evidence of sustainable, successful eco-ethical practices.

The business-as-usual faction will also spend large portions of its wealth on political candidates whose campaigns spread fear of big government, foreigners, and "socialist plots" to smash freedom of choice and economic growth. This strategy will help the faction win many battles. But, in the end, their share of the market will diminish as consumers, investors, and policy makers realize that this contingent's accounting system fosters too-many costly gaps, not least the accurate measurement of environmental liabilities. Their losses will increase resentment within the remnants of the business-as-usual camp, which will retreat from politics for a time in order to regroup, form new alliances, build a war chest and a movement to win back their access to hugely profitable business and return to their old toxic ways. That's another story.

# CONCLUSION

We don't know, Mr. C.E.O, whether or not you are aware of, or tolerate the conduct of Lian Jian Technology in using this chemical [n-hexane]. If you have known about it, then this would make us very sad. It is only for this that we have given up our youthful lives and well-being to earn all but 2000 RMB [305USD] a month. If you didn't known [sic] about this, then we hope that you can step up and using a fair approach resolve this issue. When someone says that Apple products are produced at the expense of employee's health, what do you think? No matter whether you are in this country or abroad, we don't know whether your legs are like those of our poisoned workers, unable to stand firm. Maybe there are many words that you do not want to hear, perhaps there are things that you were kept in the dark about, so let us tell you now. ... When you look down at the Apple phone you are using in your hand and you swipe it with your finger is it possible that you can feel as if it is no longer a beautiful screen to show off, but the life and the blood of us employees and victims?
—Excerpt of letter from poisoned workers at Lian Jian factory, China; Institute of Public and Environmental Affairs, 2011, 31; Steve Jobs never answered

The preceding chapter ended with a speculative fictional account that imagined conditions in which green citizenship might prosper in a world whose political-economic arrangements, while not completely favorable, at least begin to address human despoliation of the Earth's ecosystems and the pernicious exploitation of ICT/CE workers. Our choice of an "accountant of the future" as an environmental hero is somewhat counterintuitive, especially in light of the accountancy fraud that enabled criminal-finance capitalists and conspiring governments to bring down the world economy in 2007–08.[1] Moreover, the hopeful scenarios in our imagined media future were conveniently disengaged from the present crisis economy, which is hardening into a new Gilded Age of wealth concentration and hyper-consumption, even in depressed markets. These developments freeze critical thinking about climate change and the means to achieve policy and public/private investment for ecologically sound economies—public transportation works, alternative energy, low-wattage entertainment, green technologies, and so on. In the United States, right-wing demagogues rail against public investment, foreign influences, climate science, and examples of how large- and small-scale human practices are reducing greenhouse-gas emissions, pollution, and toxic waste. Green design initiatives surround us as we write, but the built environment and consumer goods seem stuck in business-as-usual processes that are defined by an overwhelming passion for fossil fuels and non-biodegradable plastic.[2]

Still, our fundamentally honest bookkeeper was drawn from present practices within media firms in which accountants have become the unlikely agents of change in greening site-specific cultural production. Our call for media accounting rooted in sustainability citizenship was provoked in large part by the fact that corporations and governments in the Global North send most of their deadly e-waste to other countries in the absence of a clear measurement of the volume of trade in these poisons. In addition, the global supply chain depicted at the outset of our accounting story is not unlike the one we find today—workers uncounted and unknown, who are living, ailing, and dying across a vast assembly line in which present-day wonders of technology are manufactured. Our fictitious militant accountants were frustrated by lacunae like those in existing policy regimes, which, although laudable in many ways fail in most attempts to find the political resources for effective accounting, policy, and enforcement. Japan, Canada, and the United States still undermine the 1995 Basel Convention on the Control of Transboundary Movements of Hazardous Wastes and Their Disposal, which prohibits the transport of dangerous material.[3] And yet, we have seen hopeful signs in legal investigations of unlawful e-waste exports to West Africa, the recodification of e-waste business as global organized crime, and EU efforts to license and oversee e-waste exporters, traders, dealers, and brokers.[4]

We have based the ethico-political values of our proposed media future on green citizenship, which presses for basic rights that include biophysical health for all organisms; clean air, land, and water; the acceptance of interterritorial and intergenerational duties of care for the Earth's ecosystems; and business corporations and governments paying for the social and environmental resources they exploit. We have tried to imagine the contradictory and complicated endeavor required to bring such rights and duties into existence with a view to the future, which in our fictionalized version ends up frequently confounding our determined green citizen.

The battle for future green citizenship against the purveyors of business-as-usual media and ICT/CE is also a battle against the current enchantment with technology, technophilia, and technological fads, which has worsened the ecological crisis. The connection between gadgetry abundance and planetary decline is only beginning to enter the consciousness of technology "experts," from academics and journalists to bureaucrats in think tanks and corporate accounting offices. They are catching up with environmental activists, who have been examining this relationship since the 1980s. The need for a new kind of accountancy and political accountability was already clear then, as activists, unionists, and concerned researchers struggled to break the informational barrier erected by media and ICT/CE businesses. Like those activists and our imaginary accountant, green citizens of the future must enact an Earth-centered ecological ethics to keep in check the managerial, human-centered tendencies of CBA and risk managerialism that fracture a holistic understanding of the relationship of media technology to the environment. Along these lines, ICT/CE manufacturers and the governmental agencies that regulate them could moderate the temptation toward pre-emptive rollouts of new technologies by using the precautionary principle that tests innovations with the existing array of standards of sustainability, as per independent and critically courageous versions of life-cycle assessment research.

Beyond production lies the problem of e-waste, which is growing as part of a profitable salvage industry that continues to flourish in the absence of global enforcement. The limits to understanding the extent of the environmental impact of e-waste, and hence the means to green ICT/CE end-of-life processing, are said to result from three reporting failures:

1. cultural workers and consumers throwing waste and by-products into the traditional waste stream, where items can't be counted and are eventually lost in landfills and incinerators;
2. nefarious forces hiding the extent of illegally procured and traded e-waste in order to continue profiting, either through global salvage or benign-sounding business-to-business trade; and
3. governmental systems of waste control that poorly inform workers and consumers about disposal of e-waste and failure to enforce laws to coerce waste-producing industries to declare all items.

All three explanations are correct. Resolutions to these problems require changes in the current system to place green citizenship and green governance at the center of e-waste reform. This means that microeconomic models that expect commodity markets to handle e-waste must be downgraded to a status that reflects their incapacity to address the urgent demands of the eco-crisis. These models rest on behavioral changes of buyers and sellers that cannot come about without an underlying cultural and political commitment to confront the stark reality of anthropogenic climate change, pollution, and destruction of ecosystems. Only a radically reconfigured notion of environmental accountancy and auditing, perhaps like the one we have envisioned here, can imagine a transformative role for markets in a future of environmentally sustainable media industries.

Clearly, the ecological problems caused by media technologies are not just a job "for the scientists." As we have seen, activists, public-health advocates, workers, unionists, and policy makers have been involved for decades in efforts to green the gadgets and planetary networks of the electronics, electrical, and energy industries.[5] Joining them is a growing number of creative artists who have come to the fore to take on cybertarians' apolitical celebrations of digital technology. Consider the art movement Arte Povera's use of found materials, railing at errant, arrogant consumption in highlighting e-waste, recycling, and ragpickers, or such artists as Jessica Millman, Miguel Rivera, Alexdromeda, Sudhu Tewari, Natalie Jeremijenko, NoMe Edonna, Chris Jordan, Erik Otto, and Jane Kim. Yona Friedman and Jorge Crowe focus on reuse rather than originality, while Julie Bargmann and Stacy Levy start with a creative cleanup rather than concluding with a painstaking one. The Carnegie Endowment's *Foreign Policy* magazine circulated Natalie Behring's stunning collection of photos from *Inside the Digital Dump* into the mainstream. Amsterdam's website Urban Screens uses electronic billboards as public space to encourage active citizenship, as do the Linz's ARS Electronica and Melbourne's Federation Square websites. Electronic billboards designed to run on solar and wind power raise awareness of the eco-crisis while working to solve it. Environmental art can cover both works that directly represent the environment—examples include Claude Monet's *London Series* or John Constable's *Clouds*—and nonrepresentational, performative works like Richard Long's *A Line Made by Walking*, James Turrell's *Skyspace*, or Olafur Eliasson's *The Weather Project*, which assume nature is occupied and shaped by humanity, and vice versa.[6] These artistic efforts can help imagine the relationship of a sustainable, democratic, and pleasurable life—a healthy Earth, a functioning global democracy, and a lot of fun—to media technologies. They strive to illustrate the balance that lightens environmental burdens while allowing us to "enjoy, invent and be free in the modern world."[7]

Many ICT/CE companies, along with the bureaucracies that regulate and lead them, are moving away from older models of unthinking industrialism. There are certainly many accommodations made with the interests of technology companies, but numerous compromises have made the dirty logic of industrial production vulnerable to critique and social reform. There is not a single big media or ICT/CE company that stands in arrogant opposition to the claims of environmentalists. They are all modifying their primitive slash-and-burn relationship to the environment with newfangled, if flawed, environmental management based on widely agreed-upon standards, though much of this languishes in milquetoast social-responsibility projects.

High-tech journalists are also beginning to temper their enthusiasm for the wonders of digital luxuries. *Wired* magazine acknowledges that we live in dangerous times with such lead features as "E-Waste: Dark Side of the Digital Age" and "1 Million Workers. 90 Million iPhones. 17 Suicides. Who's to Blame?" The BBC avows that "our shiny new technology is as dirty in its own way as a 1950's Soviet glue factory." Chris Anderson and Michael Wolff of *Wired* actually say the web is dead, because its social networks and software applications are supplanting the old fantasy of the internet as an open frontier. For them, the revolution will not erupt on Google, come from Amazon, burst through Facebook, be sold on Craigslist, or travel with Apple appliances. And they are not the only crestfallen cybertarians.[8] Cybertarian evangelists for open information such as Google and Facebook, which lead the way in social networks and applications, are immensely secretive when it comes to disclosing their environmental impact.[9] They should be held to account.

But these critical voices in the cybertarian press have been hushed by a loud chorus of playful hackers, YouTubers, bloggers, and other volunteers in the digital congregation who celebrate the blurring of recreation and work—the half-truth they recognize is amplified by such boosterism to the point where some scholars now speak of "playbor" or digital labor, a realm of creative resources that skirts the confines of wages and mind-numbing regimentation.[10] The problem with this notion is that it recapitulates an older model we have seen in the brief eco-histories of media technologies recounted throughout this book. The old model needed inexpensive, even free, resources for its revolution and the new one is no different. The idea of playbor reminds us what paper-mill owners must have said about the rivers and endless forests at their disposal, or how the first voltage barons and their banking and communications customers felt about cheap coal. It remains to be seen how long playbor can continue in its hybrid form as a resource before a wage comes to remove the fun, or copyright takes the tools away.[11] And even a casual but competent reading of high-tech history shows that the Schumpeterian fantasy of entrepreneurs leading the way simply doesn't apply. At a pedagogic level, this is entertainingly explained in the remarkable short films of Annie Leonard's *Story of Stuff Project*, especially *The Story of Electronics*. The playbor world is an adequate account of textual innovation befitting electronic games or novels, but its romanticism leads us away from an ecological orientation and the searing conditions of the global supply chain.[12]

Scholars are mostly still too dazzled by the aura surrounding media technologies to offer much help, but there are exceptions. Cultural historian and communications theorist James W. Carey looks back at the ruins of techno-utopian projections to end struggle and scarcity:

> The literature of the electrical sublime crested in the 1990s when traditional hopes were tied to the internet—a concrete, not an imagined technology—and to the instruments which were the enabling infrastructure of the internet, namely electronic networks via cables and satellites and computers. I do not have to remind you of the vast outpouring of trade books in that decade extolling not just the potential, but the reality of the internet as an agent of an unprecedented social transformation: a new economy, a new politics, a new world order, indeed a new and advanced species of men and women who were weaned on the computer and transported across all borders of space and time by the power of the internet. An enduring peace, an unprecedented rise in prosperity, an era of comfort, convenience and ease and a political world without politics or politicians—these were the hopes that cultivated a wave of belief in the magically transforming power of technology. We are now living with the consequences of those hopes and beliefs, but the age of the internet has taught us again of the fragility of politics, the brittleness of the economy and the vulnerability of the new world order. The "new" man and woman of the "new age" strikes one as the same mixture of greed, pride, arrogance and hostility that we encounter in both history and experience. (Carey, 2005, 445)[13]

Reaching back further into this tradition of techno-criticism, we find George Orwell targeting the same type of unthinking encomia of high-tech. In his day, the subjects were airplanes and the wireless:

> Reading recently a batch of rather shallowly optimistic "progressive" books, I was struck by the automatic way in which people go on repeating certain phrases which were fashionable before 1914. Two great favourites are "the abolition of distance" and "the disappearance of frontiers". I do not know how often I have met with the statements that "the aeroplane and the radio have abolished distance" and "all parts of the world are now interdependent." (Orwell, 1944)[14]

Writing in the mid-twentieth century, Orwell encouraged his readers to resist the monotonous mythologies attached to technological power. Perhaps he was thinking of Charles Knight, a major player in the development of the US book industry and popular press in the nineteenth century, who referred to the advent of the train, the telegraph, and the photograph as a "victory over time and space."[15] In the 1920s, Henry Ford rhapsodized that mechanization would increase productivity, develop transportation, and bring about "the improvement of the radio, and the coming of television," and thereby end "the lonesomeness of farm life." They would also ensure global harmony: "The airplane and radio know no boundary. They pass over the dotted lines on the map without heed or hindrance. They are binding the world together. ... Thus may we envision a United States of the World."[16] The wireless radio pioneer Guglielmo Marconi said broadcasting could "make a material contribution towards greater understanding and amity between Nations, the cementing of home life and the happiness of the individual."[17] Scores of examples of this kind point to the binding and unbinding of time and space and the visibility and audibility of signs from elsewhere, electric light as well as the telephone bringing about a new world order, transcending the chauvinism of sovereign states. To which Orwell responds:

> The effect of modern inventions has been to increase nationalism, to make travel enormously more difficult, to cut down the means of communication between one country and another, and to make the various parts of the world less, not more dependent on one another for food and manufactured goods. This is not the result of the war. The same tendencies had been at work ever since 1918, though they were intensified after the World Depression. (1944)

Writing in our own time, the distinguished political economist of communication Vincent Mosco has carried on this tradition of techno-criticism. His target is the cybertarian who unthinkingly repeats the myths of technological power in the era of ICT/CE gadgetry. Like Orwell, he criticizes the rhetoric that props up a "digital sublime." In its place, he reinstates the historical knowledge that these myths work to eliminate.[18]

Inspired by this tradition of techno-criticism, we have drawn together the work of scholarly researchers, critical-policy analysts, activists, unionists, and workers to throw some shade over cybertarian dazzle, and develop a more materialist, ecological understanding of the media and the labor that brings ICT/CE to us. We have explored how such a paradigm shift might foreground the ecological context of the long historical development of the media, calling attention to the mounting environmental burden of technology. We hope future media historians will dig deeper into the eco-history of media, their impacts on ecosystems and biophysical health, and the legacy of unthinking toxic industrialism.

Throughout this book, we have identified different points of departure for greening the media: green consumption, learning about media technology's eco-historical context, greening cultural labor and working conditions, pressing for greener governance, and cultivating forms of green citizenship rooted in eco-ethics and values of sustainability. Unbridled technology growth and the technological sublime have no place in these efforts to green the media. We have also discovered that collaboration is essential: When ecosystems and workers' lives are at stake, alliances are vital. Future work will rely on careful popular and expert contributions from the natural and social sciences, notably epidemiological, environmental, physical, and biological research; it will involve regulators of ICT/CE sectors and innovative life-cycle-assessment research; and it will improve with better ethnographic evaluations of formal and informal workers, from Delhi ragpickers to US federal prison inmates, from bureaucratic cogs to Bangalore magnates. In order to have greener media, ongoing research into the geographical and historical dimensions of the eco-crisis will be needed as well. And in order to counter the untrammeled information-society ideology that the public otherwise receives, we must begin to ask very hard questions: How much media technology is enough? Can newer designs be developed within the fixed limits of environmental sustainability? Should existing media institutions be sustained in their present size and reach or shrunk to ecologically sound dimensions?

These questions pose unique ethico-political challenges. Attempts to advance green governance and cultivate green citizenship must be mindful of the ethical dilemmas that accompany environmental sustainability. These technologies hold great value and significance for many people. But their symbolic power only helps to accelerate the speed at which media technology will reach the material limits imposed by the ecological crisis—a materiality paradox that pairs physical destructiveness and waste with a frenzied enchantment with the cultural potency of high-tech gadgetry. Moreover, strong versions of sustainability challenge precious doctrines of liberal democracy that valorize a voice for all at all times and promote the growth of media technologies as ever-expanding universes of tolerance and merriment. Additionally, new media cities such as Lagos and Delhi are emerging around the informality of production and distribution of salvage economies, with ragpicking and recycling creating low-cost, positive unoriginality—junk turned into art, parts reused in pale imitations of originals, and so on. Irregularity rather than dependability is the norm of technology in a world of precarious rather than constant infrastructure.[19]

The "smart-design" economy is not exempt from these quandaries. There is a growing list of "green" technologies compromised by the dirty industrialism from which they emerged. Despite promises of alternative-energy consumption and greener materials, solar photovoltaic panel production poses many of the same risks as the ICT/CE industry, including unsafe chemical components; toxic-waste emission with worker exposure to hazards; and poor design lacking forethought about reuse, recycling, and e-waste. With life spans of twenty-five years or so, the first generation of solar panels is reaching the end of life packed full of noxious materials that should be familiar to readers at this point—lead, selenium, cadmium, and dangerous flame retardants—and ending up in landfills in the global-waste stream. Newer solar technologies also carry some known and some under-researched environmental impacts: Thermal panels require large amounts of water diverted from current uses and dye-sensitized solar panels, and silver cells contain materials whose effects are not well known yet. And solar-power plants and wind turbines have been built in a manner reminiscent of the major transport and telecommunications projects of the nineteenth and twentieth centuries, with little regard for the habitats destroyed, species endangered, or traditional cultures disrupted.[20] The list of light-green technology can be extended to recording media like flash drives with miniature circuit boards that contain the usual toxic suspects; networks of fiber-optic cable with environmental burdens similar to copper cable; and improvements in storage batteries, which, while welcome, remain stuck in the old paradigm of resource depletion and end-of-life environmental harms. And if trends in ICT/CE innovation continue towards greener goals—high-gigabyte, low-impact, low-wattage, and high-efficiency systems—there's the strong possibility of a rebound effect, such that energy demand rises in response to lower power consumption per unit.[21]

Media technologies generate meaning, but also detritus and disease. Their industrial life cycles extend far-flung injuries into natural and biophysical environments. Their by-products travel the Earth via an international division of labor comprised of miners, smelters, assembly and transport workers, consumers, and salvage and recycling labor. Human and non-human organisms endure the same burdens caused by the old industrial products and processes—from smokestacks and chemico-mechanical methods dependent on abundant sources of electrical energy to the spreading sediment of waste and poisons.

Designers of the next round of breakthrough media technologies will have to take into account the complex and difficult problems raised in this book and those yet to be discovered. That is the precautionary tale that asks for the wisdom of doubt in place of the frenzy of innovation.

# NOTES

## INTRODUCTION

1. The terms ICT/CE and media technology will be used interchangeably throughout this book. This is not only for analytical convenience but also because there is increasing overlap between the sectors. CE connect to ICT and vice versa; televisions resemble computers; books are read on telephones; newspapers are written through clouds; and so on. Cultural forms and gadgets that were once separate are now linked. The currently fashionable notion of convergence doesn't quite capture the vastness of this integration, which includes any object with a circuit board, scores of accessories that plug into it, and a global nexus of labor and environmental inputs and effects that produce it. See Gartner, Inc., 2007; International Telecommunication Union, 2008; Malmodin et al., 2010.

2. We make this gendered point because of the shibboleth that many such items are "toys for boys."

3. Environmental Protection Agency, 2007, 1; Consumer Electronics Association, 2007, 1; Consumer Electronics Association, 2010; for ownership data see also: Grossman, 2010, 2–3; Twist, 2005; A. Smith, 2010.

4. Grossman, 2010, 24.

5. See Jackson, 2009, 13. Tim Jackson, London's Sustainable Development Commission Economics Commissioner, famously referred to economic growth as the myth by which societies have lived.

6. Organisation for Economic Co-Operation and Development, 2010, 7. In the dominant discourse of our day, technology is depicted as efficient and effective because of its reputation for allocating resources well. From this view, technology looks like the very opposite of waste—that extremely negative economic and personal characterization that veers between the incompetent and the abject. Waste is a zone in which disgust and danger oppose thrift (see Hawkins, 2006). The definition of waste depends on the social role or subject position one adopts: for economists, it refers to unused capacity; for engineers, it means maximal energy; for the critic, it "reveals the market's relation to nature" (Rogers, 2005, 231; and as Stuart Chase put it in 1925, "The conservationist knows it as any irreparable destruction of natural resources" [1929, 16]).

7. See Robinson, 2009; Herat, 2007, 305–10.

8. Environmental Protection Agency, 2007; Basel Action Network and Silicon Valley Toxics Coalition, 2002, 6; Commission of the European Communities, 2008b, 17.

9. Environmental Protection Agency, 2008, 1; Commission of the European Communities, 2008b, 31–34.

10. Leung et al., 2008, 2674–80; Wong et al., 2007, 434–42; Ray et al., 2004, 595–98; Frazzoli et al., 2010, 388–99.

11. In fact, the global recession that began in 2007 has been the main reason for any aggregate decline in energy consumption, slower turnover in gadget upgrades, and longer periods of consumer maintenance of electronic goods (see Richtel, 2011, B1).

12. David Golumbia (2009) characterizes this trend as the "cultural logic of computation."

13. David Nye is credited with coining the term "technological sublime," though he acknowledges others as sources (1994, 297, fn 8; 2007, 28). Historian Mario Biagioli also explains how a kind of technological sublime permeates everyday life through technoscience: "If around 1950 the popular imaginary placed science close to the military and away from the home, today's technoscience frames our everyday life at all levels, down to our notion of the self" (2009, 818).

14. Peters, 2006, 142–43; Walker, 1973, 34; Benjamin, 1992, 171; Nye, 2007, 69.

15. Boyce and Lewis, 2009, 5.

16. Grossman, 2010, 7–8.

17. This compulsory repetition is seemingly undertaken each time as a novelty, governed by what the cultural critic Walter Benjamin called, in his awkward but occasionally illuminating prose, "the ever-always-the-same" of "mass-production," cloaked in "a hitherto unheard-of significance" (1985, 48). Also see Science and Technology Council of the American Academy of Motion Picture Arts and Sciences, 2007, 33–50; Rogers, 2005, 202; Mattelart and Constantinou, 2008, 22.

18. A touchingly old-fashioned Facebook predictably featured "Peace on Facebook" with the promise that it would "decrease world conflict" through intercultural communication, while Twitter announced itself to be "a triumph of humanity" ("A Cyber-House Divided," 2010, 61).

19. This statement was uttered, perhaps unsurprisingly, by someone with the title Director of the Information Technologies and the Information Economy Program, Centre for Strategic Economic Studies.

20. It is important to distinguish this critique from simple attacks on certain brands of ICT/CE, such as those calling a company "evil." For example, twenty years of popular distaste for Microsoft's so-called wickedness misdirected attention away from the political-economic arrangements that made its monopoly position largely legal and lucrative. Google's mantra, "to do no evil," is another distraction from systemic matters. Still, we admit that however unhelpful as critical tools, a few of the rants directed at these brands have been quite funny. Here is satirist Charlie Brooker (2009) on Apple: "I don't care if Mac stuff is better. I don't care if Mac stuff is cool. I don't care if every Mac product comes equipped with a magic button on the side that causes it to piddle gold coins and resurrect the dead and make holographic unicorns dance inside your head. I'm not buying one, so shut up and go home. Go back to your house. I know, you've got an iHouse. The walls are brushed aluminum. There's a glowing Apple logo on the roof. And you love it there. You absolute MONSTER."

21. Marx, 1906, 83.

22. Schor, 2010: 40–41.

23. See Schiller, 1971.

24. Mosco and McKercher, 2008.

25. Barry, 2006.

26. To stay abreast of these issues, readers may wish to visit the blogs, links, and resources at http://www.ecomediastudies.org/.

27. Aslama et al., 2007, 59, 82.

28. Mattelart and Constantinou, 2008: 22–23; Hamelink, 1986.

29. James Carey, quoted in Slack and Wise, 2005, 3.

30. Descartes 1977, 225; Plumwood, 2006, 62.
31. Czitrom, 1982, 124–39; Simpson, 1996.
32. Hamelink, 1986, 23.
33. Innis, 2009: 47.
34. Steinberg, 1955, 260; Missika, 2006; De Silva, 2000.
35. Newcomb, 2005, 110; Standage, 2006.
36. "A Cyber-House," 2010; Kelly, 2008.
37. For examples, see Barnouw, 1990; Douglas, 1989; Noble, 1977; Schiller, 2007; Starr, 2004; Sterling and Kittross, 2002; Winston, 1998.
38. See Maxwell and Miller, 2008a, 2008b, 2008c, 2008d, 2008e, 2009; Miller, 2008b, 2009b; Raphael, 2003; Raphael and Smith, 2006; Smith and Raphael, 2003; Sterne, 2007; Parks, 2007; Berland, 2009a, 2009b; Gates, 2009; Hanke, 2009; Vereecken et al., 2010. A small subsection of media studies focuses on how the media frames global awareness of the transnational risks associated with climate change and other threats to the Earth's well-being: the Environmental Communication Network specializes in such questions, and publishes *Environmental Communication: A Journal of Nature and Culture* (www.esf.edu/ecn). And we admire the way that the Media, Communication and Cultural Studies Association (MeCCSA) in the United Kingdom has mobilized to make its conventions as green as possible, and has a Climate Change Network (meccsa.org.uk/climate-change-network). Attempts are underway to create similar policies in other associations, without the political-economic appreciation that guides MeCCSA.
39. See Flew and Cunningham, 2010; Keane, 2009; and Ritzer and Jurgenson, 2010 for useful incarnations and summaries of these positions. The concept is brutally skewered by a lapsed true believer in Keen (2007).
40. Castells, 1997, chapter 3.
41. Dewey stresses technology's inexorable link to "things and acts" as "instrumentalities" deployed on behalf of other goals "of which they are means and predictive signs" (1958, 122–23). Also see Czitrom, 1982, 91–112.
42. McLuhan 1964, ix. This conceptualization of media studies also informs media ecology, which the Media Ecology Association describes variously as examining how "technology and techniques, modes of information and codes of communication play a leading role in human affairs ... the interactions of communications media, technology, technique, and processes with human feeling, thought, value, and behavior" and the study of "how media of communication affect human perception, understanding, feeling, and value; and how our interaction with media facilitates or impedes our chances of survival." (http://www.media-ecology.org/media_ecology/index.html).
43. Finkelstein, 1979; Mattelart, 1994, 129.
44. McLuhan, 2009, 74.
45. Bazin, 1967, 17–18, 21. Foucault has described the period in which Bazin locates the emergent desire for cinema, roughly 1860 to 1880, as featuring "the new frenzy for images," whether on easels or tripods. Trickery and overt reassemblage were partners of reproduction, with photographers aspiring to art and painters hoping for verisimilitude (1999: 83).
46. Cultural historians Roger Chartier (1989) and Pierre Macherey (1977) turn away from reflectionism, which argues that a text's key meaning lies in its overt or covert capacity to capture the Zeitgeist, and question the claim that close readings of form, style, and theme can secure definitive interpretation. They suggest that historical and narratalogical approaches must be supplemented to take account of linguistic translations, material publications, promotional para-texts, and the like. We favor such approaches because they strive to reconstruct "the diversity of older readings from their sparse and multiple traces"; focus on "the text itself, the object that conveys it, and the act that grasps it"; and

identify "the strategies by which authors and publishers tried to impose an orthodoxy or a prescribed reading" (Chartier, [1989, 157, 161–63, 166]).

47. Streeter (2005) outlines the history of this discourse as peddled in *Wired* magazine.

48. Barbrook and Cameron, 1996; Turner, 2006; Leadbetter and Miller, 2004.

49. Ross, 2010b.

50. Baudrillard, 1988.

51. McChesney and Foster, 2003, 1.

52. Baudrillard, 2006.

53. Horkheimer, 1996, 126, 129. There are pitfalls in adapting an entirely critical stance to consumption by contrast with prosumption. Consider the historian Lesley Johnson's (1988) account of Australian radio between the 1920s and '40s. She asks what changed from the days when merely setting up a receiver that worked was a true sign of consumer mastery, to the war years, which featured sealed-set efficiencies and deskilling. The mostly male radio operators of the 1920s battled technological difficulties on a daily basis, exemplifying self-reliance and innovation. This "proper" life of initiative was replaced in the 1930s by the supposedly lazy, dependent listenership of women, when the appearance of the loudspeaker made radio an effortless listening medium. A device of consumption rather than mastery was instituted—it had been feminized—with the will to buy advertised goods being its defining quality. For a useful account of the prosumer, a preferred concept of the "new Right" of cultural studies, see Ritzer and Jurgenson, 2010.

54. Navar, 2008.

55. Benjamin, 1992, 171; Kotkin, 2001: 22; Mattelart, 2003, 177–178, 43; Hardt and Negri, 2000, 286, 290–292.

56. Webber and Wallace, 2009, 200–219.

57. Toffler, 1983; Negri, 2007.

58. Connelly, 2009a; Institution of Engineering and Technology, 2010, 3, 8.

59. Reygadas, 2002; Cowie, 1999; Ngai, 2005; Mayer, 2011. Also see Gall, 1998; Dex et al., 2000; Ursell, 2000; Blair, 2001; McKercher, 2002; Deuze, 2007; McKercher and Mosco, 2007; Miller, 1990a, 1990b; Miller et al., 2001, 2005; Mosco and McKercher, 2008; Ross, 2009; Rossiter, 2006; Day, 2005; Elmer and Gasher, 2005; Neff et al., 2005; Sholle, 2005; Chakravartty, 2007; Christopherson, 2006; "Forum," 2010, 90–113.

60. Vincent Mosco tells a similar story about his relationship with his cousin in the old Radio Row of downtown Manhattan (2004).

61. Winston, 1996, 40–43.

62. Although Chartier's words are directed at literary analysis, we think they can be addressed to media studies as well. Chartier 2005a, 38–40; Chartier, 2005b.

63. Macherey, 2007, 3–9.

64. Nader, 1972; Marcus, 1995; García Canclini, 2008, 390. See also section IV of Aguilar et al., 2009.

65. Hunter, 1988: 215; McHoul and O'Regan, 1992, 5–6; Shannon and Weaver, 1963; Eco, 1972.

66. Mattelart and Constantinou, 2008, 25; Latour, 1993.

67. Latour, 2004, 1.

68. Muecke, 2008, 95.

69. We see this enacted by Massachusetts Institute of Technology's SENSEable City Laboratory, which utilizes new surveillance technologies to comprehend urban change in a critical frame rarely encountered in that citadel of credulous cybertarianism. Its TrashTrack website follows the life of waste across space and time (http://senseable.mit.edu/trash-track; Navarro, 2009).

70. McChesney, 2009, 109.

71. As Canclini argues, "The fusion of multimedia and concentrated media ownership in cultural production correlate[s] with changes in cultural consumption" (2008, 390). This correlation is not simply one of supply and demand. It takes on the form of what Castells calls, in a paradoxical *jolie-laide* term, "mass self-communication" to capture the way that activist and affective investments by social movements and individuals match and stimulate financial and policing investments by corporations and states, and vice versa (2007, 239).

72. Beck et al., 1994; Beck, 1999; Latour with Kastrissianakis, 2007; Rikagos and Hadden, 2001; O'Malley, 2001.

73. Hacking, 1990.

74. Shah et al., 2007.

75. Interagency Task Force on Electronics Stewardship, 2011.

76. "450,000 Unsold Earth Day Issues of *Time* Trucked to Landfill," 2008; Collins, 2010; Goody and Watt, 1963, 304.

77. Nors et al., 2009; see Chartier, 1989, 2005a, 2010 and Latour, 2004.

78. Weber, 2005, 27; Sacks, 1995, 548.

# CHAPTER 1

1. Despite Jobs's arch remark, the Electronics TakeBack Coalition gave his company, Apple, a C+ in its 2010 "Report Card" based on minimal recycling being available at Apple stores. Apple declines to disclose the dimensions of its "take back" programs, expose itself to external evaluation on this score, or openly commit to recycling old products into new ones.

2. *Shop 'til You Drop!* is the name of a 1991–2006 US TV game show and a contemporary Australian women's magazine (http://www.shoptilyoudrop.com.au/magazine/in-the-magazine.htm).

3. Assadourian, 2010, 8.

4. Marx, 1906, 41.

5. Quoted in Schaefer and Durham, 2007, 44. See http://docs.info.apple.com/article. html?artnum=300406.

6. Students & Scholars Against Corporate Misbehaviour, 2010a, 4.

7. Debord, 1995, 26–27, and also 29–30.

8. Haug, 1986,17, 19, 35; Benhabib, 2002, 3.

9. Hall, 1958, 26.

10. Quotations come, respectively, from critics of these views of consumers: Nairn, 2003, 7; Mosco, 2004, 60; and Horkheimer, 1996, 4, 25. Today, such cybertarians as Jaron Lanier announce that "we tinker with your philosophy by direct manipulation of your cognitive experience, not indirectly, through argument" (2010, 6). The "we" and the "you" are not workers. They are managers and customers. As for workers, one engaged critic from the electronics production line suggests that the system in fact requires "a body without mind, a mindless body" for those who actually make the cybertarian's beloved toys (Ngai, 2005, 83). A seemingly natural class efficiency that matches different technologies to unconscious toil and full humanness has become akin to a "literature of the eighth day, the day after Genesis" (Carey, 2005, 444).

11. Zwick et al., 2008.

12. "Buy Blue's Mission," 2004; Keeter et al., 2002, 8–9, 20–21; Costanza-Chock, 2002; Capstrat/PublicPolicyPolling, 2010.

13. Dalton, 2005, 453–54; also see Maxwell and Miller, 2009. When the film version of Alice Walker's novel *The Color Purple* (Steven Spielberg, 1985) came out, it was derided by crit-

ics for a supposed inauthenticity in the eyes of African Americans. But Jacqueline Bobo's analysis of working-class black US women viewers discloses that they "sifted through the incongruent parts of the film and reacted favorably to elements with which they could identify" (1995, 3). Watching the movie and then discussing it led them to read the novel. Each interpretative occasion invoked personal experience as a yardstick. Today, Walker insists that her books be printed on postconsumer, recycled paper, a further element to understanding the life of the commodity signs that she helps generate (Transcontinental Printing, 2008, 4). That example offers a snapshot of how to understand the life cycle of a text—to know some small part of its eco-history.

14. Saied and Velasquez, 2003.

15. Woolgar et al., 2008; Einstein, 2012.

16. Weil, 2007; Cordasco, 2002; Keeler, 2002; Hawken, 2004 and 2005. For more on ISS and its promise of "enabling the financial community to manage governance risk for the benefit of shareholders," see http://www.issgovernance.com and http://www.issgovernance.com/docs/2011ESGPreview. The World Economic Forum's list of the "100 most sustainable companies in the world" includes corporations that bribe officials, provide false accounts, and are mass polluters—but are sold as appropriate for responsible investment. And there was a cringingly instrumental aspect to ISS's announcement that "the 2011 social issues proxy season may be almost as busy as last year's" (http://www.issgovernance.com/docs/2011ESGPreview, first para.).

17. Prothero et al., 2010; Bakker, 2010.

18. Basel Action Network and Silicon Valley Toxics Coalition, 2002; Tong and Wang, 2004; "Help Urged," 2006; "UN Warning," 2006; Pynn, 2006; Basel Action Network, 2007. As with so many environmental problems that are still emergent and lack "newsworthy" catastrophes, headlines come infrequently. One incident that did attract media attention occurred in the République de la Côte d'Ivoire in 2006. A toxic-waste spill cost ten people their lives and made another seventy thousand ill. This occurred at the same time as Kenya was hosting a meeting to address e-waste elements of the Basel Convention, at which the United Nations Environment Programme estimated that fifty million tons of electronic waste were being created each year.

19. Goodland, 1996, 207; Korten, 1996, 23.

20. Rockstrom et al., 2009, 4.

21. R. Smith, 2010.

22. Daly, 1996, 193.

23. Curry, 2006, 10–13; Rockstrom et al., 2009.

24. Ceruzzi, 2003, 217; Edgerton, 2007, 203; "The End of Wintel," 2010. We should note that there is debate about its scientific credentials; see Milojković and Litovski, 2011.

25. Moore, 1965, 116; see Markoff, 2011a, A1.

26. Ellick, 2008; Grossman, 2006, 121–26.

27. Cray, 2001; Betts, 2006.

28. General Electric, quoted in Anderson, 2005; see Fisher, 2005.

29. For more on this subject see: Gartner, Inc., 2007; International Telecommunication Union, 2009, 4; Malmodin et al., 2010.

30. BioRegional and London Sustainable Development Commission, 2009; "Down on the Server Farm," 2008; Organisation for Economic Co-Operation and Development, 2010, 19; Minoli, 2010; Lamb, 2009, 4–5; Corbett and Turco, 2006; Kundra, 2010; Wald, 2007; Parsley, 2008; Markoff, 2011b, B1.

31. Markoff, 2011b, B1; Koomey, 2007, i; Wald, 2007; Schäppi et al., 2007, 9; Bio Intelligence Service, with European Business Council for Sustainable Energy and Fraunhofer Institut Zuverlässigkeit and Mikrointegration, 2008; International Telecommunication Union, 2009, 10; Hancock, 2009; Thussu, 2007, 593; http://googleblog.blogspot.com/search/

label/green. Those keen on keeping up can follow a dedicated corporate Web site, http://datacenterknowledge.com.

32. Subscription records do not reliably reflect the actual units in circulation, the number of which could easily exceed the population of the world.

33. International Telecommunication Union, 2010; A. Smith, 2010; Mouawad and Galbraith, 2009; Natural Resources Defense Council, 2008; International Energy Agency, 2009, 5, 21; The Climate Group, 2008, 18–23; Hancock, 2009; Organisation for Economic Co-Operation and Development, 2010, 19.

34. Electricity consumption in general is costly because it is based on debt. Unlike during the post-War recovery, the massive economic boom between 1993 and 2007 was driven by easy credit rather than wage increases in line with productivity. The results are there for all to see in the mortgage-debt crisis that resulted from this casino consumerism (Jackson, 2009).

35. See Newell, 2001, 92, 99.

36. Van Erp and Huisman, 2010.

37. Despite the ecologically friendly aspect of green citizens buying responsibly and recycling, this position invokes a gendered notion of virtue that favors hegemonic masculinity, endorses a neoliberal focus on individual responsibility rather than collective and state-based action, and rejects participatory, deliberative democracy in favor of a moralistic republicanism—scolding the litterbug rather than passing legislation (see Arias-Maldonado, 2007; Latta, 2007; Barry, 2006; MacGregor, 2006). In this light, our own plea for dumping the doctrine of "more is better" runs the risk of pre-empting potential alliances with large numbers of progressives working to expand a counter–public sphere of alternative media; an anthropocentric ethico-politics suggests a compromise that could open a debate on the ecological context of media expansion.

38. See Assadourian, 2010, 2010, 21–53.

39. Connolly and Prothero, 2008; Carducci, 2006; Stolle et al., 2005; Conca et al., 2001; Migone, 2007; Mazar and Zhong, in press; de Pelsmacker et al., 2005.

40. A poet, visual artist, novelist, essayist, and playwright, Mayakovsky was a leading figure among the Russian Futurists.

41. Curry, 2006, 47. We have borrowed the framework for this discussion of ecological ethics from Patrick Curry.

42. Ibid., 47.

43. Ibid., 64.

44. Leopold, 1949; Connolly, 2005, 90.

45. Callicott, 1994, 36–41; Curry, 2006, 63–100.

46. Curry, 2006, 55–62.

47. Horkheimer, 1996, 32; Hobbes, 1998, 105–6.

48. Hegel, 1954, 242–3, 248–50; Hegel, 1988, 50, 154, 61.

49. Ford, 1929, 71; Bush, 1945.

50. Heidegger, 1977, 288, 296, 299; Hume, 1955, 112–13; see Bentham, 1970; Swanton, 2010.

51. Curry, 2006, chapter 6.

52. Ibid., 55–62.

53. Ibid., 113. In our time, the political role for eco-centric ethics will have to be modest unlike its unhelpful dogmatic versions, and hope at best "to acquire sufficient influence in the world to *check* anthropocentrism, instrumentalism and utilitarianism" (Curry, 2006, 67; emphasis in original).

54. Plato, 1970, 119–22; Burke, 1986, 192–95.

55. Introna, 2005; See also Sirowy, 2008.

56. Timeless time and space of flows are concepts that appear throughout Castells's recent work. Imagine being in conversation with someone who abruptly takes an incoming cell

phone call—they are no longer "with you" but have entered into the network's timeless time and space of flows, according to this theory.

57. Castells et al., 2007, 246–58.

58. International Telecommunication Union, 2009, 2, 5, and International Telecommunication Union, 2008, 67–84; Houghton, 2009; Jones, 2008.

59. Hanna and Qiang, 2010; Prahalad and Hart, 2008; Sachs, 2008; Jensen, 2007; Slater and Tacchi, 2004; Bailard, 2009; Shapiro, 2010.

60. Hutton, 2011.

61. Schiller, 2007, chapter 8.

62. Williams, 1975, 26.

63. Benjamin, 1992, 184; Innis, 1991, 60; Attali and Stourdze, 1977, 97–98.

64. Rydh, 2003; Environmental Working Group, 2009, 18–22, 28.

65. Quoted in Mooallem, 2008, 42; see also Grossman, 2006, 18–20, 44–45; Hardell, Carlberg, and Mild, 2009; Crosby, 2007; Rydh, 2003; Sadetzki et al., 2007.

66. LCA or eco-balance is an analytical tool employed unevenly by the Environmental Protection Agency and other regulators, by the International Standardization Organization, by the Society of Environmental Toxicology and Chemistry, and by numerous nongovernmental agencies involved in industry oversight around the world. The goal of LCA is to educate manufacturers and businesses about a product's connection to the environment at all stages of its existence in order to improve "environmental performance" (Scharnhorst, 2006, 1). LCA combines scientific research and studies of industry practices to assess a company's performance and indicate ways to replace old processes and components with new ones that are more ecologically sound.

67. Scharnhorst, 2006, 5; "One Small Step for Electronic Waste," 2008.

68. Quiggin, 2010; Marx, 1994, 140.

69. Kant, 1991, 54.


## CHAPTER 2

1. Collins, 2010. Collins is Academic Relations Manager at Elsevier publications.

2. Among the best, see Nixon, 2000 and Ross, 1995.

3. Plato, 2008, 68–72; see Chartier, 2010.

4. See Chartier, 2010.

5. Bacon, 1854, 370; Descartes, 1977, 56.

6. See Winston, 2007.

7. Chatfield, 2010, writing in *Prospect*; Chartier, 2010.

8. Heinzmann and Bergk, quoted in Enzensberger 1986, 89–90.

9. See Innis, 2004, 2.

10. Eco, 1994; "The Future," 2010.

11. "Edited Out," 2010.

12. Canonico et al., 2009; "Book Industry," 2009; Transcontinental Printing, 2008; Havenner, 2010.

13. À propos, "against the grain" refers not only to a form of counterindicative interpretation but also to a premium internet service that links agents, booksellers, and libraries (http://www.against-the-grain.com), as well as a short-lived Ben Affleck TV series.

14. Braudel, 1973, 285–300; Zhao, 2010, 268.

15. Braudel, 1973, 295–96; also see Adshead, 1997, 165, 193. This history is often neglected in triumphant Occidentalist history writing.

16. Marx, 2003, 63. On print history see Braudel, 1973, 295–96; Innis, 2007, 150–151; and Strasser, 1999.

17. Warde, 1955, 7, 10. On Guttenberg see Mehring, 1979, 188–94; and Braudel, 1973, 296–98.
18. Braudel, 1973, 296; Eisenstein, 1983, 13; Innis, 2007, 165.
19. Pines, 1931, 299; Starobin, 1970, 132; Outland, 2004. Wood-based turpentine is rare these days, with production shifting to the chemical kraft process by the end of the twentieth century (National Institute of Environmental Health and Science, 2002).
20. Wallwork, 1968, 147; Adshead, 1997, 193; Melville quoted in Strasser, 1999, 86.
21. Strasser, 1999, 89.
22. Roosevelt quoted in Innis, 2004, 75–77.
23. Strasser, 1999, 91–92; Burke, 1979, 175.
24. Strasser, 1999: 90–91; Kinsella, 1990.
25. Burke, 1979, 188–90; Innis, 2004, 3, 75–77; Chase, 1929, 111.
26. Burke, 1979, 180–81, 188–90.
27. Wear and Greis, 2001; Medina, 2007, 140–41; Boychuk, 2008; Borealis Centre for Environment and Trade Research, 2008; Carli, 2010a and 2010b; Smith and Pangsapa, 2008, 97.
28. Smith, 1980; U.S. Occupational Safety & Health Administration, n.d.
29. Independent Press Association et al., 2001: 6; OECD, 2001, 218; Carli, 2010a and 2010b; Environmental Protection Agency, 1995; Inform, n.d.
30. Edwards et al., 2009. See also Butler, 2009 and Transcontinental Printing, 2009.
31. Data derived from Sibley, 2009; Edwards et al., 2009; Paper Task Force, 1995: 4; and Canonico et al., 2009. On scholarly journals see Chowdhury, 2010.
32. "The Book Industry," 2008; Borealis Centre for Environment and Trade Research, 2008; bookcouncil.org.
33. BioRegional and London Sustainable Development Commission, 2009; Reichart and Hischier, 2002.
34. Independent Press Association et al., 2001: 5–10; Transcontinental Printing, n.d.; Gallagher, 2008; PPA's *Magazine Carbon Footprint Calculator* (PPA, 2009) offers members a tool for improving performance.
35. From the Alliance for Environmental Innovation/Environmental Defense, cited in Independent Press Association et al., 2001, 6.
36. For overview see Transcontinental Printing, 2009. For *National Geographic* see Boguski, 2010. For *Discover* see Barone, 2008.
37. Hunt, 1994; Winston, 1998, 19–50.
38. Marland, 1962, 32; Schallenberg, 1981, 727–729.
39. Forbes, 1947, 427.
40. We have not seen records of how this waste was disposed, but we know it contained traces of zinc, copper, and mercury.
41. Calvert, n.d.
42. Edison quoted in Schallenberg, 1981, 735–36.
43. Schallenberg, 1981; Snyder, 1992, 71.
44. Schallenberg, 1981, 735–50.
45. Penrose, 2003, 3.
46. Penrose, 2003, 11; see also Palacios et al., 2002.
47. David, 1990.
48. Blake-Coleman, 1992; Hunt, 1994; Schmitz, 1986, 394; Wikle, 2002, 48.
49. Schmitz, 1986, 398–406.
50. Walters, 1944, 133–39.
51. Charles Vidor, 1946.
52. Newell, 1997, 658–62, 688–89.
53. Calvert, n.d.; Czitrom, 1982.
54. Marland, 1962, 44.

55. Culbertson, 1924, 89; "The Value," 1902.

56. Culbertson, 1924, 89–92.

57. Culbertson, 1924, 89–92; "The Value," 1902; Headrick, 1987.

58. Kogan et al., 2003.

59. Zhao, 2010, 267.

60. U.S. Congress, 1988, 2, 9, 45–54, 82; Kogan et al., 2003.

61. Chilton, 2010.

62. Morton, 1993.

63. Meikle, 1997; Markowitz and Rosner, 2002; Corn, 1984; Strategic Counsel on Corporate Accountability, n.d.

64. "The Strange," 2010; Fairfield, 2008; Preston, 2010; Anderson, 2009; Boykoff, 2010; Carbon Disclosure Project, 2010a.

65. "The Strange," 2010; Carbon Disclosure Project, 2010a.

66. For instance, see http://www.realclimate.org/index.php/archives/2005/06/the-wall-street-journal-vs-the-consensus-of-the-scientific-community; online.wsj.com/article/SB10001424052748704007804574574101605007432.html.

67. Hearst Corporation, n.d., 1; Boguski, 2010, 642.

68. Gilson, 2008, 88; Shields, 2009; Carbon Disclosure Project, 2010b; Periodical Publishers Association, 2008.

69. Rathje and Murphy, 2001, 103; Tenner, 1996; Organisation for Economic Co-Operation and Development, 2010, 38; "Ruses," 2010.

70. Mayers et al., 2005; BioRegional and London Sustainable Development Commission, 2009; Tripsas, 1997, 124, 142; Pelta-Heller, 2007; "Ruses," 2010.

71. Electronics TakeBack Coalition, 2010.

72. See http://www.intomobile.com/2010/09/20/apple-bullies-newsday-into-taking-down-the-commercial-for-their-ipad-application. As we were writing this section, corporate apparatchiks were feverishly insisting that the clip be taken down from the internet. The last active venue we found was http://www.funnyordie.com/videos/8a3000125f/newsday-ipad-app-commercial.

73. Moberg et al. 2010,177; Teather, 2010; Kellogg, 2010; Consumer Electronics Association, 2010; "E-Publish," 2010; Grossman, 2010, 11; Robinson, 2010, 29; "From Allen Lane to Amazon," 2010; Chatfield, 2010; Lea, 2010; "E-Publish or Perish," 2010.

74. Moberg et al., 2010; Weinstein, 2010; bookcouncil.org; Tonkin, 2010; Nors et al., 2009, 55; Butler, 2009; Ritch, 2009; Goleman and Norris, 2010.

75. The Confederation of European Paper Industries has proposed a unified framework for determining carbon footprints. See http://www.cepi.org/Content/Default.asp?pageid=307.

76. http://www.ilovemountains.org/myconnection; Carli, 2010a and 2010b; Christensen and Siever, 2009; Matthews et al., 2002; Anderson, 2007; Transcontinental Printing, 2009; Collins, 2010; Milmo, 2010; Moberg et al., 2010, 180, 187.

77. See Independent Press Association et al., 2001, 5–10.

## CHAPTER 3

1. Adorno, 1981–82. Academics have written reams of textual analyses on such nature media; such works include Hochman, 1998; Mitman, 1999; Ingram, 2000; Brereton, 2005; Cubitt, 2005; Carmichael, 2006; and Chris, 2006.

2. Directed by Robert Zemeckis, 2000.

3. Directed by Roland Emmerich, 2004.

4. Directed by Davis Guggenheim, 2006.

5. Directed by Roland Emmerich, 2009.

6. Barnett et al., 2009; Balmford et al., 2004.

7. Redford, quoted in Grant, 2011, 41.

8. Till, Stanley, and Priluck, 2008, 180, 188; Thrall et al., 2008.

9. http://www.piercebrosnan.com. For a photo gallery of green entertainment industry people, see http://www.redcross.org/portal/site/en/menuitem.d229a5f06620c6052b1ecfb f43181aa0/?vgnextoid=04aeb7901438b110VgnVCM10000089f0870aRCRD&vgnextf mt=default.

10. Directed by Kim Kindersley, 2006.

11. Johnson, 2009.

12. Directed by Louie Psihoyos, 2009.

13. http://www.piercebrosnan.com/menu.php?mm=4&sm=3&pn=1

14. Directed by Tom Shadyac, 2007.

15. Boykoff and Goodman, 2009; Brockington, 2008; Roos, 2006; Gilson, 2008, 89; Wood, 2008; Universal Studios Entertainment.com, n.d.; Wells and Heming, 2009; Walsh, 2007; Corbett and Turco, 2006, 37; The Carbon Neutral Company, n.d.

16. Ventre, quoted on msnbc.com, 2008; also see Pantera, 2009.

17. Corbett and Turco, 2006, 11–14.

18. Roth and McKenny, 2007; Mitchell 2007, 117–19.

19. Carey, 2004, xvi.

20. Directed by Steven Spielberg, 1981.

21. Engardio et al., 2007; Chiang, 2010; Moore, 2009.

22. Directed by James Cameron, 1997.

23. Miller et al., 2005, 164–65; Murdoch quoted in Maxwell and Miller, 2006.

24. Miller et al., 2005, 165; Kushner, 1998.

25. Photographs are available at http://rtmark.com/popotlaimages.html.

26. *Avatar*, 2009.

27. "Popotla vs. Titanic," n.d.; Kushner, 1998; Coombe and Herman, 2000; http://gatt.org/ popotla.html; Sekula, 2001; Spagat, 2010.

28. See Cheney, 2010; Cameron, quoted in G. Miller, 2010.

29. "James Cameron is a Hypocrite," 2010.

30. Directed by Danny Boyle, 2000.

31. Law, Bunnell, and Ong, 2007; Tzanelli, 2006; Shoaib, 2001; Boyle quoted in Miller et al., 2005, 167.

32. Boyle, quoted in Gilbey, 2002.

33. "Filming, 'Damaged Beach,'" 2006.

34. Bidwai, 2005; Sharma, 2005; Shiva, 2005.

35. Motion Picture Association of America, 2009; Miller et al., 2005.

36. Reilly, 1991, 145–46.

37. Blair, 1926, 53.

38. Bean, 1939; "Twilight City," 1936; Blair, 1926; Reilly, 1991, 147.

39. Blair, 1926; United States Department of the Interior, 2008; "Twilight City," 1936; Reilly, 1991.

40. Reilly, 1991; George Eastman House, n.d.; Bowser, 1990, 21–36; Great Lakes Commission, 1992; Niman, 2003; Atlantic States Legal Foundation v. Eastman Kodak Co., 1994.

41. "Kodak Rewrites," 2006; Niman, 2003; McCarthy, n.d.; "Human and Environmental Exposure," 2010; Schoenfeld, 2007.

42. Dartmouth Toxic Metals, n.d.; Bowden and Tweedale, 2002; Viscusi, 1985; "Test-Tube Love Seat," 1940.

43. Bustamante, 2008.

44. Solomon Guggenheim worked for the family business before retiring and devoting a part of his fortune to the arts and the museum that bears his name—a backstory linking imperialist wealth, art, and film.

45. Institute of Pacific Relations, 1933; "The Smelter," 1903; Leavens, 1935; Friedman, 1992.

46. Durham, Jr., 1932; Reilly, 1991, 149; Strategic Counsel, n.d.

47. "Moguls to Direct Film's Future," 2006.

48. Head and Sterling, 1987, 106–110.

49. Strasser, 1999, 192; Grossman, 2010, 7–8.

50. Massey, 1979, 109–111.

51. Ibid., 149.

52. This validated a 1953 U.S. Air Force standard for occupational exposure to EMFs: "Ten milliwatts per centimeter squared—a measurement of power that passes through a square centimeter of space during each second," which was the marginal safety standard based on the observed dangers of exposure to 100 milliwatts per square centimeter per second (Massey, 1979, 115; Michaelson, 1968).

53. Massey, 1979, 116–20.

54. Between the 1940s and 2000, numerous epidemiological studies of microwave exposure looked for patterns of EMF effects and laboratory studies conducted on animals showed significant dangers. Human exposure could not be studied in a laboratory as easily, but post-exposure surveys analyze statistical correlations between EMFs and health risks, such as the incidence of cancer and other diseases. Research on radar (microwave) exposure included studies of 1,592 white male researchers who worked at the MIT radiation lab in the 1940s, the over-40,000 US Navy personnel said to have been exposed to varying intensities of EMF radiation in the 1950s, the hundreds of civilians living near a Soviet radar station in Latvia, the 4,600 career personnel in the Polish military exposed to radiation (out of an average population of 128,000), and the 1,827 employees working in the US Embassy in Moscow who were exposed to daily doses of microwave radiation between 1953 and 1976. The statistics proved insignificant in all but the large-scale Polish study, in which exposure to EMFs was shown to increase cancer rates (National Research Council, 2005, 133–37).

55. Massey, 1979, 121–25; Cox, 2007.

56. "Electronics: X Rays in the Living Room"; Hayashi et al., 1964.

57. Pellow and Park, 2002, chapter 4.

58. Pellow and Park, 2002, chapter 4; Kraus, 1968; Goldstine and Goldstine, 1946.

59. Kraus, 1968, 555–56; Lécuyer and Brock, 2006, 310.

60. Tajnaj, 1985, 2; Grossman, 2006, 35; Seitz, 1996, 295. Silicon was and remains a material used primarily by the steel and ferrous metals industries to add toughness. It was also used to manufacture armor-penetrating shells and by aluminum producers and the chemical industry—in fact, more silicon ends up in other electronic components than in semiconductors.

61. Williams, 2004, 5; Grossman, 2006, 36–37.

62. Lécuyer and Brock, 2006, 307.

63. Pellow and Park, 2002, 77.

64. Grossman, 2006, 37–41; Silicon Valley Toxics Coalition, n.d.; Rudolph and Swan, 1986.

65. Kaufman, 2011, D4.

66. "Deadly Spires in The Night," 1999; U.S. Fish and Wildlife Service, 1999; Wikle, 2002, 46.

67. Kessler and Cour-Palais, 1978.

68. https://www.tu-braunschweig.de/ilr/forschung/raumfahrttechnik; Mirmina, 2005, 650; European Space Agency; see also the Inter-Agency Space Debris Coordination Committee, whose members include ten national space agencies and the European Space Agency; "Junk Science," 2010.

69. Mark, quoted in Kurland and Zell, 2010, 211.

70. Science and Technology Council, 2007, 33–50.

71. Tekrati Inc., 2007; "How Marketing Missteps Stalled TV Sales," 2011; Crosbie, 2008; Russell, 2006; Roth and McKenny, 2007; International Telecommunication Union, 2008.

72. Scharnhorst, 2006, 8; Grossman, 2010, 12; Vaughan, 2011.

73. Conner and Williams, 2004; Puzzanghera, 2007.

74. Poniatowski, 2010; Baroudi et al., 2009; Lamb, 2009; Webber and Wallace, 2009; Velte, Velte, and Elsenpeter, 2008; Producers Guild of America, n.d.; "Film Studio Recycling Efforts," 2007; "Hollywood's Major Film Studios," 2008; MPAA, 2010. http://www.pgagreen.org/index.php/mobile-best-practices/11-mpaa-best-practices-for-green-production.

75. Murdoch quoted in News Corporation, 2007; Carbon Disclosure Project, 2010a.

76. Glaister, 2009; Kaufman, 2009; "Hollywood's Major Film Studios," 2008; Carbon Disclosure Project, 2010a.

77. Carbon Disclosure Project, 2010a.

78. Carbon Disclosure Project, 2010a; Murdoch, 2009.

79. Sheppard, 2010; Kurland and Zell, 2010, 212.

80. Goodell, 2011, 39.

81. Warner Brothers Studio, 2007; Carbon Disclosure Project, 2010b.

82. Directed by James Algar, 1958.

83. Liu, 2008.

84. See http://corporate.disney.go.com/environmentality/enviroport/2007/ea/oep.html; Walt Disney Company, 2008. This phrase, or a version of it, can be found in a number of Disney corporate websites, for instance: http://corporate.disney.go.com/investors/annual_reports/2008/keyBusinesses/corporateResponsibility.html

85. Gardner, 2007.

86. Gardner, 2007; http://ukfilmcouncil.org; Aftab, 2007. None of these efforts could save the UK Council from being destroyed by the Conservative Party. See also http://www.bcfilmcommission.com/community/reel_green_bc.htm, http://greeningthescreen.co.nz, http://filminflorida.com/prl/gpp.asp, http://nmfilm.com/filming/green-filming, http://oregonfilm.org/green/

87. Madrid, 2010; Science and Technology Council, 2007.

88. Jiji Press, 2009.

89. DeLillo, 1997, 285–87.

90. Sjöwall and Wahlöö, 2006, 112.

91. Deaver, 2011, 157, 277, 343.

92. Adorno, 1981–82, 199; Ventre, 2008.

93. See Murray and Heumann, 2009; Bozak, 2008; Kilpi, 2007; Moore, 2009.

## CHAPTER 4

1. Quoted in CEREAL, 2006, 6.

2. Quoted in Chan and Ho, 2008, 22.

3. Mosco and McKercher, 2008.

4. Tesh and Williams, 1996, 286–88.

5. Cole and Foster, 2001; Bullard, 2001; Goldman and Schurman, 2000; Hooks and Smith, 2004; Kottak, 1999; Mohai and Saha, 2006; Wilkinson and Pickett, 2006.

6. Pynchon, 1984. À propos, Lord Byron sought the death penalty for opponents of machines in his maiden speech in the House of Lords, just months after summering with Mary and Percy Bysshe Shelley, and even as the first Luddite piece of science fiction, *Frankenstein*,

was being created by Mary. Byron's daughter Ada is credited with writing the first computer program for Charles Babbage's proto-computer.

7. Lincoln quoted at http://www.presidency.ucsb.edu/ws/index.php?pid=29502#axzz1b Yell3oW, seventy-eighth para. For more on the powerful links between Lincoln and Marx, hear Robin Blackburn's work at http://culturalstudies.podbean.com/2011/09/24/a-conversation-with-robin-blackburn-about-slavery-marx-lincoln-and-mexico/

8. Marx, 1906, 555–56.

9. Engels, 1892.

10. Fröbel et al., 1980.

11. McLaughlin, 1993, 21.

12. Cf. Callicott, 1994.

13. Marx, 1906, 83.

14. Grossman, 2006, 99.

15. Basel Action Network, 2002, 4.

16. Miller et al., 2005.

17. Rivoli is a professor of finance and international business.

18. For the full memo, see http://www.whirledbank.org/ourwords/summers.html.

19. Lüthje, 2006.

20. Linden et al., 2007, 2–3, 6.

21. Xing and Detert, 2010; Schaefer and Durham, 2007, 49; "I'm a Mac," 2010.

22. GoodElectronics, Overeem, and CSR Platform, 2009, 19–20.

23. Although the NIDL has seen vast numbers of positions transferred offshore, there are still perhaps two hundred thousand employees in the United States making semiconductors. The exploitation of workers in US factories eludes local journalists, who might find their way to a Pulitzer prize were they to investigate the effects on local ecosystems or local populations of working twelve-hour shifts without a break and being exposed to risky chemicals such as glycol ethers or of the recycled air in work spaces specially designed to protect chips during their manufacture.

24. Silicon Valley Toxics Coalition, n.d.

25. Romundstad et al., 2001. Such risks are graphically on view through Intel's virtual tour of a factory. The lengths gone to in order to meet the needs of the chip itself and comply with European occupational-health-and-safety regulations are illuminating by contrast with the orthodoxy of thirty years ago, when protection was minimal. See http://www.intel.com/about/corporateresponsibility/education/index.htm.

26. See van Liemt, 2007, 15; http://sacom.hk.

27. Grossman, 2006, 29–33; GeSI and EICC, 2008, iii, 24–26, 34–36.

28. International Labor Organization, 2010.

29. The Dodd-Frank Act may have cut demand for Congolese minerals, but it did not change the way smugglers and international brokers combine globally mined materials, which makes it hard to track national origins—Congolese minerals can be smuggled into Rwanda or Zambia for export, for example, by the same militias the law was meant to hurt. Aronson, 2011, A19; Bengali, 2009; Global e-Sustainability Initiative and Electronic Industry Citizenship Coalition, 2008, 56; Global Witness, 2009; Montague, 2002; Cox, 2009, 21; Ma, 2009; United Nations Panel, 2002.

30. See Apple's request for confidentiality regarding the commission's inquiry BCG-E2381A, at https://fjallfoss.fcc.gov/oetcf/eas/reports/ViewExhibitReport.cfm?mode= Exhibits&RequestTimeout=500&calledFromFrame=N&application_id=258686&fcc_id=%27BCG-E2381A%27; Nimpuno et al., 2009; Apple, 2009, 2010, 2011.

31. Institute of Public and Environmental Affairs, 2011, 8–18.

32. Published news reports say that between ten and seventeen deaths resulted from suicides at Foxconn's Chinese factories. See Johnson, 2011; Branigan, 2011.

33. Chan, 2010; Moore, 2010a, 2010b; Barboza, 2010; Balfour and Culpan, 2010; Students & Scholars Against Corporate Misbehaviour, 2010a; "Light and Death," 2010; "China: Another Suicide at Foxconn," 2011.

34. Barboza, 2011; Apple, 2011.

35. Manager of a Chinese electronics factory, quoted in Catholic Agency for Overseas Development, 2004, 31.

36. See Balfour and Culpan, 2010; Institute of Public and Environmental Affairs, 2011.

37. Wong et al., reporting for *BloombergBusinessweek* 2010, 36; Balfour and Culpan, 2010; Hanna and Qiang, 2010, 137; Students & Scholars Against Corporate Misbehaviour, 2010a, 7; Johnson, 2011, 96; Branigan, 2011, 3.

38. "Union Leaders and Workers," 2010; "Massive Protest in Chennai," 2010; Kumar and Kumar, 2010; Ribeiro, 2010.

39. Ferus-Comelo, 2008, 141, 157.

40. GoodElectronics et al., 2009, 51; McKercher and Mosco, 2007; Mosco and McKercher, 2008; Mosco et al., 2010.

41. Bottini et al., 2007; van Liemt, 2007, 8; Carrillo and Zárate, 2009, 14; Johnson, 2011, 96; Branigan, 2011, 3.

42. CEREAL, 2006, 15.

43. Carrillo and Zárate, 2009; Mendoza, 2010; Reygadas, 2002; Baram, 2009.

44. Jacott et al., 2004; Simpson, 2007, 166–67.

45. CEREAL, 2009; Mendoza, 2010; García and Simpson, 2006; Gaffney, 2010; Castañeda, in press; NOTIMEX, 2010; Zoeteman et al., 2010, 424.

46. "Where is 'Away'?," 2009.

47. Greenpeace, n.d. b; Guadarrama, 2010; Moguel, 2007; Enciso, 2007.

48. Cowie, 2001, 17–18; Maxwell and Miller, 2008e.

49. Paterson, 2010; van Liemt, 2007, 12–14. For an explanation of this conduct as systematic and built into the architecture of certain sites rather than individual conduct, see Salzinger, 1997 and 2000. This research is from an earlier time when these practices may have been less common.

50. See http://lasvoces.org; García and Simpson, 2006; Simpson, 2007; Greenpeace, n.d. b; http://wiego.org; http://sewa.org; http://www.environmentalhealth.org; http://en.maquilasolidarity.org.

51. Mendoza, 2010; Malkin, 2004; "maquiladora diseases ... that bloom in wombs and spinal columns" is Urrea's phrase (1996, 12). Such "negative externalities" are part of the zero-sum calculus of Pareto optimality like that "impeccable logic" that Summers finds in dumping poisons from the United States into low-wage countries.

52. Grossman, 2006, 87–96; Ferber, 2004. A study of birth defects in children of former IBM workers was rejected for publication by Elsevier, the publisher of key medical and scientific journals, against the advice of its peer-review and editorial processes. At the time of that decision, Elsevier had a wing of its operations called Reed Exhibitions, which organized the world's largest arms fair, Defense Systems and Equipment International. Elsevier was therefore directly involved in marketing and distributing weaponry. Its valued clients include noted abusers of human rights and practitioners of terrorism, militarism, and imperialism, from Syria to the United States, with cluster bombs a specialty (Miller, 2007b). It should come as no surprise that the company adopted a protective stance toward IBM, in opposition to academic freedom, scholarly rigor, worker health, and the public interest. Fortunately, the research did emerge, despite IBM's attempts to intimidate scholars and outlets seeking to publish relevant research, thanks to open-source publishing at BioMed Central (Clapp, 2006; Clapp and Hoffman, 2008).

53. Marx sought to describe the rapid movement between production and the informal economy as a liminal life in terms of both physical borders and metaphorical exclusions that

found "sub-proletariat" classes outside the conventional reach of nineteenth-century government and commerce. Cf. Oppenheimer, 1974.

54. In Spain, *trapero* is used to refer a ragpicker; *chatarrero* to a junk man.

55. See Medina, 2007, 130.

56. Corbin, 1986, 145–46, 114–15.

57. Van Gogh, quoted in Hughes, 1985; Moser, 2007.

58. Calvino, 1994, 93, 96, 98, 102–03; Klíma, 1990.

59. Baudelaire, 1972, 141–42.

60. Black, 2006, 330–31; Palmier, 2006; Jennings, 1985.

61. Brady, 1998; Harriss, 2006; Gidwani, 2006; Medina, 2007, ix. PovertyNet quotation was fomerly at http://web.worldbank.org/WBSITE/EXTERNAL/TOPICS/EXTPOVERTY/0,,contentMDK:20161139~isCURL:Y~menuPK:373757~pagePK:148956~piPK:216618~theSitePK:336992,00.html

62. Directed by Michel Gondry, 2008.

63. Directed by Lucy Walker, João Jardim, and Karen Harley, 2010.

64. Harriss, 2006; Guillermoprieto, 1990; Gidwani, 2006; Medina, 2007; da Silva et al., 2006.

65. Corbin, 1986, 117; Nnorom and Osibanjo, 2007; Jha et al., 2008; Orisakwe and Frazzoli, 2010.

66. Basel Action Network and Silicon Valley Toxics Coalition, 2002; Lee, 2002; Tong and Wang, 2004; Pelta-Heller, 2007; Wong et al., 2007.

67. Lee, 2007, A1; van Erp and Huisman, 2010; California State Auditor, 2008; Consumers International Watch and the Danish Consumer Council, 2008, 2; Basel Action Network, 2005; also see Schluep et al., 2008.

68. Leung et al., 2008; Wong et al., 2007; Ray et al., 2004; Frazzoli et al., 2010.

69. Manhart, 2007; Wong et al., 2007.

70. Human Rights Advocates, 2008, 5; Manhart, 2007; Leung et al., 2008; Widmer et al., 2005; Wong et al., 2007.

71. In India, the names vary according to local divisions of labor and class/caste stratification. *Kabaadivala* is another spelling of the word for junk man, *raddhivala* refers to a paper recycler, and *chithda jamati* refers to a ragpicker. *Safai kamgar* is a cleaning worker. There are other words with caste implications, such as *jamadar* and *bhangi*, which are more scatological and often used as curse words. Our thanks to Anupama Kapse and Roopali Mukherjee for this clarification.

72. Mukherjee, 2003; Widmer et al., 2005; Wong et al., 2007; Ray et al., 2004; Simmons, 2005; da Silva et al., 2006; Gómez-Correa et al., 2007.

73. Medina, 2007, vii, 1, 128; Paterson, 2010.

74. Raina, 2007, 18–25.

75. Chintan Environmental Research and Action Group, 2009.

76. Zjawinski, 2008; Environmental Protection Agency, 2007, 1; Center for Environmental Health et al., 2006; Robarts, 2004; Moraff, 2007; Allen, 2007; United States Department of Justice, 2010.

77. Zoeteman et al., 2010, 428.

78. Anderson et al., 1987, 12.

79. de Nazareth, 2009; Chintan Environmental Research and Action Group, 2009, 2.

80. The recent work of McKercher and Mosco (2007), Mosco and McKercher (2008), and Mosco et al., 2010 are exceptions. Though their research addresses neither environmental aspects of media labor nor working conditions in the extractive and e-waste sectors, this work is exemplary in its comprehension of "below-the-line" labor, especially in light of the changing fortunes of the labor movement and labor organizing in the ICT/CE sectors.

## CHAPTER 5

1. Wal-Mart Stores Inc. was rebranded Walmart in 2008. The store chain is known as Walmex in México, Asda in the United Kingdom, Seiyu in Japan, and Best Price in India.
2. Papastergiadis, 2006.
3. Abrams, 2001, 49; Mattelart, 1996, 57; Standage, 1998, 6–21; Lueck, 2002, S619.
4. Weber, 1991, 228–29.
5. Attali, 2008, 31. Attali is a favored theorist of sound in cultural studies who can be listened to via the Global Speakers Bureau. See http://speakers.co.uk/csaWeb/speaker, JAQATT.
6. Kissinger, quoted in Rothkopf, 1997, 47; cf. Marcuse, 1941.
7. Schiller, 1976, 8–9, 16.
8. Tammemagi, 1999, 21–23.
9. Polanyi, 2001.
10. Colten, 1988, 15–16.
11. Schiller, 1981, and Schiller, 1984; Hamelink, 2001; Maxwell, 2003, 85–100. The OECD decreed the coming of the "information society" in 1975 and the EU followed suit in 1979, while IBM merrily declared an "information age" in 1977. Futurists theorized this technological utopia as post-ideological. Class would cease to matter (Mattelart, 2002).
12. Schiller, 1984. Typical bureaucratic thinking from this era can be found in the writings of such Cold War futurists as former National Security Advisor Zbigniew Brzezinski (1969), American Academy of Arts and Sciences prelate Daniel Bell (1977), and communications celebrant Ithiel De Sola Pool (1980). They praised the convergence of communications and information technologies for ensuring the permanent removal of grubby manufacturing from the First World to the Third and continued US cultural and technical power, provided that the blandishments of socialism, and negative reactions to global business, did not create class struggle.
13. Maxwell, 2003, 88; Lüthje, 2006.
14. United States Atomic Energy Commission, 1954, 81.
15. Miller, 2010b.
16. Foucault, 2008, 132.
17. Shabecoff, 1989. Within the United States, this is a nostrum of the Republican Party and its willfully ignorant fellow travelers, especially in the light of their intense, xenophobic nationalism and hatred of the have-nots who both service them and suffer at their hands. At such moments, it is very hard not to echo the words of the Nobel Prize–winning economist Robert Solow. When asked why he parodied neoclassical economists rather than debating them, he replied: "Suppose someone sits down where you are sitting right now and announces that he is Napoleon Bonaparte. The last thing I want to do is to get involved in a discussion of cavalry tactics at the battle of Austerlitz" (quoted in Marshall, 1988, 8). We would like to believe that few leaders outside the United States adhered to such precepts, but that would be wrong.
18. Webber and Wallace, 2009, 15, 17.
19. Charland, 1986; Lenoir, 2003; Macedonia, 2002.
20. Shachtman, 2010; Corbett and Turco, 2006; Leaning, 2000; Jorgenson, Clark, and Kentor, 2010; "Greenery on the March," 2009.
21. Directed by Sam Raimi, 2004.
22. Deck, 2004; Silver and Marwick, 2006, 50; Turse, 2008, 120; Burston, 2003; Stockwell and Muir, 2003; Andersen, 2007; Turse, 2008, 122, 119; Harmon, 2003.
23. *Armed with Science: Research Applications for the Modern Military.* Podcast March 3, 2010, edition.
24. International Telecommunication Union, 2009, 4. There are also examples of downright ridiculous thinking, typically among far Right ideologues like those at the Competitive

Enterprise Institute, whose slogan "free markets and limited government" announces in technically sweet patter that "new, better, and more powerful" technology appears in homes each year as a bounty. It warns that "the rapid spread of misinformation ... is creating an unwarranted near-panic among policy makers who fear there is no adequate policy in place for handling the growing amount of waste." Within this echo chamber of reactionary gobbledygook, landfills handle all waste, there is no contamination, and high technology ensures an end to ideology (Gattuso, 2005). The science we have discussed throughout this book is not addressed. What matters is that paymasters' material interests are satisfied.

25. Bio Intelligence Service with European Business Council for Sustainable Energy and Fraunhofer Institut Zuverlässigkeit und Mikrointegration, 2008, 257. In this vein, the Australian Council for the Humanities, Arts and Social Sciences' submission to its National Productivity Commission pleaded rather winsomely for a place at the table with corporations and governments to discuss this allegedly new "post-smokestack era of industry" (2006: 1).

26. Berkhout and Hertin, 2004.

27. Touré, quoted in Hibberd, 2009, 1; International Telecommunication Union, 2008, 67–84; International Telecommunication Union, 2009, 2, 5.

28. Touré, 2008; United Nations, 1992.

29. Houghton, 2009.

30. In 2011 China announced it would begin to use environmental "risk assessment" in the process of approving the building of new factories (Jacobs, 2011).

31. Clowney, 2006.

32. Connolly, 2005, 41–42.

33. Clowney, 2006, 109. Science's role is paradoxical and deserving of a longer discussion, but it should be noted that scientific research is the primary source of important quantitative measures of the eco-crisis. It also provides a language of critique and an array of expert activists.

34. Michaelson, 1996, 1907; Curry, 2006, 28.

35. Clowney, 2006, 125.

36. Curry, 2006, 48.

37. Clowney, 2006, 125–130.

38. Curry, 2006, 48.

39. Pepper, 2000, 451; Deutsch, 2007, C1.

40. Clinton, 2009, under "Secretary Clinton," third comment.

41. LEED is a rating standard issued by the U.S. Green Building Council (USGBC). It's the most commonly used rating system for sustainable building design. Landler, 2009.

42. Clinton, 2009, under "Secretary Clinton," third comment; Bradsher, 2009.

43. Williams, 1989, 120–21; Hazlett, 1990, 135, 135 n. 4. This blend of state power with media technology's ideological effect has survived in our own time—just substitute the internet or the cell phone for the telegraph, radio, or television. In each case, the state continues to be crucial. Who funded the Onion Router software, thereby enabling encryption of traffic to bypass Chinese censors? The Naval Research Laboratory of the US Government. Who underwrote Dynamic Internet Technology to e-mail Chinese and Vietnamese residents in ways that eluded state surveillance? The US government's International Broadcasting Bureau ("Cat and Mouse," 2006).

44. Noble, 1977; also see DuBoff, 1980; Schiller, 2007, 62, 102–06.

45. Booth, 2011; Schuler, 2010.

46. See "A Cyber-House Divided"; Organisation for Economic Co-Operation and Development, 2010, 31; http://meterpedia.com/main.

47. Barker et al., 2009.

48. Simon, 2009. Unsurprisingly, profit-seeking utilities have historically stymied advances in electrical engineering that aim to socialize low-cost, high-energy grids, like those developed at GE in the early 1900s by inventor Charles Proteus Steinmetz, who was inspired by socialist principles; a century ago, the grid was envisioned as a wireless system without metering that would be available to all. See Nye, 2007, 25; "Power," 2010.

49. Jolly, 2009.

50. U.S. Department of Energy, n.d.; McDougal, 2009; Glader, 2009; "IBM and Cisco," 2009; "GE, Cisco, and Others," 2009.

51. "General Electric," 2009; Glader, 2009; Guevarra, 2009.

52. Plepys, 2002; Bio Intelligence Service with European Business Council for Sustainable Energy and Fraunhofer Institut Zuverlässigkeit und Mikrointegration, 2008; International Telecommunication Union, 2009, 9–11.

53. Winston, 2009; "How Not to Annoy," 2008; Ingram et al., 2010, 56; Harvard Business Publisher quoted in "Data, Data Everywhere," 2010, 3.

54. Gentleman, 2007; Bellman, 2009; Gereffi and Christian, 2009; Ingram, Yue, and Rao, 2010; Vidal, 2004.

55. Directed by Robert Greenwald, 2005.

56. Littler, 2009, 105.

57. Quinn, 2005; Featherstone, 2004; incidentally, Hillary Clinton was once a member of its board.

58. Ghiami and Sorkina, 2009. Big-box retailers are "large retail stores operated by national or multinational chains. Big-box stores have been criticized for their labor market practices, their contribution to the trade deficit and many other things. On the other hand, they are popular shopping venues and have been a boon to consumers because they offer expansive product lines at low prices" (Haltiwanger et al., 2009). These stores measure between 150,000 and 250,000 square feet (Ingram et al., 2010, 56).

59. See note 66 in chapter 1.

60. Walmart, 2009; Makower, 2009; Winston, 2009.

61. Students & Scholars Against Corporate Misbehaviour, 2010b; Ghiami and Sorkina, 2009, 70–82.

62. United Nations, 2001; United Nations, 1998.

63. O'Neill, 2009, 4–5; Hurrell, 2006, 172–73; Jasanoff, 2010, 247.

64. Smith and Pangsapa, 2008, 89, 25; Porritt, 2009.

65. Thompson, quoted in Burke, 1979, 194, 195.

66. Burke, 1979, 181–84; Fairfield, 2008; http://www.cde.ca.gov/ci/cr/cf/txtbkwght.asp; http://www.defra.gov.uk/evidence/statistics/environment/waste/wrpaper.htm.

67. See International Publishers Association (http://internationalpublishers.org), the Pan African Booksellers Association (http://www.panafricanbooksellersassociation.org), the Book Industry Study Group (http://www.bisg.org), the Publishers Database for Responsible and Ethical Paper Sourcing (http://prepsgroup.com), the Federation of Indian Publishers (http://www.fipindia.org), the Fédération des Editeurs Européens (http://www.fep-fee.be), the Society of Publishers in Asia (http://www.sopasia.com), the Book Industry Environmental Council (http://www.bookcouncil.org), and the International Association of Research Organizations for the Information, Media and Graphic Arts Industries (http://www.iarigai.com). Publishers like HarperCollins began to use entirely renewable sources for electricity: 46 percent from biomass, 28 percent onshore wind, and 22 percent hydropower (Carbon Disclosure Project, 2010a).

68. Transcontinental Printing, n.d., and Transcontinental Printing, 2009; McBride, 2009, 4; Szabó et al., 2009; Puurunen and Vasara, 2007; Abou-Elela et al., 2008; Kunnari et al., 2009.

69. Greenpeace, n.d. b; United Nations Environment Programme, 1992; Osibanjo and Nnorom, 2007; Jha et al., 2008; Orisakwe and Frazzoli, 2010, 43–45.
70. United States Government Accountability Office, 2008, 23–27, 24 n. 22; Walsh, 2010; Criminal Intelligence Service Canada, 2008; van Erp and Huisman, 2010.
71. Tong and Wang, 2004; Manhart, 2007, 18; Human Rights Advocates, 2008, 5; Kumar et al., 2008; Basel Action Network and Silicon Valley Toxics Coalition, 2002; "Junk Science," 2010.
72. Commission of the European Communities, 2008, 26; Veenstra et al., 2010, 449; Pak, 2008; Jowitt, 2010; Commission of the European Communities, 2008b, 18; Mayers et al., 2005, 170.
73. Commission of the European Communities, 2008a, 18; Raphael and Smith, 2006, 247–59; Zoeteman et al., 2010; Selin and VanDeveer, 2009; Quiggin, 2010.
74. Quoted in Juan, 2008; See also Basel Action Network, 2007.
75. Zoeteman et al., 2010, 423.
76. Sénat Français, 2009.
77. Lean, 2008; Organisation for Economic Co-Operation and Development, 2007; Environmental Working Group, 2009, 18–22, 28, 3–4.
78. The data are old because the FCC no longer requires annual reports on this problem. Federal Communications Commission, 2004; Broad, 2007; http://www.crnano.org; Schoenfeld, 2007; Ornithological Council, 1999.
79. References to US Teleccommunications Act from Krasnow and Solomon, 2008, 50; Balmori, 2009; Pourlis, 2009.
80. Ornithological Council, 1999; United States Fish and Wildlife Service, 1999; Wikle, 2002, 46; Krasnow and Solomon, 2008, 62–63.
81. Pollin et al., 2009.
82. The Climate Group, 2008, 3.
83. Willard and Andjelkovic, 2005; International Telecommunication Union, 2009, 1, 5–6; Veenstra et al., 2010, 449.


## CHAPTER 6

1. Silicon Valley Toxics Coalition, quoted in Byster and Smith, 2006.
2. Baudrillard, 1999, 55; Micheletti, 2003; Hutton, 2003: 84; Hutton, in Giddens and Hutton, 2000, 47; Keeter et al., 2002, 21; Frank, 2003; Shaw, 1999, 111.
3. Barry, 2006.
4. Foster, 1999.
5. Grove, 1995; Clark, 1997; de-Shalit, 2006, 76; Hartmann, 2010; Teague, 2004; Shellenberger and Nordhaus, 2004; Haste, 2004, 419.
6. Lovato, 2004; Ross, 2010a. Anti-Mexican radio commercials offer the likes of the following from www.capsweb.org/content_elements/ … /ventura_radio_script.pdf: "Congratulations Ventura County. You're known for some of California's most polluted beaches. Ventura isn't coping with the waste products from its ongoing population explosion and associated development." See also http://www.fairus.org/site/News2/351628259?page=NewsArticle&id=22761&security=1601&news_iv_ctrl=1761.
7. Sexton, Hildyard, and Lohmann, 2005.
8. Dobson and Valencia Sáiz, 2006, 2.
9. Quiggin, 2010.
10. Meanwhile, weakened national protections of labor, land, and culture in the name of market liberalism have paralleled global social movements. Many of these movements are opposed to economic deregulation, but they like the state to keep its hands off their bodies

and private thoughts. In this sense, both social movements and forces of deregulation have pressed citizenship beyond territorial boundaries, drawing the battle lines between system-serving notions of the sovereign consumer rooted in acquisitive individualism and notions of a global common good rooted in cosmopolitan citizenship and global justice. In the more cynical versions of the neoliberal view, the consumer has become the class-less, race-less, sex-less, age-less, and unprincipled magical agent of social value in a multitude of discourses and institutions, animated by the drive to realize individual desires. But the Right's glorification of consumers rarely endorses organized political action by them because it must reflexively reject the existence of a common good. When the neoliberal *Economist* magazine proudly announces that consumers "are kings" because of new technology and transparent costs, it is referring to an "all-seeing, all-knowing" shopper (Markillie, 2005, 3)—not a socially engaged collective. Eulogies to public opinion and rational choice do not carry over to endorsements of social activism. People are sovereign when they purchase but magically transmogrify into "special interests" when they lobby. This neoliberalism offered people in the Global North diverse consumer products and diffused "rapidly evolving kinds of communications technology. . . . Citizens accustomed to a greater degree of choice in the consumer marketplace came to value this freedom in other spheres of life" (Hall, Massey, and Rustin, 1995, 8).

11. Dobson, 2003; Commission of the European Communities 2008a: 31.
12. Hopgood, 1998, 2; Frank, Hironaka, and Schofer, 2000; United Nations Environment Programme, 2007; Paterson, 1996, 2; Latour, 1993, 8; Petrini, 2002, 12.
13. Groves, 1995; Pepper, 2000; Maxwell and Miller, 2008d; Swanton, 2010, 146.
14. Martín-Barbero, 2001, 9; Miller, 2007a; Dean, 2001.
15. Dobson, 2003.
16. Rosen and Sellers 1999: 585–86; Quiggin 2010: 175–78.
17. Schor 2010.
18. See, for example, Jones, 2010; Rahaman, 2010; criticalmanagement.org; http://group.aomonline.org/cms; the journals *Critical Perspectives on Accounting*; *Accounting, Organizations and Society*; *Accounting Auditing & Accountability Journal*; and *International Journal of Critical Accounting*; and the currency of "technology foresight," which sought to address the problems caused by innovation (Miles, 2010). Scholarly work on environmental accounting began in the early 1990s. Over the next two decades, it developed to include environmental danger, corporate responsibility, new relationships between industry and the environment, systems of measurement, and reporting norms. The United Nations' Division for Sustainable Development's expert working group on the topic produced a comprehensive environmental-management accounting methodology (http://www.unep.ch/etb/areas/VRC_index.php). The US Environmental Protection Agency (2007) offers a limited but useful guide; the International Accounting Standards Board began to pay heed (Jones, 2010; Gale, 2006); and firms appeared to provide such services (http://www.greenaccountancy.com). Environmental accounting is a far cry, of course, from many norms of the industry. One of us worked as a credit analyst for a major US overseas bank in the early 1980s. As part of welcoming visiting metropolitan dignitaries to the colonies, we local operatives diligently crop dusted a barbecue area near a mine three days prior to their arrival to ensure they would not be inconvenienced by insect life. The environmental impact appears not to have made it into the historiography of the bank.
19. Schor, 2010, 18.
20. Barry, 2006, 22–23.
21. Environmental Protection Agency, 2007, 1; Hattam, 2007; Young, 2007; Okono, 2007; Robarts, 2004; International Telecommunication Union, 2009, 10–11.
22. Barry, 2006, 24.

23. Students & Scholars Against Corporate Misbehaviour, 2010a, 1–3. They also asked workers to pledge not to kill themselves and brought in monks to "exorcise the evil spirit haunting the company." Their report "reads like an Orwellian laundry list," with curfews and janitorial assignments as punishment for transgressions. But that didn't worry Apple's chief, Steve Jobs, who proudly reiterated that Apple was vigilant in assessing conditions in its supply chain and that Foxconn was not a sweatshop (Haddow, 2010). In keeping with Apple's onanism, the corporation's PR statements (Apple, 2009, 3, 6) insist that "companies we do business with must provide safe working conditions, treat employees with dignity and respect, and use environmentally responsible manufacturing processes wherever Apple products are made." Like News Corporation's dodgy vocabulary, Apple is proud to undertake such audits "through an aggressive monitoring program" even as it reveals a stunning and presumably faux naiveté that "Apple's audits revealed a complex labor supply chain."

24. Rodríguez-Garavito, 2011. Our thanks to Anamaria Tamayo Duque for these insights. See also http://www.youtube.com/watch?v=-DFHhuDy17M&feature=related; http://www.youtube.com/watch?v=sU_aKo_lyJU&feature=share

25. "Muck and Brass Plates," 2009; "A Soul-Searching Business," 2007; Rizvi, 2008; "Scavenger Hunt," 2007. This represents one of those fascinating transformations from social problem to social boon, as ragpickers shift from being regarded as unpleasant, odoriferous embodiments of the abject to model citizens of sustainable development and targets of the contemporary development discourse of microcredit. Weaker examples of green citizenship include the 2008 International Year of Sanitation, when thirty-six Indian ragpickers were invited to New York for a UN conference and strode along a catwalk as models. They were members of the Dalit caste, for whom ragpicking is a traditional but demeaned way of life. This recognition became a way of both legitimizing and transcending their lives. But, while these few dozen strolled through Gotham, 30,000 of their fellow workers remained in Mumbai picking away at waste, sorting through and categorizing rubbish in an informal *recto-verso* of a factory line that had produced "useful" products.

26. Byster and Smith, 2006, 109.

27. Smith, 2009, 13.

28. Barry, 2006, 33.

29. Frey, 2009; Shatner's phone message said, in part, "This is William Shatner speaking. You, HP, promised me a toxic-free computer by 2009. Now my friends at Greenpeace tell me that I have to wait until 2011. What's up with that? Please, ask your leader, Mark Hurd, to make computers that are free of toxic PVC plastic and brominated flame retardants just as Apple's done." See http://www.greenpeace.org/international/news/hp-reminder-28-07-09.

30. This is ethical consumption at play in civil society: developing the politics of spectacle, but eluding the search for expressive totality, so common in identity politics, by drawing on political economy and multisited knowledge (Carducci, 2006; Muldoon, 2006). That involves tracking the life of each commodity sign—establishing its eclectic, electronic legacy via design, manufacture, electricity, use, disposal, and recycling. It is a model for analysis and activism alike, of reconnecting workers and consumers to reverse the process that Marx derided as "man separated from man" (1994, 139).

31. "Greenpeace Forced Out," 2006; http://www.greenpeace.org/usa/news/tastygreenapple.

32. "Lenovo Tops Eco-Friendly Ranking," 2007.

33. Even the most neoliberally misinformed trade agreements generally provide political exceptions to laissez-faire exchange between borders for standing armies as entities of the sovereign state. They often exempt environmental matters as well.

34. Seafaring, telecommunications, football, accreditation, Catholicism, postage, airways, sea lanes, and athletics come to mind.

35. Beck and Grande, 2010, 410.
36. http://pdba.georgetown.edu/Constitutions/Ecuador/english08.html. Article 71 begins: "Nature, or Pacha Mama, where life is reproduced and occurs, has the right to integral respect for its existence and for the maintenance and regeneration of its life cycles, structure, functions and evolutionary processes."
37. Schauer, 2003.
38. Intergovernmental Panel on Climate Change, 2007, 72.
39. See Commoner, 1971.
40. Schauer, 2003, 3–6. There are two massive capitalist states in economic takeoff mode (India and China) rivaling in time and impact the remarkable ascent of the United States, the Soviet Union, and Japan. Their desire for natural resources and media technologies is matched only by their predecessors' unwillingness to pay the ecological price of this heritage.
41. Babu, Parande, and Basha, 2007; Nnorom and Osibanjo, 2008.
42. Baram, 2009; Ferus-Comelo, 2008; Schatan and Castilleja, 2007.
43. Many factors determine the viability of this model. Peace is a precondition, as is evident in eastern Congo, where armed conflict and despotism are funded by "conflict minerals," mined to feed the rapid expansion of electronics manufacturing (Global Witness, 2009). As the Colombian ragpickers' struggle has shown, the state must aggressively check corporate domination of markets and resist private capital's influence over policy to ensure that smaller firms and cooperatives with strong ecological credentials can thrive.
44. Hardin, 1968.
45. Seyfang, 2005.
46. Ostrom, 2000, 47.
47. Karpowitz et al., 2009, 584.
48. See Twentieth Century Fox, n.d.
49. "Calculating Your Carbon Footprint," 2010.
50. See note 18.
51. Zoeteman, Krikke, and Venselaar, 2010, 416 (emphasis added).
52. The Economics of Ecosystems and Biodiversity, 2010, 26.
53. The references used in our fictive account are not imagined.
54. Sy and Tinker (2010) provide a mathematical model that can be applied to this global scale of labor.
55. This radicalization would be based, somewhat ironically, in a collective realization that the quantification of populations had emerged from contradictions in the capitalist political economy that linked surveillance, social control, and liberation. This nexus would have enabled corporations to exercise absolute authority over a workforce that was technically free, in that its members could resign if they so wished. From the perspective of the radical accountant, though, it also provided information that could be used against the powerful. The division of labor that the accountants of the future would have fought to evaluate would have not evolved into the transparent system that classical economics long ago predicted, in the terms that the pioneering social scientist Émile Durkheim chided for promising a "higher law of human societies and the condition for progress" (1984, 1). Rather, as critical political economists have shown, capitalism shaped the division of labor into a key mechanism of power and control by subdividing work, multiplying its inputs, and spreading it unevenly across the planet. Marx suggests that the interconnectedness of workers that constituted the progressive dimension in the division of labor—workers of the world unite! Solidarity forever!—was obscured from those working within it, while being perverted and exploited by those with command over it (1906, 49, 83).
56. International Labor Organization, 2010; GeSI and EICC, 2008, 56; Raina, 2007, 18–25.

57. The accountants will achieve much of this new-and-improved, more labor-inclusive, accounting program by internationalizing data collection and implementing an ethnographic dimension as part of their research methodology. The new accountancy will benefit from learning world languages. Cultivating a professional delight in cultural difference, they will identify many new facets of everyday life affected by the global supply chain. Some older practitioners will see these worldly polymath characteristics as a welcome recovery of a twentieth-century notion of the humanities—one that informed interdisciplinary and internationalist ideals lost by public higher education by the end of that century. For the accountants of the future, in contrast, nostalgia and highfalutin principles will have nothing to do with acquiring these capabilities. They will be fundamental skills needed for the job ahead.

58. See Massey, 1979; National Research Council, 2005; Silicon Valley Toxics Coalition, n.d.; Grossman, 2006.

59. See Leung et al., 2008; Wong et al., 2007; Ray et al., 2004.

60. See Zoeteman et al., 2010, 418; Schor, 2010, 32–37.

61. Of course, the new accountants would be aware that it was possible to ascribe a value to the physical damage caused by exposure to toxic dust, but the cynical nature of the process sickened them. Case in point: in 2010, a US court determined that workers exposed to poisons in the ruins of the World Trade Center were worth at most about $81,000 a piece. The price was indexed to the loss of good health caused by the failure of government and business to provide protection to "first responders." In 2010, the EPA set the value of one human life at $9.1 million, though the Food and Drug Administration averred with a figure that was over a million lower, which is somewhere between where the EPA and an academic expert on these matters places the price of a human life (Appelbaum, 2011, A1).

62. The Economics of Ecosystems and Biodiversity, 2010, 26.

63. See Center for Environmental Health et al., 2006; United States Department of Justice, 2010; Leung et al., 2008; Basel Action Network, 2005; Orisakwe and Frazzoli, 2010; Chintan Environmental Research and Action Group, 2009.

## CONCLUSION

1. Taibbi, 2011.

2. Schor, 2010.

3. Van Erp and Huisman, 2010; United States Government Accountability Office, 2008, 23–27, 24 n. 22.

4. Walsh, 2010; Criminal Intelligence Service Canada, 2008; van Erp and Huisman, 2010.

5. Byster and Smith, 2006, 109.

6. Thornes, 2008; Struppek, 2006; http://www.ecorazzi.com/2011/08/01/solar-and-wind-powered-billboards-hit-london-new-york-and-sydney/. Artists also draw attention to personal multimedia messaging services by capturing passersby on electronic billboards, such as Zhang Ga's *Peoples' Portrait* in Times Square in New York City, a throwback for all the world to Judy Holliday's moment of celebrity in the classic Hollywood film *It Should Happen to You* (George Cukor, 1954), in which the main character buys advertising space to promote herself in Columbus Circle.

7. Robins and Webster, 1999, 62.

8. Mayfield, 2003; Johnson, 2011; Thompson, 2003; Anderson and Wolff, 2010; Feuz et al., 2011.

9. Greenpeace, 2011.

10. See http://digitallabor.org.

11. Ross, 2009; Carr, 2011; International Federation of Reproduction Rights Organizations, http://ifrro.org; The U.S. Digital Millennium Copyright Act, http://www.copyright.gov/legislation/dmca.pdf.

12. Edgerton, 2007, 196; Liu et al., 2009; For Leonard's work see http://storyofstuff.org/electronics; Even the OECD recommends Leonard's work! (Organisation for Economic Co-Operation and Development, 2010, 13).

13. Twenty years ago, the radical psychotherapist and philosopher Félix Guattari summed up many of these critical scholarly concerns, as follows: "The wider ecological question seems to me too important to be abandoned to the archaizing, folkloristic tendencies which choose determinedly to reject large-scale political involvement. Ecology should abandon its connotative links with images of a small minority of nature lovers or accredited experts; for the ecology I propose here questions the whole of subjectivity and capitalist power formations—formations which, moreover, can by no means be assured of continuing their successes of the last decade. … All the indicators suggest that the increased productivity engendered by current technological revolutions will continue to rise exponentially. The question is whether new ecological operators and new enunciative assemblages will succeed in orienting that growth along paths that avoid the absurdity and the impasses of integrated world capitalism." (1989, 140)

14. Orwell (1944) adds this example: "Take simply the instance of travel. In the nineteenth century some parts of the world were unexplored, but there was almost no restriction on travel. Up to 1914 you did not need a passport for any country except Russia. The European emigrant, if he could scrape together a few pounds for the passage, simply set sail for America or Australia, and when he got there no questions were asked. In the eighteenth century it had been quite normal and safe to travel in a country with which your own country was at war." Any foreigner trying to enter the United States today, for example, will smile ruefully or fume manically at such a story.

15. Knight, quoted in Briggs and Burke, 2003, 104.

16. Ford, 1929, 9, 18–19.

17. Marconi, 1924; see also Arnheim, 1969, 160–63; Marvin, 1988, 192–93.

18. Mosco, 2004; cf. Barthes, 1973, 118.

19. Sundaram, 2010, 2–3.

20. Silicon Valley Toxics Coalition, 2009; Woody, 2011; Ross, 2011, 148–84.

21. Unger and Gough, 2008.

# BIBLIOGRAPHY

"450,000 Unsold Earth Day Issues of *Time* Trucked to Landfill." Headline in *The Onion*, July 1, 2008, http://www.theonion.com/articles/450000-unsold-earth-day-issues-of-time-trucked-to,362/.

*Book Industry Treatise on Environmentally Responsible Publishing. Green Press Initiative*, April 2009. http://www.greenpressinitiative.org/documents/IndustryTreatisePaper.pdf.

"The Book Industry Unites on 'Green' Issues." *Book Business*, January 2008. http://www.bookbusinessmag.com/article/the-book-industry-unites-green-issues-90066/1#utm_source=bookbusinessmag.com&utm_medium=search_results.

"Buy Blue's Mission." December 16, 2004. http://www.buyblue.org.

"Calculating Your Carbon Footprint: How To Measure, Reduce and Offset." Panel sponsored by the Producers Guild of America East, Kodak Screening Room, New York, September 20, 2010.

"Cat and Mouse, on the Web." *Economist*, December 2, 2006. http://www.economist.com/node/8312210.

"China: Another Suicide at Foxconn." *Chinaworker*, January 20, 2011. http://www.chinaworker.info/en/content/news/1310/.

"Colour Picture Tube." *Encyclopedia Britannica Online*, n.d. http://www.britannica.com/eb/art-47985.

"Consumer Interest in Sustainability Remains Consistent Through Downturn." *Capstrat*, press release, November 19, 2010. http://www.capstrat.com/news/consumer-interest-sustainability-remains-consistent-through-downturn.

"A Cyber-House Divided." *Economist*, September 2, 2010, 61–62. http://www.economist.com/node/16943885.

"Data, Data Everywhere." *Economist*, February 27, 2010. 3–5. http://www.economist.com/node/15557443.

"Deadly Spires in The Night: The Impact of Communications Towers on Migratory Birds." *Issue Brief from the Ornithological Council* 1, no. 8 (October 1999). http://www.nmnh.si.edu/BIRDNET/orncounc/issues/OCBv1n8.html.

"Down on the Server Farm." *Economist*, May 24, 2008, 83–84. http://www.economist.com/node/11413148.

"Edited Out." *Economist*, April 3, 2010, 66. http://www.economist.com/node/15825802.

"The End of Wintel." *Economist*, July 31, 2010, 53–54. http://www.economist.com/node/16693547.

"E-Publish or Perish." *Economist*, April 3, 2010, 65–66. http://www.economist.com/node/15819008.

"Filming 'Damaged Beach.'" *Nation*, December 1, 2006. http://www.nationmultimedia. com/2006/12/01/national/national_30020443.php.

"Forum." *Communication and Critical/Cultural Studies* 7, no. 1 (2010): 90–113.

"From Allen Lane to Amazon: The Story of Publishing in the 20th Century." *Guardian*, May 25, 2010. http://www.guardian.co.uk/books/audioslideshow/2010/may/24/publishing-history-20th-century.

"The Future of the Pencil." *Economist*, September 16, 2010. http://www.economist.com/ node/17043890.

"Gartner Estimates ICT Industry Accounts for 2 Percent of Global CO2 Emissions." *Gartner*, press release, April 6, 2007. http://www.gartner.com/it/page.jsp?id=503867.

"GE, Cisco and Others Team with Miami for $200M Smart Grid Project." GreenBiz.com, April 20, 2009. http://www.greenbiz.com/news/2009/04/20/ge-cisco-miami-smart-grid.

"General Electric to Power Up New Battery Plant in Upstate New York." GreenBiz.com, May 12, 2009. http://www.greenbiz.com/news/2009/05/12/ge-battery-plant.

"Greenery on the March." *Economist*, December 12, 2009. http://www.economist.com/ node/15048783.

"Greenpeace Forced Out of Apple Mac Expo." *Greenpeace International*, press release, November 27, 2007. http://www.greenpeace.org/international/press/releases/greenpeace-forced-out-of-apple.

"Growing Concern Over India's E-Waste." *BBC News*, December 12, 2003. http://news.bbc. co.uk/2/hi/south_asia/3307815.stm.

"Help Urged for Ivory Coast Waste." *BBC News*, November 24, 2006. http://news.bbc.co.uk/2/ hi/science/nature/6180604.stm.

"How Marketing Missteps Stalled TV Sales." *Bloomberg Businessweek*, January 24, 2011, 24.

"How Not to Annoy Your Customers." *Economist*, January 5, 2008. http://www.economist. com/node/10431119.

"IBM and Cisco to Help Amsterdam Become a 'Smart City.'" *GreenBiz*, July 14, 2009. http:// www.greenbiz.com/news/2009/07/14/ibm-cisco-amsterdam-smart-city#/nl/home.

"I'm a Mac. And I'm Un-PC." *Mother Jones*, March/April, 2010.

"James Cameron is a Hypocrite." *Edmonton Sun*, September 29, 2010. http://www.edmonton-sun.com/comment/editorial/2010/09/28/15510431.html.

"Junk Science." *Economist*, August 21, 2010. http://www.economist.com/node/16843825.

"Kodak Rewrites The Book On Printing." *Businessweek*, September 4, 2006. http://www.busi-nessweek.com/magazine/content/06_36/b3999087.htm.

"Lenovo Tops Eco-Friendly Ranking." *BBC News*, April 4, 2007. http://news.bbc.co.uk/2/hi/ technology/6525307.stm.

"Let Them Eat Pollution." *Economist*, February 8, 1992.

"Light and Death." *Economist*, May 29, 2010. http://www.economist.com/node/16231588.

"Massive Protest in Chennai in Support of Foxconn Workers." International Metalworkers' Federation, October 22, 2010. http://preview.imfmetal.org/index.cfm?c=24442&l=2.

"Moguls to Direct Film's Future." *Financial Times*, November 29, 2006. http://www.ft.com/ intl/cms/s/0/d5cff1fa-7f4d-11db-b193-0000779e2340.html#axzz1cUuJnyo4.

"Muck and Brass Plates." *Economist*, June 13, 2009. http://www.economist.com/ node/13832475.

"A New Old Idea" *Economist*, September 8, 2007. http://www.economist.com/node/9719155.

"Ohio: Power Line Kills Copper Thief." *New York Times*, July 17, 2007. http://www.nytimes. com/2007/07/17/us/17brfs-copper.html.

"One Small Step for Electronic Waste." *New York Times*, March 15, 2008. http://www.nytimes. com/2008/03/15/opinion/15sat4.html.

"Out of Vogue.". *Economist*, September 29, 2007. http://www.economist.com/node/9867938.

"PC Users 'Want Greener Machines.'" *BBC News,* June 26, 2006. http://news.bbc.co.uk/2/hi/technology/5107642.stm.

"Popotla vs. Titanic." *®™ark,* n.d. http://rtmark.com/popotla.html.

"Power from Thin Air." *Economist,* June 12, 2010. http://www.economist.com/node/16295708.

"Ruses to Cut Printing Costs." *Economist,* September 4, 2010. http://www.economist.com/node/16910041.

"Scavenger Hunt." *Economist,* November 17, 2007. http://www.economist.com/node/10147690.

"A Soul-Searching Business." *Economist,* December 22, 2007. http://www.economist.com/node/10311257.

"Sony to Launch Power-Saving TVs." *Jiji Press,* January 19, 2009.

"The Strange Survival of Ink." *Economist,* June 12, 2010. http://www.economist.com/node/16322554.

"Test-Tube Love Seat." *Time,* February 26, 1940. http://www.time.com/time/magazine/article/0,9171,763265,00.html.

"The Smelter Trust and Mexican Silver—Believed the Complete Control of the Silver Mining Industry of Mexico is Contemplated." *New York Times,* April 27, 1903. http://query.nytimes.com/gst/abstract.html?res=F60F15FC345412738DDDAE0A94DC405B838CF1D3.

"Twilight City—Where Snapshots Are Born." *Modern Mechanix & Inventions Magazine,* February 1936, 84–86, 122. http://blog.modernmechanix.com/2006/06/28/twilight-city-where-snapshots-are-born/.

"Union Leaders and Workers Remain in Jail in Foxconn Dispute in India." *International Metalworkers' Federation,* October 18, 2010. http://www.imfmetal.org/index.cfm?c=24381&l=2.

"UN Warning on E-Waste 'Mountain.'" *BBC News,* November 27, 2006. http://news.bbc.co.uk/2/hi/technology/6187358.stm.

"The U.S.'s Toughest Customer." *Time,* December 12, 1969. http://www.time.com/time/magazine/article/0,9171,840502,00.html.

"The Value of Gutta Percha; The World's Supply Becoming Alarmingly Deficient. New Trees Found in German New Guinea." *New York Times,* April 6, 1902. http://query.nytimes.com/gst/abstract.html?res=F10B1EF93B591B728DDDAF0894DC405B828CF1D3.

"Where is 'Away'?" *Real Change,* December 23, 2009. http://www.realchangenews.org/index.php/site/archives/3583.

"Wiser Wires." *Economist,* October 10, 2010. http://www.economist.com/node/14586006.

"Electronics: X Rays in the Living Room." *Time,* August 4, 1967. http://www.time.com/time/magazine/article/0,9171,837185,00.html.

Abou-Elela, Sohair I., Fayza A. Nasr, Hanan S. Ibrahim, Nagwa M. Badr, and Abdul Raziq M. Askalany. "Pollution Prevention Pays Off in a Board Paper Mill." *Journal of Cleaner Production* 16, no. 3 (February 2008): 330–34.

Abrams, Herbert K. "A Short History of Occupational Health." *Journal of Public Health Policy* 22, no. 1 (2001): 34–80.

Acland, Charles, ed. *Residual Media.* Minneapolis: University of Minnesota Press, 2007.

Adorno, Theodor W. "Transparencies on Film." Translated by Thomas Y. Levin. *New German Critique* 24/25 (1981–82): 199–205.

Adshead, S. A. M. *Material Culture in Europe and China, 1400–1800: The Rise of Consumerism.* New York: St. Martin's Press, 1997.

Aftab, Kaleem. "Emission Impossible: Why Hollywood is One of the Worst Polluters." *Independent,* November 16, 2007. http://independent.co.uk/arts-entertainment/films/features/emission-impossible-why-hollywood-is-one-of-the-worst-polluters-400493.html.

Agnew, John. "Money Games: Currencies and Power in the Contemporary World Economy." *Antipode* 41, no. 8 (January 2010): 214–38.

Aguilar, Miguel Ángel, Eduardo Nivón, María Ana Portal, and Rosalía Winocur, eds. *Pensar lo contemporáneo: De la cultura situada a la convergencia tecnológica*. Barcelona: Anthropos Editorial, 2009.

Allen, Stuart. *Media, Risk and Science*. Buckingham, UK, and Philadelphia: Open University Press, 2002.

Allen, Terry J. "E-Wasting Away in China." *In These Times*, October 30, 2007, http://www.inthesetimes.com/article/3373/.

American Psychological Association. *Psychology and Global Climate Change: Addressing a Multi-Faceted Phenomenon and Set of Challenges*. 2009. Report of the American Psychological Association's Task Force on the interface between psychology and climate change. http://www.apa.org/science/about/publications/climate-change-booklet.pdf.

Andersen, Robin. "Bush's Fantasy Budget and the Military/Entertainment Complex." *PRWatch*, February 12, 2007, http://prwatch.org/node/5742.

Anderson, Benedict. *Imagined Communities: Reflections on the Origin and Spread of Nationalism*. Rev. ed. London: Verso, 1991.

Anderson, Christopher. "Little Green Men." *Flow* 2, no. 8 (July 8, 2005). http://flowtv.org/2005/07/advertising-ge-ecoimagination.

Anderson, Christopher. "Are Dead-Tree Magazines Good or Bad for the Climate?" *The Long Tail* blog, December 27, 2007, http://longtail.com/the_long_tail/2007/12/are-dead-tree-m.html.

Anderson, Christopher, and Michael Wolff. "The Web is Dead: Long Live the Internet." *Wired*, August 17, 2010, http://www.wired.com/magazine/2010/08/ff_webrip/all/1.

Anderson, Doug. "Is the Great American Newspaper Dead?" *Nielsen Wire* blog, June 1, 2009. http://blog.nielsen.com/nielsenwire/media_entertainment/is-the-great-american-newspaper-dead/.

Anderson, Perry, Folker Fröbel, Jürgen Heinrichs, and Otto Kreye. "On Some Postulates of an Anti-Systemic Policy." *Dialectical Anthropology* 12, no. 1 (1987): 1–13.

Andreola, Fernanda, Luisa Barbieri, Anna Corradi, and Isabella Lancellotti. "CRT Glass State of the Art: A Case Study: Recycling in Ceramic Glazes." *Journal of the European Ceramic Society* 27, nos. 2/3 (2007): 1623–29.

Appelbaum, Binyamin. "As U.S. Agencies Put More Value on a Life, Businesses Fret." *New York Times*, February 7, 2011. http://www.nytimes.com/2011/02/17/business/economy/17regulation.html?pagewanted=all.

Apple. *Supplier Responsibility: 2009 Progress Report. Apple*, February 2009. http://images.apple.com/supplierresponsibility/pdf/SR_2009_Progress_Report.pdf.

Apple. *Supplier Responsibility: 2010 Progress Report. Apple*, 2010. http://images.apple.com/supplierresponsibility/pdf/SR_2010_Progress_Report.pdf.

Apple. *Apple Supplier Responsibility: 2011 Progress Report. Apple*, 2011. http://images.apple.com/supplierresponsibility/pdf/Apple_SR_2011_Progress_Report.pdf.

Arias-Maldonaldo, Manuel. "An Imaginary Solution? The Green Defence of Deliberative Democracy." *Environmental Values* 16, no. 2 (2007): 233–52.

Arnheim, Rudolf. *Film as Art*. London: Faber and Faber, 1969.

Aronson, David. "How Congress Devastated Congo." *New York Times*, August 8, 2011. http://www.nytimes.com/2011/08/08/opinion/how-congress-devastated-congo.html.

Aslama, Minna, Kalle Siira, Ronald Rice, and Pekka Aula, with Philip Napoli and Katy Pearce. *Mapping Communication and Media Research in the U.S.* Helsinki: Communication Research Centre, Department of Communication, University of Helsinki, 2007. http://www.valt.helsinki.fi/blogs/crc/ReportUSA.pdf.

Assadourian, Erik. "The Rise and Fall of Consumer Cultures." In *2010 State of the World—Transforming Cultures from Consumerism to Sustainability*, edited by Worldwatch Institute, 3–20. New York: W. W. Norton, 2010.

Atlantic States Legal Foundation, Inc., Plaintiff-Appellant, v. Eastman Kodak Company. United States Court of Appeals, 12 F.3d, 353 (2nd Cir., argued June 10, 1993, decided Dec. 14, 1993; as amended Feb. 3, 1994).

Attali, Jacques. "This is Not America's Final Crisis." *New Perspectives Quarterly* 25, no. 2 (Spring 2008): 31–33.

Attali, Jacques, and Yves Stourdze. (1977). "The Birth of the Telephone and Economic Crisis: The Slow Death of Monologue in French Society." In *The Social Impact of the Telephone*, edited by Ithiel de Sola Pool, 97–111. Cambridge, MA: MIT Press.

Babbage, Charles. *On the Economy of Machinery and Manufactures.* London: Charles Knight, 1832.

Babu, Balakrishnan Ramesh, Anand Kuber Parande, and Chiya Ahmed Basha. "Electrical and Electronic Waste: A Global Environmental Problem." *Waste Management & Research* 25, no. 4 (2007): 307–18.

Bacon, Francis. *Novum Organum*, in *Francis Bacon, Selections. The Works.* Edited and translated by Basil Montague. 3 vols. Philadelphia: Parry & Macmillan, 1854.

Bailard, Catie Snow. "Mobile Phone Diffusion and Corruption in Africa." *Political Communication* 26, no. 3 (2009): 333–53.

Bakker, Gerben. "Building Knowledge about the Consumer: The Emergence of Market Research in the Motion Picture Industry." *Business History* 45, no. 1 (2003): 101–27.

Bakker, Karen. "The Limits of 'Neoliberal Natures': Debating Green Neoliberalism." *Progress in Human Geography* 34, no. 6 (December 2010): 715–35.

Balfour, Fredrik, and Tim Culpan. "The Man Who Makes Your iPhone." *Bloomberg Businessweek*, September 9, 2010. http://www.businessweek.com/magazine/content/10_38/b4195058423479.htm.

Balmford, Andrew, Andrea Manica, Lesley Airey, Linda Birkin, Amy Oliver, and Judith Schleicher. "Hollywood, Climate Change, and the Public." *Science* 305 (June 11, 2004): 1713.

Balmori, Alfonso. "Electromagnetic Pollution from Phone Masts. Effects on Wildlife." *Pathophysiology* 16, nos. 2/3 (2009): 191–99.

Bar, François, with Caroline Simard. (2006). "From Hierarchies to Network Firms." In *The Handbook of New Media: Updated Students Edition.* Edited by Leah Lievrouw and Sonia Livingstone, 350–63. Thousand Oaks, CA: Sage.

Baram, Michael. "Globalization and Workplace Hazards in Developing Nations." *Safety Science* 47, no. 6 (2009): 756–66.

Barboza, David. "String of Suicides Continues at Electronics Supplier in China." *New York Times*, May 26, 2010. http://www.nytimes.com/2010/05/26/technology/26suicide.html.

Barboza, David. "Workers Sickened at Apple Supplier Chain in China." *New York Times*, February 23, 2011. http://www.nytimes.com/2011/02/23/technology/23apple.html?pagewanted=all.

Barboza, David, and Keith Bradsher. "In China, Labor Movement Enabled by Technology." *New York Times*, June 17, 2010. http://www.nytimes.com/2010/06/17/business/global/17strike.html?pagewanted=all.

Barbrook, Richard, and Andy Cameron. "The Californian Ideology." *Science as Culture* 6, no. 1 (1996): 44–72.

Barker, Terry, Athanasios Dagoumas, and Jonathan Rubin. "The Macroeconomic Rebound Effect and the World Economy." *Energy Efficiency* 2, no. 4 (2009): 411–27.

Barnett, Jon, Peter Christoff, Haripriya Rangan, and Elissa Sutherland. (2009). "Commentary: An Inconvenient Truth (2006) (Directed by Davis Guggenheim and Al Gore, Paramount Pictures, USA): Review Symposium." *Geographical Research* 47, no. 2: 204–11.

Barnouw, Eric. *Tube of Plenty*, 2nd ed. New York: Oxford University Press, 1990.

Barone, Jennifer. "How Big is Discover's Carbon Footprint?" *Discover*, April 21, 2008. http://discovermagazine.com/2008/may/21-how-big-is-discover.s-carbon-footprint.

Baroudi, Carol, Jeffrey Hill, Arnold Reinhold, and Jhana Senxian. *Green IT for Dummies*. Hoboken: Wiley, 2009.

Barry, John. "Resistance is Fertile: From Environmental to Sustainability Citizenship." In *Environmental Citizenship*. Edited by Andrew Dobson and Derek R. Bell, 21–48. Cambridge, MA: MIT Press, 2006.

Barthes, Roland. *Mythologies*. Translated by Annette Lavers. New York: Hill and Wang, 1973.

Basel Action Network. *The Digital Dump: Exporting Re-Use and Abuse to Africa*. Seattle: Basel Action Network, 2005.

Basel Action Network. *JPEPA* [Japan-Philippines Economic Partnership Agreement] *as a Step in Japan's Greater Plan to Liberalize Hazardous Waste Trade in Asia*. Seattle: Basel Action Network, 2007.

Basel Action Network and Silicon Valley Toxics Coalition. *Exporting Harm: The High-Tech Trashing of Asia*. Seattle: Basel Action Network, February 25, 2002.

Baudelaire, Charles. *Les Fleurs du Mal*. Paris: Gallimard, 1972. Also see http://go.worldbank.org/Z6O4UP9G10.

Baudrillard, Jean. *Selected Writings*. Edited by Mark Poster. Stanford, CA: Stanford University Press, 1988.

Baudrillard, Jean. "Consumer Society." In *Consumer Society in American History: A Reader*. Edited by Lawrence B. Glickman, 33–56. Ithaca, NY: Cornell University Press, 1999.

Baudrillard, Jean. "Our Society's Judgment and Punishment." Translated by Laura Nyssola. *International Journal of Baudrillard Studies* 3, no. 2 (July 2006). http://www.ubishops.ca/baudrillardstudies/vol3_2/jb_soc.htm.

Bazin, André. *What is Cinema?* Translated by Hugh Gray. Berkeley: University of California Press, 1967.

Bean, Louis H. "Changing Trends in Cotton Production and Consumption." *Southern Economic Journal* 5, no. 4 (April 1939): 442–59.

Beaty, Bart. "My Media Studies: The Failure of Hype." *Television & New Media* 10, no. 1 (2009): 23–24.

Beck, Ulrich. *World Risk Society*. Cambridge: Polity, 1999.

Beck, Ulrich, and Edgar Grande. "Varieties of Second Modernity: The Cosmopolitan Turn in Social and Political Theory and Research." *British Journal of Sociology* 61, no. 3 (2010): 409–43.

Beck, Ulrich, Anthony Giddens, and Scott Lash. *Reflexive Modernization: Politics, Tradition and Aesthetics in the Modern Social Order*. Stanford, CA: Stanford University Press, 1994.

Behring, Natalie. "Inside the Digital Dump." *Foreign Policy*, May/June 2007. http://www.foreignpolicy.com/articles/2009/09/23/inside_the_digital_dump.

Bell, Daniel. "The Future World Disorder: The Structural Context of Crises." *Foreign Policy* 27 (1977): 109–35.

Bellman, Eric. "Wal-Mart Exports Big-Box Concept to India." *Wall Street Journal*, May 28, 2009. http://online.wsj.com/article/SB124346697277260377.html.

Bengali, Shashank. "African Workers Find Harsh Conditions in Chinese-Run Plants." *McClatchy*, July 24, 2009. http://www.mcclatchydc.com/2009/07/24/72419/african-workers-find-harsh-conditions.html.

Benhabib, Seyla. *The Claims of Culture: Equality and Diversity in the Global Era*. Princeton: Princeton University Press, 2002.

Benjamin, Walter. "Central Park." Translated by Lloyd Spencer with Mark Harrington. *New German Critique* 34 (1985): 32–58.

Benjamin, Walter. *Illuminations*. Edited by Hannah Arendt and translated by Harry Zohn. London: Fontana, 1992.

Bentham, Jeremy. *The Principles of Morals and Legislation*. Darien: Hafner, 1970.

Berkhout, Frans, and Julia Hertin. "De-Materialising and Re-Materialising: Digital Technologies and the Environment." *Futures* 36, no. 8 (2004): 903–20.

Berland, Jody. "Animal and/as Medium: Symbolic Work in Communicative Regimes." *The Global South* 3, no. 1 (2009a): 42–65.

Berland, Jody. *North of Empire: Essays on the Cultural Technologies of Space*. Durham, NC: Duke University Press, 2009b.

Berry, Sarah. *Screen Style: Fashion and Femininity in 1930s Hollywood*. Minneapolis: University of Minnesota Press, 2000.

Betts, Kellyn. "PBDEs and PCBs in Computers, Cars, and Homes." *Environmental Science & Technology* 40, no. 24 (2006): 7452.

Biagioli, Mario. "Postdisciplinary Liaisons: Science Studies and the Humanities." *Critical Inquiry* 35, no. 4 (2009): 816–33.

Bidwai, Praful. "Prevent, Prepare & Protect." *Rediff News*, January 4, 2005 http://in.rediff.com/news/2005/jan/04bidwai.htm.

Bio Intelligence Service with European Business Council for Sustainable Energy and Fraunhofer Institut Zuverlässigkeit and Mikrointegration. *European Commission DG INFSO: Impacts of Information and Communication Technologies and Energy Efficiency*. Tender no. CPP 16A-2007/2007/S 68-082361. Final report, 2008.

BioRegional and London Sustainable Development Commission. *Capital Consumption: The Transition to Sustainable Consumption and Production in London*. London: London Sustainable Development Commission, 2009.

Black, Lawrence. " 'Making Britain a Gayer and More Cultivated Country': Wilson, Lee and the Creative Industries in the 1960s." *Contemporary British History* 20, no. 3 (2006): 323–42.

Blair, George A. "The Development of the Motion Picture Raw Film Industry." *Annals of the American Academy of Political and Social Science* 128, no. 1 (November 1926): 50–53.

Blair, Helen. (2001). " 'You're Only as Good as Your Last Job': The Labour Process and Labour Market in the British Film Industry." *Work, Employment and Society* 15, no. 1: 149–69.

Blake-Coleman, B. C. *Copper Wire and Electrical Conductors: The Shaping of a Technology*. Philadelphia: Harwood Academic, 1992.

Bobo, Jacqueline. *Black Women as Cultural Readers*. New York: Columbia University Press, 1995.

Boguski, Terrie K. (2010). "Life Cycle Carbon Footprint of the *National Geographic* Magazine." *International Journal of Life Cycle Assessment* 15, no. 7: 635–43.

Booth, Jessica. "It's Not Easy Being Green, or Is It?" http://hiddenwires.co.uk/resourcesarticles2010/articles20101203-08.html

Borealis Centre for Environment and Trade Research, Book Industry Study Group, and Green Press Initiative. *Environmental Trends and Climate Impacts: Findings from the U.S. Book Industry: A Research Report Commissioned by Book Industry Study Group and Green Press Initiative*. New York: Book Industry Study Group/Green Press Initiative, 2008.

Borland, John, and Evan Hansen. "The TV is Dead. Long Live the TV." *Wired*, April 6, 2007. http://www.wired.com/entertainment/hollywood/news/2007/04/tvhistory_0406.

Bottini, Novella, Christoph Ernst, and Malta Luebker. *Offshoring and the Labor Market: What are the Issues?* Geneva: International Labor Office, 2007.

Bowden, Sue, and Geoffrey Tweedale. "Poisoned by the Fluff: Compensation and Litigation for Byssinosis in the Lancashire Cotton Industry." *Journal of Law and Society* 29, no. 4 (2002): 560–79.

Bowser, Eileen. *History of the American Cinema, Volume Two: The Transformation of Cinema, 1907–1915*. New York: Charles Scribner's Sons, 1990.

Boyce, Tammy, and Justin Lewis, eds. *Climate Change and the Media*. New York: Peter Lang, 2009.

Boychuk, Rick. "Seeing the Light." *Canadian Geographic*, June, 2008. http://www.canadiangeographic.ca/magazine/jun08/ednotebook.asp.

Boykoff, Max. "Indian Media Representations of Climate Change in a Threatened Journalistic Ecosystem." *Climatic Change* 99, nos. 1/2 (2010): 17–25.

Boykoff, Maxwell T., and Michael K. Goodman. "Conspicuous Redemption? Reflections on the Promises and Perils of the 'Celebritization' of Climate Change." *Geoforum* 40, no. 3 (2009): 395–406.

Boykoff, Maxwell T., Adam Bumpus, Diana Liverman, and Samual Randalls. "Guest Editorial." *Environment and Planning* 41, no. 10 (2009): 2299–304.

Bozak, Nadia. "The Disposable Camera: Image, Energy, Environment." PhD diss., University of Toronto, 2008.

Bradsher, Keith. "China Builds High Wall to Guard Energy Industry." *New York Times*, July 14, 2009. http://www.nytimes.com/2009/07/14/business/energy-environment/14energy.html?pagewanted=all.

Brady, Heather. Review. *South Central Review* 15, nos. 3/4 (1998): 75–77.

Branigan, Tania. "Taiwan iPhone Manufacturer Replaces Chinese Workers with Robots." *Guardian*, August 2, 2011. http://www.guardian.co.uk/world/2011/aug/01/foxconn-robots-replace-chinese-workers.

Braudel, Fernand. *Capitalism and Material Life 1400–1800*. Translated by Miriam Kochan. New York: Harper Calophon, 1973.

Brereton, Pat. *Hollywood Utopia: Ecology in Contemporary American Cinema*. Bristol, UK: Intellect, 2005.

Brigden, Kevin, David Santillo, and Paul Johnston. *Playing Dirty: Analysis of Hazardous Chemicals and Materials in Games Console Components*. Amsterdam: Greenpeace, 2008.

Briggs, Asa, and Peter Burke. *A Social History of the Media: From Gutenberg to the Internet*. Cambridge: Polity, 2003.

Broad, William J. "NASA Forced to Steer Clear of Junk in Cluttered Space." *New York Times*, July 31, 2007. http://www.nytimes.com/2007/07/31/science/space/31orbi.html.

Broadberry, Stephen, and Sayantan Ghosal. "From the Counting House to the Modern Office: Explaining Anglo-American Productivity Differences in Services, 1870–1990." *Journal of Economic History* 62, no. 4 (2002): 967–98.

Brockington, Dan. "Powerful Environmentalisms: Conservation, Celebrity and Capitalism." *Media, Culture & Society* 30, no. 4 (2008): 551–68.

Brooker, Charlie. "Microsoft's Grinning Robots or the Brotherhood of the Mac. Which is Worse?" *Guardian*, September 28, 2009. http://www.guardian.co.uk/commentisfree/2009/sep/28/charlie-brooker-microsoft-mac-windows.

Brown, K., L. Emerton, A. Maina, H. Mogaka, and E. Betser. *Enhancing the Role of Non-Wood Tree Products in Livelihood Strategies of Smallholders in Semi-arid Kenya*. Norwich: The Overseas Development Group/The School of Development Studies, University of East Anglia, 1999.

Brzezinski, Zbigniew. *Between Two Ages: America's Role in the Technotronic Era*. New York: Viking, 1969.

Bullard, Robert D. "Environmental Justice in the 21st Century: Race Still Matters." *Phylon* 49, nos. 3/4 (2001): 151–71.

Burke, Edmund. (1986). *Reflections on the Revolution in France and on the Proceedings in Certain Societies in London Relative to that Event*. Ed. Conor Cruise O'Brien. Harmondsworth: Penguin.

Burke, John G. "Wood Pulp, Water Pollution, and Advertising." *Technology and Culture* 20, no. 1 (January 1979): 175–95.

Burston, Jonathan. "War and the Entertainment Industries: New Research Priorities in an Era of Cyber-Patriotism." *War and the Media: Reporting Conflict 24/7*. Edited by Daya Kishan Thussu and Des Freedman, 163–75. London: Sage, 2003.

Bush, Vannevar. "As We May Think." *Atlantic Monthly*, July 1945.

Bustamante, Carlos. "AGFA, Kullmann, Singer & Co. and Early Cine-Film Stock." *Film History* 20, no. 1 (2008): 59–76.

Butler, Kiera. "Econundrum: Kindles vs. Books." *MotherJones*, September 21, 2009. http://motherjones.com/blue-marble/2009/09/econundrum-kindles-vs-books.

Byster, Leslie A., and Ted Smith. "From Grassroots to Global." In *Challenging the Chip: Labor Rights and Environmental Justice in the Global Electronics Industry.* Edited by Ted Smith, David A. Sonnenfeld, and David Naguib Pellow, 111–19. Philadelphia: Temple University Press, 2006.

California State Auditor. *Electronic Waste: Some State Agencies Have Discarded Their Electronic Waste Improperly, While State and Local Oversight is Limited.* Report 2008–112. Sacramento: California State Auditor, 2008.

Callicott, J. Baird. *Earth's Insights: A Multicultural Survey of Ecological Ethics from the Mediterranean Basin to the Australian Outback.* Berkeley: University of California Press, 1994.

Calvert, James B. "The Electromagnetic Telegraph." n.d. mysite.du.edu/ ~jcalvert/tel/morse/morse.htm.

Calvino, Italo. *The Road to San Giovanni.* Translated by Tim Parks. New York: Vintage International, 1994.

Canonico, Scott, Royston Sellman, and Chris Preist. "Reducing the Greenhouse Gas Emissions of Commercial Print with Digital Technologies." Proceedings of the 2009 IEEE International Symposium on Sustainable Systems and Technology, 2009.

Carbon Disclosure Project. *CDP Investor CDP 2010 Information Request: News Corporation,* (2010a). https://www.cdproject.net/en-US/Pages/HomePage.aspx.

Carbon Disclosure Project. *CDP Investor CDP 2010 Information Request: Time Warner Inc,* 2010b. https://www.cdproject.net/en-US/Pages/HomePage.aspx.

The Carbon Neutral Company. "About Us." *The Carbon Neutral Company,* n.d. http://www.carbonneutral.com/about-us/our-history/.

Cardoso, Fernando Henrique. "Scholarship and Statesmanship." *Journal of Democracy* 16, no. 2 (2005): 5–12.

Carducci, Vince. "Culture Jamming: A Sociological Perspective." *Journal of Consumer Culture* 6, no. 1 (2006): 116–38.

Carey, James. "The Internet and the End of the National Communication System." In *Television: Critical Concepts in Media and Cultural Studies.* Vol. 5, edited by Toby Miller, 185–93. London: Routledge, 2003.

Carey, James W. Introduction to *Changing Concepts of Time* by Harold A. Innis, viii–xx. Lanham, MD: Rowman & Littlefield, 2004.

Carey, James W. "Historical Pragmatism and the Internet." *New Media & Society* 7, no. 4 (2005): 443–55.

Carr, David. "At Media Companies, a Nation of Serfs." *New York Times*, February 14, 2011. http://www.nytimes.com/2011/02/14/business/media/14carr.html.

Carrillo, Jorge. *Developing the U.S.-Mexico Border Region for a Prosperous and Secure Relationship: Innovative Companies and Policies for Innovation on the U.S.-Mexico Border.* Houston: James A. Baker III Institute for Public Policy of Rice University, 2009.

Carillo, Jorge, and Robert Zárate. "The Evolution of Maquiladora Best Practices: 1965–2008." *Journal of Business Ethics* 88, Supplement 2 (2009): 335–48.

Carli, Don. "The Footprint of Print and Digital Media Supply Chains." *Sustainable Communication* (January 16, 2010a). http://www.sustainablecommunication.org/resources/articles

Carli, Don. "Print vs. Digital Media: False Dilemmas and Forced Choices." *Sustainable Communication* (April 12, 2010b). http://www.sustainablecommunication.org/resources/articles

Carmichael, Deborah A. *The Landscape of Hollywood Westerns: Ecocriticism in an American Film Genre.* Salt Lake City: University of Utah Press, 2006.

Castañeda, Mari. "Television Set Production in the Era of Digital TV." In *Companion to Media Production Studies*. Edited by Vicki Mayer. Malden, MA: Blackwell, in press.

Castells, Manuel. *The Information Age: Economy, Society, and Culture Volumes I-III*. London: Blackwell, 1996–1998.

Castells, Manuel. *The Power of Identity. The Information Age: Economy, Society, and Culture Volume II*. London: Blackwell, 1997.

Castells, Manuel. "Communication, Power and Counter-Power in the Network Society." *International Journal of Communication* 1 (2007): 238–66.

Castells, Manuel, Mireia Fernández-Ardèvol, Jack Linchuan Qiu, and Arab Sey. *Mobile Communication and Society: A Global Perspective*. Cambridge, MA: MIT Press, 2007.

Catholic Agency for Overseas Development. *Clean up your Computer: Working conditions in the electronics sector*. London: 2004. http://www.cafod.org.uk/resources/policy/private-sector/clean-up-your-computer

Center for Environmental Health, Prison Activist Resource Center, Silicon Valley Toxics Coalition, and the Computer TakeBack Campaign. *Toxic Sweatshops: How UNICOR Prison Recycling Harms Workers, Communities, the Environment, and the Recycling Industry*. 2006. http://svtc.org/svtc_prison_labor.

CEREAL (Centre for Reflection and Action on Labour Issues). *Labor Rights in a Time of Crisis: Third Report on Working Conditions in the Mexican Electronics Industry*. 2009. www.cafod. org.uk/../6/../CEREAL+REPORT-2009-ENGLISH.pdf.

CEREAL (Centre for Reflection and Action on Labour Issues). *New Technology Workers: Report on Working Conditions in the Mexican Electronics Industry*. 2006. www.cafod.org. uk/content/download/8506/../4/../Cereal+report.pdf.

Ceruzzi, Paul E. *A History of Modern Computing*. 2nd ed. Cambridge, MA: MIT Press, 2003.

Chakravartty, Paula. "Labor in or as Civil Society? Workers and Subaltern Publics in India's Information Society." In *Global Communications: Toward a Transcultural Political Economy*. Edited by Paula Chakravartty and Yuezhi Zhao, 285–307. Lanham, MD: Rowman & Littlefield, 2007.

Chan, Debby. *Apple Owes Workers and Public a Response over the Poisonings*. Hong Kong: Students & Scholars Against Corporate Misbehaviour, May 2010. http://sacom.hk/wp-content/uploads/2010/05/apple-owes-workers-and-public-a-response-over-the-poisonings.pdf.

Chan, Jenny, and Charles Ho. *The Dark Side of Cyberspace: Inside the Sweatshops of China's Computer Hardware Production*. Berlin: World Economy, Ecology & Development, 2008.

Charland, Maurice. "Technological Nationalism." *Canadian Journal of Political and Social Theory* 10, no. 1 (1986): 196–220.

Chartier, Roger. "Texts, Printings, Readings." In *The New Cultural History*. Edited by Lynn Hunt, 154–75. Berkeley: University of California Press, 1989.

Chartier, Roger. "Crossing Borders in Early Modern Europe: Sociology of Texts and Literature." Translated by Maurice Elton. *Book History* 8 (2005a): 37–50.

Chartier, Roger. "Le droit d'auteur est-il une parenthèse dans l'histoire?" *Le Monde*, December 17, 2005b. http://www.lemonde.fr/societe/article/2005/12/17/roger-chartier-le-droit-d-auteur-est-il-une-parenthese-dans-l histoire_722516 _3224.

Chartier, Roger. "Aprender a leer, leer para aprender." *Nuevo Mundo Mundos Nuevos*, 2010. http://nuevomundo.revues.org/58621.

Chase, Stuart. *The Tragedy of Waste*. New York: Grosset & Dunlap, 1929.

Chatfield, Tom. "Do Writers Need Paper?" *Prospect*, October 20, 2010. http://prospectmagazine.co.uk/2010/10/books-electronic-publishing.

Chen, Michelle. "Foxconn's Global Empire Reflects a New Breed of Sweatshop." *In These Times*, October 13, 2010. http://www.inthesetimes.com/working/entry/6550/foxconns_global_empire_reflects_a_new_breed_of_sweatshop.

Cheney, Jen. "James Cameron and the Special Edition of 'Avatar,' Eco-Conscious DVDs and BP." *Washington Post*, August 27, 2010. http://www.voices.washingtonpost.com/celebritology/2010/08/talking_with_james_cameron_abo.html.

Chiang, Oliver J. "How Green is My Game?" *GamePro*, April 5, 2010. http://www.gamepro.com/article/features/214644/how-green-is-my-game.

Chilton, Bart. "Rein in the cyber cowboys". *Financial Times*, September 6, 2010. http://www.ft.com/intl/cms/s/0/e0cf72a6-b9e1-11df-8804-00144feabdc0,s01=1.html.

Chintan Environmental Research and Action Group. *Scrap Crash! What the Crash in Prices of Scrap Means for Wastepickers and Other Recyclers*. New Delhi: Chintan Environmental Research and Action Group, 2009.

Chowdhury, Gobinda. "Carbon Footprint of the Knowledge Sector: What's the Future?" *Journal of Documentation* 66, no. 6 (2010): 934–46.

Chris, Cynthia. *Watching Wildlife*. Minneapolis: University of Minnesota Press, 2006.

Christensen, Karen, and Bill Siever. "Seeing the Forest: Why Publishers and Readers Need to Take a Fresh Look at Print and Online Publishing to Create a Sustainable Information Industry." *Serials: The Journal for the Serials Community* 23, no. 1 (2009): 20–24.

Christopherson, Susan. "Behind the Scenes: How Transnational Firms are Constructing a New International Division of Labor in Media Work." *Geoforum* 37, no. 5 (2006): 739–51.

Cieply, Michael. "The Afterlife is Expensive for Digital Movies." *New York Times*, December 23, 2007, Sunday business section. http://www.nytimes.com/2007/12/23/business/media/23steal.html?pagewanted=all.

Clapp, R. "Mortality Among U.S. Employees of a Large Computer Manufacturing Company: 1969–2001." *Environmental Health* 5, no. 30 (2006). http://ukpmc.ac.uk/classic/articlerender.cgi?artid=792764.

Clapp, R. W. and K. Hoffman. (2008). "Cancer Mortality in IBM Endicott Plant Workers, 1969–2001: An Update on a NY Production Plant." *Environmental Health* 7, no. 13 http://www.ukpmc.ac.uk/classic/articlerender.cgi?artid=1516365.

Clark, Claudia. *Radium Girls: Women and Industrial Health Reform, 1910–1935*. Chapel Hill: University of North Carolina Press, 1997.

The Climate Group. *Smart2020: Enabling the Low Carbon Economy in the Information Age*. London: Global Sustainability Initiative, 2008.

Clinton, Hillary Rodham. "Remarks Following ITC Green Building Tour and Discussion." U.S. Department of State, July 19, 2009. http://www.state.gov/secretary/rm/2009a/july/126206.htm.

Clowney, Stephen. "Environmental Ethics & Cost Benefit Analysis." *Fordham Environmental Law Review* 18 (2006): 105–50.

Cole, Luke W., and Sheila R. Foster. *From the Ground Up: Environmental Racism and the Rise of the Environmental Justice Movement*. New York: New York University Press, 2001.

Collins, Christy. "Addressing Climate Change Issues in Uncertain Times." *Elsevier Editors' Update* 29 (March 2010) http://www.elsevier.com/wps/find/editorsinfo.editors.

Colten, Craig E. "Historical Questions in Hazardous Waste Management." *Public Historian* 10, no. 1 (1988): 7–20.

Commager, Henry Steele. *The American Mind: An Interpretation of American Thought and Character Since the 1880's*. New Haven, CT: Yale University Press, 1974.

Commission of the European Communities. *Impact Assessment*. Working paper accompanying the *Proposal for a Directive of the European Parliament and of the Council on Waste Electrical and Electronic Equipment (WEEE)*. Brussels: Commission of the European Communities, 2008a.

Commission of the European Communities. *The Economics of Ecosystems & Biodiversity: An Interim Report*. Brussels: European Communities, 2008b.

Commoner, Barry. *The Closing Circle*. New York: Knopf, 1971.

Conca, Ken, Thomas Princen, and Michael F. Maniates. "Confronting Consumption." *Global Environmental Politics* 1, no. 3 (2001): 1–10.

Connelly, Michael. *El Veredicto*. Translated by Javier Guerrero. Barcelona: Roca Editorial, 2009a.

Connelly, Michael. *Nine Dragons: A Novel*. New York: Little, Brown and Company, 2009b.

Conner, Teri L., and Ronald W. Williams. "Identification of Possible Sources of Particulate Matter in the Personal Cloud Using SEM/EDX." *Atmospheric Environment* 38, no. 31 (2004): 5305–310.

Connolly, John, and Andrea Prothero. "Green Consumption: Life-Politics, Risk and Consumption." *Journal of Consumer Culture* 8, no. 1 (2008): 117–45.

Connolly, William. *Pluralism*. Durham, NC: Duke University Press, 2005.

Consumer Electronics Association. "CEA Forecasts Consumer Electronics Revenue will Surpass $155 Billion in 2007." (January 2007) Arlington, VA. http://www.businesswire.com/news/home/20070106005033/en/CEA-Forecasts-Consumer-Electronics-Revenue-Surpass-155.

Consumer Electronics Association. *Digital America 2010*. (2010). http://CE.org/Press/CEA_Pubs/1964.asp.

Consumers International, DanWatch, and the Danish Consumer Council. *The Real Deal: Exposing Unethical Behavior*. London: Consumers International, 2008.

Coombe, Rosemary, and Andrew Herman. "Trademarks, Property, and Propriety: The Moral Economy of Consumer Politics and Corporate Accountability in the World Wide Web." *DePaul Law Review* 50 (2000): 597–632.

Corbett, Charles J., and Richard P. Turco. *Sustainability in the Motion Picture Industry*. Report prepared for the Integrated Waste Management Board of the State of California, November, 2006. http://www.personal.anderson.ucla.edu/charles.corbett/papers/mpis_report.pdf.

Corbin, Alain. *The Foul and the Fragrant: Order and the French Social Imagination*. Cambridge, MA: Harvard University Press, 1986.

Cordasco, Paul. "ISS Swinging Shareholder Votes toward Social Issues." *PRWeek*, June 10, 2002.

Corn, Jacqueline Karnell. "Vinyl Chloride, Setting a Workplace Standard: An Historical Perspective on Assessing Risk." *Journal of Public Health Policy* 5, no. 4 (1984): 497–512.

Costanza-Chock, Sasha. *White Paper #1: Background and Context for the Application of coyBOTt Software to Systematic Analysis of Branding, Boycott, and Cultural Sponsorship*. 2002.

Couldry, Nick. "Does 'the Media' Have a Future?" *European Journal of Communication* 24, no. 4 (2009): 437–49.

Council for the Humanities, Arts and Social Sciences (Australia) *CHASS Submission: Productivity Commission Study on Science and Innovation*. Canberra: Council for the Humanities, Arts and Social Sciences, 2006.

Cowie, Jefferson. *Capital Moves: RCA's Seventy-Year Quest for Cheap Labor*. New York: New Press, 2001.

Cox, Stan. "Are Your Cell Phone and Laptop Bad for Your Health?" *AlterNet*, July 31, 2007. http://www.alternet.org/healthwellness/58354/?page=1.

Cox, Stan. "Cell Phones Generate Particularly Dangerous E-Waste." In *What Is the Impact of E-Waste?* Edited by Cynthia A. Bily, 18–26. Detroit: Greenhaven, 2009.

Cray, Charlie. "Toxics on the Hudson: The Saga of GE, PCBs and the Hudson River." *Multinational Monitor* 22, nos. 7/8 (July/August 2001). http://www.multinationalmonitor.org/mm2001/072001.

Criminal Intelligence Service Canada. *Report on Organized Crime*. Ottawa: Criminal Intelligence Service Canada, 2008.

Crosbie, Tracey. "Household Energy Consumption and Consumer Electronics: The Case of Television." *Energy Policy* 36, no. 6 (2008): 2191–199.

Crosby, Jackie. "iPhone Impact: The Mania Over Apple's Latest Product Could Translate into an Avalanche of Electronic Waste." *Star Tribune*, June 29, 2007.

Cubitt, Sean. *Eco Media*. Amsterdam and New York: Editions Rodopi, 2005.

Culbertson, William S. "Raw Materials and Foodstuffs in the Commercial Policies of Nations." *Annals of the American Academy of Political and Social Science* 112 (1924): 1–145.

Curry, Patrick. *Ecological Ethics: An Introduction*. Cambridge, MA: Polity, 2006.

Czitrom, Daniel J. *Media and the American Mind from Morse to McLuhan*. Chapel Hill: University of North Carolina Press, 1982.

Da Silva, Marcelo Cozzensa, Anaclaudia Gastal Fassa, C. E. Siquiera, and David Kriebel. "World at Work: Brazilian Ragpickers." *Occupational and Environmental Medicine* 62 (2005): 736–40.

Da Silva, Marcelo Cozzensa, Anaclaudia Gastal Fassa, and David Kriebel. "Minor Psychiatric Disorders Among Brazilian Ragpickers: A Cross-Sectional Study." *Environmental Health* 5, no. 17 (2006). http://www.ncbi.nlm.nih.gov/pubmed/16734911.

Dalton, Russell J. "The Greening of the Globe? Cross-National Levels of Environmental Group Membership." *Environmental Politics* 14, no. 4 (2005): 441–59.

Daly, Herman E. "'Sustainable Growth?' No Thank You." *The Case Against the Global Economy*. Edited by Jerry Mander and Edward Goldsmith, 192–96. San Francisco: Sierra Club, 1996.

Dartmouth Toxic Metals Research Program. *The Facts on Silver*. Center for Environmental Health Services, Dartmouth College. n.d. http://www.dartmouth.edu/~toxmetal/TXQAag.shtml.

Davanipour, Zoreh, and Eugene Sobel. "Long-Term Exposure to Magnetic Fields and the Risks of Alzheimer's Disease and Breast Cancer: Further Biological Research." *Pathophysiology* 16, nos. 2–3 (2009): 149–56.

David, Paul A. "The Dynamo and the Computer: An Historical Perspective on the Modern Productivity Paradox." *American Economic Review* 80, no. 2 (1990): 355–61.

Day, W.-W. "Being Part of Digital Hollywood: Taiwan's Online Gaming & 3D Animation Industry Under the New International Division of Cultural Labor." *International Journal of Comic Art* 7, no. 1 (2005): 449–61.

De Pelsmacker, Patrick, Liesbeth Driesen, and Glenn Rayp. "Do Consumers Care About Ethics? Willingness to Pay for Fair-Trade Coffee." *Journal of Consumer Affairs* 39, no. 2 (2005): 363–85.

Dean, Hartley. "Green Citizenship." *Social Policy & Administration* 35, no. 5 (2001): 490–505.

Deaver, Jeffrey. *Carte Blanche*. London: Hodder & Stoughton, 2011.

Debord, Guy. *The Society of the Spectacle*. Translated by Donald Nicolson-Smith. New York: Zone, 1995.

Deck, Andy. "Demilitarizing the Playground." *Art Context* (2004) http://artcontext.org/crit/essays/noQuarter.

DeLillo, Don. *Underworld*. New York: Scribner, 1997.

Dempster, Anna M. "An Operational Risk Framework for the Performing Arts and Creative Industries." *Creative Industries Journal* 1, no. 2 (2009): 151–70.

De Nazareth, Marianne. "Waste Pickers: Silent Friends of the Polluted Earth." *Deccan Herald*, September 9, 2009. http://www.deccanherald.com/content/17818/waste-pickers-silent-friends-polluted.html.

Descartes, René. *Philosophical Writings*. Trans. and Ed. Elizabeth Anscombe and Peter Thomas Geach. Sunbury-on-Thames: Nelson University Paperbacks/Open University, 1977.

De-Shalit, Avner. "Nationalism." In *Political Theory and the Ecological Challenge*. Edited by Andrew Dobson and Robyn Eckersley, 75–90. Cambridge, UK: Cambridge University Press, 2006.

De Silva, J. P. *La televisión ha muerto: La nueva producción audiovisual en la era de Internet: La tercera revolución industrial*. Barcelona: Editorial Gedisa, 2000.

De Sola Pool, Ithiel. "Communications Technology and Land Use." *Annals of the American Academy of Political and Social Science* 451, no. 1 (1980): 1–12.

Deutsch, Claudia H. "A Threat So Big, Academics Try Collaboration—Disciplines Cross Lines to Fight Global Warming." *New York Times*, December 25, 2007. http://www.nytimes.com/2007/12/25/business/25sustain.html?pagewanted=all.

Deuze, Mark. *Mediawork*. Cambridge: Polity, 2007.

Dewey, John. *Experience and Nature*. New York: Dover, 1958.

Dex, Shirley, Janet Willis, Richard Paterson, and Elaine Sheppard. "Freelance Workers and Contract Uncertainty: The Effects of Contractual Changes in the Television Industry." *Work, Employment and Society* 14, no. 2 (2000): 283–305.

Dinerstein, Joel. "Technology and Its Discontents: On the Verge of the Posthuman." *American Quarterly* 58, no. 3 (2006): 569–95.

Dobson, Andrew. *Citizenship and the Environment*. Oxford: Oxford University Press, 2003.

Dobson, Andrew, and Angel Valencia Sáiz, eds. *Citizenship, Environment, Economy*. New York: Routledge, 2006.

Douglas, Susan. *Inventing American Broadcasting, 1899–1922*. Baltimore: Johns Hopkins University Press, 1989.

DuBoff, Richard B. "Business Demand and the Development of the Telegraph in the United States, 1844–1860." *Business History Review* 54, no. 4 (1980): 459–79.

Durham, Walter A., Jr. "The Japanese Camphor Monopoly: Its History and Relation to the Future of Japan." *Pacific Affairs* 5, no. 9 (1932): 797–801.

Durkheim, Émile. *The Division of Labor in Society*. Translated by W. D. Halls. New York: Free Press, 1984.

Dutton, Michael. "From Culture Industry to Mao Industry: A Greek Tragedy." *boundary 2* 23, no. 2 (2005): 151–67.

Dyson, Esther, George Gilder, George Keyworth, and Alvin Toffler. *Cyberspace and the American Dream: A Magna Carta for the Knowledge Age*. Version 1.2. Progress and Freedom Foundation, 1994. http://www.pff.org/issues-pubs/futureinsights/fi1.2magnacarta.html.

Eagleton, Terry. "The Revolt of the Reader." *New Literary History* 13, no. 3 (Spring 1982): 449–52.

Eco, Umberto. "Towards a Semiotic Inquiry into the Television Message." Translated by Paolo Splendore. *Working Papers in Cultural Studies* 3 (1972): 103–21.

Eco, Umberto. "The Future of the Book." From the symposium The Future of the Book, held at the University of San Marino, July 1994. http://themodernword.com/eco/eco_future_of_book.html.

Edgar, David. "Playing Shops, Shopping Plays: The Effect of the Internal Market on Television Drama." In *British Television Drama: Past, Present and Future*. Edited by Jonathan Bignell, Stephen Lacey, and Madeleine Macmurraugh-Kavanagh, 73–77. Houndmills, UK: Palgrave Macmillan, 2000.

Edgerton, David. *The Shock of the Old: Technology and Global History since 1900*. Oxford: Oxford University Press, 2007.

Edwards, Julia, Alan McKinnon, and Sharon Cullinane. *Comparing $CO_2$ Emissions for Conventional and Online Book Retailing Channels in the UK*. Edinburgh: Heriot-Watt University, 2009.

Einstein, Mara. *Compassion, Inc.: How Corporate America Blurs the Line Between What We Buy, Who We Are, and Those We Help*. Berkeley: University of California Press, 2012.

Eisenstein, Elizabeth. *The Printing Revolution in Early Modern Europe*. Cambridge, UK: Cambridge University Press, 1983.

Electronics TakeBack Coalition. *Electronics Recycling in October 2010: Leaders Move Farther Ahead, Printer Companies Flunking*. Electronics TakeBack Coalition, 2010. http://www.electronicsTakeBack.com.

Elias, Norbert. *The Civilizing Process: The History of Manners and State Formation and Civilization*. Translated by Edmund Jephcott. Oxford: Blackwell, 1994.

Ellick, Adam B. "Tons of PCBs May Come Calling at a Down-at-the-Heels Texas City." *New York Times*, June 19, 2008. .

Ellis, John. *TV FAQ: Uncommon Answers to Common Questions About TV*. London: IB Tauris, 2007.

Elmer, Gregory, and Mike Gasher, eds. *Contracting Out Hollywood: Runaway Productions and Foreign Location Shooting*. Lanham, MD: Rowman & Littlefield, 2005.

Enciso, Angélica. "México genera cada año hasta 180 mil toneladas de basura electronica." *La Jornada*, December 24, 2007. http://www.jornada.unam.mx/2007/12/24/index.php?section=sociedad&article=033n1so.

Engardio, Pete, with Kerry Cappell, John Carey, and Kenji Hall. "Beyond the Green Corporation." *Bloomberg Businessweek*, January 29, 2007. http://www.businessweek.com/magazine/content/07_05/b4019001.htm.

Engels, Frederick. *The Condition of the Working Class in England in 1844*. London: S. Sonnenschein, 1892.

Environmental Protection Agency. *Profile of the Printing and Publishing Industry*. Washington, DC: Environmental Protection Agency, 1995.

Environmental Protection Agency. *Management of Electronic Waste in the United States*. Washington, DC: Environmental Protection Agency, 2007.

Environmental Protection Agency. *Statistics on the Management of Used and End-of-Life Electronics*. Washington, DC: Environmental Protection Agency, 2008.

Environmental Working Group. *Cell Phone Radiation: Science Review on Cancer Risks and Children's Health*. Washington, DC: Environmental Working Group, 2009. http://www.ewg.org/cellphoneradiation/fullreport.

Enzensberger, Hans Magnus. "In Praise of Illiteracy." Translated by Michael Lipson. *Grand Street* 5, no. 4 (Summer 1986): 88–96.

Enzensberger, Hans Magnus. "Constituents of a Theory of the Media." In *The New Media Reader*. Edited by Nick Montfort and Noah Wardrip-Fruin, 261–275. Cambridge, MA: MIT Press, 2003.

Erosion, Technology, Concentration Group. "Nanotech Rx Medical Applications of Nano-Scale Technologies: What Impact on Marginalized Communities?" *Erosion, Technology, Concentration Group*, September 2006. http://www.etcgroup.org/en/node/593.

European Parliament. "Resolution on health concerns associated with electromagnetic fields." Reference number INI/2008/2211. http://www.europarl.europa.eu/oeil/file.jsp?id=5680652

European Parliament and the Council of the European Union. *Directive 2002/96/EC of The European Parliament and of The Council of 27 January 2003 on Waste Electrical and Electronic Equipment (WEEE)*. Luxembourg: EU Publications Office, 2003.

European Space Agency. "Space Debris Spotlight." European Space Agency, modified September 28, 2007. http://www.esa.int/esaCP/SEMHDJXJD1E_FeatureWeek_0.html

Fairfield, Hannah. "Pushing Paper out the Door." *New York Times*, February 10, 2008, Sunday Business Section 1. http://www.nytimes.com/2008/02/10/business/10metrics.html?pagewanted=all.

Featherstone, Liza. *Selling Women Short: The Landmark Battle for Workers' Rights at Wal-Mart*. New York: Basic Books, 2004.

Federal Communications Commission. *Avian/Communication Tower Collisions*. Prepared for FCC. West Chester, PA: Avatar Environmental, September 30, 2004.

Ferber, Dan. "Authors Turn Up Heat Over Disputed Paper." *Science* 304, no. 5679 (2004): 1891. http://www.sciencemag.org/content/304/5679/1891.2.summary.

Ferus-Comelo, Anibel. "Mission Impossible? Raising Labor Standards in the ICT Sector." *Labor Studies Journal* 33, no. 2 ( January 11, 2008): 141–62.

Feuz, Martin, Matthew Fuller, and Felix Stalder. "Personal Web Searching in the Age of Semantic Capitalism: Diagnosing the Mechanisms of Personalisation." *First Monday* 16, no. 2 (February 2011). http://firstmonday.org/htbin/cgiwrap/bin/ojs/index.php/fm/article/view/3344/2766.

Finkelstein, Sidney. "McLuhan's Totalitarianism and Human Resilience." *Communication and Class Struggle*. Edited by Armand Mattelart and Seth Seiglaub, 176–82. New York: International General, 1979.

Fisher, Daniel. "GE Turns Green." *Forbes*, August 15, 2005, 80–85.

Flew, Terry and Stuart Cunningham. "Creative Industries After the First Decade of Debate." *Information Society* 26, no. 2 (2010): 113–23.

Flowerdew, John, and Alina Wan. "Genre Analysis of Tax Computation Letters: How and Why Accountants Write the Way They Do." *English for Specific Purposes* 25, no. 2 (2006): 133–53.

Forbes, Gilbert. "Some Observations on Occupational Markings." *Journal of Criminal Law and Criminology* 38, no. 4 (November/December 1947): 423–36.

Ford, Henry. *My Philosophy of Industry: An Authorized Interview by Ray Leone Faurote*. New York: Coward-McCann, 1929.

Forster, E. M. *The Machine Stops and Other Stories*. Abinger Edition of E. M. Forster Volume 7. London: André Deutsche, 1997. Originally published in *The Oxford and Cambridge Review* in November 1909.

Foster, John Bellamy. *The Vulnerable Planet: A Short Economic History of the Environment*. Rev. ed. New York: Monthly Review Press, 1999.

Foucault, Michel. "Revisions: Photogenic Painting; Gilles Deleuze, Michel Foucault, Gérard Fromanger." In *Gérard Fromanger*, edited by Sarah Wilson and translated by Dafydd Roberts, 83–104. London: Black Dog, 1999.

Foucault, Michel. "Qu'est-ce que les Lumières?" *Dits et Écrits 1954–1988 Volume II: 1976–1988*. Edited by Daniel Defert and François Ewald with Jacques Lagrange, 1381–397. Paris: Quarto Gallimard, 2001.

Foucault, Michel. *The Birth of Biopolitics: Lectures at the Collège de France, 1978–79*. Edited by Michel Senellart and translated by G. Burchell. Houndmills, UK: Palgrave Macmillan, 2008.

Fox Filmed Entertainment. *Guide to Greening Film & Television Production*, n.d. http://www.greenproductionguide.com/media/documents/Fox_Guide_to_Greening_Film_and_TV_production.pdf.

Frank, Dana. "Where are the Workers in Consumer-Worker Alliances? Class Dynamics and the History of Consumer-Labor Campaigns." *Politics & History* 31, no. 3 (2003): 363–79.

Frank, David John, Ann Hironaka, and Evan Schofer. "The Nation-State and the Natural Environment Over the Twentieth Century." *American Sociological Review* 65, no. 1 (2000): 96–116.

Frazzoli, Chiara, Orish Ebere Orisakwe, Roberto Dragone, and Alberto Mantovani. "Diagnostic Health Risk Assessment of Electronic Waste in Developing Countries' Scenarios." *Environmental Impact Assessment Review* 30, no. 6 (2010): 388–99.

Frey, Michelle. "Finger Painting for a Good Cause." *Greenpeace*, July 28, 2009. http://www.greenpeace.org/usa/en/news-and-blogs/campaign-blog/finger-painting-for-a-good-cause/blog/25680/.

Friedman, Milton. "Franklin D. Roosevelt, Silver, and China." *Journal of Political Economy* 100, no. 1 (1992): 62–83.

Fröbel, Folker, Jürgen Heinrichs, and Otto Kreye. *The New International Division of Labor: Structural Unemployment in Industrialised Countries and Industrialisation in Developing Countries*.

Translated by P. Burgess. Cambridge: Cambridge University Press, 1980; Paris: Éditions de la Maison des Sciences de l'Homme.

Frow, John. "Intellectual Property Rights and the Public Domain in the New World Order." *Indian Journal of Law and Technology* 2 (2006): 106–27.

Gaffney, Sean. "Rise in Maquiladora Jobs May Signal Wider Rebound." *Monitor*, January 8, 2010. http://www.themonitor.com/articles/signal-34204-jobs-wider.html.

Galbraith, John Kenneth. *The New Industrial State*. Boston: Houghton Mifflin, 1967.

Gale, Robert. "Environmental Management Accounting as a Reflexive Modernization Strategy in Cleaner Production." *Journal of Cleaner Production* 14, no. 14 (2006): 1228–236.

Gall, Gregor. "The Changing Relations of Production: Union Derecognition in the UK Magazine Industry." *Industrial Relations Journal* 29, no. 2 (1998): 151–61.

Gallagher, Rachael. "PPA Estimates Magazine Industry's Carbon Footprint." *Press Gazette*, May 19, 2008. http://www.pressgazette.co.uk/story.asp?storyCode=41177&section code=1.

García Canclini, Néstor. *Diferentes, desiguales y desconectados: Mapas de la interculturalidad*. Barcelona: Editorial Gedisa, 2004.

García Canclini, Néstor. "Interview for the 9th Spanish Sociology Conference, 2007." Translated by Toby Miller. *Social Identities* 14, no. 3 (2008): 389–94.

García, Connie, and Amelia Simpson. "Community-Based Organizing for Labor Rights, Health, and the Environment." *Challenging the Chip: Labor Rights and Environmental Justice in the Global Electronics Industry*. Edited by Ted Smith, David A. Sonnenfeld, and David Naguib Pellow, 150–60. Philadelphia: Temple University Press, 2006.

García, Dorde Cuvardic. "El *Trapero*: El Otro Marginal en la Historia de la Literatura y de la Cultura Popular." *Káñina: Revista de las Artes y Letras* 31 (2007): 217–27.

Gardner, Emma. *Developing an Environmental Strategy for UK Film*. London: UK Film Council, 2007.

Garnham, Nicholas. "From Cultural to Creative Industries: An Analysis of the Implications of the 'Creative Industries' Approach to Arts and Media Policy Making in the United Kingdom." *International Journal of Cultural Policy* 11, no. 1 (2005): 15–29.

Gates, Kelly. "New Media Addiction." *Television & New Media* 10, no. 1 (2009): 58–60.

Gattuso, Dana Joel. "Mandated Recycling of Electronics: A Lose-Lose-Lose Proposition." *Issue Analysis* 2 (February 1, 2005). http://cei.org/studies-issue-analysis/mandated-recycling-electronics-lose-lose-lose-proposition.

Gentleman, Amelia. "Indians Protest Wal-Mart's Wholesale Entry." *New York Times*, August 9, 2007. http://www.nytimes.com/2007/08/09/business/worldbusiness/09iht-walmart.4.7061818.html.

George Eastman House. *Pumping Station at Kodak Park Connected with Private Water Supply System of 12,000,000 Gallons Daily Capacity*. Still photograph archive. Catalog record 87:0026:0029. n.d.

Gereffi, Gary, and Michelle Christian. "The Impacts of Wal-Mart: The Rise and Consequence of the World's Dominant Retailer." *Annual Review of Sociology* 35 (2009): 573–91.

Global e-Sustainability Initiative (GeSI) and Electronic Industry Citizenship Coalition (EICC). *Social and Environmental Responsibility in Metals Supply to the Electronic Industry*. Electronic Industry Citizenship Coalition, 2008. http://www.eicc.info/PDF/Report%20 on%20Metal%20Extraction.pdf.

Ghiami, Yousef, and Edith Sorkina. "Sustainability in Retail Supply Chains: A Study On The Ten World's Largest Retailers." Thesis for master of science in logistics and transport management, Graduate School of Business, Economics and Law, University of Gothenburg, 2009. Master degree project no. 2009.

Gibson, William. *The Science in Science Fiction*. NPR Talk of the Nation, November 30, 1999. http://www.npr.org/templates/story/story.php?storyId=1067220.

Gibson, William. *Pattern Recognition*. New York: GP Putnam's Sons, 2003.

Giddens, Anthony, and Will Hutton. "In Conversation." In *Global Capitalism*. Edited by Will Hutton and Anthony Giddens, 1–51. New York: New Press, 2000.

Gidwani, Vinay K. "Subaltern Cosmopolitanism as Politics." *Antipode* 38, no. 1 (2006): 7–21.

Gilbey, Ryan. "Danny Boyle: 'Yes, We did Betray Ewan.'" *Independent*, October 25, 2002. http://www.independent.co.uk/arts-entertainment/films/features/danny-boyle-yes-we-did-betray-ewan-608347.html.

Gilson, Dave. "Project Green Lite." *Mother Jones*, March/April 2008: 87–89.

Glader, Paul. "GE Says 'Green' Business Revenue Grew 21 percent." *Wall St Journal*, May 27. 2009. http://online.wsj.com/article/SB124339691665357611.html#articleTabs%3Darticle.

Glaister, Dan. "Jack Bauer Saves the World Again: *24* Goes Carbon Neutral." *Guardian*, March 3, 2009. http://www.guardian.co.uk/world/2009/mar/03/24-fox-television-carbon-emissions.

Global e-Sustainability Initiative and Electronic Industry Citizenship Coalition. *Social and Environmental Responsibility in Metals Supply to the Electronic Industry*. Guelph, Ontario, 2008. http://www.eicc.info/PDF/Report%20on%20Metal%20Extraction.pdf.

Global Witness. *"Faced with a Gun, What Can You Do?": War and the Militarisation of Mining in Eastern Congo*. London: Global Witness, 2009.

Goldman, Michael, and Rachel A. Schurman. "Closing the 'Great Divide': New Social Theory on Society and Nature." *Annual Review of Sociology* 26 (August 2000): 563–84.

Goldsmith, Ben, and Tom O'Regan. *The Film Studio: Film Production in the Global Economy*. Lanham, MD: Rowman & Littlefield, 2005.

Goldstine, H. H., and Adele Goldstine. "The Electronic Numerical Integrator and Computer (ENIAC)." *Mathematical Tables and Other Aids to Computation* 2, no. 15 (1946): 97–110.

Goleman, Daniel, and Gregory Norris. "How Green is My iPad?" *New York Times*, April 4, 2010. http://www.nytimes.com/interactive/2010/04/04/opinion/04opchart.html.

Golumbia, David. *The Cultural Logic of Computation*. Cambridge, MA: Harvard University Press, 2009.

Gómez-Correa, Jaime Arturo, Andrés Alonso Agudelo-Suárez, Juan Ignacio Sarmiento-Gutiérreza, and Elena Ronda-Pérez. "Condiciones de trabajo y salud de los recicladores urbanos de Medellín (Colombia)." *Archivos de Prevención de Riesgos Laborales* 10, no. 4 (2007): 181–87.

GoodElectronics, Paula Overeem, and CSR Platform (MVO Platform). *Reset: Corporate Social Responsibility in the Global Electronics Supply Chain*. Amsterdam: GoodElectronics, 2009.

Goodell, Jeff. "Who's to Blame—The 12 Politicians and Corporate Executives Most Responsible for Blocking Efforts to Halt Global Warming." *Rolling Stone*, February 3, 2011: 39–42.

Goodland, Robert. "Growth Has Reached its Limits." *The Case Against the Global Economy*. Edited by Jerry Mander and Edward Goldsmith, 207–17. San Francisco: Sierra Club, 1996.

Goody, Jack, and Ian Watt. "The Consequences of Literacy." *Comparative Studies in Society and History* 5, no. 3 (1963): 304–45.

Grant, Meg. "Redford Unedited." *AARP: The Magazine*, March/April 2011: 38–42, 82–83.

Grantham, Bill. *"Some Big Bourgeois Brothel": Contexts for France's Culture Wars With Hollywood*. Luton, UK: University of Luton Press, 2000.

Great Lakes Commission des Grands Lacs. *Liquid Asset: Great Lakes Water Quality and Industry Needs*. Great Lakes Commission des Grands Lacs, 1992. http://www.glc.org/docs/liqasset/liqasset.html .

Greek, Dinah. "Green Computing: How to Watch Your Waste." *Computer Active*, November 24, 2005. http://www.computeractive.co.uk/computeractive/features/2146583/green-computing-waste-watchers.

Greenpeace. *Guide to Greener Electronics.* http://www.greenpeace.org/electronics. (n.d. a).

Greenpeace. "Tóxicos en la producción y basura electronica (e-waste)." (n.d. b). http://www.greenpeace.org/mexico/campaigns/t-xicos/copy-of-acerca-de-la-campa-a.

Greenpeace. *Playing Dirty: Analysis of Hazardous Chemicals and Materials in Games Console Components.* Amsterdam: Greenpeace, 2008.

Greenpeace. *How Dirty is Your Data? A Look at the Energy Choices that Power Cloud Computing.* Amsterdam: Greenpeace, 2011.

Grossman, Elizabeth. *High Tech Trash: Digital Devices, Hidden Toxics, and Human Health.* Washington: Island, 2006.

Grossman, Elizabeth. *Tackling High-Tech Trash: The E-Waste Explosion & What We Can Do About It.* New York: Dēmos, 2010. http://www.demos.org/publication/tackling-high-tech-trash-e-waste-explosion-what-we-can-do.

Groves, Richard H. *Green Imperialism: Colonial Expansion, Tropical Island Edens and the Origins of Environmentalism 1600–1860.* Cambridge, UK: Cambridge University Press, 1995.

Guadarrama, Rafael H. " 'Reciclotrón', este fin de semana en el Valle de México." *Once TV Mexico,* January 28, 2010. http://oncetv-ipn.net/noticias/index.php?modulo=despliegue&dt_fecha=2010-01-28&numnota=43.

Guattari, Félix. "The Three Ecologies." Translated by Chris Turner. *New Formations* 8 (1989): 131–47.

Guevarra, Leslie. "DOD Enlists GE for $2M Project to Make Military Base a Smart Microgrid Model." *GreenBiz,* July 8, 2009. http://www.greenbiz.com/news/2009/07/09/dod-enlists-ge-for-microgrid-model.

Guillermoprieto, Alma. "Letter from Mexico City." *New Yorker,* September 17, 1990: 93.

Hacking, Ian. *The Taming of Chance.* Cambridge, UK: Cambridge University Press, 1990.

Haddow, Douglas. "Do We Still Care About Sweatshops?" *Guardian,* October 14, 2010. http://www.guardian.co.uk/commentisfree/2010/oct/14/apple-foxconn-china-workers.

Hall, Stuart. "A Sense of Classlessness." *Universities & Left Review* 5 (1958): 26–31.

Hall, Stuart, Doreen Massey, and Michael Rustin. "Uncomfortable Times." *Soundings* 1 (1995): 5–18.

Haltiwanger, John, Ron Jarmin, and C. J. Krizan. *Mom-and-Pop Meet Big-Box: Complements or Substitutes?* United States Census Bureau, Center for Economic Statistics. CES 09-34. 2009.

Hamelink, Cees. "Is Information Technology Neutral?" In *Communication and Domination: Essays to Honor Herbert I. Schiller.* Edited by Jörg Becker, Göran Hedebro, and Leena Paldan, 16–24. Norwood, NJ: Ablex, 1986.

Hamelink, Cees. "Remembering Herbert Schiller: Our Common Efforts." *Television & New Media* 2, no. 1 (2001): 11–16.

Hancock, Simon. "Iceland New Home of Server Farms?" *BBC News,* October 10, 2009. http://news.bbc.co.uk/go/pr/fr/-/2/hi/programmes/click_online/8297237.stm.

Hanke, Bob. "Reflections on the Academic Milieu of Media Studies." *International Journal of Communication* 3 (2009):551–77. http://ijoc.org/ojs/index.php/ijoc/article/view/422.

Hanna, Nagy K., and Christine Zhen-Wei Qiang. "China's Emerging Informatization Strategy." *Journal of the Knowledge Economy* 1, no. 2 (2010): 128–64.

Hardell, Lennart, Michael Carlberg, and Kjell Hansson Mild. "Epidemiological Evidence for an Association Between Use of Wireless Phones and Tumor Diseases." *Pathophysiology* 16, nos. 2/3 (2009): 113–22.

Hardin, Garrett. "The Tragedy of the Commons." *Science* 162 (1968): 1243–248.

Hardt, Michael, and Antonio Negri. *Empire.* Cambridge, MA: Harvard University Press, 2000.

Harmon, Amy. "More Than Just a Game, but How Close to Reality?" *New York Times*, April 3, 2003. http://www.nytimes.com/2003/04/03/technology/more-than-just-a-game-but-how-close-to-reality.html?pagewanted=all&src=pm.

Harney, Stefano. *State Work: Public Administration and Mass Intellectuality*. Durham, NC: Duke University Press, 2002.

Harriss, John. "Middle-Class Activism and the Politics of the Informal Working Class: A Perspective on Class Relations and Civil Society in Indian Cities." *Critical Asian Studies* 38, no. 4 (2006): 445–65.

Hartmann, Betsy. "The Greening of Hate: An Environmentalist's Essay." *Southern Poverty Law Center*, July 2010. http://www.splcenter.org/greenwash-nativists-environmentalism-and-the-hypocrisy-of-hate/the-greening-of-hate-an-essay.

Hassan, Rashid, Robert Scholes, and Neville Ash, eds. *The Millennium Ecosystem Assessment Series: Current State and Trends*. Vol. 1, *Findings of the Condition and Trends Working Group of the Millennium Ecosystem Assessment*. Washington: Island, 2005.

Haste, Helen. "Constructing the Citizen." *Political Psychology* 25, no. 3 (2004): 413–39.

Hattam, Jennifer. "The Top 10 Greenest Colleges and Universities in the U.S." *Sierra Magazine*, November 6, 2007.

Haug, Wolfgang F. *Critique of Commodity Aesthetics: Appearance, Sexuality and Advertising in Capitalist Society*. Translated by Robert Bock. Cambridge: Polity, 1986.

Havenner, Jennifer. "How the Book Industry Can Save $3 Billion Dollars and 12 Million Trees." *Huffington Post*, June 22, 2010. http://www.huffingtonpost.com/jennifer-havenner/how-the-book-industry-can_b_620449.html.

Hawken, Paul. "Green is Good." *AlterNet*, October 8, 2004. http://www.alternet.org/story/20119/green_is_good/.

Hawken, Paul. "The Truth about Ethical Investing." *AlterNet*, April 29, 2005. http://www.alternet.org/story/21888/the_truth_about_ethical_investing/.

Hawkins, Gay. *The Ethics of Waste: How We Relate to Rubbish*. Lanham, MD: Rowman & Littlefield, 2006.

Hay, James. "My Space?" *Television & New Media* 10, no. 1 (January 2009): 72–76.

Hayashi S, T. Kitao, M. Hayashi, I. Oki, and A. Oshino. "X-rays from Color Television Receivers." *Journal of Radiation Research* 5, no. 3 (1964): 147–58.

Hazlett, Thomas W. "The Rationality of U.S. Regulation of the Broadcast Spectrum." *Journal of Law and Economics* 33, no. 1 (April 1990): 133–75.

Head, Sydney W. and Christopher H. Sterling. *Broadcasting in America*. Fifth edition. Boston, MA: Houghton Mifflin, 1987.

Headrick, Daniel R. "Gutta-Percha: A Case of Resource Depletion and International Rivalry." *IEEE Technology and Society Magazine* 6 (1987): 12–16.

Healy, Michael. "Experimentation and Innovation in U.S. Publishing Today: Findings from the Book Industry Study Group." *Publishing Research Quarterly* 24, no. 4 (2008): 233–39.

Hearst Corporation. "Being Green," n.d. http://hearst.com/beinggreen.

Hegel, Georg Wilhelm Friedrich. (1954). *The Philosophy of Hegel*. Edited by Carl J. Friedrich and translated by Carl J. Friedrich, Paul W. Friedrich, W. H. Johnston, L. G. Struthers, B. Bosanquet, W. M. Bryant, and J. B. Baillie. New York: Modern Library.

Hegel, Georg Wilhelm Friedrich. Introduction to *Lectures on the Philosophy of World History*. Translated by Hugh Barr Nisbet. Cambridge, UK: Cambridge University Press, 1988.

Heidegger, Martin. *Basic Writings from Being and Time (1927) to The Task of Thinking (1964)*. Edited by David Farrell Krell and translated by Joan Stambaugh, J. Glenn Gray, David Farrell Krell, John Sallis, Frank A. Capuzzi, Albert Hofstadter, W. B. Barton, Jr., Vera Deutsch, William Lovitt, and Fred D. Wieck. New York: Harper & Row, 1977.

Herat, Sunil. "Review: Sustainable Management of Electronic Waste (e-Waste)." *Clean* 35, no. 4 (2007): 305–10.

Hiatt, Brian. "How iTunes Conquered the Music Biz." *Rolling Stone*, September 20, 2007: 15–16.

Hibberd, Mike. "Public Private Partnership." Telecoms.com, September 15, 2009. http://www.telecoms.com/14505/public-private-partnership.

Hobbes, Thomas. *On the Citizen*. Edited by Richard Tuck and Michael Silverthorne. Cambridge, UK: Cambridge University Press, 1998.

Hochman, Jhan. *Green Cultural Studies: Nature in Film, Novel, and Theory*. Moscow: University of Idaho Press, 1998.

Hooks, Gregory, and Chad L. Smith. "The Treadmill of Destruction: National Sacrifice Areas and Native Americans." *American Sociological Review* 69, no. 4 (August 2004): 558–75.

Hopgood, Stephen. *American Foreign Environmental Policy and the Power of the State*. New York and London: Oxford University Press, 1998.

Horkheimer, Max. *Critique of Instrumental Reason: Lectures and Essays Since the End of World War II*. Translated by Matthew J. O'Connell, et al. (unnamed). New York: Continuum, 1996.

Houghton, J. "ICT and the Environment in Developing Countries: Opportunities and Developments." Paper prepared for the Organization for Economic Cooperation and Development, 2009.

Hughes, Robert. "The Urban Poet." *Time Magazine*, September 9, 1985. http://www.time.com/time/magazine/article/0,9171,959792,00.html.

Human Rights Advocates. *The Human Rights Impact of the Illicit Transfer and Dumping of Toxic Wastes and Dangerous Substances: E-Waste, Sham Recycling, and the Need for Effective Regulation*. Report presented at the United Nations Human Rights Council, 7th Session. Berkley: Human Rights Advocates, 2008.

Human Rights Watch. "No Guarantees: Sex Discrimination in Mexico's Maquiladora Sector." Refworld, August 1, 1996. http://www.unhcr.org/refworld/docid/3ae6a7f110.html.

Hume, David. *An Inquiry Concerning Human Understanding with a Supplement: An Abstract of a Treatise of Human Nature*. Edited by Charles W. Hendel. Indianapolis: Bobbs-Merrill, 1955.

Humphreys, David. "Environmental and Ecological Citizenship in Civil Society." *International Spectator* 44, no. 1 (2009): 171–83.

Hundt, Reed, and Gregory L. Rosston. "Communications Policy for 2006 and Beyond." *Federal Communications Law Journal* 58, no. 1 (2006): 1–34.

Hunt, Bruce J. "The Ohm Is Where the Art Is: British Telegraph Engineers and the Development of Electrical Standards." *Osiris: A Journal Dedicated to the History of Science and its Cultural Influences* 9 (1994): 48–63.

Hunter, Ian. "Providence and Profit: Speculations in the Genre Market." *Southern Review* 22, no. 3 (November 1989): 211–23.

Hurrell, Andrew. "The State." In *Political Theory and the Ecological Challenge*. Edited by Andrew Dobson and Robyn Eckersley, 165–82. Cambridge: Cambridge University Press 2006.

Hutton, Jan. "Mobile Phones Dominate in South Africa." *Nielsen Wire* September 30, 2011 http://blog.nielsen.com/nielsenwire/global/mobile-phones-dominate-in-south-africa.

Hutton, Will. *A Declaration of Interdependence: Why America Should Join the World*. New York: W. W. Norton, 2003.

Independent Press Association, Conservatree, and Co-op America. *Turning the Page: Environmental Impacts of the Magazine Industry and Recommendations for Improvement*. Washington, DC: The Paper Project, 2001.

Inform. *The Secret Life of Paper*. Video, Inform, n.d. http://www.informinc.org/pages/media/the-secret-life-series/the-secret-life-of-paper.html.

Ingram, David. *Green Screen: Environmentalism and Hollywood Cinema*. Exeter, UK: University of Exeter Press, 2000.

Ingram, Paul, Lori Qingyuan Yue, and Hayagreeva Rao. "Trouble in Store: Probes, Protests, and Store Openings by Wal-Mart, 1998–2007." *American Journal of Sociology* 116, no. 1 (July 2010): 53–92.

Innis, Harold A. *The Bias of Communication*. Toronto: University of Toronto Press, 1991.

Innis, Harold A. *Changing Concepts of Time*. Lanham, MD: Rowman & Littlefield, 2004.

Innis, Harold A. *Empire and Communications*. Toronto: Dundurn, 2007.

Innis, Harold A. "A Plea for Time." In *Canadian Cultural Studies: A Reader*. Edited by Sourayan Mookerjea, Imre Szeman, and Gail Faurschou, 7–53. Durham, NC: Duke University Press, 2009.

Institute of Aerospace Systems. "Space Debris." *Technische Universität Braunschweig*, n.d. https://www.tu-braunschweig.de/ilr/forschung/raumfahrttechnik.

Institute of Engineering and Technology. *Rebound: Unintended Consequences from Transport Policies and Technology Innovations. The Institute of Engineering and Technology*, 2010. http://www.theiet.org/factfiles/transport/index.cfm.

Institute of Pacific Relations. "Memorandum on Silver—Conflicting American and Chinese Interests." *Memorandum* 3, no. 21/22 (October 26, 1934).

Institute of Public and Environmental Affairs. *The Other Side of Apple*. Beijing: IPE Reports, 2011. http://www.ipe.org.cn/En/about/report.aspx.

Inter-Agency Space Debris Coordination Committee. n.d. http://www.iadc-online.org.

Interagency Task Force on Electronics Stewardship: White House Council on Environmental Quality, Environmental Protection Agency, and General Services Administration. *National Strategy for Electronics Stewardship*. United States Environmental Protection Agency, 2011. http://www.epa.gov/wastes/conserve/materials/ecycling/taskforce/docs/strategy.pdf.

Intergovernmental Panel on Climate Change. *Climate Change 2007: Synthesis Report Summary for Policymakers*. Geneva: World Meteorological Organization, 2007.

International Energy Agency. *Gadgets and Gigawatts: Policies for Energy Efficient Electronics—Executive Summary*. Paris: Organization for Economic Cooperation and Development, 2009.

International Labour Organization. *Sectoral Activities Department (SECTOR)*. International Labour Organization, 2010. http://www.ilo.org/public/english/dialogue/sector/sectors/mining/emp.htm.

International Peace Bureau. *The Military's Impact on the Environment: A Neglected Aspect of the Sustainable Development Debate*. Geneva: International Peace Bureau, 2002. http://www.ipb.org/i/pdf-files/The_Militarys_Impact_on_the_Environment.pdf.

International Telecommunication Union. *ICTs for Environment: Guidelines for Developing Countries, with a Focus on Climate Change*. Geneva: ICT Applications and Cybersecurity Division Policies and Strategies Department ITU Telecommunication Development Sector, 2008.

International Telecommunication Union. *ITU Background Report*. Paper presented at the ITU Symposium on ICTs and Climate Change. Hosted by CTIC, Quito, Ecuador, July 8–10, 2009.

International Telecommunication Union. *World Telecommunication/ICT Development Report 2010. Monitoring the WSIS Targets: A Mid-Term Review. International Telecommunication Union*, 2010. http://itu.int/dms_pub/itu-d/opb/ind/D-IND-WTDR-2010-PDF-E.pdf.

Introna, Lucas. *Stanford Encyclopedia of Philosophy*, 2005, s.v. "Phenomenological Approaches to Ethics and Information Technology." http://plato.stanford.edu/entries/ethics-it-phenomenology.

Jackson, Tim. *Prosperity Without Growth? The Transition to a Sustainable Economy*. London: Sustainable Development Commission, 2009.

Jacobs, Andrew. "China Issues Warning on Climate and Growth." *New York Times*, March 1, 2011. http://www.nytimes.com/2011/03/01/world/asia/01beijing.html.

Jacott, Marisa, Cyrus Reed, and Mark Winfield. *The Generation and Management of Hazardous Wastes and Transboundary Hazardous Waste Shipments Between Mexico, Canada and the United States Since 2004: A 2004 Update*. Austin: Texas Center for Policy Studies, 2004.

Jasanoff, Sheila. "A New Climate for Society." *Theory, Culture & Society* 27, nos. 2/3 (2010): 233–53..

Jennings, Humphrey. *Pandaemonium: The Coming of the Machine as Seen by Contemporary Observers, 1660–1886*. Edited by Mary-Lou Jennings and Charles Madge. New York: Free Press, 1985.

Jensen, Robert. "The Digital Provide: Information Technology, Market Performance, and Welfare in the South Indian Fisheries Sector." *Quarterly Journal of Economics* 122, no. 3 (2007): 879–924.

Jha, Arvind K., C. Sharma, Nahar Singh, R. Ramesh, R. Purvaja, and Prabhat K. Gupta. "Greenhouse Gas Emissions from Municipal Solid Waste Management in Indian Mega-Cities: A Case Study of Chennai Landfill Sites." *Chemosphere* 71, no. 4 (March 2008): 750–58.

Johansson, Olle. "The London Resolution." *Pathophysiology* 16, nos. 2/3 (2009): 247–48.

Johnson, Joel. "1 Million Workers. 90 Million iPhones. 17 Suicides. Who's to Blame?" *Wired*, March 30, 2011, 96. http://www.wired.com/magazine/2011/02/ff_joelinchina/all/1.

Johnson, Lesley. *The Unseen Voice: A Cultural Study of Early Australian Radio*. London: Routledge, 1988.

Johnson, Ted. "Hollywood: Causes and Effects." *Variety*, June 12, 2009. http://www.variety.com/article/VR1118004913?refCatId=13.

Jolly, David. "France Resists a Power-Monitoring Business." *New York Times*, July 22, 2009. http://www.nytimes.com/2009/07/22/business/energy-environment/22green.html.

Jones, Candace. "Co Evolution of Entrepreneurial Careers, Institutional Rules and Competitive Dynamics in American Film." *Organization Studies* 22, no. 6 (November 2001): 911–44.

Jones, Michael John. "Accounting for the Environment: Towards a Theoretical Perspective for Environmental Accounting and Reporting." *Accounting Forum* 34, no. 2 (June 2010): 123–38.

Jones, Van. *The Green-Collar Economy: How One Solution Can Fix Our Two Biggest Problems*. New York: HarperOne, 2008.

Jorgenson, Andrew K., Brett Clark, and Jeffrey Kentor. "Militarization and the Environment: A Panel Study of Carbon Dioxide Emissions and the Ecological Footprints of Nations, 1970–2000." *Global Environmental Politics* 10, no. 1 (February 2010): 7–29.

Jowitt, Tom. "European E-Waste Directive Delayed Until 2011." *eWEEK Europe UK*, October 21, 2010. http://www.eweekeurope.co.uk/news/european-e-waste-directive-delayed-until-2011-10805.

Juan, Shan. "Bearing the Brunt of Globalization." *China Daily*, July 3, 2008. http://www.chinadaily.com.cn/china/2008-07/03/content_6815829.htm.

Kalm, Sara. "Emancipation or Exploitation? A Study of Women Workers in Mexico's Maquiladora Industry." *Statsveteskaplig Tidskrift* 104 (2001): 225–58.

Kant, Immanuel. *Kant: Political Writings*, 2nd ed. Edited by Hans Siegbert Reiss and translated by H. B. Nisbet. Cambridge, UK: Cambridge University Press, 1991.

Karpowitz, Christopher F., Chad Raphael, and Allen S. Hammond IV. "Deliberative Democracy and Inequality: Two Cheers for Enclave Deliberation Among the Disempowered." *Politics & Society* 37, no. 4 (December 2009): 576–615.

Kaufman, Leslie. "Car Crashes to Please Mother Nature." *New York Times*, March 2, 2009. http://www.nytimes.com/2009/03/02/arts/television/02twen.html.

Kaufman, Leslie. "Conspiracies Don't Kill Birds. People, However, Do." *New York Times*, January 18, 2011. http://www.nytimes.com/2011/01/18/science/18birds.html.

Keane, Michael. "Understanding China: Navigating the Road Ahead." *Economia della cultura* 1, no. 1 (2009): 19–34.

Keeler, Dan. "Spread the Love and Make it Pay." *Global Finance*, May 2002. 20–25.

Keen, Andrew. *The Cult of the Amateur: How Today's Internet is Killing Our Culture and Assaulting Our Economy*. London: Nicholas Brealey, 2007.

Keeter, Scott, Cliff Zukin, Molly Andolina, and Krista Jenkins. *The Civic and Political Health of the Nation: A Generational Portrait*. College Park, MD: Center for Information & Research on Civic Learning & Engagement, 2002.

Kellogg, Carolyn. "7.5 Million iPads. How Many Kindles?" *Los Angeles Times*, October 19, 2010. http://latimesblogs.latimes.com/jacketcopy/2010/10/75-million-ipads-how-many-kindles.html.

Kelly, John. *Pride of Place: Mainstream Media and the Networked Public Sphere*. Cambridge, MA: Berkman Center for Internet and Society at Harvard University, 2008.

Kennan, George F. "To Prevent a World Wasteland." *Foreign Affairs* 48, no. 3 (1970): 401–13. http://www.foreignaffairs.com/articles/24149/george-f-kennan/to-prevent-a-world-wasteland.

Kessler, Donald J., and Burton G. Cour-Palais. "Collision Frequency of Artificial Satellites: The Creation of a Debris Belt." *Journal of Geophysical Research* 83, no. A6 (June 1, 1978): 2637–646.

Kilpi, Harri. "Green Frames: Exploring Cinema Ecocritically." *WiderScreen* 3, no. 7 (2007). http://www.widerscreen.fi/2007/1/green_frames-exploring_cinema_ecocritically.htm.

Kinsella, Susan. "The History of Paper." *Resource Recycling*, June 1990. http://conservatree.com/learn/Papermaking/History.shtml.

Klíma, Ivan. *Love and Garbage*. Translated by Ewald Osers. New York: Vintage, 1990.

Kogan, Irina, Charles K. Paull, Linda Kuhnz, Erica J. Burton, Susan Von Thun, H. Gary Green, and James P. Barry. *Environmental Impact of the ATOC/Pioneer Seamount Submarine Cable*. Moss Landing, CA: Monterey Bay Aquarium Research Institute, 2003. http://montereybay.noaa.gov/research/techreports/cablesurveynov2003.pdf.

Koh, D., G. Chan, and E. Yap. "World at Work: The Electronics Industry." *Occupational and Environmental Medicine* 61, no. 2 (2004): 180–83.

Koomey, J. G. *Estimating Total Power Consumption by Servers in the U.S. and the World*. Oakland, CA: Analytics, 2007.

Korten, David C. (1996). "The Failures of Bretton Woods." In *The Case Against the Global Economy*. Edited by Jerry Mander and Edward Goldsmith, 20–30. San Francisco: Sierra Club.

Kotkin, Joel. *The New Geography: How the Digital Revolution is Reshaping the American Landscape*. New York: Random House, 2001.

Kottak, Conrad P. "The New Ecological Anthropology." *American Anthropologist* 101, no. 1 (1999): 23–35.

Kramer, Andrew E. "For One Business, Polluted Clouds Have Silvery Linings." *New York Times*, July 12, 2007. http://www.nytimes.com/2007/07/12/world/europe/12norilsk.html.

Krasnow, E. G. and H. A. Solomon. "Communication Towers: Increased Demand Coupled with Increased Regulation." *Media Law & Policy* 18, no. 1 (2008): 45–68.

Kraus, Jerome. "The British Electron-Tube and Semiconductor Industry, 1935–62." *Technology and Culture* 9, no. 4 (October 1968): 544–61.

Krugman, Paul. "Chinese New Year." *New York Times*, January 1, 2010. http://www.nytimes.com/2010/01/01/opinion/01krugman.html.

Kumar, Arun, and Nanda Kumar. "Government Seeks to Crush Strike of Foxconn Workers in India." *World Socialist*, October 25, 2010. http://wsws.org/articles/2010/oct2010/foxc-o25.shtml.

Kumar, Sunil, Somnath Mukherjee, Tapan Chakrabarti, and Sukumar Devotta. "Hazardous Waste Management System in India: An Overview." *Critical Reviews in Environmental Science and Technology* 38, no. 1 (2007): 43–71.

Kundra, Vivek. *Memorandum for Chief Information Officers*. Office of Management and Budget, Executive Office of the President. CIO.gov, February 26, 2010. http://www.cio.gov/documents/Federal-Data-Center-Consolidation-Initiative-02-26-2010.pdf.

Kunnari, Esa, Jani Valkama, Marika Keskinen, and Pauliina Mansikkamaäki. "Environmental Evaluation of New Technology: Printed Electronics Case Study." *Journal of Cleaner Production* 17, no. 9 (2009): 791–99.

Kurland, Nancy B., and Deone Zell. "The Green in Entertainment: A Conversation." *Journal of Management Inquiry* 19, no. 3 (September 2010): 209–18.

Kushner, David. "Titanic vs. Popotla." *Wired*, August 7, 1998. http://www.wired.com/culture/lifestyle/news/1998/08/14294.

Lamb, John. *The Greening of IT: How Companies Can Make a Difference for the Environment*. Upper Saddle River, NJ: IBM, 2009.

Landler, Mark. "Meeting Shows U.S.-India Split on Emissions." *New York Times*, July 20, 2009. http://www.nytimes.com/2009/07/20/world/asia/20diplo.html.

Lanier, Jaron. *You Are Not a Gadget: A Manifesto*. New York: Alfred A Knopf, 2010.

Latour, Bruno. *We Have Never Been Modern*. Translated by Catherine Porter. Cambridge, MA: Harvard University Press, 1993.

Latour, Bruno. *Politics of Nature: How to Bring the Sciences into Democracy*. Translated by Catherine Porter. Cambridge, MA: Harvard University Press, 2004.

Latour, Bruno, with Konstantin Kastrissianakis. "We Are All Reactionaries Today." *Re-Public: Re-Imagining Democracy—English Version*. March 22, 2007. http://www.re-public.gr.

Latta, P. Alex. "Locating Democratic Politics in Ecological Citizenship." *Environmental Politics* 16, no. 3 (2007): 377–93

Law, Lisa, Tim Bunnell, and Chin-Ee Ong. "*The Beach*, the Gaze and Film Tourism." *Tourist Studies* 7, no. 2 (August 2007): 141–64.

Lea, Richard. "Books Overtake Games as Most Numerous iPhone Apps." *Guardian*, March 9, 2010. http://www.guardian.co.uk/books/2010/mar/09/books-overtake-games-iphone-apps.

Leadbetter, Charles, and Paul Miller. *The Pro-Am Revolution: How Enthusiasts are Changing Our Economy and Society*. London: Demos, 2004.

Lean, Geoffrey. "Mobile Phones 'More Dangerous Than Smoking.'" *Independent*, March 30, 2008. http://www.independent.co.uk/life-style/health-and-wellbeing/health-news.

Leaning, Jennifer. "Environment and Health: 5. Impact of War." *Canadian Medical Association Journal* 163, no. 9 (October 31, 2000): 1157–61. http://www.cmaj.ca/content/163/9/1157.full.

Leavens, Dickson H. "The Distribution of the World's Silver." *Review of Economics and Statistics* 17, no. 6 (November 1935): 131–38.

Lebel, Louis, and Sylvia Lorek. "Enabling Sustainable Production-Consumption Systems." *Annual Review of Environment and Resources* 33 (2008): 241–75.

Lécuyer, Christophe, and David C. Brock. "The Materiality of Microelectronics." *History and Technology* 22, no. 3 (2006): 301–325.

Lee, Mike. "Our Electronic Waste is Piling Up Overseas." *San Diego Union-Tribune*, June 19, 2007. http://www.signonsandiego.com/uniontrib/20070619/news_1n19ewaste.html.

Lee, Sherry. "Ghosts in the MACHINES." *South China Morning Post Magazine*, May 12, 2002.

Lenoir, Timothy. "Programming Theaters of War: Gamemakers as Soldiers." *Bombs and Bandwidth: The Emerging Relationship Between Information Technology and Security*. Edited by Robert Latham, 175–98. New York: New Press, 2003.

Leopold, Aldo. *A Sand County Almanac*. New York: Oxford University Press, 1949.

Leung, Anna O. W., Nurdan S. Duzgoren-Aydin, K. C. Cheung, and Ming H. Wong. "Heavy Metals Concentrations of Surface Dust from E-Waste Recycling and its Human Health Implications in Southeast China." *Environmental Science and Technology* 42, no. 7 (March 4, 2008): 2674–680.

Levins, Hoag. "Video: Making TV Commercials the Carbon-Neutral Way." *AdvertisingAge,* October 17, 2007. http://www.adage.com/article?article_id=121206.

Levitt, Joshua. "Cash from Waste." *Electronics Supply & Manufacturing,* March 1, 2007. http://www.usedcisco.com/cash_from_waste.

Linden, Greg, Kenneth L. Kraemer, and Jason Dedrick. *Who Captures Value in a Global Innovation System? The Case of Apple's iPod.* Personal Computing Industry Center, Alfred P. Sloan Foundation Industry Center, Paul Merage School of Business, University of California, Irvine, 2007. http://paginaspersonales.deusto.es/aminondo/Materiales_web/Linden_et_al_IPod_2007.pdf.

Littler, Jo. *Radical Consumption: Shopping for Change in Contemporary Culture.* New York and Maidenhead, UK: McGraw-Hill/Open University Press, 2009.

Liu, Connie. "A Look Behind the Scenes: How Green is Hollywood?" *Deliberations* (Spring 2008): 51–57.

Liu, W. L., C. F. Shen, Z. Zhang, and C. B. Zhang. "Distribution of Phthalate Esters in Soil of E-Waste Recycling Sites from Taizhou City in China." *Bulletin of Environmental Contamination and Toxicology* 82, no. 6 (March 17, 2009): 665–67.

Liu, Yu. "Maoist Discourse and the Mobilization of Emotions in Revolutionary China." *Modern China* 36, no. 3 (2010): 329–62.

Lohr, Steve. "For Today's Graduate, Just One Word: Statistics." *New York Times,* August 6, 2009. http://www.nytimes.com/2009/08/06/technology/06stats.html.

Lovato, Roberto. "Fear of a Brown Planet." *The Nation,* June 28, 2004, 17–21.

Lueck, Dean. "The Extermination and Conservation of the American Bison." *Journal of Legal Studies* 1, no. 2 (2002): S609–52.

Lüthje, Boy. "The Changing Map of Global Electronics: Networks of Mass Production in the New Economy." *Challenging the Chip: Labor Rights and Environmental Justice in the Global Electronics Industry.* Edited by Ted Smith, David A. Sonnenfeld, and David Naguib Pellow, 17–30. Philadelphia: Temple University Press, 2006.

Ma, Tiffany. "China and Congo's Coltan Connection." Project 2049 Institute Futuregram 09-003 (2009). http://www.project2049.net/publications.html.

Macauley, David. "Hanna Arendt and the Politics of Place: From Earth Alienation to *Oikos.*" *Minding Nature: The Philosophers of Ecology.* Edited by David Macauley, 102–33. New York: Guilford, 1996.

Macedonia, Mike. "Games, Simulation, and the Military Education Dilemma." In *The Internet and the University: 2001 Forum,* 157–67. Boulder, CO: Educause, 2002.

MacGregor, Sherilyn. *Beyond Mothering Earth: Ecological Citizenship and the Politics of Care.* Vancouver: University of British Columbia Press, 2006.

Macherey, Pierre. "Culture and Politics: Interview with Pierre Macherey." Edited and translated by Colin Mercer and Jean Radford. *Red Letters* 5 (1977): 3–9.

Macherey, Pierre. "The Literary Thing." Translated by Audrey Wasser. *diacritics* 37, no. 4 (2007): 21–30.

Madrid, Carolina. "Hollywood Greens Up with Environmental Database." *Reuters,* August 11, 2010. http://www.reuters.com/article/idUSTRE67A53K20100811.

Makower, Joel. "Walmart's Sustainability Index: The Hype and the Reality." *GreenBiz,* July 16, 2009. http://www.greenbiz.com/blog/2009/07/16/Walmart-sustainability-index.

Malaby, Thomas. "Parlaying Value: Capital in and Beyond Virtual Worlds." *Games & Culture: A Journal of Interactive Media* 1, no. 2 (2006): 141–62.

Malkin, Elisabeth. "A Boom Along the Border." *New York Times,* August 26, 2004. http://www.nytimes.com/2004/08/26/business/a-boom-along-the-border.html.

Malmodin, Jens, Åsa Moberg, Dag Lundén, Göran Finnveden, and Nina Lövehagen. "Greenhouse Gas emissions and Operational Electricity Use in the ICT and Entertainment & Media Sectors." *Journal of Industrial Ecology* 4, no. 5 (2010): 770–90.

Manhart, Andreas. *Key Social Impacts of Electronics Production and WEEE-Recycling in China.* Freiburg, Germany: Institute for Applied Ecology, 2007.

Marconi, Guglielmo. Foreword of *The Story of Broadcasting* by A. R. Burrows, vii. London: Cassell, 1924.

Marcus, George. "Ethnography in/of the World System: The Emergence of Multi-Sited Ethnography." *Annual Review of Anthropology* 24 (October 1995): 95–117.

Marcuse, Herbert. "Some Social Implications of Modern Technology." *Studies in Philosophy and Social Sciences* 9, no. 3 (1941): 414–39.

Marcuse, Herbert. "Ecology and Revolution." *Liberation* 16 (1972): 10–12.

Markillie, Paul. "Crowned at Last." *Economist*, April 2, 2005, 3–6. http://www.economist.com/node/3785166.

Markoff, John. "Progress Hits a Snag: Tiny Chips Use Outsize Power." *New York Times*, July 31, 2011a. http://www.nytimes.com/2011/08/01/science/01chips.html?pagewanted=all.

Markoff, John. "Data Centers' Power Use Less Than Was Expected." *New York Times*, July 31, 2011b. http://www.nytimes.com/2011/08/01/technology/data-centers-using-less-power-than-forecast-report-says.html.

Markowitz, Gerald, and David Rosner. "Corporate Responsibility for Toxins." *Annals of the American Academy of Political and Social Science* 584, no. 1 (November 2002): 159–74.

Marland, E. A. "British and American Contributions to Electrical Communications." *British Journal for the History of Science* 1, no. 1 (1962): 31–48.

Marshall, Eliot. "Nobel Economist Robert Solow." *Dialogue* 82 (1988): 8–9.

Martín-Barbero, Jesús. Introduction to *Imaginarios de Nación: Pensar en Medio de la Tormenta.* Edited by Jesús Martín-Barbero, 7–10. Bogotá, Colombia: Ministerio de Cultura, 2001.

Martínez-Alier, Joan. *The Lack of General Economic Equivalency in Ecological Economics.* Vol. 7 of *The Milano Papers.* Edited by Michele Cangiani, 209–24. Montreal and New York: Black Rose, 1997.

Marvin, Carolyn. *When Old Technologies Were New: Thinking About Electronic Communication in the Late Nineteenth Century.* New York: Oxford University Press, 1988.

Marx, Karl. *Capital* Vol. 1: *A Critique of Political Economy.* Edited by Frederick Engels and Translated by Samuel Moore and Edward Aveling. New York: Modern Library, 1906.

Marx, Karl. "Human Emancipation." In *Citizenship.* Edited by Paul Barry Clarke, 137–40. London: Pluto, 1994.

Marx, Karl. *The Eighteenth Brumaire of Louis Bonaparte.* Translated by Daniel De Leon. Mountain View: New York Labor News, 2003.

Massey, Karen A. "The Challenge of Nonionizing Radiation: A Proposal for Legislation." Tenth annual administrative law issue, *Duke Law Journal* 1 (February 1979): 105–89.

Mattelart, Armand. *Mapping World Communication: War, Progress, Culture.* Translated by Susan Emanuel and James A. Cohen. Minneapolis: University of Minnesota Press, 1994.

Mattelart, Armand. *The Invention of Communication.* Translated by Susan Emanuel. Minneapolis: University of Minnesota Press, 1996.

Mattelart, Armand. "Cómo nació el mito de Internet." Translated by Yanina Guthman. In *El mito internet.* Edited by Victor Hugo de la Fuente, 25–32. Santiago, Chile: Editorial aún creemos en los sueños, 2002.

Mattelart, Armand. *The Information Society: An Introduction.* Translated by S. G. Taponier and J. A. Cohen. London: Sage, 2003.

Mattelart, Armand, and Costas M. Constantinou. "Communications/Excommunications: An Interview with Armand Mattelart." Translated by Amandine Bled, Jacques Guot, and Costas Constantinou. *Review of International Studies* 34 (2008): 21–42.

Matthews, H. Scott, Eric Williams, Takashi Tagami, and Chris T. Henderson. "Energy Implications of Online Book Retailing in the United States and Japan." *Environmental Impact Assessment Review* 22, no. 5 (October 2002): 493–507.

Maxwell, Richard. *Herbert Schiller*. Lanham, MD: Rowman & Littlefield, 2003.

Maxwell, Richard. "El Papel de la Comunicación en Nuestra Sociedad." *Documentación Social: Revista de Estudios Sociales y Sociología Aplicada* 140 (2006): 11–24.

Maxwell, Richard, and Toby Miller. "Film and Globalization." *Communications Media, Globalization and Empire*. Edited by Oliver Boyd-Barrett, 33–52. Eastleigh, UK: John Libbey, 2006.

Maxwell, Richard, and Toby Miller. "La mano visible." *Página 12*, August 6, 2008a. http://www.pagina12.com.ar/diario/laventana/26-109121-2008-08-06.html.

Maxwell, Richard, and Toby Miller. "Creative Industries or Wasteful Ones?" *Urban China* 33 (2008b): 122.

Maxwell, Richard, and Toby Miller. "E-Waste: Elephant in the Living Room." *Flow* 9, no. 3 (2008c). http://flowtv.org/?p=2194.

Maxwell, Richard, and Toby Miller. "Ecological Ethics and Media Technology." *International Journal of Communication* 2 (2008d): feature 331–53. http://ijoc.org/ojs/index.php/ijoc/article/viewFile/320/151.

Maxwell, Richard, and Toby Miller. "Green Smokestacks?" *Feminist Media Studies* 8, no. 3 (2008e): 324–29.

Maxwell, Richard, and Toby Miller. "Talking Rubbish: Green Citizenship, Media, and the Environment." *Climate Change and the Media*. Edited by Tammy Boyce and Justin Lewis, 17–27. New York: Peter Lang, 2009.

Mayer, Vicki. *Below the Line: Producers and Production Studies in the New Television Economy.* Durham, NC: Duke University Press, 2011.

Mayers, C. Kieren, Chris M. France, and Sarah J. Cowell. "Extended Producer Responsibility for Waste Electronics." *Journal of Industrial Ecology* 9, no. 3 (2005): 169–89.

Mayfield, Kendra. "E-Waste: Dark Side of Digital Age." *Wired*, January 10, 2003. http://www.wired.com/science/discoveries/news/2003/01/57151?currentPage=all.

Mazar, Nina and Chen-Bo Zhong. "Do Green Products Make Us Better People?" *Psychological Science*, February 2010.

McBride, Edward. "Talking Rubbish." *Economist*, February 28, 2009, 3–5. http://www.economist.com/node/13135349.

McCarthy, Vance. "Kodak—A Picture of Nano-Driven Innovation." Nano Science and Technology Institute, n.d. http://www.nsti.org/news/item.html?id=179.

McChesney, Robert W. "My Media Studies: Thoughts from Robert W. McChesney." *Television & New Media* 10, no. 1 (January 2009): 108–09.

McChesney, Robert W., and John Bellamy Foster. "The Commercial Tidal Wave." *Monthly Review* 54, no. 10 (March 2003): 1–16. http://monthlyreview.org/2003/03/01/the-commercial-tidal-wave.

McDougall, Paul. "IBM's Green Shoots: Government, Healthcare, India." *Information Week*, July 20, 2009. http://www.informationweek.com/blog/main/archives/2009/07/ibms_green_shoo.html;jsessionid=543FTGYCLUVHEQSNDLPSKHSCJUNN2JVN.

McHoul, Alec, and Tom O'Regan. "Towards a Paralogics of Textual Technologies: Batman, Glasnost and Relativism in Cultural Studies." *Southern Review* 25, no. 1 (1992): 5–26.

McKercher, Catherine. *Newsworkers Unite: Labor, Convergence and North American Newspapers.* Lanham, MD: Rowman & Littlefield, 2002.

McKercher, Catherine, and Vincent Mosco, eds. *Knowledge Workers in the Information Society.* Lanham, MD: Lexington, 2007.

McLaughlin, Andrew. *Regarding Nature: Industrialism and Deep Ecology.* Albany: State University of New York Press, 1993.

McLean, Craig. "The Importance of Being Earnest." *Guardian*, May 28, 2005. http://www.guardian.co.uk/music/2005/may/28/popandrock.coldplay.

McLuhan, Marshall. *Understanding Media: The Extensions of Man.* New York: Mentor, 1964.

McLuhan, Marshall. "Canada as Counter-Environment." *Canadian Cultural Studies: A Reader.* Edited by Sourayan Mookerjea, Imre Szeman, and Gail Faurschou, 71–86. Durham, NC: Duke University Press, 2009.

McNeill, J. R. "Observations on the Nature and Culture of Environmental History." *History and Theory* 42, no. 4 (2003): 5–43.

Medina, Martin. *The World's Scavengers: Salvaging for Sustainable Consumption and Production.* Lanham, MD: AltaMira, 2007.

Mehring, Franz. "In Memory of Gutenberg's 500th Birthday (Germany 1900)." *Communication and Class Struggle.* Edited by Armand Mattelart and Seth Seiglaub, 188–94. New York: International General, 1979.

Meikle, Jeffrey L. "Material Doubts: The Consequences of Plastic." *Environmental History* 2, no. 3 (1997): 278–300.

Melville, Herman. "The Paradise of Bachelors and the Tartarus of Maids." *Harper's New Monthly Magazine* 10 (1855): 670–78.

Mendoza, Jorge Eduardo. "The Effect of the Chinese Economy on Mexican Maquiladora Employment." *International Trade Journal* 24, no. 1 (2010): 52–83.

Michaelson, Jay. "Rethinking Regulatory Reform: Toxics, Politics, and Ethics." *Yale Law Journal* 105, no. 7 (May 1996): 1891–925.

Michaelson, S. M. "The Tri-Service Program—A Tribute to George M. Knauf, USAF (MC)." *IEEE Transactions on Microwave Theory and Techniques* 19, no. 2 (1968): 131–46.

Micheletti, Michele. *Political Virtue and Shopping: Individuals, Consumerism, and Collective Action.* New York: Palgrave Macmillan, 2003.

Migone, Andrea. "Hedonistic Consumerism: Patterns of Consumption in Contemporary Capitalism." *Review of Radical Political Economics* 39, no. 2 (Spring 2007): 173–200.

Miles, Ian. "The Development of Technology Foresight: A Review." *Technological Forecasting & Social Change* 77, no. 9 (November 2010): 1448–456.

Miller, Gerri. "On the Green Carpet at the Environmental Media Association Awards." *Mother Nature Network,* October 19, 2010. http://www.mnn.com/lifestyle/arts-culture/stories/on-the-green-carpet-at-the-environmental-media-association-awards.

Miller, Toby. "*Mission Impossible* and the new international division of labour." *Metro,* 82: 21–28, 1990a.

Miller, Toby. "*Mission Impossible*: How do you turn Indooroopilly into Africa?" *Queensland images in film and television.* Edited by Jonathan Dawson and Bruce Malloy, 122–31. St. Lucia: University of Queensland Press, 1990b.

Miller, Toby. *The Well-Tempered Self: Citizenship, Culture, and the Postmodern Subject.* Baltimore: Johns Hopkins University Press, 1993.

Miller, Toby. "A View From a Fossil: The New Economy, Creativity and Consumption—Two or Three Things I Don't Believe in." *International Journal of Cultural Studies* 7, no. 1 (March 2004): 55–65.

Miller, Toby. "Hollywood, Cultural Policy Citadel." *Understanding Film: Marxist Perspectives.* Edited by Mike Wayne, 182–93. London: Pluto, 2005.

Miller, Toby. *Cultural Citizenship: Cosmopolitanism, Consumerism, and Television in a Neoliberal Age.* Philadelphia: Temple University Press, 2007a.

Miller, Toby. "'Drowning in Information and Starving for Knowledge': 21st Century Scholarly Publishing." *International Journal of Communication* 1 (2007b): feature 123–35. http://www.ijoc.org/ojs/index.php/ijoc/article/download/121/56.

Miller, Toby. "Face Up to Tech Waste." *Press-Enterprise,* December 16, 2007c. http://pe.com/localnews/opinion/localviews/stories/PE_OpEd_Opinion_D_op_1216_miller_loc.1b11b81.html.

Miller, Toby. "'Step Away from the Croissant': Media Studies 3.0." *The Media and Social Theory.* Edited by David Hesmondhalgh and Jason Toynbee, 213–30. London: Routledge, 2008a.

Miller, Toby. "La mano visible: Apuntes sobre la incorporación del impacto ambiental de las tecnologías mediaticas en la investigación sobre medios y globalización." *Comunicación*, Edited by José Carlos Lozano Rendón, 121–25. Monterrey, Mexico: Fondo Editorial de Nuevo León, 2008b.

Miller, Toby. *Makeover Nation: The United States of Reinvention*. Columbus: Ohio State University Press, 2008c.

Miller, Toby. "Media Studies 3.0." *Television & New Media* 10, nos. 5/6 (January 2009a): 5–6.

Miller, Toby. "Cybertarians of the World Unite: You Have Nothing to Lose but Your Tubes!" *The YouTube Reader*. Edited by Pelle Snickars and Patrick Vondereau, 424–40. Stockholm: National Library of Sweden, 2009b.

Miller, Toby. "The Oldest New Network: The Division of Cultural Labor and its Ecological Impact." *International Review of Information Ethics* 11 (2009c): 31–35.

Miller, Toby. "A Future for Media Studies: Cultural Labour, Cultural Relations, Cultural Politics." *How Canadians Communicate III: Contexts of Canadian Popular Culture*. Edited by Bart Beaty, Derek Briton, Gloria Filax, and Rebecca Sullivan, 35–53. Edmonton, Alberta: Athabasca University Press, 2010a.

Miller, Toby. *Television Studies: The Basics*. London: Routledge, 2010b.

Miller, Toby, and George Yúdice. "O Copyright: Instrumento de Expropiação e Resistência Onde de Encontram a Economia Política e os Estudos Culturais." Translated by Robervan Barbosa de Santana. *Comunicação e a Crítica da Economia Política: Perspectivas Teóricas e Epistemológicas*. Edited by César Bolaño, 173–91. São Cristovão, Brazil: Editora-UFS, 2009.

Miller, Toby, Nitin Govil, John McMurria, and Richard Maxwell. *Global Hollywood*. London: British Film Institute, 2001.

Miller, Toby, Nitin Govil, John McMurria, Richard Maxwell, and Ting Wang. *Global Hollywood 2*. London: British Film Institute, 2005.

Milmo, Sean. "Ink Industry Faces Challenges in Determining Carbon Footprints." *Ink World*, January/February 2010. http://www.inkworldmagazine.com/articles.

Milojković, Jelena and Vančo Litovski. "Short-Term Forecasting in Electronics." *International Journal of Electronics* 98, no. 2 (2011): 161–72.

Minoli, Daniel. "Designing Green Networks with Reduced Carbon Footprints." *Journal of Telecommunications Management* 3, no. 1 (April 2010): 15–35.

Miranda, Marta, Philip Burris, Jessie Froy Bingcang, Phil Shearman, Jose Oliver Briones, Antonio La Viña, and Stephen Menard. *Mining and Critical Ecosystems: Mapping the Risks*. Washington: World Resources Institute, November 2003.

Mirmina, Steven A. "Reducing the Proliferation of Orbital Debris: Alternatives to a Legally Binding Instrument." *American Journal of International Law* 99, no. 3 (July 2005): 649–62.

Missika, Jean-Louis. *La fin de la télévision*. Paris: Seuil, 2006.

Mitchell, Stacey. *Big-Box Swindle: The True Cost of Mega-Retailers and the Fight for America's Independent Business*. Boston: Beacon, 2007.

Mitman, Gregg. *Reel Nature: America's Romance with Wildlife on Film*. Cambridge, MA: Harvard University Press, 1999.

Moberg, Åsa, Martin Johansson, Göran Finnveden, and Alex Jonsson. "Printed and E-Tablet Newspaper from an Environmental Perspective—A Screening Life Cycle Assessment." *Environmental Impact Assessment Review* 30, no. 3 (April 2010): 177–91.

Miguel, Guillermo J. Román. *Diagnóstico sobre la generación de basura electrónica en México*. Mexico City: Instituto Nacional de Ecología, 2007.

Mohai, Paul, and Robin Saha. "Reassessing Racial and Socioeconomic Disparities in Environmental Justice Research." *Demography* 43, no. 2 (May 2006): 383–99.

Monbiot, George. *The Age of Consent: A Manifesto for a New World Order*. London: Flamingo, 2003.

Montague, Dena. "Stolen Goods: Coltan and Conflict in the Democratic Republic of Congo." *SAIS Review* 22, no. 1 (Winter/Spring 2002): 103–18.

Mooallem, Jon. "The Afterlife of Cellphones." *New York Times*, January 13, 2008. http://www.nytimes.com/2008/01/13/magazine/13Cellphone-t.html?pagewanted=all.

Moore, Christopher Luke. "Digital Games Distribution: The Presence of the Past and the Future of Obsolescence." *M/C Journal* 12, no. 3 (2009). http://www.journal.media-culture.org.au/index.php/mcjournal/article/viewArticle/166.

Moore, Gordon E. "Cramming More Components onto Integrated Circuits." *Electronics* 38, no. 8 (April 9, 1965): 114–17. http://download.intel.com/research/silicon/moorespaper.pdf.

Moore, Malcolm. "Apple Admits Using Child Labour." *Telegraph*, February 27, 2010a. http://www.telegraph.co.uk/technology/apple/7330986/Apple-admits-using-child-labour.html.

Moore, Malcolm. "Four Suicide Attempts in a Month at Foxconn, the Makers of the iPad." *Telegraph*, April 7, 2010b. http://blogs.telegraph.co.uk/news/malcolmmoore/100033036/four-suicide-attempts-in-a-month-at-foxconn-the-makers-of-the-ipad.

Moraff, Christopher. "America's Slave Labor." *In These Times*, January 2007.

Morton, David L. "'The Rusty Ribbon': John Herbert Orr and the Making of the Magnetic Recording Industry, 1945–1960." *Business History Review* 67, no. 4 (1993): 589–622.

Mosco, Vincent. *The Political Economy of Communication*. London: Sage, 1996.

Mosco, Vincent. *The Digital Sublime: Myth, Power, and Cyberspace*. Cambridge, MA: MIT Press, 2004.

Mosco, Vincent. "The Future of Journalism." *Journalism* 10, no. 3 (2009): 350–52.

Mosco, Vincent, and Catherine McKercher. *The Laboring of Communication: Will Knowledge Workers of the World Unite?* Lanham, MD: Lexington, 2008.

Mosco, Vincent, Catherine McKercher, and Ursula Huws, eds. *Getting the Message: Communications Workers and Global Value Chains*. Special issue *Work Organisation Labour & Globalisation* 4, no. 2 (2010).

Moser, Walter. "Garbage and Recycling: From Literary Theme to Mode of Production." *Other Voices: The eJournal of Cultural Criticism* 3, no. 1 (2007) http://www.othervoices.org/3.1/wmoser/index.php.

Motion Picture Association of America. "Film Studio Recycling Efforts Keep 20,000 Tons out of Landfills, Prevent Harmful Greenhouse Gas Emissions." April 20, 2007.

Motion Picture Association of America, "Hollywood's Major Film Studios Put Environmental Guide to Use." Press release, April 18, 2008. http://greenopolis.com/files/earth_day_release_2008_final.pdf.

Motion Picture Association of America. *The Economic Impact of the Motion Picture & Television Industry on the United States*. Washington, DC: Motion Picture Association of America, 2009.

Motion Picture Association of America, *Best Practices Guide for Green Production*, 2010. http://www.pgagreen.org/index.php/mobile-best-practices/11-mpaa-best-practices-for-green-production

Mouawad, Jad, and Kate Galbraith. "Plugged-In Age Feeds Hunger for Electricity." *New York Times*, September 20, 2009. http://www.nytimes.com/2009/09/20/business/energy-environment/20efficiency.html?pagewanted=all.

Muecke, Stephen. *Joe in the Andamans and Other Fictocritical Stories*. Sydney: Local Consumption Publications, 2008.

Mukherjee, Sanjukta, with Central Department for Development Studies, Tribhuvan University. *Child Ragpickers in Nepal: A Report on the 2002–2003 Baseline Survey*. Bangkok: International Labour Organization, 2003.

Muldoon, Annie. "Where the Green is: Examining the Paradox of Environmentally Conscious Consumption." *Electronic Green Journal* 1, no. 23 (2006): article 3.

Murashov, Vladimir. "Human and Environmental Exposure Assessment for Nanomaterials: An Introduction to This Issue." *International Journal of Occupational and Environmental Health* 16, no. 4 (2010). http://www.ijoeh.com/index.php/ijoeh/article/view/1651.

Murdoch, James. "Clean Energy Conservatives Can Embrace." *Washington Post*, December 4, 2009. http://www.washingtonpost.com/wp-dyn/content/article/2009/12/03/AR2009120303698.html.

Murray, Robin L., and Joseph K. Heumann. *Ecology and Popular Film: Cinema on the Edge.* Albany: State University of New York Press, 2009.

Nader, Laura. "Up the Anthropologist—Perspectives Gained from Studying Up." *Reinventing Anthropology.* Edited by Dell H. Hymes, 284–311. New York: Pantheon, 1972.

Nairn, Tom. "Democracy & Power: American Power & the World." *OpenDemocracy* January 9, 16, 23, 2003, and February 4 and 20, 2003. http://www.opendemocracy.net/conflict-americanpower/debate.jsp.

National Grid. *The Power Behind the World Cup!* London: National Grid, 2006.

National Institute of Environmental Health Sciences. *Turpentine (Turpentine Oil, Wood Turpentine, Sulfate Turpentine, Sulfite Turpentine) [8006-64-2]. Review of Toxicological Literature. National Toxicology Program,* 2002. http://ntp.niehs.nih.gov/ntp/htdocs/chem_background/exsumpdf/turpentine.pdf.

National Research Council. *An Assessment of Potential Health Effects from Exposure to PAVE PAWS Low-Level Phased Array Radiofrequency Energy.* Washington, DC: National Academies, 2005.

Natural Resources Defense Council. *Lowering the Cost of Play: Improving the Energy Efficiency of Video Game Consoles. National Resources Defense Council,* 2008. http://www.nrdc.org/energy/consoles/contents.asp.

Nautilus Institute, Natural Heritage Institute, and Human Rights Advocates. *Dodging Dilemmas? Environmental and Social Accountability in the Global Operations of California-Based High Tech Companies.* San Francisco: Nautilus Institute, 2002.

Navar, Murgesh. "The New TV Ecosystem." *Media Post's Video Insider,* June 30, 2008. http://www.mediapost.com/publications/blogs.

Navarro, Mireya. "Following Trash and Recyclables on Their Journey." *New York Times,* September 17, 2009. http://www.nytimes.com/2009/09/17/science/earth/17trash.html.

Neale, Steve. *Cinema and Technology: Image, Text, Ideology.* Chicago: University of Chicago Press, 1985.

Neff, Gina, Elizabeth Wissinger, and Sharon Zukin. "Entrepreneurial Labor Among Cultural Producers: 'Cool' Jobs in 'Hot' Industries." *Social Semiotics* 15, no. 3 (2005): 307–34.

Negri, Antonio. *goodbye mister socialism*. Paris: Seuil, 2007.

Neuman, W. Russell. *The Future of the Mass Audience.* Cambridge, UK: Cambridge University Press, 1993.

Newcomb, Horace. "Studying Television: Same Questions, Different Contexts." *Cinema Journal* 45, no. 1 (2005): 107–11.

Newell, Edmund. "Atmospheric Pollution and the British Copper Industry, 1690–1920." *Technology and Culture* 38, no. 3 (1997): 655–89.

Newell, Peter. "Environmental NGOs, TNCs, and the Question of Governance." *The International Political Economy of the Environment: Critical Perspectives.* Edited by Dimitris Stevis and Valeire J. Assetto, 85–107. Boulder, CO: Lynne Rienner, 2001.

News Corporation. "0 in 2010." *News Corporation,* n.d. http://www.newscorp.com/energy/index.html.

Ngai, Pun. *Made in China: Women Factory Workers in a Global Workplace.* Hong Kong and Durham, NC: Hong Kong University Press/Duke University Press, 2005.

Niman, Michael I. "Kodak's Toxic Moments." *AlterNet,* May 29, 2003. http://www.alternet.org/story/16030/kodak's_toxic_moments.

Nimpuno, Nardono, Alexandra McPherson, and Tanvir Sadique. *Greening Consumer Electronics—Away from Chlorine and Bromine.* Göteborg/Montréal: ChemSec and Clean Production Action, 2009.

Nixon, Robert. *Dreambirds: The Natural History of a Fantasy.* London: Picador, 2000.

Nnorom, I. C., and O. Osibanjo. "Overview of Electronic Waste (E-Waste) Management Practices and Legislations, and Their Poor Applications in the Developing Countries." *Resources Conservation & Recycling* 52, no. 6 (2008): 843–58.

Noble, David F. *America by Design: Science, Technology and the Rise of Corporate Capitalism.* Oxford, UK: Oxford University Press, 1977.

Nors, Minna, Tiina Pajula, and Hanna Pihkola. "Calculating the Carbon Footprint of a Finnish Newspaper and Magazine from Cradle to Grave." *Life Cycle Assessment of Products and Technologies: LCA Symposium.* Edited by Heli Koukkari and Minna Nors, 55–65. Espoo, Finland: VTT, 2009.

NOTIMEX. "22 Maquiladoras Closed in 2009 Due to the Economic Crisis." *Maquila Portal,* February 24, 2010. http://www.maquilaportal.com/index.php/blog/show/22-maquiladoras-closed-in-2009-due-to-the-economic-crisis.html.

Nunn, Kem. *Tijuana Straits: A Novel.* New York: Scribner, 2005.

Nye, David E. *American Technological Sublime.* Cambridge, MA: MIT Press, 1994.

Nye, David E. "Technology and the Production of Difference." *American Quarterly* 58, no. 3 (2006): 597–618.

Nye, David E. *Technology Matters: Questions to Live With.* Cambridge, MA: MIT Press, 2007.

Okono, Fred. "The Complete Package." *ICT Update* 38 (July 2007). http://ictupdate.cta.int/en/Feature Articles/The-complete-package.

O'Malley, Pat. "Discontinuity, Government and Risk: A Response to Rigakos and Hadden." *Theoretical Criminology* 5, no. 1 (2001): 85–92.

O'Neill, Kate. *The Environment and International Relations.* Cambridge, UK: Cambridge University Press, 2009.

Oppenheimer, Martin. "The Sub-Proletariat: Dark Skins and Dirty Work." *Critical Sociology* 4 (January 1974): 7–20.

Organisation de Coopération et de Développement Economiques. "OECD Environmental Outlook (2001)." http://www.oecd.org/document/26/0,3746,fr_2649_34283_1863386_1_1_1_1,00.html

Organisation for Economic Co-Operation and Development. *Environmental Outlook.* Paris: Organisation for Economic Co-Operation and Development, 2001.

Organisation for Economic Co-Operation and Development. *Extended Producer Responsibility.* Paris: Organisation for Economic Co-Operation and Development, 2007.

Organisation for Economic Co-Operation and Development. *Greener and Smarter: ICTs, the Environment and Climate Change.* Paris: Organisation for Economic Co-Operation and Development, 2010.

Orisakwe, Orish Ebere, and Chiara Frazzoli. "Electronic Revolution and Electronic Wasteland: The West/Waste Africa Experience." *Journal of Natural & Environmental Sciences* 1, no. 1 (2010): 43–47.

Ornithological Council. "Deadly Spires in the Night: The Impact of Communications Towers on Migratory Birds." *Issue Brief* 1, no. 8 (1999).

Orwell, George. "As I Please." *Tribune,* May 12, 1944. http://orwell.ru/library/articles/As_I_Please/english/

Orwell, George. *The Lion and the Unicorn: Socialism and the English Genius.* Harmondsworth: Penguin, 1982.

Osibanjo, O. and I. C. Nnorom. "The Challenge of Electronic Waste (e-waste) Management in Developing Countries." *Waste Management & Research* 25, no. 6 (December 2007): 489–501.

Ostrom, Elinor. "Reformulating the Commons." *Swiss Political Science Review* 6, no. 1 (2000): 29–52.

Outland III, Robert B. *Tapping the Pines: The Naval Stores Industry in the American South.* Baton Rouge: Louisiana State University Press, 2004.

Pak, Phoenix. "Haste Makes E-Waste: A Comparative Analysis of How the United States Should Approach the Growing E-Waste Threat." *Cardozo Journal of International and Comparative Law* 16 (Spring 2008): 241–78.

Palacios, H., I. Iribarren, M.J. Olalla, and V. Cala. "Lead poisoning of Horses in the Vicinity of a Battery Recycling Plant." *Science of the Total Environment* 290 (May 6, 2002): 81–89.

Palmier, Jean-Michel. *Walter Benjamin: Le chiffonier, l'Ange et le Petit Bossu—Esthétique et politique chez Walter Benjamin.* Edited by Florent Perrier. Paris: Klincksieck, 2006.

Pantera, Gabrielle. "Hollywood Goes Green." *Hollywood Today,* May 6, 2009 http://hollywoodtoday.net/2009/05/06/hollywood-goes-green/.

Papastergiadis, Nikos. "Modernism and Contemporary Art." *Theory, Culture & Society* 23, nos. 2/3 (2006): 466–69.

Paper Task Force. *Paper Task Force Recommendations for Purchasing and Using Environmentally Preferable Paper: Project Synopsis.* New York: Environmental Defense Fund, 1995.

Parks, Lisa. "Falling Apart: Electronics Salvaging and the Global Media Economy." *Residual Media.* Edited by Charles Acland, 32–47. Minneapolis: University of Minnesota Press, 2007.

Parsley, David. "Server Farms: Where the Internet Lives." *Building* 11 (2008).

Paterson, Kent. "Temping Down Labor Rights: The Manpowerization of Mexico." *CorpWatch,* January 6, 2010. http://www.corpwatch.org/article.php?id=15496.

Paterson, Matthew. *Global Warming and Global Politics.* London: Routledge, 1996.

Pellow, David Naguib, and Lisa Sun-Hee Park. *The Silicon Valley of Dreams: Environmental Justice, Immigrant Workers, and the High-Tech Global Economy.* New York: New York University Press, 2002.

Pelta-Heller, Zack. "HP's Printer Cartridges Are an E-Waste Disaster—Does the Company Really Care?" *AlterNet,* October 29, 2007. http://www.alternet.org/environment/65945.

Penrose, Beris. "Occupational Lead Poisoning in Battery Workers: The Failure to Apply the Precautionary Principle." *Labour History* 84 (May 2003): 1–20.

Pepper, David. "Environmentalism." *Understanding Contemporary Society: Theories of the Present.* Edited by Gary Browning, Abigail Halci, and Frank Webster, 445–62. London: Sage, 2000.

Periodical Publishers Association. *PPA Annual Report to DEFRA: Progress on Voluntary Producer Responsibility Agreement 2008.*

Periodical Publishers Association. *PPA Magazine Carbon Footprint Calculator: User Guide,* 2009.

Peters, John Durham. "Technology and Ideology: The Case of the Telegraph Revisited." *Thinking with James Carey: Essays on Communications, Transportation, History.* Edited by Jeremy Packer and Craig Robertson, 137–55. New York: Peter Lang, 2006.

Petrini, Carlo. "Slow Down: The Return to Local Food." *Demos Collection* 18 (2002): 25–30.

Pines, Charles C. "The Story of Ink." *American Journal of Police Science* 2, no. 4 (1931): 290–301.

Plato. *The Laws.* Translated by Trevor J. Saunders. London: Penguin, 1970.

Plato. *Phaedrus.* Translated by Benjamin Jowett. Charleston, SC: Forgotten, 2008.

Plepys, Andrius. "The Grey Side of ICT." *Environmental Impact Assessment Review* 22, no. 5 (2002): 509–23.

Plumwood, Val. "Feminism." *Political Theory and the Ecological Challenge.* Edited by Andrew Dobson and Robyn Eckersley, 51–74. Cambridge, UK: Cambridge University Press, 2006.

Polanyi, Karl. *The Great Transformation: The Political and Economic Origins of Our Time.* Boston: Beacon, 2001.

Political Economy Research Institute. *The Misfortune 100: Top Corporate Air Polluters in the United States*. Amherst: University of Massachusetts, 2004.

Pollin, Robert, James Heintz, and Heidi Garrett-Peltier. *The Economic Benefits of Investing in Clean Energy*. Amherst: Center for American Progress and Political Economy Research Institute of the University of Massachusetts, 2009.

Poniatowski, Marty. *Foundations of Green IT: Consolidation, Virtualization, Efficiency, and ROI in the Data Center*. Upper Saddle River, NJ: Prentice Hall, 2010.

Pope John Paul II. "Peace with God the Creator, Peace with All of Creation." Message of His Holiness for the Celebration of the World Day of Peace, the Vatican, Rome, December 8, 1989. http://conservation.catholic.org/ecologicalcrisis.htm.

Porritt, Jonathon. "Living Within Our Means." *Forum for the Future*, 2009. http://www.forum-forthefuture.org/blog/living-within-our-means.

Pourlis, Aris F. (2009). "Reproductive and Developmental Effects of EMF in Vertebrate Animal Models." *Pathophysiology* 16, nos. 2–3: 179–89.

Prahalad, Coimbatore Krishnarao, and Stuart L. Hart. "The Fortune at the Bottom of the Pyramid." *Revista Electrônica de Estratégia & Negócios* 1, no. 2 (2008). http://portaldeperiodicos.unisul.br/index.php/EeN/article/viewArticle/39.

Preston, Peter. "We Thought the Internet Was Killing Print. But It Isn't." *Guardian*, October 17, 2010. http://www.guardian.co.uk/media/2010/oct/17/newspaper-abcs-websites-internet-news.

Producers Guild of America. *Green Production Guide*, n.d. http://www.greenproductionguide.com.

Prothero, Andrea, Pierre McDonagh, and Susan Dobscha. "Is Green the New Black? Reflections on a Green Commodity Discourse." *Journal of Macromarketing* 30, no. 2 (2010): 147–59.

Puurunen, Karina, and Petri Vasara. "Opportunities for Utilising Nanotechnology in Reaching Near-Zero Emissions in the Paper Industry." *Journal of Cleaner Production* 15, nos. 13/14 (2007): 1287–294.

Puzzanghera, Jim. "High-Tech TV Upgrades Will Create Low-Tech Trash." *Los Angeles Times*, May 24, 2007. http://www.latimes.com/business/la-fi-digitaltv24-2007may24,0,1022143.story.

Pynchon, Thomas. "Is it O.K. to be a Luddite?" *New York Times Book Review*, October 28, 1984.

Pynn, Larry. "Dangerous Waste Bund for China is Intercepted." *Vancouver Sun*, December 22, 2006.

Quiggin, John. *Zombie Economics: How the Dead Still Walk Among Us*. Princeton, NJ: Princeton University Press, 2010.

Quinn, Bill. *How Wal-Mart is Destroying America (and the World)*, 3rd ed. New York: Random House, 2005.

Rahaman, Abu Shiraz. "Critical Accounting Research in Africa: Whence and Whither." *Critical Perspectives on Accounting* 21, no. 5 (2010): 420–27.

Raina, Ravi. *ICT Human Resource Development in Asia and the Pacific: Current Status, Emerging Trends, Policies and Strategies*. Incheon, Republic of Korea: United Nations Asian and Pacific Training Centre for Information and Communication Technology for Development, 2007. http://www.unapcict.org/ecohub/resources/ict-human-resource-development-in-asia-and-the.

Raphael, Chad, and Ted Smith. "Importing Extended Producer Responsibility for Electronic Equipment into the United States." In *Challenging the Chip: Labor Rights and Environmental Justice in the Global Electronics Industry*. Edited by Ted Smith, David A. Sonnenfeld, and David Naguib Pellow, 247–59. Philadelphia: Temple University Press, 2006.

Raphael, Chad. "E-Waste and the Greening of the Information Age." *STS Nexus* 3, no. 2 (2003): 23–28. http://www.scu.edu/sts/nexus/summer2003/RaphaelArticle.cfm.

Rathje, William, and Cullen Murphy. *Rubbish! The Archaeology of Garbage*. Tucson: University of Arizona Press, 2001.

Ray, Manas Ranjan, Gopeshwar Mukherjee, Sanghita Roychowdhury, and Twisha Lahiri. "Respiratory and General Health Impairments of Ragpickers in India: A Study in Delhi." *International Archives of Occupational and Environmental Health* 77, no. 8 (2004): 595–98.

Reichart, Inge, and Roland Hischier. "The Environmental Impact of Getting the News: A Comparison of On-Line, Television, and Newspaper Information Delivery." *Journal of Industrial Ecology* 6, nos. 3–4 (2002): 185–200.

Reilly, Julie A. "Celluloid Objects: Their Chemistry and Preservation." *Journal of the American Institute for Conservation* 30, no. 2 (1991): 145–62.

Reygadas, Luis. *Ensamblando culturas: Diversidad y conflicto en la globalización de la industria.* Barcelona: Gedisa, 2002.

Ribeiro, John. "Foxconn Workers Exploited in India, Activists Say." *Computerworld*, October 27, 2010. http://www.computerworld.com/s/article/9193298/Foxconn_workers_exploited_in_India_activists_say.

Ricardo, Jorge. "Cuestionan el mercado." *Reforma*, May, 2008.

Richtel, Matt. "Consumers Hold on to Products Longer." *New York Times*, February 26, 2011. http://www.nytimes.com/2011/02/26/business/26upgrade.html?pagewanted=all.

Rigakos, George S. and Richard Hadden, W. "Crime, Capitalism and the 'Risk Society.'" *Theoretical Criminology* 5, no. 1 (2001): 61–84.

Riis, Jacob. *How the Other Half Lives: Studies Among Tenements of New York*. New York: Hill and Wang, 1957.

Ritch, Emma. "Cutting the CO2 from E-Readers with Solar." *Cleantech*, October 12, 2009. http://www.cleantech.com/news/5141/cutting-co2-e-readers-solar-lpl.

Ritzer, George, and Nathan Jurgenson. "Production, Consumption, Prosumption: The Nature of Capitalism in the Age of the Digital 'Prosumer.'" *Journal of Consumer Culture* 10, no. 1 (2010): 13–36.

Rivoli, Pietra. *The Travels of a T-Shirt in the Global Economy: An Economist Examines the Markets, Power, and Politics of World Trade*. Hoboken, NJ: John Wiley, 2008.

Rizvi, Salim. "From Clearing Excrement to New York Modeling." *BBC News*, July 4, 2008. http://news.bbc.co.uk/2/hi/7489296.stm.

Robarts, Guy. "Bridging the Global Computer Divide." *BBC News*, March 15, 2004. http://news.bbc.co.uk/2/hi/business/3535583.stm.

Robertson, Craig. *The Passport in America: The History of a Document*. Oxford, UK: Oxford University Press, 2010.

Robins, Kevin, and Frank Webster. *Times of the Technoculture: From the Information Society to the Virtual Life*. London: Routledge, 1999.

Robinson, Brett H. "E-Waste: An Assessment of Global Production and Environmental Impacts." *Science of the Total Environment* 408, no. 2 (2009): 183–91.

Robinson, Colin. "The Trouble with Amazon." *Nation*, August 2–9, 2010, 29–32. http://www.thenation.com/article/37484/trouble-amazon.

Rockstrom, Johan, Will Steffen, Kevin Noone, Åsa Persson, F. Stuart III Chapin, Eric Lambin, Timothy M. Lenton, Martin Scheffer, Carl Folke, Hans Joachim Schellnhuber, B. Nykvist, C. A. de Wit, T. Hughes, S. van der Leeuw, H. Rodhe, S. Sörlin, P. K. Snyder, R. Costanza, U. Svedin, M. Falkenmark, L. Karlberg, R. W. Corell, V. J. Fabry, J. Hansen, B. Walker, L. Liverman, K. Richardson, P. Crutzen, and J. A. Foley "Planetary Boundaries: Exploring the Safe Operating Space for Humanity." *Ecology and Society* 14, no. 2 (2009). http://www.ecologyandsociety.org/vol14/iss2/art32.

Rogers, Heather. *Gone Tomorrow: The Hidden Life of Garbage*. New York: New Press, 2005.

Romundstad, Pål, Aage Andersen, and Tor Haldorsen. "Cancer Incidence Among Workers in the Norwegian Silicon Carbide Industry." *American Journal of Epidemiology* 153, no. 10 (2001): 978–86.

Roos, Dave. "Hollywood Goes Green." *MovieMaker,* July 24, 2006. http://www.moviemaker.com/directing/article/hollywood_goes_green_2881.

Rose, Deborah B., and Libby Robin. "The Ecological Humanities in Action: An Invitation." *Australian Humanities Review* 31–32 (2004). http://lib.latrobe.edu.au/AHRarchive/issue-April-2004/rose.html.

Rosen, Christine Meisner, and Christopher C. Sellers. "The Nature of the Firm: Towards an Ecocultural History of Business." *Business History Review* 73, no. 4 (Winter 1999): 577–600.

Ross, Andrew. *The Chicago Gangster Theory of Life: Nature's Debt to Society.* New York: Verso, 1995.

Ross, Andrew. *Nice Work if You Can Get It: Life and Labor in Precarious Times.* New York: New York University Press, 2009.

Ross, Andrew. "Greenwashing Nativism." *Nation,* August 16–23, 2010a: 18–20. http://www.thenation.com/article/38036/greenwashing-nativism.

Ross, Andrew. "The Corporate Analogy Unravels." *Chronicle of Higher Education,* October 17, 2010b. http://chronicle.com/article/Farewell-to-the-Corporate/124919.

Ross, Andrew. *Bird on Fire: Lessons from the World's Least Sustainable City.* New York: Oxford University Press, 2011.

Rossiter, Ned. *Organized Networks: Media Theory, Creative Labour, New Institutions.* Rotterdam: NAi, 2006.

Roth, Kurt W., and Kurtis McKenny. *Energy Consumption by Consumer Electronics in U.S. Residences.* Final report for the Consumer Electronics Association. Cambridge, UK: Tiax, 2007. http://www.ce.org/pdf/Energy%20Consumption%20by%20CE%20in%20U.S.%20Residences%20(January%202007).pdf.

Rothkopf, David. "In Praise of Cultural Imperialism?" *Foreign Policy* 107 (1997): 38–53.

Royte, Elizabeth. "E-Waste@Large." *New York Times,* January 27, 2006. http://www.nytimes.com/2006/01/27/opinion/27royte.html.

Rudolph, L., and Shanna H. Swan. "Reproductive Hazards in the Microelectronics Industry." *Occupational Medicine* 1, no. 1 (1986): 135–43.

Russell, Ben. "Flat Screen Televisions 'Will Add to Global Warming.'" *Independent,* November 1, 2006. http://www.independent.co.uk/environment/climate-change/flat-screen-televisions-will-add-to-global-warming-422424.html.

Rydh, Carl Johan. "Environmental Assessment of Battery Systems: Critical Issues for Established and Emerging Technologies." Master's thesis, Department of Environmental Systems Analysis, Chalmers University of Technology, Göteborg, Sweden, 2003 ESA200316.pdf.

Sachs, Jeffrey. "The Digital War on Poverty." *Guardian,* August 21, 2008. http://www.guardian.co.uk/commentisfree/2008/aug/21/digitalmedia.mobilephones.

Sacks, Harvey. *Lectures on Conversation.* Vols. I and II. Edited by Gail Jefferson. Malden, MA: Blackwell, 1995.

Sadetzki, Siegal, Angela Chetrit, Avital Jarus-Hakak, Elisabeth Cardis, Yonit Deutch, Shay Duvdevani, Ahuva Zultan, Laurence Freedman, and Michael Wolf. "Cellular Phone Use and Risk of Benign and Malignant Parotid Gland Tumors—A Nationwide Case-Control Study." *American Journal of Epidemiology* 167, no. 4 (2007): 457–67.

Sage, Cindy, and David O. Carpenter. "Public Health Implications of Wireless Technologies." *Pathophysiology* 16, no. 2 (August 2009): 233–46.

Saied, Mohamed, and German T. Velasquez. "PCs and Consumers—A Look at Green Demand, Use, and Disposal." In *Computers and Environment: Understanding and Managing Their Impacts.* Edited by Ruediger Kuehr and Eric Williams, 161–81. Dordrecht, Netherlands: Kluwer Academic, 2003.

Salzinger, Leslie. "From High Heels to Swathed Bodies: Gendered Meanings Under Production in Mexico's Export-Processing Industry." *Feminist Studies* 23, no. 3 (1997): 549–74.

Salzinger, Leslie. "Manufacturing Sexual Subjects: 'Harassment', Desire and Discipline on a Maquiladora Shopfloor." *Ethnography* 1, no. 1 (2000): 67–92.

Schaefer, Peter D., and Meenakshi Gigi Durham. "On the Social Implications of Invisibility: The iMac G5 and the Effacement of the Technological Object." *Critical Studies in Media Communication* 24, no. 1 (2007): 39–56.

Schallenberg, Richard H. "The Anomalous Storage Battery: An American Lag in Early Electrical Engineering." *Technology and Culture* 22, no. 4 (1981): 725–52.

Schäppi, Bernd, Bernhard Przywara, Frank Bellosa, Thomas Bogner, Silvio Weeren, and Alain Anglade. *Energy Efficient Servers in Europe: Energy Consumption, Saving Potentials, Market Barriers and Measures.* Part I, *Energy Consumption and Saving Potentials.* Vienna: Austrian Energy Agency, The Efficient Servers Consortium, 2007.

Scharnhorst, Wolfram. "Life Cycle Assessment in the Telecommunication Industry: A Review." *International Journal of Life-Cycle Assessment* 13, no. 1 (2006): 75–86.

Schatan, Claudia, and Liliana Castilleja. "The Maquiladora Electronics Industry on Mexico's Northern Boundary and the Environment." *International Environmental Agreements* 7, no. 2 (2007): 109–35.

Schauer, Thomas. *The Sustainable Information Society: Vision and Risks.* Vienna: European Support Centre of the Club of Rome, 2003.

Schiller, Dan. *How to Think About Information.* Urbana: University of Illinois Press, 2007.

Schiller, Herbert I. *Mass Communication and American Empire.* Boston: Beacon, 1971.

Schiller, Herbert I. *Communication and Cultural Domination.* New York: International Arts and Sciences Press, 1976.

Schiller, Herbert I. *Who Knows: Information in the Age of the Fortune 500.* Norwood, NJ: Ablex, 1981.

Schiller, Herbert I. *Information and the Crisis Economy.* Norwood, NJ: Ablex, 1984.

Schluep, Mathias, David Rochat, Alice Wanjira Munyua, Salah Eddine Laissaoui, Salimata Wone, Cissé Kane, and Klaus Hieronymi. "Assessing the E-Waste Situation in Africa." Paper presented at the Electronics Goes Green 2008+ conference, Berlin, September 8–10, 2008. http://ewasteguide.info/files/Schluep_2008_EGG.pdf.

Schmitz, Christopher. "The Rise of Big Business in the World Copper Industry 1870–1930." *Economic History Review* 39, no. 3 (1986): 392–410.

Schoenfeld, Amy. "Everyday Items, Complex Chemistry." *New York Times*, December 22, 2007. http://www.nytimes.com/2007/12/22/business/22chemicals.html.

Schor, Juliet B. *Plenitude: The New Economics of True Wealth.* New York: Penguin, 2010.

Schwarzenegger, Arnold. "The Clean Air Act Keeps Us Healthy." *Wall Street Journal*, April 21, 2011. http://online.wsj.com/article/SB10001424052748703789104576273120525192318.html.

Schuler, Richard E. "The Smart Grid: A Bridge Between Emerging Technologies, Society, and the Environment." *Bridge* 40, no. 1 (2010): 42–49.

Science and Technology Council of the American Academy of Motion Picture Arts and Sciences. *The Digital Dilemma: Strategic Issues in Archiving and Accessing Digital Motion Picture Materials.* Los Angeles: Academy Imprints, 2007.

Seitz, Frederick. "The Tangled Prelude to the Age of Silicon Electronics." *Proceedings of the American Philosophical Society* 140, no. 3 (1996): 289–337.

Sekula, Allan. "TITANIC's Wake." *Art Journal* 60, no. 2 (2001): 26–37.

Selin, Henrik, and Stacy D. VanDeveer. "European Regulations Prove That E-Waste Can be Managed Responsibly." In *What Is the Impact of E-Waste?* Edited by Cynthia A. Bily, 48–56. Detroit: Greenhaven, 2009.

Sénat Français. *Projet de loi portant engagement (urgence déclarée), national pour l'environnement.* Paris: Sénat Français, 2009. http://www.senat.fr/leg/pjl08-155.pdf.

Sexton, Sarah, Nicholas Hildyard, and Larry Lohmann. "We're a Small Island: The Greening of Intolerance." *The Corner House*, April 7, 2005. http://www.thecornerhouse.org.uk/resource/were-small-island-0.

Seyfang, Gill. "Shopping for Sustainability: Can Sustainable Consumption Promote Ecological Citizenship?" *Environmental Politics* 14, no. 2 (2005): 290–306.

Shabecoff, Philip. "Reagan and Environment: To Many, a Stalemate." *New York Times,* January 2, 1989. http://www.nytimes.com/1989/01/02/us/reagan-and-environment-to-many-a-stalemate.html?pagewanted=all&src=pm.

Shabi, Rachel. "The E-Waste Land." *Guardian,* November 30, 2002.

Shachtman, Noah. "Green Monster." *Foreign Policy,* May/June 2010. http://www.foreignpolicy.com/articles/2010/04/26/green_monster?page=full.

Shah, Dhavan V., Douglas M. McLeod, Lewis Friedland, and Michelle R. Nelson. "The Politics of Consumption/The Consumption of Politics." *Annals of the American Academy of Political and Social Science* 611 (2007): 6–15.

Shannon, Claude E., and Warren Weaver. *The Mathematical Theory of Communication.* Urbana: University of Illinois Press, 1963.

Shapiro Judy. "Why Mobile Technology Is Still Going to Save the World." *Advertising Age,* July 26, 2010 http://adage.com/article/digitalnext/mobile-technology-save-world/145084/

Sharma, Devinder. "Tsunamis, manglares y economía de mercado." Translated by Felisa Sastre. *Rebelión,* January 14, 2005. http://www.rebelion.org/noticia.php?id=10010.

Shaw, Randy. *Reclaiming America: Nike, Clean Air, and the New National Activism.* Berkeley: University of California Press, 1999.

Shellenberger, Michael, and Ted Nordhaus. "The Death of Environmentalism: Global Warming Politics in a Post-Environmental World." *Grist,* January 13, 2005. http://www.grist.org/article/doe-reprint/PALL.

Sheppard, Kate. "Fair and … Carbon Neutral?" *Mother Jones,* July/August 2010, 42–43.

Shields, Rachel. "It's So Last Year: *Vanity Fair* Abandons the 'Green Issue.'" *Independent,* April 5, 2009. http://www.independent.co.uk/news/media/its-so-last-year-vanity-fair-abandons-the-green-issue-1662661.html.

Shiva, Vandana. *Water Wars: Privatization, Pollution, and Profit.* Boston: South End, 2002.

Shiva, Vandana. "Lecciones del tsunami para quienes menosprecian a la madre tierra." *Rebelión,* January 15, 2005. http://www.rebelion.org/noticia.php?id=10045.

Shoaib, Mahwash. "The Heart of Whiteness: The Allure of Tourism in *Vertical Limit* and *the Beach.*" *Bad Subjects* 54 (2001). http://www.bad.eserver.org/issues/2001/54/shoaib.html.

Sholle, David. "Informationalism and Media Labour." *International Journal of Media & Cultural Politics* 1, no. 1 (2005): 137–41.

Sibley, Lisa. "Cleantech Group Report: E-Readers a Win for Carbon Emissions." *Cleantech,* August 19, 2009. http://www.cleantech.com/

Siegel, Lenny, and John Markoff. "The High Cost of High-Tech: The Dark Side of the Chip." *Questioning Technology: A Critical Anthology.* Edited by John Zerzan and Alice Cares, 54–60. London: Freedom, 1988.

Silicon Valley Toxics Coalition. *Electronic Industry Overview.* San Jose, CA: Silicon Valley Toxics Coalition, n. d.

Silicon Valley Toxics Coalition. *Toward a Just and Sustainable Solar Energy Industry. Silicon Valley Toxics Coalition,* January 14, 2009. Silicon Valley Toxics Coalition white paper. http://svtc.org/wp-content/uploads/Silicon_Valley_Toxics_Coalition_-_Toward_a_Just_and_Sust.pdf.

Silver, David, and Alice Marwick. "Internet Studies in Times of Terror." *Critical Cyberculture Studies.* Edited by David Silver and Adrienne Massanari, 47–54. New York: New York University Press, 2006.

Simmons, Dan. "India's Poor Tackle E-Waste." *BBC News,* October 14, 2005. http://news.bbc.co.uk/2/hi/programmes/click_online/4341494.stm.

Simon, Stephanie. "The More You Know … ." *Wall Street Journal,* February 9, 2009. http://online.wsj.com/article/SB123378462447149239.html.

Simpson, Amelia. "Warren County's Legacy for Mexico's Border Maquiladoras." *Golden Gate University Environmental Law Journal* 1 (2007): 153–74.

Simpson, Christopher. *Science of Coercion: Communication Research and Psychological Warfare, 1945–1960.* New York: Oxford University Press, 1996.

Sirowy, Beata. "Understanding the Information Society: The Potentials of Phenomenological Approach." *Media and Urban Space: Understanding, Investigating, and Approaching Media-city.* Edited by Frank Eckardt, 45–64. Berlin: Frank & Timme GmbH, 2008.

Sjöwall, Maj, and Per Wahlöö. *Roseanna: A Martin Beck Mystery.* Translated by Lois Roth. New York: Vintage, 2006.

Slack, Jennifer D., and J. Macgregor Wise. *Culture and Technology: A Primer.* New York: Peter Lang, 2005.

Slade, Giles. "iWaste." *Mother Jones,* March/April 2007.

Slater, Don, and Jo Tacchi. *RESEARCH: ICT Innovations for Poverty Reduction.* New Delhi: UNESCO, 2004.

Smith, Aaron. *Gadget Ownership.* Pew Research Center Publications, October 14, 2010. http://pewresearch.org/pubs/1763/americans-and-their-gadgets-technology-devices.

Smith, Anthony. *Goodbye Gutenberg: The Newspaper Revolution of the 1980s.* Oxford, UK: Oxford University Press, 1980.

Smith, Christopher Holmes. "'I Don't Like To Dream About Getting Paid': Representations of Social Mobility and the Emergence of the Hip-Hop Mogul." *Social Text* 77, vol. 21, no. 4 (2003): 69–97.

Smith, Kimberly K. *African American Environmental Thought: Foundations.* Lawrence: University of Kansas Press, 2007.

Smith, Mark J., and Piya Pangsapa. *Environment and Citizenship: Integrating Justice, Responsibility and Civic Engagement.* London: Zed, 2008.

Smith, Richard. "Beyond Growth or Beyond Capitalism?" *Real-World Economics Review* 53 (2010): 28–42.

Smith, Ted. "Why We are 'Challenging the Chip': The Challenges of Sustainability in Electronics." *International Review of Information Ethics* 11 (2009). http://i-r-i-e.net/issue11.htm.

Smith, Ted, and Chad Raphael. "High Tech Goes Green." *Yes!,* March 21, 2003: 28–30.

Smith, Ted, David A. Sonnenfeld, and David Naguib Pellow, eds. *Challenging the Chip: Labor Rights and Environmental Justice in the Global Electronics Industry.* Philadelphia: Temple University Press, 2006a.

Smith, Ted, David A. Sonnenfeld, and David Naguib Pellow. "The Quest for Sustainability and Justice in a High-Tech World." *Challenging the Chip: Labor Rights and Environmental Justice in the Global Electronics Industry.* Edited by Ted Smith, David A. Sonnenfeld, and David Naguib Pellow, 1–11. Philadelphia: Temple University Press, 2006b.

Snyder, John W. "Historic Preservation and Hazardous Waste: A Legacy of the Industrial Past." *APT Bulletin* 24, nos. 1–2 (1992): 67–73.

Spagat, Eliot. "As Borders Tighten, Illegals Turn to the Sea." *Washington Times,* August 26, 2010 http://www.washingtontimes.com/news/2010/aug/26/as-borders-tighten-illegals-turn-to-sea.

Standage, Tom. *The Victorian Internet: The Remarkable Story of the Telegraph and the Nineteenth Century's On-Line Pioneers.* New York: Berkley, 1998.

Standage, Tom. "Your Television is Ringing." *Economist,* October 12, 2006 http://www.economist.com/node/7995312.

Stanley, Allesandra. "Sounding the Global-Warming Alarm Without Upsetting the Fans." *New York Times,* July 9, 2009. http://www.nytimes.com/2007/07/09/arts/television/09watc.html.

Starobin, Robert S. "The Economics of Industrial Slavery in the Old South." *Business History Review* 44, no. 2 (1970): 131–74.

Starr, Paul. *The Creation of the Media: Political Origins of Modern Communications.* New York: Basic, 2004.

Steinberg, S. H. *Five Hundred Years of Printing.* Harmondsworth: Penguin, 1955.

Sterling, Christopher H., and John Michael Kittross. *Stay Tuned: A History of American Broadcasting,* 3rd ed. Mahwah: Lawrence Erlbaum Associates, 2002.

Sterne, Jonathan. "Out with the Trash: On the Future of New Media." *Residual Media.* Edited by Charles Acland, 16–31. Minneapolis: University of Minnesota Press, 2007.

Stockwell, Stephen, and Adam Muir. "The Military-Entertainment Complex: A New Facet of Information Warfare." *Fibreculture* 1 (2003). http://one.journal.fibreculture.org/issue1/issue1_stockwellmuir.html.

Stolle, Dietlind, Marc Hooghe, and Michele Micheletti. "Politics in the Supermarket: Political Consumerism as a Form of Political Participation." *International Political Science Review* 26, no. 3 (2005): 245–69.

Strasser, Susan. *Waste and Want: A Social History of Trash.* New York: Metropolitan, 1999.

Strategic Counsel on Corporate Accountability. *Formosa Plastics: A Briefing Paper on Waste, Safety and Financial Issues Including U.S. Campaign Finance Abuses.* Waverly, MA: Strategic Counsel on Corporate Accountability, n.d.

Streeter, Tom. "The Moment of *Wired.*" *Critical Inquiry* 31, no. 4 (2005): 755–79.

Struppek, Mirjam. "The Social Potential of Urban Screens." *Visual Communication* 5, no. 2 (2006): 173–88.

Students & Scholars Against Corporate Misbehaviour. *Workers as Machines: Military Management in Foxconn.* Hong Kong: Students & Scholars Against Corporate Misbehaviour, 2010a.

Students & Scholars Against Corporate Misbehaviour. *Disney, Walmart and ICTI: Together Make Workers Rights Violations Normal and Sustainable.* Hong Kong: Students & Scholars Against Corporate Misbehaviour, 2010b.

Suarez, Daniel. *Daemon: A Novel.* New York: Dutton, 2009.

Sundaram, Ravi. *Pirate Modernity: Delhi's Media Urbanism.* London: Routledge, 2010.

Sutter, Paul. "Reflections: What Can U.S. Environmental Historians Learn from Non-U.S Environmental Historiography?" *Environmental History* 8, no. 1 (January 2003): 109–30.

Swanton, Christine. "Heideggerian Environmental Virtue Ethics." *Journal of Agricultural and Environmental Ethics* 23, nos. 1–2 (2010): 145–66.

Sy, Aida, and Tony Tinker. "Labor Processing Labor: A New Critical Literature for Information Systems Research." *International Journal of Accounting Information Systems* 11, no. 2 (2010): 120–33.

Szabó, Laszlo, Antonio Ramirez Soria, Juha Forsström, Janne T. Keränen, and Eemeli Hytönen. "A World Model of the Pulp and Paper Industry: Demand, Energy Consumption and Emissions Scenarios to 2030." *Environmental Science & Policy* 12, no. 3 (2009): 25–69.

Taibbi, Matt. "Why Isn't Wall Street in Jail?" *Rolling Stone,* March 3, 2011. 44–51. http://www.rollingstone.com/politics/news/why-isnt-wall-street-in-jail-20110216.

Tajnaj, Carolyn. "Fred Terman, the Father of Silicon Valley." *IEEE Design & Test of Computers* 2, no. 2 (March 1985).

Tammemagi, Hans. *The Waste Crisis: Landfills, Incinerators, and the Search for a Sustainable Future.* New York: Oxford University Press, 1999.

Teague, Peter. Foreword of *The Death of Environmentalism: Global Warming Politics in a Post-Environmental World* by Michael Shellenberger and Ted Nordhaus. CA: Breakthrough Institute, 2004.

Teather, David. "Amazon's Ebook Milestone: Digital Sales Outstrip Hardbacks for First Time in U.S." *Guardian,* July 20, 2010. http://www.guardian.co.uk/books/2010/jul/20/amazon-ebook-digital-sales-hardbacks-us.

The Economics of Ecosystems and Biodiversity (TEEB). *The Economics of Ecosystems and Biodiversity: Mainstreaming the Economics of Nature: A Synthesis of the Approach, Conclusions, and Recommendations of TEEB* 2010. http://www.teebweb.org/LinkClick. aspx?fileticket=bYhDohL_TuM%3D.

Tekrati Inc. "Samsung Holds Lead in Global Television Market in Q2 2007, Says iSuppli." Tekrati.com, September 25, 2007. http://ce.tekrati.com/research/9371.

Tenner, Edward. *Why Things Bite Back: Technology and the Revenge of Unintended Consequences.* New York: Alfred A. Knopf, 1996.

Tesh, Sylvia N., and Bruce A. Williams. "Identity Politics, Disinterested Politics, and Environmental Justice." *Polity* 28, no. 3 (Spring 1996): 285–305.

Thompson, Anne. "Hollywood Goes Green." *Variety*, April 27, 2007. http://www.variety.com/article/VR1117963892.

Thompson, Bill. "Taxing Times for E-Waste." *BBC News*, September 26, 2003. http://news.bbc.co.uk/2/hi/technology/3141988.stm.

Thrall, A. Trevor, Jaime Lollio-Fahkreddine, Jon Berent, Lana Donnelly, Wes Herrin, Zachary Paquette, Rebecca Wenglinski, and Amy Wyatt. "Star Power: Celebrity Advocacy and the Evolution of the Public Sphere." *International Journal of Press/Politics* 13, no. 4 (2008): 362–85.

Thussu, Daya Kishan. "The 'Murdochization' of News? The Case of Star TV in India." *Media, Culture & Society* 29, no. 4 (2007): 593–611.

Till, Brian D., Sarah M. Stanley, and Randi Priluck. "Classical Conditioning and Celebrity Endorsers: An Examination of Belongingness and Resistance to Extinction." *Psychology & Marketing* 25, no. 2 (2008): 179–96.

Time Warner. *2008 Corporate Social Responsibility Report.* New York: Time Warner, 2008. http://b2bcdn.timeinc.com/tw/ourcompany/corporate-responsibility/pdf/tw_csr_report08.pdf.

Thornes, John E. "A Rough Guide to Environmental Art." *Annual Review of Environment and Resources* 33 (2008): 391–411.

TMZ. "Celebs Who Claim They're Green but Guzzle Gas." *TMZ*, October 18, 2006. http://www.tmz.com/2006/10/18/celebs-who-claim-theyre-green-but-guzzle-gas

Toffler, Alvin. *Previews and Premises.* New York: William Morrow, 1983.

Tong, Xin, and Jici Wang. "Transnational Flows of E-Waste and Spatial Patterns of Recycling in China." *Eurasian Geography and Economics* 45, no. 8 (2004): 608–21.

Tonkin, Emma. "eBooks: Tipping or Vanishing Point?" *Ariadne* 62 ( January 30, 2010). http://www.ariadne.ac.uk/issue62/tonkin.

Touré, Hamadoun I. *ITU Secretary-General's Declaration on Cybersecurity and Climate Change.* Geneva: International Telecommunication Union, November 12–13, 2008. http://www.itu.int/council/C2008/hls/statements/closing/sg-declaration.html.

Transcontinental Printing. *Reducing the Carbon Footprint of Books.* An industry-trends white paper. Transcontinental Printing, September 2008. http://img.en25.com/Web/TranscontinentalPrinting/Reducing_the_Carbon_Eng.pdf.

Transcontinental Printing. *Reducing the Carbon Footprint of Magazines.* An industry-trends white paper. Transcontinental Printing, May 2009. http://www.unisourcegreen.com/pdf/wp_carbon_footprint.pdf.

Transcontinental Printing. *Reducing the Carbon Footprint of Print Communications. An industry-trends white paper.* Transcontinental Printing, n.d. http://img.en25.com/Web/TranscontinentalPrinting/Comm_Reducing_the_Carbon_En.pdf.

Tripsis, Mary. "Unraveling The Process of Creative Destruction: Complementary Assets and Incumbent Survival in the Typesetter Industry." *Strategic Management Journal* 18, no. S1 (1997): 119–42.

Turner, Fred. *From Counterculture to Cyberculture: Stewart Brand, the Whole Earth Network, and the Rise of Digital Utopianism.* Chicago: University of Chicago Press, 2006.

Turse, Nick. *The Complex: How the Military Invades Our Everyday Lives.* New York: Metropolitan, 2008.

Twist, Jo. "Gadget Market 'to Grow in 2005.'" *BBC News,* January 10, 2005. http://news.bbc.co.uk/2/hi/technology/4161639.stm.

Tzanelli, Rodanthi. "Reel Western Fantasies: Portrait of a Tourist Imagination in *The Beach* (2000)." *Mobilities* 1, no. 1 (2006): 121–42.

UK Film Industry. *Environmental Strategy.* London: UK Film Council, n.d.

Unger, Nicole, and Oliver Gough. "Life cycle considerations about optic fibre cable and copper cable systems: a case study." *Journal of Cleaner Production* 16, no. 14 (2008): 1517–525.

Union of Concerned Scientists. "What's in Space? Satellites: Types, Orbits, Countries, and Debris." *Nuclear Weapons & Global Security,* May 2006. http://www.ucsusa.org/global_security/space_weapons/whats-in-space.html.

United Nations. *United Nations Framework Convention On Climate Change.* Bonn: United Nations Climate Change Secretariat, 1992.

United Nations. *Kyoto Protocol to The United Nations Framework Convention on Climate Change (1997).* Bonn, Germany: United Nations Climate Change Secretariat, 1998.

United Nations. *Stockholm Convention on Persistent Organic Pollutants.* Geneva: Secretariat of the Stockholm Convention, 2001.

United Nations Environmental Programme. *Basel Convention on the Control of Transboundary Movements of Hazardous Wastes and Their Disposal.* Geneva: The Secretariat of the Basel Convention, 1992.

United Nations Environmental Programme. *UNEP 2006 Annual Report.* Nairobi, Kenya: United Nations Environmental Programme, 2007.

United Nations. *Report of the Panel of Experts on the Illegal Exploitation of Natural Resources and Other Forms of Wealth of the Democratic Republic of the Congo.* United Nations, 2002. http://www.un.org/News/dh/latest/drcongo.htm.

United States Atomic Energy Commission. *In the Matter of J. Robert Oppenheimer: Transcript of hearing before personnel security board and texts of principal documents and letters.* Boston, MA: MIT Press, 1971.

United States Congress. *Copper: Technology and Competitiveness.* Washington, DC: Office of Technology Assessment, 1988.

United States Department of the Interior. *2006 Minerals Yearbook, Silver.* United States Geological Survey, 2008.

United States Department of Labor. *OSHA Assistance for the Printing Industry,* n.d. http://www.osha.gov/SLTC/printing_industry/index.html.

United States Fish and Wildlife Service. *Bird Kills at Towers and Other Human-Made Structures: An Annotated Partial Bibliography (1960–1998).* Washington, DC: Office of Migratory Bird Management, 1999.

United States Government Accountability Office. *Electronic Waste: EPA Needs to Better Control Harmful U.S. Exports Through Stronger Enforcement and More Comprehensive Regulation.* Report to the Chairman, Committee on Foreign Affairs, House of Representatives. GAO-08-1044. Washington, DC: Government Accountability Office, 2008.

Universal Studios Entertainment.com. "Evan Almighty," Universal Studios Entertainment.com, n.d. http://www.universalstudiosentertainment.com/evan-almighty.

Urrea, Luis Alberto. *By the Lake of Sleeping Children: The Secret Life of the Mexican Border.* New York: Anchor, 1996.

Ursell, Gillian. "Television Production: Issues of Exploitation, Commodification and Sub-jectivity in UK Television Labour Markets." *Media, Culture & Society,* 22 no. 6 (2000): 805–26.

U.S. Department of Energy. "Federal Smart-Grid Taskforce." Energy.gov, n.d. http://energy. gov/oe/technology-development/smart-grid/federal-smart-grid-task-force.

U.S. Department of Justice, Office of the Inspector General. *A Review of the Federal Prisons Industries' Electronic-Waste Recycling Program.* The United States Department of Justice, October 2010. http://www.justice.gov/oig/reports/BOP/o1010.pdf.

V., Vinutha. "The E-Waste Problem." *Express Computer,* November 21, 2005. http://www. expresscomputeronline.com/20051121/management01.shtml.

Van Erp, Judith, and Wim Huisman. "Smart Regulation and Enforcement of Illegal Disposal of Electronic Waste." *Criminology & Public Policy* 9, no. 3 (2010): 579–90.

Vaughan, Adam. "Flat-Screen TV Electricity Consumption Falls by 60%." *Guardian,* July 29, 2011. http://www.guardian.co.uk/environment/2011/jul/29/flat-screen-tv-electricity.

Van Liemt, Gijsbert. *Recent Developments on Corporate Social Responsibility (CSR) in Informa-tion and Communications Technology (ICT) Hardware Manufacturing.* Geneva: Interna-tional Labour Office, 2007.

Van Loon, Joost. *Media Technology: Critical Perspectives.* Maidenhead, UK: Open University Press, 2008.

Veenstra, Albert, Cathy Wang, Wenji Fan, and Yihong Ru. "An Analysis of E-Waste Flows in China," *The International Journal of Advanced Manufacturing Technology* 47, nos. 5–8 (2010): 449–459.

Velte, Toby J., Anthony T. Velte, and Robert Elsenpeter. *Green IT: Reduce Your Information System's Environmental Impact While Adding to the Bottom Line.* New York: McGraw Hill, 2008.

Ventre, Michael. "It's Not Easy Being Green, Hollywood Discovers." Msnbc.com, April 23, 2008. http://msnbc.msn.com/id/24256817/ns/business-going_green.

Vereecken, Willem, Ward Van Heddeghem, Didier Colle, Mario Pickavet, and Piet Demeester. "Overall ICT Footprint and Green Communication Technologies." Proceedings of the 4th International Symposium on Communications 2010, Control and Sign Processing, Limassol, Cyprus, March 3–5, 2010.

Vidal, Míriam. "Comenzó a operar ayer el Wal-Mart de Teotihuacán." *El Universal,* November 5, 2004. http://www2.eluniversal.com.mx/pls/impreso/noticia.html?id_ nota=63622&tabla=ciudad.

Virilio, Paul. *War and Cinema: The Logistics of Perception.* Translated by Patrick Camiller. Lon-don: Verso, 1989.

Viscusi, W. Kip. "Cotton Dust Regulation: An OSHA Success Story?" *Journal of Policy Analysis and Management* 4, no. 3 (1985): 325–43.

Wajcman, Judy. *Feminism Confronts Technology.* University Park: Pennsylvania State University Press, 1991.

Wajcman, Judy. *TechnoFeminism.* Oxford, UK: Polity, 2004.

Walmart. "Sustainability Milestone Meeting—July 16, 2009." Walmart Web cast. July 16, 2009. http://www.walmartstores.com/Sustainability/9264.aspx?p=9191.

Wald, Matthew L. "Taming the Guzzlers that Power the World Wide Web." *New York Times,* November 7, 2007. http://query.nytimes.com/gst/fullpage.html?res=9F02E7D8113C F934A35752C1A9619C8B63&pagewanted=all.

Walker, R. R. *The Magic Spark: The Story of the First Fifty Years of Radio in Australia.* Melbourne: Hawthorn, 1973.

Wallwork, K. L. "The Calico Printing Industry of Lancastria in the 1840s." *Transactions of the Institute of British Geographers* 45 (1968): 143–56.

Walters, Adelaide. "The International Copper Cartel." *Southern Economic Journal* 11, no. 2 (1944): 133–56.

Walsh, Bryan. "Living with Ed—In a Green Hollywood." *Time*, November 30, 2007. http://www.time.com/time/health/article/0,8599,1689569,00.html.

Walsh, Luke. "Two Year Investigation Sees Nine Charged Over International WEEE Dumping." *edieWaste*, October 14, 2010. http://www.edie.net/news/news_story.asp?id=18819&channel=5&title=Two+year+investigation+sees+nine+charged+over+international+WEEE+dumping+.

Walt Disney Company. *2008 Corporate Responsibility Report*. Disney, 2008. http://disney.go.com/crreport/overview/messagefromceo.html.

Warde, Beatrice. Foreword to *Five Hundred Years of Printing* by S. H. Steinberg, 7–10. Harmondsworth: Penguin, 1955.

Warner Brothers Studio. "Warner Home Video Product Packaging to Go Green." *WB Entertainment Corporate Responsibility*, 2007. http://wbenvironmental.warnerbros.com.

Warner Brothers Studio. "Environmental Initiatives." *WB Entertainment Corporate Responsibility*, n.d. http://wbenvironmental.warnerbros.com.

Waters, Mary C. "Once Again, Strangers on Our Shores." In *The Fractious Nation? Unity and Division in American Life*. Edited by Jonathan Rieder and Stephen Steinlight, 117–30. Berkeley: University of California Press, 2003.

Wear, David N., and John G. Greis. *The Southern Forest Resource Assessment Summary Report*. USDA Forest Service, 2001.

Webber, Lawrence, and Michael Wallace. *Green Tech: How to Plan and Implement Sustainable IT Solution*. New York: American Management Association, 2009.

Weber, Max. "Commerce on the Stock and Commodity Exchanges." Translated by Steven Lestition. *Theory and Society* 29, no. 3 (2000): 339–71.

Weber, Max. (1991). From Max Weber: Essays in Sociology. Edited by H.H Gerth and C. Wright Mills. Preface by Brian S. Turner. Abingdon: Routledge.

Weber, Max. "Remarks on Technology and Culture." Edited by Thomas M. Kemple and translated by Beatrix Zumsteg and Thomas M. Kemple. *Theory, Culture & Society* 22, no. 4 (2005): 23–38.

Weil, Nancy. "The Realities of Green Computing." *PC World*, August 3, 2007. http://www.pcworld.com/businesscenter/article/135509/the_realities_of_green_computing.html.

Weinstein, Andrew. "A Look at Global Expansion for E-Books." *Publishing Research Quarterly* 26, no. 1 (2010): 11–15.

Wells, H. G. *When the Sleeper Awakes*. New York: Modern Library, 2003. Originally published in 1899.

Wells, Peter, and Liz Heming. "Green Celebrity: Oxymoron, Fashion or Pioneering Sustainability?" *International Journal of Innovation and Sustainable Development* 4, no. 1 (2009): 61–73.

Wheaton, Ken. "Reports of Mag-Industry Demise Greatly Exaggerated." *AdvertisingAge*, April 2, 2007. http://adage.com/article/print-edition/reports-mag-industry-demise-greatly-exaggerated/115827/.

Widmer, Rolf, Heidi Oswald-Krapf, Deepali Sinha-Khetriwal, Max Schnellmann, and Heinz Böni. "Global Perspectives on E-Waste." *Environmental Impact Assessment Review* 25, no. 5 (2005): 436–58.

Wikle, Thomas A. (2002). "Cellular Tower Proliferation in the United States." *Geographical Review* 92, no. 1: 45–62.

Wilkinson, Richard G., and Kate E. Pickett. "Income Inequality and Population Health: A Review and Explanation of the Evidence." *Social Science & Medicine* 62, no. 7 (2006): 1768–784.

Willard, Terri and Maja Andjelkovic, eds. *A Developing Connection: Bridging the Policy Gap Between the Information Society and Sustainable Development*. Winnipeg: Institute for Sustainable Development, 2005.

Williams, Chris. *Ecology and Socialism: Solutions to Capitalist Ecological Crisis*. New York: Haymarket, 2010.

Williams, Eric D. "Environmental Impacts of Microchip Manufacture." *Thin Solid Films* 461, no. 1 (2004): 2–6.

Williams, Martyn. "Greenpeace Says E-Waste from U.S. Stopped in Hong Kong." About.com, June 15, 2008. http://pcworld.about.com/od/businesscenter/Greenpeace-Says-E-waste-From-U.htm.

Williams, Raymond. *Television: Technology and Cultural Form*. New York: Schocken, 1975.

Williams, Raymond. *The Politics of Modernism: Against the New Conformists*. Edited by Tony Pinkney. London: Verso, 1989.

Winner, Langdon. *The Whale and the Reactor: A Search for Limits in an Age of High Technology*. Chicago: University of Chicago Press, 1986.

Winocur, Rosalía. *Ciudadanos mediáticos*. Barcelona: Editorial Gedisa, 2002.

Winseck, Dwayne R. and Robert M. Pike. *Communication and Empire: Media, Markets, and Globalization, 1860–1930*. Durham, NC: Duke University Press, 2007.

Winston, Andrew "How the Wal-Mart Eco-Ratings will Save Money." *Harvard Business Review*, July 17, 2009. http://blogs.harvardbusiness.org/winston/2009/07/how-the-Wal-Mart-ecoratings-wil.html.

Winston, Brian. *Technologies of Seeing: Photography, Cinematography, and Television*. London: British Film Institute, 1996.

Winston, Brian. *Media Technology and Society: A History from the Telegraph to the Internet*. London: Routledge, 1998.

Winston, Brian. "Let Them Eat Laptops: The Limits of Technicism." *International Journal of Communication* 1 (2007): 170–76. http://ijoc.org/ojs/index.php/ijoc/article/viewFile/150/72.

Winston, Brian. "'Caging the Copycat': Wie neue Technologien eingeschrän werdem. Eine Fallstudie: Das Google Book Search Settlement." In *Kulturen des Kopierschutzes II Navigationen: Zeitschrift für Medien- und Kulturwissenschaften*. Edited by Jens Schroeter *et al.* Siegen, Germany: Universitatsverlag Siegen, 2010.

Wollen, Peter. "Cinema and Technology: A Historical Overview." *The Cinematic Apparatus*. Edited by Teresa de Lauretis and Stephen Heath, 14–22. Basingstoke: Macmillan, 1985.

Wong, Coby S. C., S. C. Wu, Nurdan S. Duzgoren-Aydin, Adnan Aydin, and Ming H. Wong. "Trace Metal Contamination of Sediments in an E-Waste Processing Village in China." *Environmental Pollution* 145, no. 2 (2007): 434–42.

Wong, Stephanie, John Liu, and Tim Culpan. "Life and Death at the iPad Factory." *Bloomberg Businessweek*, June 7–13, 2010. 35–36.

Wood, Daniel B. "Hollywood Rolls Out the Green Carpet." *Christian Science Monitor*, December 21, 2008. http://www.csmonitor.com/Environment/Living-Green/2008/1221/hollywood-rolls-out-the-green-carpet.

Woody, Todd. "Solar Energy Faces Tests on Greenness." *New York Times*, February 24, 2011.

Woolgar, Steve, Daniel Neyland, Peter Healey, João Arriscado Nunes, Marisa Matias, Ana Raquel Matos, Daniel Neves, and Rob Hagendijk. *Articulating New Accountability Systems: Integrated Framework*. James Martin ResIST Working Paper 13/ResIST Project deliverable # 17. CITS-CT-2006-029052. *ResIST*, 2008. http://www.resist-research.net/cms/site/docs/Integrated%20Framework%20WP3%20final.pdf.

Xing, Yuqing, and Neal Detert. *How the iPhone Widens the United States Trade Deficit with the People's Republic of China*. ADBI working paper 257. Tokyo: Asian Development Bank Institute, 2010. http://www.adbi.org/working-paper/2010/12/14/4236.iphone.widens.us.trade.deficit.prc/.

Young, Tom. "Eaga Sends PCs to Africa." *Computing*, September 13, 2007. http://www.computing.co.uk/computing/analysis/2198569/case-study-eaga.

Zhao, Quansheng, and Guoli Liu. "Managing the Challenges of Complex Interdependence: China and the United States in the Era of Globalization." *Asian Politics & Policy* 2, no. 1 (2010): 1–23.

Zhao, Yuezhi. "China's Pursuits of Indigenous Innovations in Information Technology Developments: Hopes, Follies and Uncertainties." *Chinese Journal of Communication* 3, no. 3 (2010): 266–89.

Zjawinski, Sonia. "Garbage In, Garden Out: Inside the High Tech Trash Disassembly Line." *Wired*, March 24, 2008. http://www.wired.com/special_multimedia/2008/st_wastestream.

Zoeteman, Bastiaan C. J., Harold R. Krikke, and Jan Venselaar. "Handling WEEE Waste Flows: On the Effectiveness of Producer Responsibility in a Globalizing World." *International Journal of Manufacturing Technology* 47, nos. 5–8 (2010): 415–36.

Zwick, Detlev, Samuel K. Bonsu, and Aron Darmody. "Putting Consumers to Work: 'Co-Creation' and New Marketing Governmentality." *Journal of Consumer Culture* 8, no. 2 (2008): 163–96.

## FILMS

*2012*, directed by Roland Emmerich, 2009.

*An Inconvenient Truth*, directed by Davis Guggenheim, 2006.

*Avatar*, directed by James Cameron, 2009.

*Be Kind Rewind*, directed by Michel Gondry, 2008.

*Cast Away*, directed by Robert Zemeckis, 2000.

*E.T.: The Extra-Terrestrial*, directed by Steven Spielberg, 1981.

*Evan Almighty*, directed by Tom Shadyac, 2007.

*Gilda*, directed by Charles Vidor, 1946.

*It Should Happen to You, directed by George Cukor, 1954.*

*Spider-Man 2*, directed by Sam Raimi, 2004.

*The Beach*, directed by Danny Boyle, 2000.

*The Color Purple*, directed by Steven Spielberg, 1985.

*The Cove*, directed by Louie Psihoyos, 2009.

*The Day After Tomorrow*, directed by Roland Emmerich, 2004.

*Titanic*, directed by James Cameron, 1997.

*Wal-Mart: The High Cost of Low Price*, directed by Robert Greenwald, 2005.

*Waste Land*, directed by Lucy Walker, João Jardim, and Karen Harley, 2010.

*Whaledreamers*, directed by Kim Kindersley, 2006.

*White Wilderness*, directed by James Algar, 1958.

# INDEX

Printed in the USA/Agawam, MA
February 18, 2013

572926.070